Copyright © 2o20 by Isla Finlay -All rights reserved.

No part of this book may be reproduced or transmitted in any form or by any means, electronic or mechanical, including photocopying and recording, or by any information storage and retrieval system, without permission in writing from the publisher. This is a work of fiction. Names, places, characters and incidents are either the product of the author's imagination or are used fictitiously, and any resemblance to any actual persons, living or dead, organizations, events or locales is entirely coincidental. The unauthorized reproduction or distribution of this copyrighted work is ilegal.

Please note the information contained within this document is for educational and entertainment purposes only. All effort has been executed to present accurate, up to date, reliable, complete information. No warranties of any kind are declared or implied. Readers acknowledge that the author is not engaged in the rendering of legal, financial, medical, or professional advice. The content within this book has been derived from various sources. Please consult a licensed professional before attempting any techniques outlined in this book. By reading this document, the reader agrees that under no circumstances is the author responsible for any losses, direct or indirect, that are incurred as a result of the use of the information contained within this document, including, but not limited to, errors, omissions, or inaccuracies.

CONTENTS

INTRODUCTION 7	57. Fuss-free Beef Roast.............................. 27
BREAKFAST RECIPES 12	58. Creamy Chicken Breasts....................... 27
1. Cheesy Hash 12	59. Short Ribs And Veggies 27
2. Bacon, Avocado And Cheese.................. 12	60. Beef Ribs 27
3. Eggs Benedict Bread Pudding................. 12	61. Beef Stew Recipe From Ethiopia........... 28
4. Easy Glazed Doughnuts 13	62. Green Curry Chicken Thai Style 28
5. Raspberry Breakfast Cake 13	63. Easy Kung Pao Chicken 28
6. Strawberries & Cream Quinoa................ 13	64. Beef Cooked In Mango-turmeric Spice 29
7. Cauliflower Hash Browns 13	65. Whole Roasted Chicken 29
8. Onion Tofu Scramble 14	66. Mexican Taco Casserole 29
9. Bacon, Tomato And Eggs 14	67. Easter Dinner Ham 30
10. Walnut Date Oatmeal............................ 14	68. Chili Rubbed Chicken 30
11. Sausage Solo 14	69. Mustard Pork Chops 30
12. Almond French Toast Bites................... 14	70. Chicken Jerky 30
13. Baked Biscuits & Gravy......................... 15	71. Tender Chops In Sweet 'n Sour Sauce 31
14. Bacon Veggies Combo 15	72. Beef Roast 31
15. Bacon And Egg Hash 15	73. One-pot Thai Red Curry......................... 31
16. Ham Spinach Ballet............................... 15	74. Thanksgiving Dinner Turkey 31
17. Three Cheese Eggs 16	75. Soy Glazed Pork Tenderloin.................. 32
18. Almond Muffins..................................... 16	76. Lemon Drumsticks................................. 32
19. Pumpkin Spice Breakfast Cake 16	77. Ham Stuffed Turkey Rolls 32
20. Ham And Eggs Casserole..................... 17	78. Stuffed Whole Chicken.......................... 32
21. Almond Spice Oatmeal 17	79. Potatoes, Beefy-cheesy Way 32
22. French Toast & Cream Cheese Casserole 17	80. Creamy 'n Tasty Chicken Chowder 33
23. Sweet And Savory Oatmeal 17	81. Thai Egg Rolls... 33
24. Cheesy Ham & Egg Casserole 18	82. Special Thanksgiving Roast................... 33
25. Veggie Egg Casserole 18	83. Braised Shredded Beef.......................... 34
26. Caramel Pumpkin Oatmeal 18	84. Pulled Pork With Apple-bacon-bbq Sauce 34
27. Bacon, Broccoli And Cheddar Frittata 18	85. Salsa Chicken Breast 34
28. Bacon And Egg Bites 18	86. Not Your Ordinary Beef Pot Pie............. 34
29. Almond French Toast 19	87. Ropa Vieja 35
30. Maple Sausage Bread Pudding 19	88. Cheesy Chicken Breast 35
31. Cherry Fritters....................................... 19	89. Indian Keema Matar Chicken 35
32. Sausage And Spinach Breakfast Casserole 20	90. Favorite Beef Taquitos 36
33. Spinach Quiche..................................... 20	91. Inspiring Pork Platter 36
34. Blackberry Muffins................................ 20	92. Caprese Hasselback Chicken 36
35. Double Meat Breakfast Casserole....... 20	93. St. Louis Style Beef Ribs....................... 36
36. Breakfast Stuffed Baked Potatoes 21	94. Traditional Chicken 'n Dumplings......... 37
37. Coconut Oatmeal 21	95. Pork Jerky 37
38. Pepperoni Omelet................................. 21	96. Porkchops Down South 37
39. Blueberry Bagels................................... 21	97. Irresistible Chicken Drumsticks............ 37
40. Avocado Eggs 22	98. Pork Tenderloin In Teriyaki Sauce 38
MEAT RECIPES...23	99. Christmas Dinner Platter 38
41. Everyday Chicken Breast...................... 23	100. Slow Cooking Beef Fajitas 38
42. Pulled Bbq Chicken............................... 23	101. Pork Carnita 39
43. Chicken Shawarma Middle-east........... 23	102. Yummy Turkey Tenderloins 39
44. Veggie Chicken Soup 23	103. Simple Homestyle Chicken Thighs 39
45. Luscious Chicken Breasts 24	104. Pot Roast Recipe With An Asian Twist 39
46. St. Patty's Corned Beef Recipe 24	105. Bacon Swiss Pork Chops 40
47. Out Of World Deer 24	106. Tender Duck Legs 40
48. Buffalo Chicken Wings 24	107. Mexican Style Pork Chops.................. 40
49. Lamb Roast.. 25	108. Chinese Pork Chops 40
50. Ninja Foodi Salsa Verde Chicken 25	109. Beef Covered In Herbs....................... 41
51. Drunken Duck Breast............................ 25	110. Tasty Chicken Tetrazzini 41
52. Ginger-balsamic Glazed Chicken 25	111. Teriyaki Chicken & Broccoli............... 41
53. Spice Crusted Chicken Breasts 26	112. Spicy Beef Jerky................................... 42
54. Chili Pork 26	113. Chicken Meatballs Buffalo Flavored 42
55. Mediterranean Turkey Cutlets 26	114. Lemon Pork Chops.............................. 42
56. Savory 'n Aromatic Chicken Adobo 26	115. Beef Jerky... 42

116. Glazed Turkey Breast 43
117. Creamy Shredded Venison 43
118. Pork Ribs 43
119. Citrus Pork Carnitas 44
120. Beef Stew 44
121. Cauliflower Corned Beef Hash 44
122. Apple Glazed Bbq Ribs 44
123. Chicken Congee 45
124. Shining Dinner Meal 45
125. Easiest Turkey Breast 45
126. Subtly Sweet Chicken Breasts 46
127. Braised Chuck Roast 46
128. Garlic Creamy Beef Steak 46
129. Pork Nachos 46
130. Roasted Crisp Whole Chicken 47
131. Tender Chicken Thighs 47
132. Festive Fajita Beef 47
133. Creamy Tomato Chicken 48
134. Asian Beef & Broccoli 48
135. Mexican Style Chicken Breast 48
136. 3-ingredients Duck Legs 48
137. Pork Meatballs 49
138. Garlic Chicken In Creamy Tuscan Style 49
139. Ketogenic Beef Sirloin Steak 49
140. Perfect Fall Dinner Pork 49
141. Richly Cheesy Sausage 50
142. Chili Chicken Wings 50
143. Zingy Chicken Wings 50
144. Tasty Sesame-honeyed Chicken 50
145. Bbq Turkey Legs 51
146. Jamaican Style Curried Chicken 51
147. Crispy Fried Chicken 51
148. Classic Sausage & Bell Peppers 52
149. Garlicky Leg Of Lamb 52
150. Nutritious Beef Curry 52
151. Chicken Soup 52
152. Garlicky-ginger Drumsticks 52
153. Flavor-packed Beef Curry 53
154. Zesty Lamb Chops 53
155. Bacon 'n Broccoli Frittata 53
156. Spicy Chicken Jerky 53
157. Hawaiian Lamb Chops 54
158. Mexican Cheesy Chicken Ole 54
159. Italian Chicken Dinner 54
160. Sweet And Sour Chicken Wings 54
161. Creamy Turkey Breast 55
162. Family Dinner Pork Shoulder 55
163. Quick Shredded Buffalo Chicken 55
164. Ranch Flavored Tender Wings 55
165. The Shiny Chicken Stock 56
166. Beef Taco Casserole 56
167. Bacon Spaghetti Squash 56
168. Crispy Pork Carnitas 56
169. Mild Flavored Rabbit 57
170. Pulled Pork Slathered In Bbq Sauce 57
171. Hk Mushroom Gravy Over Chops 57
172. Zesty Lamb Chops(2) 57
173. Crispy Garlic-parmesan Wings 58
174. Almonds Coated Lamb 58
175. Holiday Luncheon Meal 58
176. Breaded Chicken Tenders 59
177. Herb Infused Leg Of Lamb 59
178. Succulent Roasted Chicken 59
179. Dinner Party Turkey Breast 59
180. Keto Chicken Chili 60
181. Beefy Stew Recipe From Persia 60
182. Sweet & Sour Pork Chops 60
183. Beef ' N Mushrooms In Thick Sauce 61
184. Zesty Lamb Chops(1) 61
185. Awesome Beef Enchilada 61
186. Ny Strip Steak 61
187. Mother's Day Special Steak 62
188. Texas Steak 62
189. Refreshingly Tasty Steak 62
190. Herbed Lamb Chops 62
191. Jamaican Jerk Pork 63
192. Filet Mignon Ala Carribé 63
193. Pork Chili 63
194. Beef Chili 63
195. Chicken Taco Filling 64
196. Jamaican Jerk Pork Roast 64
197. Deliciously Spicy Turkey Legs 64
198. Chicken Alfredo Pasta 64
199. Smoky Roasted Chicken 65
200. French Style Duck Breast 65
FISH AND SEAFOOD RECIPES 66
201. Fancy "rich" Guy Smoked Lobster 66
202. Spicy Shrimp Soup 66
203. Cajun Spiced Salmon 66
204. Coconut Curry Sea Bass 66
205. Lemon Pepper Salmon 67
206. Rosemary Scallops 67
207. Salmon Stew 67
208. Sweet And Sour Fish 67
209. Family Feast Shrimp 67
210. Buttered Halibut 68
211. Bbq Shrimp 68
212. Jambalaya 68
213. Butter Shrimp 69
214. Tomato-basil Dressed Tilapia 69
215. Ketogenic Butter Fish 69
216. Bok Choy On Ginger-sesame Salmon 69
217. Well-seasoned Catfish 70
218. Easy Veggie-salmon Bake 70
219. Green Chili Mahi-mahi Fillets 70
220. Shrimp Magic 70
221. Sweet 'n Spicy Mahi-mahi 71
222. Mesmerizing Salmon Loaf 71
223. Everyday Flounder 71
224. Cod Topped With Mediterranean-spiced Tomatoes 71
225. Coconut Curry Fish 72
226. Paprika Shrimp 72
227. Black Pepper Scallops 72
228. Salmon With Orange-ginger Sauce 72
229. Stewed Mixed Seafood 72
230. Pepper Crusted Tuna 73
231. Salmon-pesto Over Pasta 73
232. Wine Braised Salmon 73
233. Mexican Swordfish 74
234. Lemon Cod 74
235. Seafood Gumbo New Orleans Style 74
236. Salsa Tuna Steaks 74
237. Tilapia Filet Topped With Mango-salsa 75

238. Buttered Scallops 75
239. Creamy Herb 'n Parm Salmon 75
240. Flavorsome Salmon 75
241. Miso Glazed Salmon 76
242. Chili Lime Salmon 76
243. Buffalo Fish 76
244. Pasta 'n Tuna Bake 77
245. Eggs 'n Smoked Ramekin 77
246. Veggie Fish Soup 77
247. Spicy Flounder 77
248. French Salmon Meal 77
249. Salmon And Asparagus 78
250. Tomato Lime Tilapia 78

SOUPS & STEWS 79
251. Creamy Chicken & Mushroom Soup 79
252. Tuscan-style Veggie Soup 79
253. Irish Lamb Stew 79
254. Jamaican Chicken Stew 79
255. Venison Stew 80
256. Spiced Potato-cauliflower Chowder 80
257. Filling Cauli-squash Chowder 80
258. Chili-quinoa 'n Black Bean Soup 81
259. Tipsy Potato Chowder 81
260. Seafood Stew 81
261. Shrimp & Mango Curry 81
262. Sunchoke & Asparagus Soup 82
263. Sweet Potato 'n Garbanzo Soup 82
264. Autumn Stew 82
265. Greens & Beans Soup 82
266. Coconut, Apple 'n Squash Chowder 83
267. Sweet Potato & Black Bean Stew 83
268. Lamb Provencal 83
269. Verde Pork Stew 84
270. Chickpea And Potato Soup 84
271. Duck Ale Chili 84
272. White Chicken Chili 84
273. Vegan Approver Tortilla Soup 85
274. Deliciously Traditional Clam Chowder 85
275. Poblano Beef Stew 85
276. Healthy Celery 'n Kale Soup 86
277. Beefy White Cream Soup 86
278. Sausage & Spinach Stew 86
279. Mushroom & Wild Rice Soup 87
280. Cheesy Onion Soup 87

DESSERT RECIPES 88
281. Easy Peasy Applesauce 88
282. Lemon Ricotta Cake 88
283. Coconutty-blueberry Cake 88
284. Carrot Pecan 88
285. Strawberry Cake 89
286. Chocolate Peanut Butter Cups 89
287. Flourless Chocolate Brownies 89
288. Super Simple Chocolate Brownies 89
289. Fudge Divine 89
290. Chocolate Mug Cake 90
291. Orange-cranberry Pudding 90
292. Coconut Cake 90
293. Meyer Lemon Hand Pies 90
294. Turtle Fudge Pudding 91
295. Key Lime Curd 91
296. Choco-coffee Cake 91
297. Banana Bundt Cake 92
298. Blueberry & Peach Streusel Pie 92
299. Blackberry Brioche Bread Pudding 92
300. Cherry Cobbler 93
301. Crème Brûlée 93
302. Hot Fudge Cake 93
303. Bananas Foster 93
304. Chocolatey 'n Peanut Butter Cakes 94
305. Raspberry Mug Cake 94
306. Sweet Sticky Coco-rice 94
307. Reece's Cookie Bars 94
308. Surprising Campfire S'mores 95
309. Strawberry Chocolate Chip Mug Cake 95
310. Scrumptiously Molten Lava Cake 95
311. Pineapple Pecan Bread Pudding 95
312. Chocolate Cheese Cake(2) 96
313. Cream Crepes 96
314. Excellent Strawberry Toast Pastries 96
315. Balsamic Roasted Strawberries 96
316. Almond Cheese Cake 96
317. Coconut Cream Cake 97
318. Almond Cake 97
319. Chocolate Cheese Cake(1) 97
320. Lemon Mousse 98
321. Chocolate Pecan Pie 98
322. Nutty Cinnamon 'n Cranberry Cake 98
323. Lemon Sponge Pie 98
324. Individual S'mores Pies 99
325. Noodle Kugel 99
326. Vanilla Yogurt 99
327. Caramel Apple Chimichangas 99
328. Nut Porridge 100
329. Fruity And Tasty Vegan Crumble 100
330. Crunchy Cinnamon Topped Peaches 100

OTHER FAVORITE RECIPES 101
331. Ninja Foodi Chili 101
332. Steamed Lemon Grass Crab Legs 101
333. Easy Chow Mein Topped With Green Onions 101
334. Steamed Brisket In Guinness 101
335. Lemon Pepper Wings 102
336. Fragrant Steamed Pork 102
337. Hot Pepper Jelly Cheese Dip With Bacon 102
338. Ninja Foodie Short Ribs 102
339. Beer Braised Brisket 103
340. Mediterranean Spinach With Cheese 103
341. Lamb Marsala 103
342. Deliciously Dehydrated Apple Chips 103
343. Louisiana Style Banana Foster 104
344. Bacon And Cabbage 104
345. Dessert Fruity Tacos 104
346. Simple Pot Roast And Potatoes 104
347. French Onion Soup 105
348. Zucchini Cream Cheese Fries 105
349. Elegant Mushroom Sautee 105
350. Thai Sweet Pork 105
351. Ninja Foodi Cola Roast 106
352. Cheesy Spinach Bake 106
353. Cauliflower Gratin 106
354. Pork Loin With Onion Beer Sauce 106
355. Hard Steamed Eggs 107
356. Broiled Cranberry Pork 107
357. Jalapeno & Cheese Wontons 107
358. Spiced Roasted Broccoli 107

#	Recipe	Page
359.	Quinoa 'n Lime-cilantro Salad	108
360.	Stunning Broccoli Florets	108
361.	Chili Tomatoes 'n Black Beans	108
362.	Eggplant Parmesan	108
363.	Chicken-parm Fettucine Alfredo	109
364.	Spicy Green Beans	109
365.	Scalloped Pineapple	109
366.	Coffee-flavored Chuck Roast	109
367.	Simple Beer-marinated Pork Roast	109
368.	Apple Butter Pork Loin	110
369.	Herb Roasted Pork Loin With Potatoes	110
370.	Cinnamon Apple Chips	110
371.	Roasted Whole Chicken	110
372.	Dad's Beef Jerky	111
373.	Lemony Steamed Fish	111
374.	Easy Baked Beef & Pasta	111
375.	Amazing Beef Sauerbraten	111
376.	Pressure Cooker Red Beans And Sausages	112
377.	Tasty Mushroom Ala Bourguignon	112
378.	Baked Beans	112
379.	Vegetarian-approved Meatballs In Bbq Sauce	112
380.	Easy Garlic Broiled Chicken	113
381.	Makhanidaal (butterfly Lentils)	113
382.	Luncheon Green Beans	113
383.	Bacon Cheeseburger Dip	113
384.	Breakfast Oats With Apricots 'n Nuts	114
385.	Cauliflower Mash	114
386.	Air Fried Zucchini Chips	114
387.	Homemade Sweet Yogurt	114
388.	Chinese Style Steamed Fish	115
389.	Vanilla-espresso Flavored Oats	115
390.	Cheesy Artichoke & Crab Dip	115
391.	Dehydrated Beet Chips	115
392.	Crispy Fried Green Tomatoes	116
393.	Simple Roasted Veggie Stock	116
394.	Seafood Casserole	116
395.	Tasty Asparagus Fries	116
396.	Low-carb Zucchini Chips	117
397.	Mexican Beef And Vegetable Stew	117
398.	The Easy Watermelon Jerky	117
399.	Cheesy Mozzarella Sticks	117
400.	Southwest Chicken Egg Rolls	118
401.	Chicken Poblano	118
402.	Creamy Braised Oxtails	118
403.	Light Luncheon Meal	119
404.	Pressure Cooker Lamb Stew	119
405.	Flavorsome Baked Bananas	119
406.	Salsa Verde Slow Cooker Dip	119
407.	Crispy Fried Crumbed Fish	120
408.	Spanish Rice Pudding	120
409.	Braised Artichokes	120
410.	Savory Roasted Vegetables	120
411.	Buffalo Air Fried Chicken	121
412.	Vegetable Masala Indian Style	121
413.	Delicate Stuffed Tomatoes	121
414.	Chipotle Chicken Bowls	122
415.	Easy Foiled Baked Salmon	122
416.	Capers 'n Olives On Red Sauce Pasta	122
417.	Juicy Corned Beef	122
418.	Steamed Broccoli And Carrots With Lemon	123
419.	Heart-felt Caramelized Onions	123
420.	Filipino-style Bistek Tagalog	123
421.	Lemon Orzo With Asparagus	123
422.	Chinese Steamed Buns	124
423.	Ninja Foodi Chinese Ribs	124
424.	Sole Steamed With Tomatoes And Leaks	124
425.	Ninja Foodie Pressure Cooked Adobo	124
426.	Scrumptious Sausage Dinner	125
427.	Easy 'n Crispy Egg Rolls	125
428.	Creamy Cheesy Polenta	125
429.	Baked Teriyaki Chicken	125
430.	Kids Favorite Pasta	126
431.	Appetizing Baked Pompano	126
432.	Greek Style Stew	126
433.	Mexican Pork In Annatto Sauce	127
434.	Asian Spiced Chicken Wings	127
435.	Carrot Pudding	127
436.	Bbq Oysters With Bacon	127
437.	Cheese Casserole	127
438.	Cheesy Cauliflower	128
439.	Buffalo Cauliflower Bites	128
440.	Spicy Pressure Cooker Short Ribs	128
441.	Ninja Foodi Pressure Cooked BBQ Chicken	128
442.	Asparagus Bites	129
443.	Buffalo Chicken Soup	129
444.	Easy Ninja Foodi Pot Roast	129
445.	Fried Meatballs With Tomato Sauce	129
446.	Mini Meatballs	130
447.	Crunchy Tortilla Chips	130
448.	Cheesy Green Chili Rice	130
449.	Roasted Corn	130
450.	Crab Frittata	131
451.	Ginger-soy On Tuna Fish	131
452.	Creamy Tomato-basil Soup	131
453.	Spicy Honey Mustard Pork Roast	131
454.	Brekky Bacon 'n Egg Risotto	132
455.	Tomato ' N Eggplant Pasta	132
456.	Broiled & Buttered Scallops	132
457.	Chinese Steamed Fish	132
458.	Southwest Short Ribs	133
459.	Cheesy 'n Milky Haddock	133
460.	Pressure Cooker Pork Tenderloin	133
461.	Nutty Brussels Sprouts	134
462.	Ninja Foodi Baked Fudge	134
463.	Flaky Broiled Salmon	134
464.	Chinese Pork Roast	134
465.	Root Veggie Mix	135
466.	Steamed Egg Chawan Mushi	135
467.	Chicken Potato & Broccoli Casserole	135
468.	Seafood With Chorizo 'n Chicken Spanish Rice	135
469.	Tasty 'n Easy To Make Baked Potatoes	136
470.	Summertime Mousse	136
471.	Olive-brined Air Fryer Turkey Breasts	136
472.	Crispy Brussel Sprouts	136
473.	Crispy Sweet Potato Fries	137
474.	Tiger Shrimp A La Bang Bang	137
475.	Jicama Fries	137
476.	Roasted Beets	137
477.	Buttery Corn	138
478.	Steamed Egg Chawanmushi	138
479.	Crispy Kale Chips In Ninja Foodi	138
480.	Avocado Chips	138
481.	Crunchy Onion Rings	138
482.	Spicy Short Ribs	139

483. Spicy 'n Steamy Shrimps 139
484. Easy Crab Wontons 139
485. Herbed Pork Rump Roast 139
486. Southwest's Chickpea Gumbo 140
487. Easy-steam Lobster Tails 140
488. Salt-encrusted Prime Rib Roast 140
489. Baked Calamari & Shrimp Pasta 140
490. Pressure Cooker Fenugreek Chicken 141
491. Broiled Short Ribs 141
492. Wonderful Side Dish 141
493. Unique Apple Pastries 142
494. Spicy Cauliflower Bites 142
495. Hearty Egg And Sausage Bake 142
496. Asparagus, Shrooms 'n Shrimp Risotto 142
497. Bangladeshi Beef Curry 143
498. Holiday Brussels Sprouts With Nuts & Cranberries 143
499. Parmesan 'n Garlic Fries 143
500. Garden Fresh Veggie Combo 144
501. Cheesy Shepherd's Pie 144
502. Butter-lemon On Walleye Pickerel 144
503. Artichoke Dip 145
504. Rum Spiced Nuts 145
505. Crusty Sweet Potato Hash 145
506. Beef, Veggie 'n Barley Stew 145
507. Cajun Style Blue Crabs 146
508. Cool Beet Chips 146
509. Chive 'n Parsnips Chowder 146
510. Sugar-glazed Carrots 146
511. Zucchini Pasta With Walnuts & Basil 147
512. Squash With Cherries 147
513. Pressure Cooker Pasta Stew 147
514. Fall-time Vegetarian Dish 147
515. Orange Lobster Tail 147
516. Eggs Stuffed With Avocado & Watercress 148
517. Spicy Salmon Jerky 148
518. Balsamic Roasted Pork Loin 148
519. Soy-glazed Mushrooms 148
520. Steamed Garlic Prawn Chinese Style 149
521. Sausage Onions & Peppers 149
522. Authentic French Potato Gratin 149
523. Steamed Mussels With Fennel And Tomatoes 149
524. Sweet & Spicy Balsamic Beef 150
525. Red Wine Braised Short Ribs 150
526. Coconut Carrots 150
527. Flaky Fish With Ginger 150
528. Sumptuous Breakfast Frittata 151
529. Tastiest Cauliflower 151
530. Pressure Cooker Pork Carnitas 151
531. Speedy Paella 151
532. Celery Root Fried Crisped 152
533. Vegan-approved Fajita Pasta 152
534. Crispy 'n Tasty Cauliflower Bites 152
535. Healthy Asparagus Bake 152
536. Zucchini Fries 153
537. Kale Chips 153
538. Mixed Nuts 153
539. Pumpkin & Bacon Risotto 153
540. Loaded Nachos 154
541. Portuguese Steamed Clams 154
542. Spicy Red Potatoes 154
543. Duck Confit 154
544. Popular Finger Food 155
545. Easy Broiled Lobster Tails 155
546. Korean Chicken 155
547. Teriyaki Green Beans & Mushrooms 156
548. Herb Roasted Pork 156
549. Great Snacking Nuts 156
550. Almond Cheddar Cornbread 156
551. Veggie 'n Shrimp Fried Rice 157
552. Vegetable And Tilapia Dinner 157
553. Pressure Cooker Bone-in Pork Chops With Vegetables 157
554. Veal Marengo 158
555. Marinated Tofu 158

INTRODUCTION

Over the years, we see the continuous trend of millennials moving into condominiums and high-rise developments in cities to be closer to their work places and other urban necessities.

Millennials value practically hence the rise of new lifestyles such as minimalism and tiny house living. The behavior and purchasing pattern of this generation has also given birth to innovations to suit their style of living.

More people nowadays prefer portable appliances that are also multi-purpose to minimize costs and save space at home. Conventional kitchen appliances not only take up space but can also be quite expensive. Outdoor cookers such as coal-fired grills can be a hassle to operate during the winter or inclement weather.

These challenges led to the advancement of electric-powered cookers. Electric grills like the Ninja Foodi can grill indoors throughout the year. It is an excellent option for people who love grilled food but do not have access nor the luxury of outdoor spaces. It is perfect for people who cannot grill outside due to harsh weather conditions.

Understanding the Ninja Foodi Grill

The Ninja Foodi Grill is a tabletop multi-function appliance that can grill, air crisp, bake, roast, and even dehydrate.

It makes use of their cyclonic grilling technology that utilizes rapidly circulating hot air to cook and sea food.

The Foodi grill is an electric grill, air fryer, convection oven, oven toaster, and dehydrator all rolled into one.

The Benefits of Using an Electric Grill

Whether it is a trend or the general convenience of it, more people are appreciating smaller and more portable indoor cookers due to a number of benefits from owning one.

- Compact – Electric grills are small enough to fit most kitchen counters and tables. It is also portable enough to be easily transported or moved around.
- Smokeless – This is probably one of the best things about indoor electric grills. People who do not have any access to open areas can still enjoy grilling since it does not produce smoke like standard grillers.
- Multi-function – Most indoor cookers come with various functionalities giving you more value for your money. It can also eliminate the need to purchase other appliances and save you essential kitchen space.
- Easy to clean and operate – Indoor grills are plug and play appliances making them user-friendly to a wider demographic. The cooking components are coated with a non-stick ceramic material that can be effortlessly taken apart and cleaned using a standard dishwasher.
- Grill marks - Like traditional outdoor grills, indoor grills can also give meat and other foods those appetizing grill marks. Although, the Ninja Foodi's grill marks are curved, unlike the typical straight markings you get from regular outdoor grills.
- Browns and crisps food – Indoor grills like the Ninja Foodi use the circulating hot air to cook the food thoroughly. This creates delectable flavors through a browning process called the Maillard reaction. Similar to convection ovens and toasters, the Ninja Foodi is excellent at making food crunchy when you need it to be.

- Capable of high temperatures – A wide range of temperature settings let you cook a variety of foods from char-grilled vegetables to restaurant-level steaks. Unlike other tabletop cookers, the Ninja Grill will let you cook frozen foods without the need to defrost. It can also get as hot as 500 to 510 degrees Fahrenheit.

Structural Composition of the Ninja Foodi Grill

Although the Ninja Foodi is a countertop cooker, it does come in a hefty size. But given its multi-purpose functionality and convenience over conventional single-purpose appliances, the size can easily be excused.

The hood houses the heating element and convection fans that help sear meat and eliminate the need to flip food. The grill grates, crisper basket, and cooking pot are all coated with a non-stick ceramic finish.

All cooking components are safe to use as it is manufactured without harmful chemicals such as PTFE, PFOA, and BPA.

A grease collector at the back prevents any spillage and makes cleaning a breeze. The kebab skewers and roasting rack are all made of food-safe stainless steel as well.

The power cable is 3 meters long and is intended to keep the grill close to an outlet and prevent people from tripping over lengthy cords.

How to Use the Ninja Foodi Grill

When you are cooking for the first time with your Foodi grill, you must first wash the detachable cooking parts with warm soapy water to remove any oil and debris. Let them air dry and place them back inside once you are ready to cook. An easy-to-follow instruction guide comes with each unit, so make sure to go over it prior to cooking.

Position your grill on a level and secure surface. Leave at least 6 inches of space around it, especially at the back where the air intake vent and air socket are located. Ensure that the splatter guard is installed whenever the grill is in use. This is a wire mesh that covers the heating element on the inside of the lid.

For grilling

- Plug your unit into an outlet and power on the grill.
- Use the grill grate over the cooking pot and choose the grill function. This has four default temperature settings of low at 400 degrees F, medium at 450 degrees F, high at 500 degrees F, and max at 510 degrees F.
- Set the time needed to cook. You may check the grilling cheat sheet that comes with your unit to guide you with the time and temperature settings. It is best to check the food regularly depending on the doneness you prefer and to avoid overcooking.
- Once the required settings are selected, press start and wait for the digital display to show 'add food'. The unit will start to preheat similar to an oven and will show the progress through the display. This step takes about 8 minutes.
- If you need to check the food or flip it, the timer will pause and resume once the lid is closed.
- The screen will show 'Done' once the timer and cooking has completed. Power off the unit and unplug the device. Leave the hood open to let the unit cool faster.

For roasting
- Remove the grill grates and use the cooking pot that comes with the unit. You may also purchase their roasting rack for this purpose.
- Press the roast option and set the timer between 1 to 4 hours depending on the recipe requirements. The Foodi will preheat for 3 minutes regardless of the time you have set.
- Once ready, place the meat directly on the roasting pot or rack.
- Check occasionally for doneness. A meat thermometer is another useful tool to get your meats perfectly cooked.

For baking
- Remove the grates and use the cooking pot.
- Choose the bake setting and set your preferred temperature and time. Preheating will take about 3 minutes.
- Once done with preheating, you may put the ingredients directly on the cooking pot, or you may use your regular baking tray. An 8-inch baking tray can fit inside as well as similar-sized oven-safe containers.

For air frying / air crisping
- Put the crisper basket in and close the lid.
- Press the air crisp or air fry option then the start button. The default temperature is set at 390° F and will preheat at about 3 minutes. You can adjust the temperature and time by pressing the buttons beside these options.
- If you do not need to preheat, just press the air crisp button a second time and the display will show you the 'add food' message.
- Put the food inside and shake or turn every 10 minutes. Use oven mitts or tongs with silicone tips when doing this.

For dehydrating
- Place the first layer of food directly on the cooking pot.
- Add the crisper basket and add one more layer.
- Choose the dehydrate setting and set the timer between 7 to 10 hours.
- You may check the progress from time to time.

For cooking frozen foods
- Choose the medium heat, which is 450° F using the grill option. You may also use the air crisp option if you are cooking fries, vegetables, and other frozen foods.
- Set the time needed for your recipe. Add a few minutes to compensate for the thawing.
- Flip or shake after a few minutes to cook the food evenly.

Cleaning and Maintenance
Components are dishwasher-safe and are fabricated with a non-stick ceramic coating, to make clean-up and maintenance easier. Plus, the grill conveniently comes with a plastic cleaning brush with a scraper at the other end.

Cleaning tips
1. Let the grill cool down completely and ensure that it is unplugged from the power outlet before trying to clean the unit.

2. Take out the splatter guard, grill grates and cooking pot and soak in soapy water for a few hours to let the debris soften and make cleaning easier. Wash only the removable parts.

3. Gently brush off dirt and debris using the plastic brush that comes with your grill. Use the other end of the brush to dislodge food in hard to reach areas.

4. Let the parts dry thoroughly.

5. Clean the insides and exterior of the unit with a clean damp cloth.

Maintenance tips

1. Always keep your unit clean, especially before putting in a new batch for cooking. You should clean the parts and the unit after each use.

2. Never use cleaning instruments or chemicals that are too harsh and can damage the coating.

3. Keep the electrical cords away from children and any traffic in your kitchen.

4. Avoid getting the unit and electrical components wet and place it away from areas that constantly get soaked or damp.

5. Always unplug the unit when not in use.

Troubleshooting

Smoke coming out of the grill

Although the Ninja Foodi is virtually smokeless as advertised, you may see some smoke from time to time for a number of reasons.

One is the type of oil you use for cooking. Ideally, canola, grapeseed, and avocado oil should be used since they have a high smoke point. This means that they do not produce smoke or burn at high temperatures. Other oils with high smoke points include corn, almond, safflower, sesame, and sunflower oils.

Another reason is the accumulation of grease at the bottom of the pot. If you continuously cook foods that produce a lot of grease and oil, this will burn and create smoke. Empty and clean the pot before cooking the next batch.

The grill is showing 'Add Food'

This means that the unit has finished preheating and that you can now put food inside the grill.

The control panel is showing 'Shut Lid'

Try opening the lid and closing it securely until the message is gone.

Unit is unresponsive and only showing 'E' on the panel

Your unit is damaged and you need to contact customer service.

Tips and Frequently Asked Questions

Here are some useful tips you can use when cooking with the Ninja Foodi as well as some commonly asked questions to guide you if you are planning to purchase one for yourself.

Useful tips

- Brush or spray the grates with some canola, corn or avocado oil to avoid smoke.
- A light coating of oil will make your air-fried French fries taste better.
- Use the time charts as a guide, but make sure you check the food regularly since the grill gets hot and can cook quickly. You may also use a meat thermometer into your food to cook exactly the way you want.

- Use silicone or wooden utensils. Never stick metal tongs or cutleries on your grill to avoid electric shock and damaging the ceramic coating.
- If you are planning to do a lot of dehydrating and baking, it will be helpful to purchase their food rack and baking pan.
- If the timer was up but you need to cook the food longer, simply adjust the timer and press the start button to continue cooking.
- Although preheating is recommended to get the finest results, you can skip this step by pressing the option a second time.
- To get juicier meat, let it rest at least 5 minutes before slicing.

FAQs

1.   Is it worth the price?

If you are getting the Foodi grill as a secondary appliance, it may seem pricey. But given the various functions you are getting with one equipment, the value for money will be apparent with continuous use.

2.   Can it heat up the kitchen as most ovens do?

No. One great thing about portable cookers like the Ninja Foodi grill is that it does not make the kitchen uncomfortably hot making it ideal for use even during the summer time.

3.   What button should I press to pause the timer?

Opening the lid will automatically pause the timer.

4.   Why my food is not evenly cooked when air fried?

It is best not to overcrowd food inside the crisper basket and create an even layer to get better results. You need to flip or shake the food every few minutes to have even browning.

5.   How do I convert cooking temperatures from recipes meant for regular ovens?

You can simply reduce the temperature required by 25 degrees Fahrenheit when using the Ninja Foodi grill. You will have to check the food regularly to make sure it will not get overcooked.

BREAKFAST RECIPES

1. Cheesy Hash

Servings: 6
Cooking Time: 30 Minutes
Ingredients:
- 6 eggs
- 4 cups riced cauliflower
- ¼ cup milk
- 1 onion, chopped
- 3 Tbsp butter
- 1 ½ cups cheddar cheese

Directions:
1. Press the saute button on your Ninja Foodi and add the butter and the onions. Cook, stirring occasionally until the onions are soft, about 5 minutes.
2. Add the iced cauliflower to the pot and stir. Turn on the air crisper for 15 minutes, turning the cauliflower halfway through.
3. In a small bowl, mix the eggs and milk together then pour over the browned cauliflower.
4. Sprinkle the cheddar cheese on top and close the lid of the Ninja Foodi for one minute to just melt the cheese. Serve while hot
- **Nutrition Info:** Calories: 291g, Carbohydrates: 8g, Protein: 18g, Fat: 22 g, Sugar: 1g, Sodium: 729g

2. Bacon, Avocado And Cheese

Servings: 4
Cooking Time: 7 Minutes
Ingredients:
- 8 slices bacon
- 2 Avocados, sliced
- ½ cup cheddar cheese
- ¼ tsp ground black pepper

Directions:
1. Prepare a baking pan that fits in your Ninja Foodi bowl by greasing the pan with butter. Set aside
2. Lay the bacon strips inside the Ninja Foodi, trying not to layer them on top of each other.
3. Set the Ninja Foodi to air crisp at 325 for 7 minutes.
4. Remove the pan of bacon from the Ninja Foodi and place the sliced avocado on top. Sprinkle the top with the cheese and with the ground black pepper. Return to the Foodi and cook for another 2 minutes to melt the cheese. Remove and enjoy while hot!
- **Nutrition Info:** Calories: 265g, Carbohydrates: 8g , Protein: 10g, Fat: 23g, Sugar: 2g, Sodium: 431 g

3. Eggs Benedict Bread Pudding

Servings: 4 – 6 Servings
Cooking Time: 90 Minutes
Ingredients:
- ½ pound Canadian bacon, cubed
- 4 asparagus spears, ends trimmed and cut into ½ inch pieces
- 3 English muffins, separated and cut into quarters
- 1 ½ cups milk
- 1 ½ cups half-and-half
- 6 eggs
- 1 package Hollandaise sauce mix
- 2 tablespoons fresh chives, chopped fine
- 1 teaspoon salt
- ¾ teaspoon white pepper
- For the Hollandaise Sauce
- ¾ cup butter, cubed
- 3 large egg yolks
- 1 ½ teaspoons fresh lemon juice
- ½ teaspoon salt
- Pinch of white pepper
- Pinch of cayenne

Directions:
1. Make the main part of the dish the night before serving. Heat oven to 375 degrees.
2. Place muffin pieces on a baking sheet and cook for 10 – 12 minutes or till toasted and crunchy.
3. Set the cooker to sauté on med-high heat. Add bacon and cook till lightly browned. Add in asparagus and cook, stirring often, about 4 minutes. Add toasted muffin pieces to bacon mix and toss well.
4. In a large mixing bowl, whisk together sauce mix packet and milk. Add eggs, half-and-half, salt, and pepper and whisk till thoroughly combined. Add the bacon mixture and stir well. Cover with foil and refrigerate 6 hours or overnight.
5. In the morning, remove the pudding mix from the fridge and let come to room temperature.
6. Lightly spray the cooking pot with cooking spray and attach the Tender Crisp lid. Transfer the egg mixture to the cooking pot and top with chives. Secure the lid and set temperature to 350 degrees. Bake for 45 minutes or it passes the toothpick test.
7. While it is baking prepare the Hollandaise sauce: place the butter in a saucepan over medium heat and melt till frothy, but not boiling.
8. Place remaining ingredients in a blender and process till combined. Keep the blender running as you slowly add the melted butter. The sauce will thicken, it is best to make the

sauce during the last 10 minutes of baking time.
9. To serve, cut the bread pudding into wedges and top with the sauce. Enjoy.

4. Easy Glazed Doughnuts

Servings: 8 Doughnuts & 8 Doughnut Holes
Cooking Time: 5 Mins
Ingredients:
- 2 cups flour
- ½ cup milk, room temperature
- ¼ cup sugar
- 1 egg, beaten
- 2 tablespoons butter, melted
- 1 ½ teaspoons fast acting yeast
- ¼ teaspoon nutmeg, optional
- salt
- Glaze:
- 1 cup powdered sugar
- 4 teaspoons water
- candy sprinkles

Directions:
1. Combine dry ingredients in a large bowl. Stir in milk, butter and egg to form a soft dough.
2. Transfer dough to a lightly floured surface and knead 2-3 minutes till smooth. Place the dough in a lightly oiled bowl, cover and let rise in a warm place till double in size, about 30 minutes.
3. Turn dough out onto a lightly floured surface and roll out to 1/4-inch thickness. Cut out 8 doughnuts using a 3-inch round cutter. Then use a 1-inch round cutter to remove center.
4. Leave the doughnuts and holes on the lightly floured surface and loosely cover with a cloth, let rise till double again.
5. Lightly spray the basket with cooking spray. Place half the doughnuts in the basket, in a single layer. Secure the Tender Crisp lid and set the temperature to 350 degrees. Cook 4 -5 minutes till golden brown. Repeat
6. To make the glaze, whisk the powdered sugar and water together till thoroughly mixed. Dip the doughnuts and holes in the glaze and place on a wire rack. Top with candy sprinkles. Let set about 10 minutes, till glaze hardens, then serve.

5. Raspberry Breakfast Cake

Servings: 6
Cooking Time: 25 Minutes
Ingredients:
- 8 Tbsp butter
- ½ cup Baking Stevia
- 1 egg
- 1 tsp vanilla
- 2 cups almond flour
- 2 tsp baking powder
- 1 tsp salt
- 1 cup fresh raspberries
- ½ cup buttermilk

Directions:
1. Use an electric mixer to cream the butter and stevia together until they are light and fluffy.
2. Mix the vanilla and eggs in a small bowl then add to the mixer with the butter blend. Ix until just combined
3. In a separate bowl, toss the raspberries and ¼ cup almond flour to coat the berries.
4. Add the remaining dry ingredients to the mixer and fold together by hand. Add the buttermilk and mix until smooth.
5. Add the raspberries to the batter and mix briefly.
6. Pour the cake batter into your Ninja Foodi and place the lid on.
7. Press the air crisp button and set the temperature to 350 degrees and program the timer to 25 minutes.
8. Once cooked, a toothpick should come out of the center of the cake cleanly. Allow to cool and serve.
- **Nutrition Info:** Calories: 183 g, Carbohydrates: 8g, Protein: 3g, Fat: 16 g, Sugar: 3g, Sodium: 464 g

6. Strawberries & Cream Quinoa

Servings: 3-4 Servings
Cooking Time: 8 Hours
Ingredients:
- 2 cups milk
- 1 ½ cups strawberries, halved
- 1 cup dry quinoa, rinsed
- 1 medium banana, sliced
- 2 tablespoons butter
- Honey to taste

Directions:
1. Add all ingredients to cooking pot and stir to combine.
2. Secure the lid and select slow cooking function on low heat. Cook 6 – 8 hours.
3. Serve warm topped with honey.

7. Cauliflower Hash Browns

Servings: 6
Cooking Time: 30 Minutes
Ingredients:
- 6 eggs
- 4 cups riced cauliflower
- ¼ cup milk
- 1 onion, chopped
- 3 Tbsp butter
- 1 ½ cups chopped, cooked ham
- ½ cup shredded cheese

Directions:

1. Press the saute button on your Ninja Foodi and add the butter and the onions. Cook, stirring occasionally until the onions are soft, about 5 minutes.
2. Add the iced cauliflower to the pot and stir. Turn on the air crisper for 15 minutes, turning the cauliflower halfway through.
3. In a small bowl, mix the eggs and milk together then pour over the browned cauliflower.
4. Sprinkle the ham over the top of the egg mix.
5. Press the air crisp button again and set the timer for 10 minutes.
6. Sprinkle the cheddar cheese on top and close the lid of the Ninja Foodi for one minute to just melt the cheese. Serve while hot

- **Nutrition Info:** Calories: 166g, Carbohydrates: 3g, Protein: 9g, Fat: 14 g, Sugar: 1g, Sodium: 278 g

8. Onion Tofu Scramble

Servings: 4
Cooking Time: 8 Minutes
Ingredients:
- 4 tbsps. butter
- 2 blocks tofu, cubed
- Salt and black pepper
- 1 c. grated cheddar cheese
- 2 medium sliced onions

Directions:
1. Mix together tofu, salt and black pepper in a bowl.
2. Press "Sauté" on Ninja Foodi and add butter and onions.
3. Sauté for about 3 minutes and add seasoned tofu.
4. Cook for about 2 minutes and add cheddar cheese.
5. Lock the lid and set the Ninja Foodi on "Air Crisp" for about 3 minutes at 340 degrees F.
6. Dish out in a serving plate and serve hot.

- **Nutrition Info:** 184 calories, 12.7g fat, 6.3g carbs, 12.2g protein

9. Bacon, Tomato And Eggs

Servings: 4
Cooking Time: 7 Minutes
Ingredients:
- 4 eggs
- 1 Tbsp milk
- ½ cup crumbled bacon
- 1 tomato, diced
- ¼ tsp salt
- ¼ tsp ground black pepper

Directions:
1. Prepare a baking pan that fits in your Ninja Foodi bowl by greasing the pan with butter. Set aside
2. In a medium bowl, whisk together the eggs, milk, salt and pepper and then add the ham and cheese to the bowl and stir briefly.
3. Pour the egg mix into the prepared baking pan and lower the pan into the Ninja Foodi.
4. Set the Ninja Foodi to air crisp at 325 for 7 minutes.
5. Remove the pan of eggs from the Ninja Foodi and enjoy while hot!

- **Nutrition Info:** Calories: 157g, Carbohydrates: 2g , Protein: 11g, Fat: 12g, Sugar: 3g, Sodium: 957 g

10. Walnut Date Oatmeal

Servings: 2 -3 Servings
Cooking Time: 3 Minutes
Ingredients:
- 2 ¼ cups water
- 1 cup old-fashioned rolled oats
- 2 tablespoons walnuts, chopped
- 2 tablespoons dates, pitted and chopped
- ½ banana, sliced

Directions:
1. Add all ingredients to the cooking pot.
2. Secure lid and select pressure cooker setting with high pressure. Set timer for 3 minutes. When timer goes off use quick release to remove the lid. Stir and serve drizzled with honey or brown sugar.

11. Sausage Solo

Servings: 4
Cooking Time: 35 Minutes
Ingredients:
- 4 eggs
- 4 cooked and sliced sausages
- 2 tbsps. butter
- ½ c. grated mozzarella cheese
- ½ c. cream

Directions:
1. Mix together eggs and cream in a bowl and beat well.
2. Put the egg mixture in the pot of Ninja Foodi and top evenly with cheese and sausage slices.
3. Press "Bake/Roast" and set the timer to 20 minutes at 345 degrees F.
4. Dish out after 20 minutes and serve immediately.

- **Nutrition Info:** 180 calories, 12.7g fat, 3.9g carbs, 12.4g protein

12. Almond French Toast Bites

Servings: 3 Serving
Cooking Time: 15 Minutes
Ingredients:
- 8 pieces of bread
- 6 eggs
- 1/3 cup sugar

- 2 tablespoons almond milk
- 2 tablespoons cinnamon

Directions:
1. Whisk the eggs and almond milk together in a small bowl.
2. In a separate small bowl mix the sugar and cinnamon together.
3. Tear the bread in half and roll the halves into balls, pressing them firmly together.
4. Soak the balls in the egg till it starts to soak into the bread, then roll them in the cinnamon sugar.
5. Place the balls, 8 at a time, in the basket for the air fryer. Lock the Tender Crisp lid in place and set the temperature to 360 degrees. Cook the bites 15 minutes, or till they are crisp.
6. Serve them with maple syrup for dipping or eat them as they are.

13. Baked Biscuits & Gravy

Servings: 4 Servings
Cooking Time: 1 Hour
Ingredients:
- 1 tube refrigerated biscuits
- 1 pound sausage, cooked and drained
- 4 eggs
- 1 cup cheddar cheese, grated
- 1/3 cup milk
- ½ teaspoon pepper
- ½ teaspoon salt
- For the gravy
- 2 cups milk
- 4 tablespoons butter
- 4 tablespoons flour
- ½ teaspoon salt
- ½ teaspoon pepper

Directions:
1. Cut each biscuit into 8 pieces. Set aside.
2. Mix the eggs, milk, salt and pepper in a bowl till combined.
3. Set the cooker to sauté on medium heat. Add butter and melt. Stir in flour, salt and pepper and while stirring, slowly pour in the milk.
4. Increase the heat to med-high and simmer gravy till it thickens. Transfer to a small bowl.
5. Wipe out the inside of the cooker and spray it lightly with cooking spray.
6. Add biscuit pieces to the cooker, then add sausage, cheese, egg mix and top with gravy.
7. Lock the Tender Crisp lid in place and set the temperature to 350 degrees. Bake for 35 – 45 minutes or eggs are cooked through.

14. Bacon Veggies Combo

Servings: 4
Cooking Time: 25 Minutes
Ingredients:
- 1 chopped green bell pepper, seeded
- 4 bacon slices
- ½ c. Parmesan Cheese
- 1 tbsp. avocado mayonnaise
- 2 chopped scallions

Directions:
1. Arrange bacon slices in the pot of Ninja Foodi and top with avocado mayonnaise, bell peppers, scallions and Parmesan Cheese.
2. Press "Bake/Roast" and set the timer to 25 minutes at 365 degrees F.
3. Remove from the Ninja Foodi after 25 minutes and dish out to serve.
- **Nutrition Info:** 197 calories, 13.8g fat, 4.7g carbs, 14.3g protein

15. Bacon And Egg Hash

Servings: 6
Cooking Time: 30 Minutes
Ingredients:
- 6 eggs
- 4 cups riced cauliflower
- ¼ cup milk
- 1 cup crumbled, cooked bacon
- 1 onion, chopped
- 3 Tbsp butter
- ½ cups cheddar cheese

Directions:
1. Press the saute button on your Ninja Foodi and add the butter and the onions. Cook, stirring occasionally until the onions are soft, about 5 minutes.
2. Add the riced cauliflower to the pot and stir. Turn on the air crisper for 15 minutes, turning the cauliflower halfway through.
3. In a small bowl, mix the eggs and milk together then pour over the browned cauliflower.
4. Sprinkle the cheddar cheese on top and close the lid of the Ninja Foodi for one minute to just melt the cheese. Serve while hot
- **Nutrition Info:** Calories: 301g, Carbohydrates: 3g, Protein: 18g, Fat: 26 g, Sugar: 1g, Sodium: 595g

16. Ham Spinach Ballet

Servings: 8
Cooking Time: 35 Minutes
Ingredients:
- 3 lbs. fresh baby spinach
- ½ c. cream
- 28 oz. sliced ham
- 4 tbsps. melted butter
- Salt and freshly ground black pepper

Directions:

1. Press "Sauté" on Ninja Foodi and add butter and spinach.
2. Sauté for about 3 minutes and top with cream, ham slices, salt and black pepper.
3. Lock the lid and set the Ninja Foodi to "Bake/Roast" for about 8 minutes at 360 degrees F.
4. Remove from the Ninja Foodi after 8 minutes and dish out to serve.
- **Nutrition Info:** 188 calories, 12.5g fat, 4.9g carbs, 14.6g protein

17. Three Cheese Eggs

Servings: 4
Cooking Time: 7 Minutes
Ingredients:
- 4 eggs
- 1 Tbsp milk
- ¼ cup Shredded cheddar cheese
- ¼ cup swiss cheese
- ¼ cup American cheese
- ¼ tsp salt
- ¼ tsp ground black pepper

Directions:
1. Prepare a baking pan that fits in your Ninja Foodi bowl by greasing the pan with butter. Set aside
2. In a medium bowl, whisk together the eggs, milk, salt and pepper and then add the ham and cheese to the bowl and stir briefly.
3. Pour the egg mix into the prepared baking pan and lower the pan into the Ninja Foodi.
4. Set the Ninja Foodi to air crisp at 325 for 7 minutes.
5. Remove the pan of eggs from the Ninja Foodi and enjoy while hot!
- **Nutrition Info:** Calories: 138g, Carbohydrates: 1g, Protein: 11g, Fat: 10g, Sugar: 2g, Sodium: 711 g

18. Almond Muffins

Servings: 6
Cooking Time: 25 Minutes
Ingredients:
- 8 Tbsp butter
- ½ cup Baking Stevia
- 1 egg
- 1 tsp vanilla
- 2 cups coconut flour
- 2 tsp baking powder
- 1 tsp salt
- ½ cup chopped almonds
- ½ cup buttermilk

Directions:
1. Use an electric mixer to cream the butter and stevia together until they are light and fluffy.
2. Mix the vanilla and eggs in a small bowl then add to the mixer with the butter blend. Mix until just combined
3. Add the remaining dry ingredients to the mixer and fold together by hand. Add the buttermilk and mix until smooth.
4. Add the almonds to the batter and mix briefly.
5. Pour the muffin batter into eight silicone muffin cups. Place the muffin cups inside the Ninja Foodi on top of a metal trivet.
6. Press the air crisp button and set the temperature to 350 degrees and program the timer to 25 minutes.
7. Once cooked, a toothpick should come out of the center of the cake cleanly. Allow to cool and serve.
- **Nutrition Info:** Calories: 2386g, Carbohydrates: 29g, Protein: 6g, Fat: 26g, Sugar: 5g, Sodium: 699 g

19. Pumpkin Spice Breakfast Cake

Servings: 6
Cooking Time: 25 Minutes
Ingredients:
- 8 Tbsp butter
- ½ cup Baking Stevia
- 1 egg
- 1 tsp vanilla
- 2 cups almond flour
- 2 tsp baking powder
- 1 tsp salt
- 1 tsp cinnamon
- ¼ tsp nutmeg
- ¼ tsp ginger
- 1 cup pumpkin puree

Directions:
1. Use an electric mixer to cream the butter and stevia together until they are light and fluffy.
2. Mix the vanilla and eggs in a small bowl then add to the mixer with the butter blend. Ix until just combined
3. Add the remaining dry ingredients to the mixer and fold together by hand. Add the pumpkin puree and mix until smooth.
4. Pour the cake batter into your Ninja Foodi and place the lid on.
5. Press the air crisp button and set the temperature to 350 degrees and program the timer to 25 minutes.
6. Once cooked, a toothpick should come out of the center of the cake cleanly. Allow to cool and serve.
- **Nutrition Info:** Calories: 176g, Carbohydrates: 8g, Protein: 3g, Fat: 16 g, Sugar: 2g, Sodium: 127 g

20. Ham And Eggs Casserole

Servings: 4
Cooking Time: 7 Minutes
Ingredients:
- 4 eggs
- 1 Tbsp milk
- 1 cup cooked, chopped ham
- ½ cup Shredded cheddar cheese
- ¼ tsp salt
- ¼ tsp ground black pepper

Directions:
1. Prepare a baking pan that fits in your Ninja Foodi bowl by greasing the pan with butter. Set aside
2. In a medium bowl, whisk together the eggs, milk, salt and pepper and then add the ham and cheese to the bowl and stir briefly.
3. Pour the egg mix into the prepared baking pan and lower the pan into the Ninja Foodi.
4. Set the Ninja Foodi to air crisp at 325 for 7 minutes.
5. Remove the pan of eggs from the Ninja Foodi and enjoy while hot!
- **Nutrition Info:** Calories: 169g, Carbohydrates: 1g, Protein: 12g, Fat: 13g, Sugar: 1g, Sodium: 455 g

21. Almond Spice Oatmeal

Servings: 6
Cooking Time: 10 Minutes
Ingredients:
- 1 ½ cups chopped almonds
- 3 cups almond milk
- 2 cups water
- ½ cup psyllium husks
- 1 ½ tsp vanilla extract
- ½ tsp cinnamon
- ¼ tsp nutmeg
- ½ cup granulated stevia

Directions:
1. Add all of the ingredients into the Ninja Foodi and stir together briefly
2. Place the lid on and set the steamer valve to seal. Set the pressure cooker function to 1 minute (it will take about 10 minutes to come to pressure).
3. When the oatmeal is done, do a quick pressure release by opening the steamer valve carefully. Serve while hot
- **Nutrition Info:** Calories: 136g, Carbohydrates: 3g, Protein: 4g, Fat: 9g, Sugar: 1g, Sodium: 66 g

22. French Toast & Cream Cheese Casserole

Servings: 4 - 6 Servings
Cooking Time: 45 Minutes
Ingredients:
- 1 small loaf of bread, sourdough or challah is ideal
- 1 cup milk
- 4 eggs
- ½ cup cream cheese, soft
- ½ cup brown sugar, packed
- 1 tablespoon powdered sugar
- 1 ½ teaspoons vanilla, divided
- ½ teaspoon cinnamon
- Streusel Topping
- ¼ cup brown sugar
- ¼ cup flour
- 3 tablespoons butter, cold and cubed
- ½ teaspoon cinnamon

Directions:
1. Lightly spray cooking pot with cooking spray.
2. Slice the bread then cut it into 1-inch cubed. Layer half of them in the prepared cooking pot.
3. In a mixing bowl, beat the cream cheese till smooth. Add powdered sugar and ¼ teaspoon of the vanilla and mix till combined. Drop by spoonful's on top of the bread. Add remaining bread cubes.
4. In a separate bowl, whisk together eggs, milk, cinnamon, brown sugar and remaining vanilla till combined and no lumps remain. Pour over the bread. Cover tightly with plastic wrap and refrigerate 3 hours or overnight.
5. Before baking, remove from refrigerator and prepare the topping: In a small bowl, stir together the dry ingredients. Cut in butter with a pastry knife or two forks. Sprinkle over the bread mixture.
6. Place the pot in the cooker and secure the Tender Crisp lid. Set the temperature to 350 degrees and bake for 45 minutes or golden brown on top. Serve it while warm with fruit or syrup.

23. Sweet And Savory Oatmeal

Servings: 6
Cooking Time: 10 Minutes
Ingredients:
- 3 cups almond milk
- 2 cups water
- ½ cup psyllium husks
- 1 ½ tsp vanilla extract
- ½ tsp cinnamon
- ¼ tsp nutmeg
- ½ cup granulated stevia
- ½ cup crumbled, cooked bacon

Directions:
1. Add all of the ingredients into the Ninja Foodi and stir together briefly
2. Place the lid on and set the steamer valve to seal. Set the pressure cooker function to 1

minute (it will take about 10 minutes to come to pressure).
3. When the oatmeal is done, do a quick pressure release by opening the steamer valve carefully. Serve while hot
- **Nutrition Info:** Calories: 65g, Carbohydrates: 4g, Protein: 1g, Fat: 8g, Sugar: 0g, Sodium: 316 g

24. Cheesy Ham & Egg Casserole

Servings: 8 Servings
Cooking Time: 4 -8 Hours
Ingredients:
- 1 bag O'Brien potatoes, frozen
- 1 dozen eggs
- ½ pound ham, diced
- 1 cup cheddar cheese, grated
- ½ cup milk
- Salt & pepper

Directions:
1. Lightly spray the inside of the cooking pot with cooking spray.
2. Place the potatoes in the pot. Then top with ham and the cheese.
3. Beat the eggs in a large bowl. Stir in milk, salt and pepper and pour over the other ingredients.
4. Secure the lid and select slow cooker function. The casserole will be done in 4 hours on high heat or 8 hours on low.

25. Veggie Egg Casserole

Servings: 4
Cooking Time: 7 Minutes
Ingredients:
- 4 eggs
- 1 Tbsp milk
- 1 tomato, diced
- ½ cup spinach
- ¼ tsp salt
- ¼ tsp ground black pepper

Directions:
1. Prepare a baking pan that fits in your Ninja Foodi bowl by greasing the pan with butter. Set aside
2. In a medium bowl, whisk together the eggs, milk, salt and pepper and then add the veggies to the bowl and stir briefly.
3. Pour the egg mix into the prepared baking pan and lower the pan into the Ninja Foodi.
4. Set the Ninja Foodi to air crisp at 325 for 7 minutes.
5. Remove the pan of eggs from the Ninja Foodi and enjoy while hot!
- **Nutrition Info:** Calories: 78g, Carbohydrates: 1g, Protein: 7g, Fat: 5g, Sugar: 2g, Sodium: 660 g

26. Caramel Pumpkin Oatmeal

Servings: 10 Servings
Cooking Time: 2 Hours
Ingredients:
- 5 -7 cups milk
- 2 cups rolled oats
- ½ cup pumpkin
- ½ cup date paste
- 2 teaspoon cinnamon
- ½ teaspoon ginger
- ¼ teaspoon nutmeg

Directions:
1. Add all ingredients to the cooking pot. Secure the lid and select slow cooker function on high heat. Set timer for 2 hours.
2. Stir before serving. Store any left overs in an airtight container in the refrigerator.

27. Bacon, Broccoli And Cheddar Frittata

Servings: 4
Cooking Time: 7 Minutes
Ingredients:
- 6 eggs
- 2 Tbsp milk
- ½ cup chopped, cooked bacon
- 1 cup cooked broccoli
- ½ cup shredded cheddar cheese
- ¼ tsp salt
- ¼ tsp ground black pepper

Directions:
1. Prepare a baking pan that fits in your Ninja Foodi bowl by greasing the pan with butter. Set aside
2. In a medium bowl, whisk together the eggs, milk, salt and pepper and then add the bacon, broccoli and cheese to the bowl and stir briefly.
3. Pour the egg mix into the prepared baking pan and lower the pan into the Ninja Foodi.
4. Set the Ninja Foodi to air crisp at 325 for 7 minutes.
5. Remove the pan of eggs from the Ninja Foodi and enjoy while hot!
- **Nutrition Info:** Calories: 269g, Carbohydrates: 3g, Protein: 19g, Fat: 20g, Sugar: 2g, Sodium: 370 g

28. Bacon And Egg Bites

Servings: 6
Cooking Time: 20 Minutes
Ingredients:
- 5 slices bacon
- ½ cup milk
- 1 cup chopped spinach
- 6 eggs

Directions:
1. Place the bacon strips in the Ninja Foodi air crisper basket and use the air crisp function, set for 10 minutes to cook the bacon.

Remove the basket and the strips and pour the bacon grease into a separate small bowl.
2. Add the eggs to the bacon grease along with the spinach, crumbled cooked bacon and milk.
3. Spray an egg bite mold and pour the egg mix evenly into each mold. Place the mold on top of the metal trivet inside the Ninja Foodi. Lower the crisper lid and set the temperature for 375 for 17 minutes.
4. Once cooked, remove the egg mold from the Ninja Foodi and let cool. Pop the egg bites out of the mold and serve hot or cold.
- **Nutrition Info:** Calories: 118g, Carbohydrates: 2g, Protein: 9g, Fat: 8 g, Sugar: 2g, Sodium: 216 g

29. Almond French Toast

Servings: 4
Cooking Time: 7 Minutes
Ingredients:
- 6 eggs
- 1 cup milk
- 4 cups keto almond bread, cut in cubes
- ¼ tsp salt
- 1 tsp vanilla extract
- ½ tsp cinnamon

Directions:
1. Prepare a baking pan that fits in your Ninja Foodi bowl by greasing the pan with butter. Set aside
2. In a medium bowl, whisk together the eggs, milk, salt, vanilla and cinnamon and then add the almond bread to the bowl and stir briefly. Let sit for one hour
3. Pour the egg mix into the prepared baking pan and lower the pan into the Ninja Foodi.
4. Set the Ninja Foodi to air crisp at 325 for 18 minutes.
5. Remove the pan of French toast from the Ninja Foodi and enjoy while hot!
- **Nutrition Info:** Calories: 220g, Carbohydrates: 8g, Protein: 22g, Fat: 11g, Sugar: 5g, Sodium:708 g

30. Maple Sausage Bread Pudding

Servings: 4-6 Servings
Cooking Time: 7-8 Hours
Ingredients:
- 1 pound sausage, casings removed
- 1 small baguette, cubed
- 2 cups milk
- 1 ½ cups cheddar cheese, cubed
- ½ cup heavy cream
- ½ cup maple syrup
- 4 eggs

Directions:
1. Set cooker to sauté on med heat and add sausage. Cook, breaking it up into bite-size pieces, do not crumble it. Transfer to strainer and drain off fat. Cool completely.
2. In a large mixing bowl, whisk together eggs, milk, cream and syrup till smooth. Add the bread pieces, sausage and cheese and stir to combine, most of the liquid should soak into the bread.
3. Set the cooker to slow cooking function on low heat. Secure the lid and cook 7-8 hours, or overnight. Serve warm drizzled with more maple syrup.

31. Cherry Fritters

Servings: 12 Fritters
Cooking Time: 30 Minutes
Ingredients:
- 2 ¾ cups flour
- 1 ¼ cups sweet cherries, pitted and chopped
- 1 cup milk
- 1 egg
- 3 tablespoons sugar
- 2 tablespoons butter, soft
- 2 ¼ teaspoons instant yeast
- 1 teaspoon vanilla
- ½ teaspoon salt
- ½ teaspoon almond extract
- Glaze
- 1 ¼ cups powdered sugar
- 3 tablespoons milk
- 1 teaspoon vanilla extract
- ½ teaspoon almond extract

Directions:
1. Make the dough the night before. In a large bowl, mix flour, sugar, yeast and salt together. Beat in milk, butter, extracts and egg till dough forms.
2. Transfer dough to a lightly floured surface and knead about 6 minutes. Place the dough into a buttered bowl and cover with plastic. Chill overnight.
3. Next day, transfer dough to a well-floured work surface. Press into a rectangle about 12 x 8 inches. Sprinkle the cherries over the dough being sure to leave about ½ inch at the edges plain. Roll up along the widest side. Slice into 12 pieces, place on flour dusted, line cookie sheet and loosely cover. Let rise for 20-30 minutes or till double in size.
4. Lightly spray the rolls with cooking spray, then add 2 at a time to the fryer basket. Place in the cooker and secure the Tender Crisp lid. Set the temperature for 360 degrees and cook 1-2 minutes on each side, or till they are golden brown. Remove to a wire rack and repeat with remaining rolls.
5. Whisk the glaze ingredients together in a medium bowl. Dip the top of each fritter in

glaze then place back on the rack. Allow several minutes for the glaze to set before serving.

32. Sausage And Spinach Breakfast Casserole

Servings: 6 -8 Servings
Cooking Time: 6 – 8 Hours
Ingredients:
- 1 pound breakfast sausage, casings removed
- 5 cups baby spinach, packed
- 1 bag of O'Brien potatoes, frozen
- 2 cups milk
- 8 eggs
- 1 ¼ cups Swiss cheese, grated
- 1 small onion, chopped fine
- ¼ cup Parmesan cheese, grated
- 2 teaspoons Dijon mustard
- 1 ½ teaspoons oregano
- 1 ½ teaspoons salt
- ¼ teaspoon freshly ground black pepper
- Red pepper flakes or hot sauce, for serving

Directions:
1. Set cooker to sauté on med-high heat. Add sausage, onion, and oregano and cook, breaking up the sausage till no longer pink, about 8 minutes. Add spinach and stir till wilted. Drain off the excess fat.
2. Add potatoes, 1 cup Swiss cheese, and the Parmesan cheese and stir to combine.
3. In a large bowl, whisk eggs, milk, mustard, salt and pepper together. Pour over sausage mix making sure you have an even layer.
4. Secure the lid and select slow cooker function on low heat. Cook 6 -8 hours or till the eggs are set. Top with remaining Swiss cheese and replace lid till it melts. Serve with pepper flakes or hot sauce if you like.

33. Spinach Quiche

Servings: 6
Cooking Time: 45 Minutes
Ingredients:
- 1 tbsp. melted butter
- 10 oz. frozen and thawed spinach
- 5 beaten eggs
- Salt and black pepper
- 3 c. shredded Monterey Jack cheese

Directions:
1. Press "Sauté" on Ninja Foodi and add butter and spinach.
2. Sauté for about 3 minutes and dish out in a bowl.
3. Add eggs, Monterey Jack cheese, salt and black pepper to a bowl and transfer into greased molds.
4. Place the molds inside the pot of Ninja Foodi and press "Bake/Roast".
5. Set the timer to 30 minutes at 360 degrees F and press "Start".
6. Remove from the Ninja Foodi after 30 minutes and cut into equal sized wedges to serve.
- **Nutrition Info:** 349 calories, 27.8g fat, 3.2g carbs, 23g protein

34. Blackberry Muffins

Servings: 6
Cooking Time: 25 Minutes
Ingredients:
- 8 Tbsp butter
- ½ cup Baking Stevia
- 1 egg
- 1 tsp vanilla
- 2 cups coconut flour
- 2 tsp baking powder
- 1 tsp salt
- 1 cup fresh blackberries
- ½ cup buttermilk

Directions:
1. Use an electric mixer to cream the butter and stevia together until they are light and fluffy.
2. Mix the vanilla and eggs in a small bowl then add to the mixer with the butter blend. Mix until just combined
3. In a separate bowl, toss the blackberries and ¼ cup almond flour to coat the berries.
4. Add the remaining dry ingredients to the mixer and fold together by hand. Add the buttermilk and mix until smooth.
5. Add the blackberries to the batter and mix briefly.
6. Pour the muffin batter into eight silicone muffin cups. Place the muffin cups inside the Ninja Foodi on top of a metal trivet.
7. Press the air crisp button and set the temperature to 350 degrees and program the timer to 25 minutes.
8. Once cooked, a toothpick should come out of the center of the cake cleanly. Allow to cool and serve.
- **Nutrition Info:** Calories: 285g, Carbohydrates: 2g , Protein: 6g, Fat: 17g, Sugar: 3g, Sodium: 590 g

35. Double Meat Breakfast Casserole

Servings: 4 -6 Servings
Cooking Time: 50 Minutes
Ingredients:
- ½ pound breakfast sausage
- 2 cups hash browns, shredded and thawed
- 4 slices bacon, chopped
- 6 eggs
- ¾ cup Velveeta, cubed
- ½ cup cheddar cheese, grated
- ½ cup mushrooms, sliced

- ¼ cup red bell pepper, chopped
- ¼ cup green bell pepper, chopped
- ¼ cup onion, chopped fine
- 2 -3 tablespoons sour cream

Directions:
1. Set the cooker to saute on med-high heat. Add the sausage and cook till brown. Remove with a slotted spoon and set aside.
2. Add bacon and cook, the remove it and set aside too. Drain all but 2 tablespoons of fat from the cooking pot.
3. Add vegetables and hash browns to the pot and cook till vegetables soften, stirring often. Stir in Velveeta cheese and continue cooking till it is melted and combined.
4. Meanwhile, in a large mixing bowl, whisk together eggs, sour cream, cheddar cheese and cooked bacon together.
5. Once the Velveeta is melted, top with sausage then pour the egg mixture over that.
6. Lock the Tender Crisp lid in place and set the temperature to 350 degrees. Bake the casserole for 35 -40 minutes or the center is set. Let rest 10 minutes before serving.

36. Breakfast Stuffed Baked Potatoes

Servings: 4 Servings
Cooking Time: 8 Hours 10 Minutes
Ingredients:
- 4 potatoes, scrubbed and pricked all over
- 4 strips bacon, cooked and crumbled
- 4 eggs
- ½ cup cheddar cheese, grated
- 1 avocado, sliced
- ¼ cup chives, chopped
- 1 teaspoon olive oil
- Salt & pepper

Directions:
1. Rub the potatoes with oil and sprinkle with salt and pepper. Wrap in foil and place them in the cooking pot. Lock the lid in place and select slow cooking function on low heat. Cook potatoes overnight.
2. In the morning, carefully remove the potatoes and set the cooker to saute on med-high heat. Cook bacon till crisp, drain on paper towel and crumble when cool enough to do so.
3. Fry the eggs how you like them.
4. To assemble, cut the potatoes open, sprinkle cheese over them. Top with bacon, an egg, a slice of avocado and the chives. Salt and pepper to taste and enjoy.

37. Coconut Oatmeal

Servings:6
Cooking Time: 10 Minutes
Ingredients:
- 1 cup shredded dried coconut flakes
- 3 cups coconut milk
- 3 cups water
- ¼ cup psyllium husks
- ½ cup coconut flour
- 1 ½ tsp vanilla extract
- ½ tsp cinnamon
- ½ cup granulated stevia

Directions:
1. Add all of the ingredients into the Ninja Foodi and stir together briefly
2. Place the lid on and set the steamer valve to seal. Set the pressure cooker function to 1 minute (it will take about 10 minutes to come to pressure).
3. When the oatmeal is done, do a quick pressure release by opening the steamer valve carefully. Serve while hot
- **Nutrition Info:** Calories: 202g, Carbohydrates: 6g , Protein: 3g, Fat: 16g, Sugar: 2g, Sodium: 52 g

38. Pepperoni Omelet

Servings: 4
Cooking Time: 5 Minutes
Ingredients:
- 4 tbsps. heavy cream
- 15 pepperoni slices
- 2 tbsps. butter
- Salt and black pepper
- 6 eggs

Directions:
1. Whisk together the eggs, heavy cream, pepperoni slices, salt and black pepper in a bowl.
2. Press "Sauté" on Ninja Foodi and add butter and egg mixture.
3. Sauté for about 3 minutes and flip the side of the omelette.
4. Lock the lid and set the Ninja Foodi on "Air Crisp" for about 2 minutes at 350 degrees F.
5. Dish out in a serving plate and serve with low carb bread.
- **Nutrition Info:** 141 calories, 11.3g fat, 0.6g carbs, 8.9g protein

39. Blueberry Bagels

Servings: 4 Bagels
Cooking Time: 25 Mins
Ingredients:
- 1 cup flour
- 1 cup yogurt
- ¼ cup dried blueberries
- 2 tablespoons sugar
- 1 egg white
- 2 teaspoons baking powder
- 2 teaspoons water
- ¼ teaspoon sea salt

Directions:

1. Combine dry ingredients, except berries, in a small bowl.
2. In a medium bowl, stir together the yogurt and berries. Fold in the dry ingredients till combined.
3. Knead the dough, on a lightly floured surface, several times till it is no longer sticky. Cut it into 4 pieces and roll each piece into an 8-inch long rope.
4. In a separate small bowl, stir together the egg white and water.
5. Form a loop with each dough piece and pinch the ends together.
6. Brush with the egg white mixture and add them to the fryer basket, 2 at a time.
7. Lock the Tender Crisp lid in place and set the temperature to 330 degrees. Bake 12 minutes, then repeat with remaining bagels.
8. Serve warm or let cool and store tightly wrapped for later.

40. Avocado Eggs

Servings: 4

Cooking Time: 7 Minutes
Ingredients:
- 4 eggs
- 2 Avocados, sliced
- ¼ tsp salt
- ¼ tsp ground black pepper

Directions:
1. Prepare a baking pan that fits in your Ninja Foodi bowl by greasing the pan with butter. Set aside
2. Crack the eggs into the prepared baking pan and sprinkle with the salt and pepper. Lower the pan into the Ninja Foodi.
3. Set the Ninja Foodi to air crisp at 325 for 7 minutes.
4. Remove the pan of eggs from the Ninja Foodi and place the sliced avocado on top. Enjoy while hot!
- **Nutrition Info:** Calories: 190g, Carbohydrates: 7g , Protein: 8g, Fat: 15g, Sugar: 2g, Sodium: 657 g

MEAT RECIPES

41. Everyday Chicken Breast

Servings: 4 Servings
Cooking Time: 8 Minutes
Ingredients:
- 4 boneless skinless chicken breasts
- ½ cup water

Directions:
1. Place the chicken breast in the Ninja Foodi pot and add the water.
2. Close the pressure seal lid and set the steamer valve to seal.
3. Cook on high pressure for 8 minutes then do a quick pressure release. Serve the chicken while hot.
- **Nutrition Info:** Calories: 249g, Carbohydrates: 0g, Protein: 52g, Fat: 2g, Sugar: 0g, Sodium: 149mg

42. Pulled Bbq Chicken

Servings: 6 Servings
Cooking Time: 15 Minutes
Ingredients:
- 1 ½ pounds boneless, skinless chicken thighs
- 1 Tbsp olive oil
- 1 tsp ground paprika
- ¼ tsp salt
- ¼ tsp ground black pepper
- 1 onion, chopped
- ¼ cup hot sauce
- ¼ cup water
- 2 Tbsp vinegar

Directions:
1. Turn the Ninja Foodi on to saute and add the olive oil. Once hot, add the chicken thighs and sear on each side for 2 minutes.
2. Sprinkle the salt and pepper on the chicken and then add all the remaining ingredients to the pot.
3. Cover the Foodi and use the pressure cooker function to cook the chicken for 15 minutes under high heat pressure.
4. Release the pressure using a natural steam release and then use two forks to pull he chicken apart. Serve warm or chilled
- **Nutrition Info:** Calories: 215g, Carbohydrates: 1g, Protein: 17g, Fat: 16g, Sugar: 1g, Sodium: 1672 mg

43. Chicken Shawarma Middle-east

Servings: 2
Cooking Time: 20 Minutes
Ingredients:
- ¼ teaspoon coriander
- ¼ teaspoon cumin
- ½ teaspoon paprika
- 1 teaspoon cardamom
- ½ teaspoon cinnamon powder
- ¼ teaspoon cloves
- ¼ teaspoon nutmeg
- ¼ cup lemon juice
- ¼ cup yogurt
- 2 tablespoons garlic, minced
- 1-pound boneless chicken breasts, cut into strips
- 2 bay leaves
- Salt and pepper to taste
- 2 pita bread
- ¼ cup greek yogurt
- For garnish: tomatoes, lettuce, and cucumber

Directions:
1. Place in the Ninja Foodi the coriander, cumin, paprika, cardamom, cinnamon powder, cloves, nutmeg, lemon juice, yogurt, garlic, and chicken breasts. Add the bay leaves and season with salt and pepper to taste.
2. Install pressure lid. Close Ninja Foodi, press the pressure button, choose high settings, and set time to 20 minutes.
3. Once done cooking, do a quick release. Place the chicken in the pita bread and drizzle with Greek yogurt. Garnish with tomatoes, lettuce, and cucumber.
4. Serve and enjoy.
- **Nutrition Info:** Calories: 372; carbohydrates: 21.8g; protein: 55.1g; fat: 7.1g

44. Veggie Chicken Soup

Servings: 4 Servings
Cooking Time: 12 Minutes
Ingredients:
- 1 pound chicken breast
- 6 cups chicken broth
- 2 cloves of garlic, chopped
- 1 carrot, chopped
- 1 Bell pepper, chopped
- 1 sweet potato, peeled, diced
- 2 celery stalks, chopped
- ½ white onion, chopped
- ¼ tsp salt
- 1/8 tsp ground black pepper
- ¼ cup shredded cheddar cheese

Directions:
1. Add all the ingredients to the pot and place the pressure cooker lid on the Ninja Foodi.
2. Cook on high pressure for 12 minutes. Do a quick steam release and remove the lid.
3. Remove the chicken from the pot and shred the chicken using two forks.
4. Serve while hot or freeze to use at a later date.

- **Nutrition Info:** Calories: 310g, Carbohydrates: 14g, Protein: 37g, Fat: 6g, Sugar: 5g, Sodium: 376 mg

45. Luscious Chicken Breasts

Servings: 4
Cooking Time: 20 Minutes
Ingredients:
- 2 (8-oz.) skinless, boneless chicken fillets
- Salt and freshly ground black pepper, to taste
- 4 brie cheese slices
- 1 tbsp. fresh chive, minced
- 4 cured ham slices

Directions:
1. Cut each chicken fillet in 2 equal sized pieces.
2. Carefully, make a slit in each chicken piece horizontally about ¼-inch from the edge.
3. Open each chicken piece and season with the salt and black pepper.
4. Place 1 cheese slice in the open area of each chicken piece and sprinkle with chives.
5. In the pot of Ninja Foodi, place 1 C. of water.
6. Place the rolled chicken breasts into "Cook & Crisp Basket".
7. Arrange the "Cook & Crisp Basket" in the pot.
8. Cover the Ninja Foodi with the pressure lid and place the pressure valve to "Seal" position. Select "Pressure" and set to "High" for about 5 minutes.
9. Press "Start/Stop" to begin. Switch the valve to "Vent" and do a "Quick" release.
10. Once all the pressure is released, open the lid
11. Now, close the Ninja Foodi with the crisping lid and Select "Air Crisp".
12. Set the temperature to 355 degrees F for 15 minutes. Press "Start/Stop" to begin.
13. Open the lid and transfer the rolled chicken breasts onto a cutting board.
14. Cut into desired sized slices and serve.
- **Nutrition Info:** Calories: 271; Carbohydrates: 1.2g; Protein: 35.2g; Fat: 13.4g; Sugar: 0.1g; Sodium: 602mg; Fiber: 0.4g

46. St. Patty's Corned Beef Recipe

Servings: 2
Cooking Time: 60 Minutes
Ingredients:
- 2 cloves of garlic, chopped
- 1/2 onion, quartered
- 1 1/4 pounds corned beef brisket, cut in large slices
- 3-oz. Beer
- 1 cup water
- 2 small carrots, roughly chopped
- 1 small potato, chopped
- 1/2 head cabbage, cut into four pieces

Directions:
1. In the Ninja Foodi, place the garlic, onion, corned beef brisket, beer, and water. Season with salt and pepper to taste.
2. Install pressure lid. Close Ninja Foodi, press the pressure button, choose high settings, and set time to 50 minutes.
3. Once done cooking, do a quick release. Open the lid and take out the meat. Shred the meat using fork and place it back into the Ninja Foodi.
4. Stir in the vegetables.
5. Install pressure lid. Close the lid and seal the vent and press the pressure button. Cook for another 10 minutes. Do quick release.
6. Serve and enjoy.
- **Nutrition Info:** Calories:758; carbohydrates: 45.8g; protein: 43.1g; fat: 44.7g

47. Out Of World Deer

Servings: 10
Cooking Time: 2½ Hours
Ingredients:
- 3-4 lb. deer, thawed
- Salt and freshly ground black pepper, to taste
- 1 (12-oz.) can beer
- ¼ C. Worcestershire sauce
- 1 tbsp. honey

Directions:
1. Grease the pot of Ninja Foodi generously.
2. Select "Sauté/Sear" setting of Ninja Foodi and place the deer meat.
3. Press "Start/Stop" to begin and cook, uncovered for about 15 minutes per side.
4. Press "Start/Stop" to stop the cooking and stir in the remaining ingredients.
5. Close the crisping lid and select "Slow Cooker".
6. Set on "High" for about 2 hours.
7. Press "Start/Stop" to begin.
8. Open the lid and with 2 forks, shred the meat.
9. Serve hot.
- **Nutrition Info:** Calories: 242; Carbohydrates: 4.1g; Protein: 41.3g; Fat: 4.3g; Sugar: 2.9g; Sodium: 156mg; Fiber: 0g

48. Buffalo Chicken Wings

Servings: 4
Cooking Time: 20 Minutes
Ingredients:
- 2 lb. frozen chicken wings, drums and flats separated
- 2 tbsp. canola oil

- 2 tbsp. Buffalo sauce
- 2 tsp. kosher salt

Directions:
1. In the pot of Ninja Foodi, place ½ C. of water.
2. Place the chicken wings into "Cook & Crisp Basket".
3. Arrange the "Cook & Crisp Basket" in the pot.
4. Cover the Ninja Foodi with the pressure lid and place the pressure valve to "Seal" position. Select "Pressure" and set to "High" for about 5 minutes.
5. Press "Start/Stop" to begin. Switch the valve to "Vent" and do a "Quick" release.
6. Once all the pressure is released, open the lid
7. Remove the wings from the pot and with paper towels, pat dry them.
8. In the basket, place the wings and drizzle with the oil evenly.
9. Now, close the Ninja Foodi with the crisping lid and select "Air Crisp".
10. Set the temperature to 390 degrees F for 15 minutes.
11. Press "Start/Stop" to begin. After 7 minutes, flip the wings.
12. Meanwhile, in a large bowl, add Buffalo sauce and salt and mix well.
13. Open the lid and transfer the wings into the bowl of Buffalo sauce.
14. Then, toss the wings well to coat with the Buffalo sauce.
15. Serve immediately.
- **Nutrition Info:** Calories: 495; Carbohydrates: 0.5g; Protein: 65.6g; Fat: 23.8g; Sugar: 0g; Sodium: 1400mg; Fiber: 0g

49. Lamb Roast

Servings: 6
Cooking Time: 1 Hour 10 Mins
Ingredients:
- 2 lbs. lamb roasted wegmans
- 1 c. onion soup
- 1 c. beef broth
- Salt and black pepper

Directions:
1. Put the lamb roast in the pot of Ninja Foodi and add onion soup, beef broth, salt and black pepper.
2. Lock the lid and set the Ninja Foodi to "Pressure" for about 55 minutes at "Md:Hi".
3. Release the pressure naturally and dish out.
- **Nutrition Info:** 349 calories, 18.8g fat, 2.9g carbs, 39.9g protein

50. Ninja Foodi Salsa Verde Chicken

Servings: 2
Cooking Time: 20 Minutes
Ingredients:
- 1-pound boneless chicken breasts
- 1/4 teaspoon salt
- 1 cup commercial salsa verde

Directions:
1. Place all ingredients in the Ninja Foodi.
2. Install pressure lid. Close Ninja Foodi, press the manual button, choose high settings, and set time to 20 minutes.
3. Once done cooking, do a quick release.
4. Serve and enjoy.
- **Nutrition Info:** Calories: 273; carbohydrates: 2.5g; protein: 51.4g; fat: 6.3g

51. Drunken Duck Breast

Servings: 2
Cooking Time: 20 Minutes
Ingredients:
- 1 (10½-oz.) duck breast
- 1 tsp. mustard
- 1 tbsp. fresh thyme, chopped
- 1 C. beer
- Salt and freshly ground black pepper, to taste

Directions:
1. Spray the duck breast with cooking spray evenly.
2. In a bowl, mix together mustard, thyme, beer, salt and black pepper. Add duck breast ad coat with marinade generously. Refrigerate, covered for about 4 hours.
3. Arrange the "Cook & Crisp Basket" in the pot of Ninja Foodi.
4. Close the Ninja Foodi with crisping lid and select "Air Crisp".
5. Press "Start/Stop" to begin and set the temperature to 390 degrees F.
6. Set the time for 5 minutes to preheat. With a piece of foil, cover the duck breast
7. Now, place the duck breast into "Cook & Crisp Basket". Close the Ninja Foodi with crisping lid and select "Air Crisp". Set the temperature to 390 degrees F for 15 minutes.
8. Press "Start/Stop" to begin. Open the lid and remove the foil from the breast.
9. Close the Ninja Foodi with crisping lid and set the temperature to 355 degrees F for 5 minutes. Press "Start/Stop" to begin. Open the lid and serve hot.
- **Nutrition Info:** Calories: 255; Carbohydrates: 5.7g; Protein: 33.8g; Fat: 6.g; Sugar: 0.1g; Sodium: 83mg; Fiber: 0.7g

52. Ginger-balsamic Glazed Chicken

Servings: 2
Cooking Time: 15 Minutes
Ingredients:
- 4 chicken thighs, skinless
- 1/4 cup balsamic vinegar

- 1 1/2 tablespoons mustard
- 1 tablespoon ginger garlic paste
- 4 cloves of garlic, minced
- 1-inch fresh ginger root
- 2 tablespoons honey
- Salt and pepper to taste

Directions:
1. Place all ingredients in the Ninja Foodi. Stir to combine everything.
2. Install pressure lid. Close Ninja Foodi, press the manual button, choose high settings, and set time to 15 minutes.
3. Once done cooking, do a quick release. Remove pressure lid.
4. Mix and turnover chicken.
5. Cover, press roast, and roast for 5 minutes.
6. Serve and enjoy.
- **Nutrition Info:** Calories: 476; carbohydrates:12.5g; protein: 32.4g; fat: 32.9g

53. Spice Crusted Chicken Breasts

Servings: 4
Cooking Time: 35 Minutes
Ingredients:
- 1½ tbsp. smoked paprika
- 1 tsp. ground cumin
- Salt and freshly ground black pepper, to taste
- 2 (12-oz.) bone-in, skin-on chicken breasts
- 1 tbsp. olive oil

Directions:
1. In a small bowl, mix together paprika, cumin, salt and black pepper.
2. Coat the chicken breasts with oil evenly and then season with the spice mixture generously. Arrange the "Cook & Crisp Basket" in the pot of Ninja Foodi.
3. Close the Ninja Foodi with crisping lid and select "Air Crisp".
4. Press "Start/Stop" to begin and set the temperature to 375 degrees F.
5. Set the time for 5 minutes to preheat.
6. Now, place the chicken breasts into the "Cook & Crisp Basket".
7. Close the Ninja Foodi with crisping lid and select "Air Crisp".
8. Set the temperature to 375 degrees F for 35 minutes.
9. Press "Start/Stop" to begin。 Open the lid and transfer the chicken breasts onto a cutting board for about 5 minutes.
10. Cut each breast in 2 equal sized pieces and serve.
- **Nutrition Info:** Calories: 363; Carbohydrates: 1.7g; Protein: 49.7g; Fat: 16.6g; Sugar: 0.3g; Sodium: 187mg; Fiber: 1g

54. Chili Pork

Servings: 2
Cooking Time: 10 Minutes
Ingredients:
- 2 tsp salt
- 1 Tbsp paprika
- 1 tbsp chili powder
- T tsp ground black pepper
- 1 tsp onion powder
- 1 tsp garlic powder
- 1 tsp ground cumin
- 2 pounds bone in Pork Chops
- 1 tbsp olive oil

Directions:
1. Mix all of the spices together in a bowl and then set aside.
2. Rub the pork chops with the olive oil and then coat in the spice seasoning.
3. Place the spiced chicken in the cook and crisp basket and turn the Ninja Foodi to 375 degrees. Place the basket in the Foodi and set the timer for 30 minutes. Serve while hot straight out of the pot.
- **Nutrition Info:** Calories: 340, Carbohydrates: 5g, Protein: 20g, Fat: 7g, Sugar: 5g, Sodium: 270 mg

55. Mediterranean Turkey Cutlets

Servings: 4
Cooking Time: 25 Minutes
Ingredients:
- 1 tsp. Greek seasoning
- 1 lb. turkey cutlets
- 2 tbsps. olive oil
- 1 tsp. turmeric powder
- ½ c. almond flour

Directions:
1. Combine Greek seasoning, turmeric powder and almond flour in a bowl.
2. Dredge turkey cutlets in it and set aside for about 30 minutes.
3. Press "Sauté" on Ninja Foodi and add oil and turkey cutlets.
4. Sauté for about 2 minutes and add turkey cutlets.
5. Press "Pressure" and set to "Lo:Md" for about 20 minutes.
6. Dish out in a serving platter.
- **Nutrition Info:** 340 calories, 19.4g fat, 3.7g carbs, 36.3g protein

56. Savory 'n Aromatic Chicken Adobo

Servings: 2
Cooking Time: 20 Minutes
Ingredients:
- 1-pound boneless chicken thighs
- 1/4 cup white vinegar
- ½ cup water
- 1/4 cup soy sauce

- 1/2 head garlic, peeled and smashed
- 2 bay leaves
- ½ teaspoon pepper
- 1 tsp oil

Directions:
1. Place all ingredients in the Ninja Foodi.
2. Install pressure lid. Close Ninja Foodi, press the pressure button, choose high settings, and set time to 10 minutes.
3. Once done cooking, do a quick release.
4. Open the lid and press the sauté button. Allow the sauce to reduce so that the chicken is fried slightly in its oil, around 10 minutes.
5. Serve and enjoy.
- **Nutrition Info:** Calories: 713; carbohydrates: 3.2g; protein: 43.9g; fat: 58.3g

57. Fuss-free Beef Roast

Servings: 6
Cooking Time: 8 Hours
Ingredients:
- 1 (2 lb.) beef round roast
- 3 large carrots, chopped
- 1 large onion, thinly sliced
- Salt and freshly ground black pepper, to taste
- 1 C. BBQ sauce

Directions:
1. In the pot of Ninja Foodi, place all the ingredients and mix well.
2. Close the crisping lid and select "Slow Cooker".
3. Set on "Low" for about 6-8 hours.
4. Press "Start/Stop" to begin.
5. Open the lid and transfer the roast onto a cutting board.
6. Cut into desired sized slices and serve.
- **Nutrition Info:** Calories: 263; Carbohydrates: 21g; Protein: 33g; Fat: 5.6g; Sugar: 13.7g; Sodium: 164mg; Fiber: 1.7g

58. Creamy Chicken Breasts

Servings: 4
Cooking Time: 25 Minutes
Ingredients:
- 1 small onion
- 2 tbsps. butter
- 1 lb. chicken breasts
- ½ c. sour cream
- Salt

Directions:
1. Apply salt to the chicken breasts generously and keep aside.
2. Heat butter in a skillet on medium-low heat and add onions.
3. Sauté for 3 minutes and add chicken breasts.
4. Cover the lid and cook for about 10 minutes.
5. Stir in the sour cream and cook for about 4 minutes.
6. Stir gently and dish out to serve.
- **Nutrition Info:** 447 calories, 26.9g fat, 3.8g carbs, 45.3g protein

59. Short Ribs And Veggies

Servings: 4
Cooking Time: 1 Hour
Ingredients:
- 3 pounds bone in beef short ribs
- 2 tsp salt
- 1 tsp ground black pepper
- 1 cup chopped onion
- ¼ cup Marsala wine
- ½ cup beef broth
- 2 Tbsp stevia
- 4 cloves garlic, chopped
- 1 tbsp chopped thyme
- 2 parsnips, chopped
- 1 cup pearl onions
- 1 cup chopped beets

Directions:
1. Season ribs with the salt and pepper and then add to the Ninja Foodi pot with 1 Tbsp of oil. Select the sear function and let the ribs sear for 5 minutes, flip and sear for another 5 minutes.
2. Add the onion, wine, broth, stevia, garlic and thyme and place the pressure cooker lid on the Foodi. Set the pressure to high and the timer to 40 minutes. Once the timer is complete, quickly release the steam and open the lid.
3. Place the reversible rack over the top of the ribs in the pot. Place the veggies on the rack and drizzle with some extra oil.
4. Close the crisper lid and set the temperature to 350 for 15 minutes.
5. Remove the veggies and ribs and set aside. Press the sauté function and let the sauce in the pot cook for two more minutes before serving with the ribs and veggies.
- **Nutrition Info:** Calories: 506g, Carbohydrates: 14g, Protein: 47g, Fat: 27g, Sugar: 10g, Sodium: 1647 mg

60. Beef Ribs

Servings: 4
Cooking Time: 40 Minutes
Ingredients:
- 2 pounds beef spare ribs, boneless
- 1 ½ cup beef broth
- ½ tsp ground black pepper
- 1 ½ tsp paprika
- 1 tsp onion powder
- 1 tsp garlic powder
- 1 cup tomato sauce
- 1 ½ tbsp. butter, melted

- 2 Tbsp apple cider vinegar
- 1 tbsp Worcestershire sauce
- 2 tbsp stevia powder
- ½ tsp salt
- ½ tsp onion powder

Directions:
1. In a small bowl, mix together the melted butter, tomato sauce, vinegar, Worcestershire sauce, stevia, ½ tsp salt and ½ tsp onion powder.
2. Place the ribs in the Ninja Foodi bowl and sprinkle with the remaining spices. Toss to coat completely.
3. Pour the homemade BBQ sauce into the bowl with the ribs and place the pressure cooker lid on the pot. Set the timer for 30 minutes at high heat. Once the cooking cycle is complete, let the pressure naturally release from the pot, about another 15 minutes.
4. Brush the ribs with the sauce from the bottom of the pot and then place the crisper lid on the pot. Set the temperature for 400 and set the timer for 10 minutes. Let the ribs brown and then serve hot.
- **Nutrition Info:** Calories: 610 g, Carbohydrates: 6g, Protein: 41g, Fat: 46g, Sugar: 5g, Sodium: 1490 mg

61. Beef Stew Recipe From Ethiopia

Servings: 2
Cooking Time: 55 Minutes
Ingredients:
- 1-pound beef stew meat, cut into chunks
- ¼ teaspoon turmeric powder
- 1 tablespoon garam masala
- 1 tablespoon coriander powder
- 1 teaspoon cumin
- ¼ teaspoon ground nutmeg
- 2 teaspoons smoked paprika
- ¼ teaspoon black pepper
- 2 tablespoons ghee
- 1 onion, chopped
- 1 tablespoon ginger, grated
- 2 cloves of garlic, grated
- 1 tablespoon onions
- 3 tablespoons tomato paste
- ½ teaspoon sugar
- Salt and pepper to taste
- 1 cup water

Directions:
1. In a mixing bowl, combine the first 8 ingredients and allow to marinate in the fridge for at least 4 hours.
2. Press the sauté button and heat the oil. Sauté the onion, ginger, and garlic until fragrant. Stir in the marinated beef and allow to sear button for 3 minutes.
3. Stir in the rest of the ingredients.
4. Install pressure lid. Close Ninja Foodi, press the pressure button, choose high settings, and set time to 50 minutes.
5. Once done cooking, do a quick release.
6. Serve and enjoy.
- **Nutrition Info:** Calories: 591; carbohydrates: 11.5g; protein: 83.5g; fat: 23.4g

62. Green Curry Chicken Thai Style

Servings: 2
Cooking Time: 15 Minutes
Ingredients:
- 1 tablespoon Thai green curry paste
- 1/3 cup coconut milk
- 1/2 teaspoon coriander powder
- ½ teaspoon cumin powder
- 1/3-pound chicken breasts, bones removed and cut into chunks
- ¼ cup chicken broth
- 1 tablespoon fish sauce
- 1/4 tablespoon sear button sugar
- 1/2 tablespoon lime juice
- 1 lime leaves, crushed
- 1/4 cup bamboo shoots, sliced
- 1/4 cup onion, cubed
- Salt and pepper to taste
- 1/3 cup green bell pepper
- 1/3 cup zucchini, sliced
- 2 tbsp Thai basil leaves

Directions:
1. Press the sauté button on the Ninja Foodi. Place the Thai green curry paste and the coconut milk. Stir until the mixture bubbles. Stir in the coriander and cumin powder and cook for 30 seconds.
2. Stir in the chicken and coconut broth. Season with fish sauce, sear button sugar, lime juice, bamboo shoots, lime leaves, and onion. Season with salt and pepper to taste.
3. Install pressure lid. Close Ninja Foodi, press the manual button, choose high settings, and set time to 10 minutes.
4. Once done cooking, do a quick release. Open the lid and press the sauté button. Stir in the green bell pepper, zucchini, and basil leaves. Allow to simmer for at least 5 minutes to cook the vegetables.
5. Serve and enjoy.
- **Nutrition Info:** Calories: 208; carbohydrates:9 g; protein:16 g; fat: 12g

63. Easy Kung Pao Chicken

Servings: 2
Cooking Time: 20 Minutes
Ingredients:
- 1 tablespoon olive oil
- 1 clove garlic, minced
- 1/2 teaspoon grated ginger

- 1/2 teaspoon crushed red pepper
- 1/2 onion, chopped
- 1-pound chicken breasts, cut into bite-sized pieces
- 1/4 cup soy sauce
- 2 tbsp honey
- 2 tbsp hoisin sauce
- 1/2 zucchini, diced
- 1/2 red bell pepper, chopped

Directions:
1. Press the sauté button on the Ninja Foodi and heat the oil. Sauté the garlic, ginger, red pepper, and onion until fragrant.
2. Add the chicken breasts and stir for 3 minutes until lightly golden.
3. Stir in the soy sauce, honey, and hoisin sauce.
4. Close Ninja Foodi, press bake button, set temperature to 350 ºF, and set time to 20 minutes. Halfway through cooking time, stir and continue cooking.
5. Open the lid and press the sauté button. Stir in the zucchini and bell pepper. Allow to simmer until the vegetables are cooked.
6. Serve and enjoy.
- **Nutrition Info:** Calories: 501; carbohydrates: 29.4g; protein: 40.7g; fat: 24.5g

64. Beef Cooked In Mango-turmeric Spice

Servings: 2
Cooking Time: 50 Minutes
Ingredients:
- 1-pound beef shin, cut into chunks
- ½ teaspoon ground cinnamon
- ¼ teaspoon ground cloves
- 1 teaspoon dried mango powder
- 1 teaspoon ground turmeric
- ½ teaspoon ground cumin
- 3 cloves of garlic, minced
- 1 tablespoon lemon juice
- 1 teaspoon honey
- 12 cardamom pods, bashed
- Salt and pepper to taste
- 2 tablespoons ghee
- 1 cup onions, cut into wedges
- 2 green chilies, sliced
- 2 tomatoes, chopped
- 1 cup water

Directions:
1. In a mixing bowl, combine the first 11 ingredients and allow to marinate in the fridge for at least 2 hours.
2. Press the sauté button on the Ninja Foodi and add the ghee. Stir in the marinated beef and sear button on all sides for at least 5 minutes.
3. Stir in the rest of the ingredients.
4. Install pressure lid. Close Ninja Foodi, press the pressure button, choose high settings, and set time to 45 minutes.
5. Once done cooking, do a quick release.
6. Serve and enjoy.
- **Nutrition Info:** Calories: 463; carbohydrates: 19.3g; protein: 51.5g; fat: 20g

65. Whole Roasted Chicken

Servings: 6 Servings
Cooking Time: 40 Minutes
Ingredients:
- Whole 5 pounds Chicken
- 2 Tbsp salt
- ¼ cup lemon juice
- ¼ cup water
- 1 Tbsp stevia powder
- 1 tsp salt
- ½ tsp ground black pepper
- 1 Tbsp dried thyme
- 4 garlic cloves, minced
- 1 Tbsp olive oil

Directions:
1. Add the salt, lemon juice, water, stevia, black pepper, thyme and garlic to the Ninja Foodi Pot.
2. Place the chicken inside the pot as well and brush with the seasoning mix.
3. Move the chicken to the air crisper basket and place back into the pot.
4. Put the pressure cooker lid on the Foodi and seal. Set the pressure cooker function to high for 15 minutes. Once the cooking cycle is complete, do a quick pressure release and open the top.
5. Coat the chicken with the olive oil and put the crisper lid on and sue the air crisper function set to 400 degrees for 15 minutes.
6. Check the chicken after 15 minutes and make sure the internal temperature is 165.
7. Slice and serve while hot.
- **Nutrition Info:** Calories: 235 g, Carbohydrates: 4g, Protein: 18g, Fat: 17g, Sugar: 2g, Sodium: 592 mg

66. Mexican Taco Casserole

Servings: 6
Cooking Time: 35 Minutes
Ingredients:
- 1 c. shredded cheddar cheese
- 1 c. cottage cheese
- 2 lbs. beef, ground
- 1 c. salsa
- 2 tbsps. taco seasoning

Directions:
1. Mix together the taco seasoning and ground beef in a bowl.

2. Stir in salsa, cottage cheese and cheddar cheese.
3. Place ground beef mixture in the pot of Ninja Foodi and lock the lid.
4. Press "Bake/Roast" and set the timer to about 25 minutes at 370 degrees F.
5. Bake for about 25 minutes and dish out to serve immediately.
- **Nutrition Info:** 409 calories, 16.5g fat, 5.7g carbs, 56.4g protein

67. Easter Dinner Ham

Servings: 8
Cooking Time: 1½ Hours
Ingredients:
- 1 (4-lb.) bone-in, fully cooked ham
- 2 C. apple cider
- 1 (3-inch) piece fresh ginger, grated finely
- ¼ C. packed brown sugar
- ¼ C. bourbon

Directions:
1. Select "Bake/Roast" of Ninja Foodi and set the temperature to 375 degrees F.
2. Press "Start/Stop" to begin and preheat the Ninja Foodi for about 10 minutes.
3. With a knife, score the ham on all sides in a diamond pattern.
4. In the pot of Ninja Foodi, place the ham and top with the apple cider.
5. Close the Ninja Foodi with crisping lid and set the time for 1½ hours.
6. Press "Start/Stop" to begin.
7. Open the lid and transfer the ham onto a platter.
8. With a piece of foil, cover the ham to and keep warm.
9. Discard the cooking liquid from the pot, reserving 1 C. inside.
10. Now, select "Sauté/Sear" setting of Ninja Foodi and stir in the remaining ingredients.
11. Cook, uncovered for about 10 minutes or until desired thickness of glaze.
12. Coat the ham with glaze and serve.
- **Nutrition Info:** Calories: 590; Carbohydrates: 11.8g; Protein: 32.5g; Fat: 36.5g; Sugar: 11.2g; Sodium: 3000mg; Fiber: 0.1g

68. Chili Rubbed Chicken

Servings: 2 Servings
Cooking Time: 10 Minutes
Ingredients:
- 2 tsp salt
- 1 Tbsp paprika
- 1 tbsp chili powder
- T tsp ground black pepper
- 1 tsp onion powder
- 1 tsp garlic powder
- 1 tsp ground cumin
- 2 chicken thighs, bone in
- 1 tbsp olive oil

Directions:
1. Mix all of the spices together in a bowl and then set aside.
2. Rub the chicken thighs with the olive oil and then coat in the spice seasoning.
3. Place the spiced chicken in the cook and crisp basket and turn the Ninja Foodi to 375 degrees. Place the basket in the Foodi and set the timer for 30 minutes. Serve while hot straight out of the pot.
- **Nutrition Info:** Calories: 230g, Carbohydrates: 7g, Protein: 15g, Fat: 16g, Sugar: 1g, Sodium: 473 mg

69. Mustard Pork Chops

Servings: 4
Cooking Time: 40 Minutes
Ingredients:
- 2 tbsps. butter
- 2 tbsps. Dijon mustard
- 4 pork chops
- Salt and black pepper
- 1 tbsp. fresh rosemary, chopped

Directions:
1. Marinate the pork chops with Dijon mustard, fresh rosemary, salt and black pepper for about 2 hours.
2. Put the butter and marinated pork chops in the pot of Ninja Foodi and cover the lid.
3. Press "Pressure" and cook for about 30 minutes on Lo:Md.
4. Release the pressure naturally and dish out in a platter.
- **Nutrition Info:** 315 calories, 26.1g fat, 1g carbs, 18.4g protein

70. Chicken Jerky

Servings: 6 Servings
Cooking Time: 7 Hours
Ingredients:
- ½ pound Chicken breast, sliced into 1/8" Thick strips
- ½ cup coconut aminos
- 2 Tbsp Worcestershire sauce
- 2 tsp ground black pepper
- 1 tsp liquid smoke
- 1 tsp onion powders
- ½ tsp garlic powder
- 1 tsp kosher salt

Directions:
1. Place all the ingredients in a large Ziploc bag and seal shut. Shake to mix. Leave in the fridge overnight.
2. Lay the strips on the dehydrator trays, being careful not to overlap them.

3. Place the cook and crisp lid on and set the temperature for 135 degrees for 7 hours. Once done, store in an airtight containers.
- **Nutrition Info:** Calories: 67g, Carbohydrates: 9g, Protein: 4g, Fat: 1g, Sugar: 7g, Sodium: 938 mg

71. Tender Chops In Sweet 'n Sour Sauce

Servings: 2
Cooking Time: 35 Minutes
Ingredients:
- 1/2 tablespoon olive oil
- 1-pound pork chops, pounded
- 1 onion, chopped
- 3 cloves of garlic minced
- 1/3 cup pineapple chunks
- 1 green bell pepper, chopped
- 1/3 cup water
- 2 tbsp ketchup
- 2 tbsp white vinegar
- 1 ½ teaspoons white sugar
- 1/2 tablespoon soy sauce
- 1 tablespoon tomato paste
- 1 teaspoon worcestershire sauce
- 1 tablespoon cornstarch + 1 1/2 tablespoons water

Directions:
1. Press the sauté button in the Ninja Foodi and heat the oil. Sear the pork chops on both sides for 5 minutes and add the onions and garlic until fragrant.
2. Stir in the rest of the ingredients except for the cornstarch and water.
3. Install pressure lid. Close Ninja Foodi, press the pressure button, choose high settings, and set time to 30 minutes.
4. Once done cooking, do a quick release.
5. Press the sauté button and stir in the cornstarch. Allow to simmer for a minute to thicken the sauce.
6. Serve and enjoy.
- **Nutrition Info:** Calories: 405; carbohydrates:35 g; protein: 46g; fat: 9g

72. Beef Roast

Servings: 6
Cooking Time: 25 Minutes
Ingredients:
- 2 pound chuck roast
- 1 Tbsp olive oil
- 1 tsp salt
- 1 tsp ground black pepper
- 1 tsp onion powder
- 1 tsp garlic powder
- 4 cups beef stock

Directions:
1. Place the roast in the Ninja Foodi pot and season with the salt and pepper. Add the oil and then use the saute function to sear each side of the roast for 3 minutes to brown.
2. Add the beef broth, onion powder and garlic powder.
3. Close the pressure cooker lid and set the timer for high pressure, 40 minutes.
4. Once the timer has gone off, naturally release the pressure from the pot.
5. Open the lid and serve while hot.
- **Nutrition Info:** Calories: 308g, Carbohydrates: 2g, Protein: 24g, Fat: 22g, Sugar: 2g, Sodium: 1142mg

73. One-pot Thai Red Curry

Servings: 2
Cooking Time: 20 Minutes
Ingredients:
- 1 1/2 tablespoon Thai red curry paste
- 1/2 can coconut milk
- 3/4-pound chicken breasts, sliced into chunks
- ¼ cup chicken broth
- 1 tablespoon fish sauce
- 1 teaspoon sear button sugar
- 1/2 tablespoon lime juice
- 1/2 cup red and green bell pepper
- 1/2 cup carrots, peeled and sliced
- ½ cup cubed onion
- 2 lime leaves
- 6 thai basil leaves

Directions:
1. Place all ingredients in the Ninja Foodi and give a good stir.
2. Install pressure lid. Close Ninja Foodi, press the manual button, choose high settings, and set time to 20 minutes.
3. Once done cooking, do a quick release.
4. Serve and enjoy.
- **Nutrition Info:** Calories: 528; carbohydrates: 15.9g; protein: 53.4g; fat: 27.8g

74. Thanksgiving Dinner Turkey

Servings: 8
Cooking Time: 1 Hour 23 Minutes
Ingredients:
- ¼ C. butter
- 5-6 carrots, peeled and cut into chunks
- 1 (6-lb.) boneless turkey breast
- Salt and freshly ground black pepper, to taste
- 1-2 C. chicken broth

Directions:
1. Select "Sauté/Sear" setting of Ninja Foodi and place the butter into the pot.
2. Press "Start/Stop" to begin and heat for about 2-3 minutes.
3. Add the carrots and cook, uncovered for about 4-5 minutes.

4. Add turkey breast and cook for about 10-15 minutes or until golden brown from both sides.
5. Press "Start/Stop" to stop cooking and stir in salt, black pepper and broth.
6. Close the Ninja Foodi with the crisping lid and select "Bake/Roast".
7. Set the temperature to 375 degrees F for 1 hour and press "Start/Stop" to begin.
8. Open the lid and transfer the turkey onto a cutting board for about 5 minutes before slicing.
9. Cut into desired sized slices and serve alongside carrots.
- **Nutrition Info:** Calories: 402; Carbohydrates: 3.9g; Protein: 8.3g; Fat: 7.4g; Sugar: 2g; Sodium: 347mg; Fiber: 0.9g

75. Soy Glazed Pork Tenderloin

Servings: 8
Cooking Time: 8 Hours
Ingredients:
- 3 lb. pork tenderloin
- 1 envelope dry onion soup mix
- Salt and freshly ground black pepper, to taste
- 3 tbsp. soy sauce
- 1¾ C. chicken broth

Directions:
1. In the pot of Ninja Foodi, place all ingredients and stir to combine.
2. Close the crisping lid and select "Slow Cooker".
3. Set on "Low" for about 8 hours.
4. Press "Start/Stop" to begin.
5. Open the lid and transfer the pork tenderloin onto a cutting board.
6. Cut into desired sized slices and serve.
- **Nutrition Info:** Calories: 276; Carbohydrates: 5.3g; Protein: 46.5g; Fat: 6.3g; Sugar: 0.6g; Sodium: 1100mg; Fiber: 0.5g

76. Lemon Drumsticks

Servings: 2 Servings
Cooking Time: 28 Minutes
Ingredients:
- ½ cup water
- ½ cup hot sauce
- 2 Tbsp butter
- 1/3 cup lemon juice
- 1 pound drumsticks
- ½ tsp paprika

Directions:
1. Add all the ingredients into the cook and crisp basket and place the basket inside the Ninja Foodi.
2. Place the pressure cooker lid on top of the pot and close the pressure valve to the seal position. Set the pressure cooker function to high heat and set the timer for 5 minutes.
3. Once the coking cycle is complete, release the pressure quickly by carefully opening the steamer valve. Enjoy while hot
- **Nutrition Info:** Calories: 414g, Carbohydrates: 3g, Protein: 42g, Fat: 26g, Sugar: 1g, Sodium: 4571 mg

77. Ham Stuffed Turkey Rolls

Servings: 8
Cooking Time: 30 Minutes
Ingredients:
- 4 tbsps. fresh sage leaves
- 8 ham slices
- 8 turkey cutlets
- Salt and black pepper
- 2 tbsps. melted butter

Directions:
1. Season the turkey cutlets with salt and black pepper.
2. Roll the turkey cutlets and wrap each one with ham slices tightly.
3. Coat each roll with butter and place the sage leaves evenly over each cutlet.
4. Press "Bake/Roast" on Ninja Foodi and add turkey rolls.
5. Bake for about 10 minutes at 360 degrees F and flip the sides.
6. Bake for another 10 minutes and dish out to serve.
- **Nutrition Info:** 467 calories, 24.8g fat, 1.7g carbs, 56g protein

78. Stuffed Whole Chicken

Servings: 6
Cooking Time: 8 Hours 10 Minutes
Ingredients:
- 1 c. mozzarella cheese
- 4 peeled garlic cloves,
- 2 lbs. whole chicken, clean and dried
- Salt and black pepper
- 2 tbsps. fresh lemon juice

Directions:
1. Stuff the chicken cavity with garlic cloves mozzarella cheese.
2. Season the chicken with salt and black pepper.
3. Transfer the chicken in the Ninja Foodi and drizzle lemon juice.
4. Press "Slow Cooker" and cook on Low for about 8 hours.
5. Dish out and serve hot.
- **Nutrition Info:** 309 calories, 12.1g fat, 1.6g carbs, 45.8g protein

79. Potatoes, Beefy-cheesy Way

Servings: 2
Cooking Time: 25 Minutes

Ingredients:
- ½ pounds ground beef
- 2 large potatoes, peeled and chopped
- 3/4 cup cheddar cheese, shredded
- 1/4 cup chicken broth
- 1/2 tablespoon Italian seasoning mix
- Salt and pepper to taste

Directions:
1. Press the sauté button on the Ninja Foodi and stir in the beef. Sear button the meat until some of the oil has rendered.
2. Add the rest of the ingredients.
3. Install pressure lid.
4. Close Ninja Foodi, press the pressure button, choose high settings, and set time to 20 minutes.
5. Once done cooking, do a quick release.
6. Serve and enjoy.
- **Nutrition Info:** Calories: 801; carbohydrates: 66.8g; protein: 53.4g; fat: 35.6g

80. Creamy 'n Tasty Chicken Chowder

Servings: 2
Cooking Time: 20 Minutes
Ingredients:
- 1/2-pound chicken thighs, cut into bite-sized pieces
- 3 strips of bacon, chopped
- ½ cup diced onions
- ½ cup chopped celery
- 1 teaspoon minced garlic
- ½ teaspoon dried thyme
- ½ teaspoon dried oregano
- 2 cups chicken stock
- 1/2 cup heavy cream
- Salt and pepper to taste
- 1 cup spinach

Directions:
1. Press the sauté button on the Ninja Foodi and stir in the chicken and bacon. Add the onions, celery, garlic, thyme, and oregano until fragrant.
2. Add the stock and heavy cream. Season with salt and pepper to taste.
3. Install pressure lid. Close Ninja Foodi, press the manual button, choose high settings, and set time to 15 minutes.
4. Once done cooking, do a quick release.
5. Open the lid and stir in the spinach last.
6. Serve and enjoy.
- **Nutrition Info:** Calories: 485; carbohydrates: 13.9g; protein: 27.2g; fat: 35.6g

81. Thai Egg Rolls

Servings: 4
Cooking Time: 8 Minutes
Ingredients:
- 2 C. cooked beef, shredded
- ¼ C. Thai peanut sauce
- 1 medium carrot, peeled and julienned
- 1 red bell pepper, seeded and julienned
- 4 egg roll wrappers

Directions:
1. In a bowl, add the beef and peanut sauce and toss to coat well.
2. In another bowl, mix together the carrot and bell pepper.
3. With a damp cloth, cover the wrappers to avoid the drying.
4. Arrange 1 wrapper onto a clean, smooth surface.
5. Place about ¼ of the carrot mixture onto the bottom third of 1 wrapper, followed by ½ C. of the beef mixture. With wet fingers, moisten the outside edges of wrapper. Fold the sides of the wrapper over the filling, then roll up from the bottom.
6. Pinch the center to create a round, sausage-like roll.
7. Repeat with the remaining wrappers and filling.
8. Spray each egg roll with cooking spray evenly.
9. Arrange the "Cook & Crisp Basket" in the pot of Ninja Foodi.
10. Close the Ninja Foodi with crisping lid and select "Air Crisp".
11. Press "Start/Stop" to begin and set the temperature to 390 degrees F.
12. Set the time for 5 minutes to preheat.
13. Now, place the rolls into "Cook & Crisp Basket".
14. Close the Ninja Foodi with crisping lid and select "Air Crisp".
15. Set the temperature to 390 degrees F for 8 minutes.
16. Press "Start/Stop" to begin.
17. Open the lid and cut each roll in 2 equal sized portions before serving.
- **Nutrition Info:** Calories: 461; Carbohydrates: 42.3g; Protein: 42.8g; Fat: 12.9g; Sugar: 10.8g; Sodium: 741mg; Fiber: 2.9g

82. Special Thanksgiving Roast

Servings: 12
Cooking Time: 8 Hours
Ingredients:
- 12-oz. beef broth
- 1 (14-oz.) can whole berry cranberries
- 5 tsp. horseradish
- Salt and freshly ground black pepper, to taste
- 1 (4-lb.) venison roast

Directions:

1. For sauce: in a pan, add all the ingredients except the roast over medium heat and bring to a boil, stirring frequently.
2. In the pot of Ninja Foodi, place the roast and top with the hot sauce.
3. Close the crisping lid and select "Slow Cooker".
4. Set on "Low" for about 6-8 hours.
5. Press "Start/Stop" to begin.
6. Open the lid and transfer the roast onto a cutting board.
7. Cut into desired sized slices and serve.
- **Nutrition Info:** Calories: 346; Carbohydrates: 12.2g; Protein: 55.5g; Fat: 6.1g; Sugar: 10.6g; Sodium: 192mg; Fiber: 0.5g

83. Braised Shredded Beef

Servings: 6
Cooking Time: 10 Hours
Ingredients:
- 2 lb. boneless beef
- 4 garlic cloves, peeled
- 1 large onion, sliced
- Salt and freshly ground black pepper, to taste
- ½ C. beef broth

Directions:
1. With a sharp knife, make 4 deep cuts in different places of beef.
2. Press the garlic cloves into each cut.
3. In the pot of Ninja Foodi, place the onion slices and top with the beef.
4. Sprinkle with salt and black pepper and top with the broth.
5. Close the crisping lid and select "Slow Cooker".
6. Set on "Low" for about 8-10 hours.
7. Press "Start/Stop" to begin.
8. Open the lid and with 2 forks, shred the meat.
9. Serve hot.
- **Nutrition Info:** Calories: 297; Carbohydrates: 3.1g; Protein: 46.7g; Fat: 9.6g; Sugar: 1.1g; Sodium: 192mg; Fiber: 0.6g

84. Pulled Pork With Apple-bacon-bbq Sauce

Servings: 2
Cooking Time: 25 Minutes
Ingredients:
- 1 slice of bacon, chopped
- ½ cup onion, chopped
- 1 medium apple, chopped
- ½ cup ketchup
- 1 tablespoon sear button sugar
- 2 tbsp Worcestershire sauce
- 1 tablespoon apple cider vinegar
- 1/2 teaspoon salt
- 1-pound pork tenderloin

Directions:
1. Press the sauté button on the Ninja Foodi and add the chopped bacon. Cook until the bacon has rendered its fat. Set aside.
2. Sauté the onions and apples for a minute. Add the ketchup, sear button sugar, Worcestershire sauce, and apple cider vinegar. Season with salt.
3. Add the pork tenderloin.
4. Install pressure lid.
5. Close the lid and press the manual button. Cook on high for 25 minutes.
6. Do a complete natural pressure release.
7. Remove the pork from the pot and shred using a fork.
8. Garnish with crispy bacon.
- **Nutrition Info:** Calories: 246; carbohydrates: 19.0g; protein: 25.7g; fat: 7.4g

85. Salsa Chicken Breast

Servings: 4 Servings
Cooking Time: 8 Minutes
Ingredients:
- 4 boneless skinless chicken breasts
- ½ cup water
- 1 cup chopped tomatoes
- ½ cup chopped onion
- 1 tbsp lemon juice
- ½ tsp salt
- ¼ tsp ground black pepper

Directions:
1. Place the chicken breast in the Ninja Foodi pot and add all the ingredients to the bowl.
2. Close the pressure seal lid and set the steamer valve to seal.
3. Cook on high pressure for 8 minutes then do a quick pressure release. Serve the chicken while hot.
- **Nutrition Info:** Calories: 271g, Carbohydrates: 5g, Protein: 53g, Fat: 2g, Sugar: 4g, Sodium: 731 mg

86. Not Your Ordinary Beef Pot Pie

Servings: 2
Cooking Time: 25 Minutes
Ingredients:
- 1 1/2 tablespoons butter
- 1/2 cup diced onion
- 1/2 cup diced celery
- 2 cloves of garlic, minced
- 6-oz beef
- 1 teaspoon dried thyme
- 3/4 cup potatoes, diced
- 1/3 cup carrots, diced
- 1/3 cup frozen peas
- 3/4 cups beef broth

- 2 tbsp milk
- 1 tablespoon cornstarch + 1 1/2 tablespoons water
- 1/2 box puff pastry
- 1 egg white

Directions:
1. Press the sauté button on the Ninja Foodi and heat the butter. Sauté the onion, celery and garlic until fragrant. Add the beef and sear button for 5 minutes.
2. Stir in the thyme, potatoes, carrots, frozen peas, beef broth and milk.
3. Install pressure lid. Close Ninja Foodi, press pressure button, choose high settings, and set time to 10 minutes.
4. Once done cooking, do a quick release.
5. Ladle into two ramekins and cover the top of the ramekins with puff pastry. Brush the top with egg whites.
6. Place in Ninja Foodi, bake at 350 ºF for 10 minutes or until tops are lightly browned.
7. Serve and enjoy.

- **Nutrition Info:** Calories: 328; carbohydrates: 26.6g; protein: 20.8g; fat: 15.3g

87. Ropa Vieja

Servings: 6
Cooking Time: 00 Minutes
Ingredients:
- 2 Pounds chuck roast
- 1 sliced onion
- 4 cloves garlic, minced
- 2 tsp oregano
- 1 tsp cumin
- 1 tsp paprika
- 2 tsp salt
- ½ tsp ground black pepper
- 1/8 tsp ground cloves
- 2 bay leaves
- 1 can diced tomatoes
- 2 red bell peppers

Directions:
1. Add all the ingredients to the Ninja Foodi except the green bell peppers.
2. Close the pressure cooker lid and seal the steamer valve. Set the timer for 90 minutes on low pressure.
3. Allow the pressure to naturally release and then open the lid and shred the beef with two forks.
4. Add the bell peppers and place the crisper lid on the pot. Cook at 350 for 5 minutes.
5. Serve hot

- **Nutrition Info:** Calories: 358g, Carbohydrates: 3g, Protein: 28g, Fat: 26 g, Sugar: 3g, Sodium: 855 mg

88. Cheesy Chicken Breast

Servings: 4 Servings
Cooking Time: 8 Minutes
Ingredients:
- 4 boneless skinless chicken breasts
- ½ cup water
- 1 cup chopped tomatoes
- ½ cup chopped onion
- 1 tbsp lemon juice
- ½ tsp salt
- ¼ tsp ground black pepper
- 1 cup Mexican Blend shredded cheese

Directions:
1. Place the chicken breast in the Ninja Foodi pot and add all the ingredients to the bowl.
2. Close the pressure seal lid and set the steamer valve to seal.
3. Cook on high pressure for 8 minutes then do a quick pressure release.
4. Sprinkle the cheese on top of the hot chicken and place the air crisper lid on. Set to broil and the timer for 5 minutes. The cheese should be melted and beginning to brown. Serve the chicken while hot.

- **Nutrition Info:** Calories: 301g, Carbohydrates: 6g, Protein: 46g, Fat: 11g, Sugar: 4g, Sodium: 788mg

89. Indian Keema Matar Chicken

Servings: 2
Cooking Time: 25 Minutes
Ingredients:
- 2 tablespoons oil
- 1 tablespoon garlic paste
- 1 tablespoon ginger paste
- 1 onion, chopped
- 1-pound ground chicken
- 2 teaspoon coriander powder
- 1 teaspoon cayenne pepper
- 1 teaspoon garam masala
- ½ teaspoon ground cumin
- Salt and pepper to taste
- 2 tomatoes, diced
- ½ cup green peas
- ¼ cup water
- 1 tablespoon lemon juice
- ½ cup mint leaves

Directions:
1. Press the sauté button on the Ninja Foodi and heat the oil and sauté the garlic and ginger paste. Add the onion and sauté until fragrant.
2. Stir the chicken and season with coriander powder, cayenne pepper, garam masala, and cumin. Season with salt and pepper to taste. Stir for 3 minutes.
3. Add the tomato, green peas, water, and lemon juice.

4. Install pressure lid. Close Ninja Foodi, press the manual button, choose high settings, and set time to 20 minutes.
5. Once done cooking, do a quick release. Garnish with chopped mint leaves.
6. Serve and enjoy.
- **Nutrition Info:** Calories: 560; carbohydrates:20.7g; protein: 44.8g; fat: 33.1g

90. Favorite Beef Taquitos

Servings: 12
Cooking Time: 15 Minutes
Ingredients:
- 8-oz. cream cheese, softened
- 2 tbsp. buffalo sauce
- 2 C. cooked beef, shredded
- 12 small corn tortillas

Directions:
1. In a bowl, add cream cheese and buffalo sauce and mix until smooth.
2. Add the shredded beef and mix well. Arrange the corn tortillas onto a clean, smooth surface. Spread about 2-3 tbsp. of the chicken mixture onto center of each tortillas in a thin layer. Roll each tortilla up tightly around the chicken mixture.
3. Arrange the greased "Cook & Crisp Basket" in the pot of Ninja Foodi.
4. Close the Ninja Foodi with crisping lid and select "Air Crisp".
5. Press "Start/Stop" to begin and set the temperature to 360 degrees F.
6. Set the time for 5 minutes to preheat.
7. Now, place the rolls into the greased "Cook & Crisp Basket". Close the Ninja Foodi with crisping lid and select "Air Crisp". Set the temperature to 400 degrees F for 15 minutes.
8. Press "Start/Stop" to begin. Open the lid and cut each roll in 2 equal sized portions. Serve warm.
- **Nutrition Info:** Calories: 202; Carbohydrates: 11.9g; Protein: 14.3g; Fat: 10.8g; Sugar: 0.4g; Sodium: 92mg; Fiber: 1.5g

91. Inspiring Pork Platter

Servings: 6
Cooking Time: 12 Minutes
Ingredients:
- 2 lb. boneless pork chops
- Salt and freshly ground black pepper, to taste
- 1 small head cabbage, cut into thick chunks
- 2 C. chicken broth
- ¼ C. butter

Directions:
1. Season the pork chops with salt and black pepper evenly.
2. In the pot of Ninja Foodi, place the chops and top with the cabbage, followed by broth and butter.
3. Cover the Ninja Foodi with the pressure lid and place the pressure valve to "Seal" position. Select "Pressure" and set to "High" for about 12 minutes.
4. Press "Start/Stop" to begin. Switch the valve to "Vent" and do a "Natural" release. Once all the pressure is released, open the lid.
5. Serve hot.
- **Nutrition Info:** Calories: 330; Carbohydrates: 8g; Protein: 43g; Fat: 13.6g; Sugar: 4.5g; Sodium: 446mg; Fiber: 3.3g

92. Caprese Hasselback Chicken

Servings: 8
Cooking Time: 1 Hour 10 Minutes
Ingredients:
- 4 tbsps. butter
- Salt and black pepper
- 2 c. freshly sliced mozzarella cheese
- 8 large chicken breasts
- 4 roma tomatoes, sliced

Directions:
1. Make a few deep slits in the chicken breasts and season with salt and black pepper.
2. Stuff the mozzarella cheese slices and tomatoes in the chicken slits.
3. Grease the pot of Ninja Foodi with butter and arrange stuffed chicken breasts.
4. Press "Bake/Roast" and bake for about 1 hour at 365 degrees F.
5. Dish out and serve hot.
- **Nutrition Info:** 287 calories, 15g fat, 3.8g carbs, 33.2g protein

93. St. Louis Style Beef Ribs

Servings: 4
Cooking Time: 34 Minutes
Ingredients:
- 2 tbsp. brown sugar
- Salt and freshly ground black pepper, to taste
- 1 (3-3½-lb.) rack beef ribs, cut into thirds
- ½ C. beer
- 1 C. BBQ sauce

Directions:
1. In a small bowl, mix together the brown sugar, salt and black pepper.
2. Rub the ribs with sugar mixture evenly.
3. In the pot of Ninja Foodi, place the beer. Place the ribs into "Cook & Crisp Basket". Arrange the "Cook & Crisp Basket" in the pot.
4. Cover the Ninja Foodi with the pressure lid and place the pressure valve to "Seal"

position. Select "Pressure" and set to "High" for about 19 minutes.
5. Press "Start/Stop" to begin. Switch the valve to "Vent" and do a "Quick" release.
6. Once all the pressure is released, open the lid
7. Now, close the Ninja Foodi with the crisping lid and select "Air Crisp".
8. Set the temperature to 400 degrees F for 15 minutes.
9. Press "Start/Stop" to begin. After 10 minutes, open lid and coat the ribs with BBQ sauce generously.
10. Close the lid and cook for 5 minutes further. Open the lid and serve hot.
- **Nutrition Info:** Calories: 861; Carbohydrates: 28.1g; Protein: 120.6g; Fat: 24.9g; Sugar: 20.7g; Sodium: 900mg; Fiber: 0.4g

94. Traditional Chicken 'n Dumplings

Servings: 2
Cooking Time: 25 Minutes
Ingredients:
- 1-pound chicken breasts, cut into cubes
- 2 cloves of garlic, minced
- 1/2 cup chopped onion
- 1/2 cup chopped celery
- 1/2 teaspoon dried thyme
- 1/2 tablespoon bouillon
- 1 cup frozen vegetables (peas and carrots)
- 1 1/2 cups chicken stock
- 1 can cream of chicken
- Salt and pepper to taste
- 1/2 can southern homestyle biscuits
- 2 tbsp parsley, chopped

Directions:
1. Press the sauté button on the Ninja Foodi and stir in the chicken, garlic, onion, celery, and thyme. Stir constantly and allow the onions to sweat.
2. Stir in bouillon, vegetables, stock, and cream of chicken. Stir in the cream of chicken and season with salt and pepper to taste. Allow to simmer for a few minutes. Add the biscuits on top.
3. Install pressure lid. Close Ninja Foodi, press the pressure button, choose high settings, and set time to 15 minutes.
4. Once done cooking, do a quick release.
5. Remove pressure lid. Cover, press roast, and roast for 5 minutes at 400 ºF.
6. Garnish with parsley.
7. Serve and enjoy.
- **Nutrition Info:** Calories: 726; carbohydrates: 51.2g; protein: 63.8g; fat: 29.6g

95. Pork Jerky

Servings: 6
Cooking Time: 10 Minutes
Ingredients:
- ½ pound pork chops, sliced into 1/8" Thick strips
- ½ cup soy sauce
- 2 Tbsp Worcestershire sauce
- 2 tsp ground black pepper
- 1 tsp onion powder
- ½ tsp garlic powder
- 1 tsp kosher salt

Directions:
1. Place all the ingredients in a large Ziploc bag and seal shut. Shake to mix. Leave in the fridge overnight.
2. Lay the strips on the dehydrator trays, being careful not to overlap them.
3. Place the cook and crisp lid on and set the temperature for 135 degrees for 7 hours. Once done, store in an airtight containers.
- **Nutrition Info:** Calories: 61g, Carbohydrates: 2g, Protein: 8g, Fat: 2g, Sugar: 1g, Sodium: 1531 mg

96. Porkchops Down South

Servings: 2
Cooking Time: 20 Minutes
Ingredients:
- 2 4-ounces lean pork loin chop, boneless and fat trimmed
- 1 tbsp vegetable oil
- 1/3 cup salsa
- 1 tablespoon lime juice
- ½ cup water
- 2 tbsp fresh cilantro

Directions:
1. Flatten the pork chops with your hand.
2. Add oil to the Ninja Foodi set at the sauté setting. Place the pork chops and cook for one minute on each side.
3. Pour the salsa and lime juice over the pork chops. Add the water and mix well.
4. Install pressure lid. Close the lid and press the pressure button and choose high setting.
5. Cook for 15 minutes. Do natural pressure release.
6. Sprinkle with cilantro on top.
- **Nutrition Info:** Calories: 270; carbohydrates: 2.1g; protein: 29.4g; fat: 16.0g

97. Irresistible Chicken Drumsticks

Servings: 4
Cooking Time: 28 Minutes
Ingredients:
- ¼ C. Dijon mustard
- 1 tbsp. honey
- 2 tbsp. olive oil

- Salt and freshly ground black pepper, to taste
- 4 (6-oz.) boneless chicken drumsticks Marinated the chicken drumsticks with all the above ingredients for overnight. Preheat Philips Air fryer at 160 degrees.

Directions:
1. In Baked the drumstick for 12 minutes at 160 degrees. Then baked for 5 to 10 minutes at 180 degree for crispy skin a bowl, add all ingredients except the drumsticks and mix until well combined.
2. Add drumsticks and coat with the mixture generously.
3. Refrigerate, covered o marinate overnight.
4. In the pot of Ninja Foodi, place 1 C. of water.
5. Place the chicken drumsticks into the "Cook & Crisp Basket".
6. Arrange the "Cook & Crisp Basket" in the pot.
7. Cover the Ninja Foodi with the pressure lid and place the pressure valve to "Seal" position.
8. Select "Pressure" and set to "High" for about 6 minutes.
9. Press "Start/Stop" to begin.
10. Switch the valve to "Vent" and do a "Quick" release.
11. Once all the pressure is released, open the lid
12. Now, close the Ninja Foodi with the crisping lid and Select "Air Crisp".
13. Set the temperature to 320 degrees F for 12 minutes.
14. Press "Start/Stop" to begin.
15. Now, set the temperature to 355 degrees F for 10 minutes.
16. Remove the id and serve hot.
- **Nutrition Info:** Calories: 374; Carbohydrates: 5.2g; Protein: 47.5g; Fat: 17.3g; Sugar: 4.4g; Sodium: 352mg; Fiber: 0.5g

98. Pork Tenderloin In Teriyaki Sauce

Servings: 2
Cooking Time: 20 Minutes
Ingredients:
- 1 tablespoon olive oil
- 1-pound pork tenderloin, cut into strips
- 2 cloves of garlic, minced
- ½ large onion, chopped
- 1 red chili pepper, chopped
- ¼ teaspoon black pepper
- ½ cup teriyaki sauce
- 1/2 cup chicken broth
- 2 tbsp sear button sugar

Directions:
1. Press the sauté button on the Ninja Foodi.
2. Heat the oil and add the tenderloins. Stir constantly for 5 minutes or until they become sear button.
3. Add garlic, onion, red chili pepper and black pepper.
4. Add the remaining ingredients.
5. Install pressure lid.
6. Close the lid and press the pressure button. Choose high settings and cook for 20 minutes.
7. Do natural pressure release.
8. Serve with rice.
- **Nutrition Info:** Calories: 383; carbohydrates: 16.9g; protein: 50.3g; fat: 12.7g

99. Christmas Dinner Platter

Servings: 6
Cooking Time: 8 Hours
Ingredients:
- 1 (3¼ lb.) bone-in leg of lamb
- 4-5 medium Desiree potatoes, chopped into chunks
- 1 head garlic, peeled
- Salt and freshly ground black pepper, to taste
- 1 C. wine

Directions:
1. Grease the pot of Ninja Foodi generously. Press "Start/Stop" to begin and heat for about 2-3 minutes. Add the lamb and cook, uncovered for about 10 minutes or until browned completely.
2. Press "Start/Stop" to stop the cooking and transfer the lamb onto a plate.
3. In the bottom of pot, place the potatoes and about half of the garlic cloves.
4. Place the lamb on top of the potatoes and rub with remaining garlic cloves.
5. Sprinkle with salt and black pepper and pour wine on top.
6. Close the crisping lid and select "Slow Cooker". Set on "Low" for about 6-8 hours.
7. Press "Start/Stop" to begin. Open the lid and transfer the leg of lamb onto a cutting board. Cut into desired sized pieces and serve alongside the potatoes.
- **Nutrition Info:** Calories: 946; Carbohydrates: 24.7g; Protein: 74.9g; Fat: 55.1g; Sugar: 2g; Sodium: 270mg; Fiber: 3.5g

100. Slow Cooking Beef Fajitas

Servings: 8
Cooking Time: 7 Hours 8 Minutes
Ingredients:
- 2 tbsps. butter
- 2 sliced bell peppers
- 2 lbs. sliced beef

- 2 tbsps. fajita seasoning
- 2 sliced onions

Directions:
1. Press "Sauté" on Ninja Foodi and add butter, onions, fajita seasoning, bell pepper and beef.
2. Sauté for about 3 minutes and press "Slow Cooker".
3. Cook for 7 hours on Low and dish out to serve hot.

- **Nutrition Info:** 353 calories, 13.4g fat, 8.5g carbs, 46.7g protein

101. Pork Carnita

Servings: 6
Cooking Time: 35 Minutes
Ingredients:
- 2 pounds pork shoulder
- 1 tbsp tapioca starch
- 2 tsp garlic powder
- 2 tsp cumin
- 1 tsp ground coriander
- 1 tsp salt
- 2 cups green Keto salsa
- ½ cup lime juice

Directions:
1. Mix the dry spices together and then rub all over the pork.
2. Add the pork to the Ninja Foodi bowl and seal the top. Press the pressure cook button and place the pressure cooker lid on top. Cook on high pressure for 35 minuts.
3. Open the pressure cooker lid and press saute to bring the liquid in the pot to a boil. Shred the pork with two forks and mix into the thickened sauce.

- **Nutrition Info:** Calories: 113g, Carbohydrates: 3g, Protein: 8g, Fat: 8g, Sugar: 1g, Sodium: 480 mg

102. Yummy Turkey Tenderloins

Servings: 6
Cooking Time: 23 Minutes
Ingredients:
- 1 tsp. dried thyme, crushed
- 1 tsp. garlic powder
- Salt and freshly ground black pepper, to taste
- 1 (24-oz.) package boneless turkey breast tenderloins
- 2 tbsp. olive oil

Directions:
1. In a small bowl, mix together the thyme, garlic powder, salt and black pepper.
2. Rub the turkey tenderloins with thyme mixture evenly.
3. Select "Sauté/Sear" setting of Ninja Foodi and place the oil into the pot.
4. Press "Start/Stop" to begin and heat for about 2-3 minutes.
5. Add the turkey tenderloins and cook, uncovered for about 10 minutes or until golden brown.
6. Press "Start/Stop" to stop cooking and transfer the turkey breast onto a plate.
7. Arrange a roasting rack into the pot. Place the turkey tenderloins over the rack.
8. Now, close the Ninja Foodi with the crisping lid and select "Bake/Roast".
9. Set the temperature to 350 degrees F for 10 minutes and press "Start/Stop" to begin.
10. Open the lid and transfer the turkey onto a cutting board for about 5 minutes before slicing. Cut into desired sized slices and serve.

- **Nutrition Info:** Calories: 162; Carbohydrates: 0.5g; Protein: 28.2g; Fat: 6.2g; Sugar: 0.1g; Sodium: 93mg; Fiber: 0.1g

103. Simple Homestyle Chicken Thighs

Servings: 4
Cooking Time: 14 Minutes
Ingredients:
- 4 (6-oz.) boneless skin-on chicken thighs
- 1 tbsp. extra-virgin olive oil
- 2 tsp. poultry seasoning
- 1 tsp. salt

Directions:
1. In the pot of Ninja Foodi, place 1 C. of water.
2. In the pot, arrange the reversible rack in higher position.
3. Arrange the chicken thighs over the rack, skin side up.
4. Cover the Ninja Foodi with the pressure lid and place the pressure valve to "Seal" position.
5. Select "Pressure" and set to "High" for about 4 minutes.
6. Press "Start/Stop" to begin.
7. Switch the valve to "Vent" and do a "Quick" release.
8. Once all the pressure is released, open the lid
9. Coat the chicken thighs with oil evenly and season with poultry seasoning and salt.
10. Now, close the Ninja Foodi with the crisping lid and select "Broil".
11. Set time to 10 minutes and select "Start/Stop" to begin.
12. Open the lid and serve hot.

- **Nutrition Info:** Calories: 394; Carbohydrates: 0.5g; Protein: 30.2g; Fat: 29.2g; Sugar: 0g; Sodium: 710mg; Fiber: 0.1g

104. Pot Roast Recipe With An Asian Twist

Servings: 2
Cooking Time: 50 Minutes

Ingredients:
- 1-pound beef pot roast
- 1/2 tablespoon Chinese five-spice powder
- ¼ cup soy sauce
- ¼ cup black bean sauce
- 2 pieces star anise
- 2 bay leaves
- 1 cup water
- 1 onion, diced
- 3 cloves of garlic, minced
- Sesame seeds for garnish

Directions:
1. Place all ingredients in the Ninja Foodi except for the sesame seeds.
2. Install pressure lid.
3. Close Ninja Foodi, press pressure button, choose high settings, and set time to 20 minutes.
4. Once done cooking, do a quick release.
5. Garnish with sesame seeds.
6. Serve and enjoy.
- **Nutrition Info:** Calories: 354; carbohydrates: 6.5; protein: 51.9g; fat: 13.3g

105. Bacon Swiss Pork Chops

Servings: 4
Cooking Time: 23 Minutes
Ingredients:
- ½ c. shredded Swiss cheese
- 4 pork chops
- 6 bacon strips, cut in half
- Salt and black pepper
- 1 tbsp. butter

Directions:
1. Apply black pepper and salt to the pork chops generously.
2. Press "Sauté" on Ninja Foodi and add butter and pork chops.
3. Sauté for about 3 minutes on each side and add bacon strips and Swiss cheese.
4. Press "Pressure" and set the timer to 15 minutes on Medium Low.
5. Transfer the steaks in a serving platter and serve hot.
- **Nutrition Info:** 483 calories, 40g fat, 0.7g carbs, 27.7g protein

106. Tender Duck Legs

Servings: 2
Cooking Time: 30 Minutes
Ingredients:
- 2 garlic cloves, minced
- 1 tbsp. fresh parsley, chopped
- 1 tsp. five spice powder
- Salt and freshly ground black pepper, to taste
- 2 duck legs

Directions:
1. In a bowl, mix together garlic, parsley, five spice powder, salt and black pepper.
2. Rub the duck legs with garlic mixture generously.
3. Arrange the "Cook & Crisp Basket" in the pot of Ninja Foodi.
4. Close the Ninja Foodi with crisping lid and select "Air Crisp".
5. Press "Start/Stop" to begin and set the temperature to 340 degrees F.
6. Set the time for 5 minutes to preheat.
7. Now, place the duck legs into "Cook & Crisp Basket".
8. Close the Ninja Foodi with crisping lid and select "Air Crisp".
9. Set the temperature to 340 degrees F for 25 minutes.
10. Press "Start/Stop" to begin. Set the temperature to 390 degrees F for 5 minutes.
11. Press "Start/Stop" to begin. Open the lid and serve hot.
- **Nutrition Info:** Calories: 139; Carbohydrates: 1.1g; Protein: 22.1g; Fat: 4.5g; Sugar: 0.1g; Sodium: 160mg; Fiber: 0.1g

107. Mexican Style Pork Chops

Servings: 4
Cooking Time: 8 Minutes
Ingredients:
- 2 pounds pork chops
- ½ cup water
- 1 cup chopped tomatoes
- ½ cup chopped onion
- 1 jalapeno, seeds removed, minced
- 1 tbsp lime juice
- ½ tsp salt
- ¼ tsp ground black pepper

Directions:
1. Place the pork chop in the Ninja Foodi pot and add all the ingredients to the bowl.
2. Close the pressure seal lid and set the steamer valve to seal.
3. Cook on high pressure for 8 minutes then do a quick pressure release. Serve the pork while hot.
- **Nutrition Info:** Calories: 155g, Carbohydrates: 7g, Protein: 24g, Fat: 5g, Sugar: 5g, Sodium: 793 mg

108. Chinese Pork Chops

Servings: 4
Cooking Time: 19 Minutes
Ingredients:
- 4 (8-oz.) frozen boneless pork chops
- ¼ C. hoisin sauce
- 1/3 C. honey
- 1½ tbsp. soy sauce
- 1 tsp. Chinese five spice powder

Directions:
1. In the pot of Ninja Foodi, place ½ C. of water.
2. In the pot, arrange the reversible rack in higher position.
3. Place the chops over the rack.
4. Cover the Ninja Foodi with the pressure lid and place the pressure valve to "Seal" position. Select "Pressure" and set to "High" for about 4 minutes.
5. Press "Start/Stop" to begin. Switch the valve to "Vent" and do a "Quick" release.
6. Meanwhile, in a bowl add the hoisin sauce, honey, soy sauce and Chinese five spice powder and beat until well combined.
7. Once all the pressure is released, open the lid. Coat the top of pork chops with ½ of sauce generously. Now, close the Ninja Foodi with crisping lid and select "Broil". Set time to 5 minutes and select "Start/Stop" to begin.
8. Open the lid and coat the chops with the remaining sauce.
9. Close the Ninja Foodi with the crisping lid and cook for 10 minutes more.
10. Open the lid and serve.
- **Nutrition Info:** Calories: 449; Carbohydrates: 30.8g; Protein: 60.3g; Fat: 8.5g; Sugar: 27.7g; Sodium: 727mg; Fiber: 0.6g

109. Beef Covered In Herbs

Servings: 2
Cooking Time: 35 Minutes
Ingredients:
- 3/4-pound lean beef roast
- ½ teaspoon black pepper, ground
- ½ teaspoon salt
- 2 tbsp dijon mustard
- 1 teaspoon prepared horseradish
- 1 tablespoon low-calorie mayonnaise
- 2 cloves of garlic, minced
- 1 cup water
- 2 tbsp fresh parsley, chopped
- 1 thyme, chopped
- 1 tablespoon dill, chopped

Directions:
1. Mix all ingredients in the Ninja Foodi.
2. Install pressure lid. Close the lid and press the pressure button, choose high settings, and cook for 20 minutes.
3. Do natural pressure release.
4. Serve and enjoy.
- **Nutrition Info:** Calories: 362; carbohydrates: 5.8g; protein: 46.9g; fat: 16.8g

110. Tasty Chicken Tetrazzini

Servings: 2
Cooking Time: 15 Minutes
Ingredients:
- 1 tablespoon butter
- 1 tablespoon flour
- 2 tbsp heavy cream
- 1/3 cup parmesan cheese
- ¼ cup cheddar cheese
- 2 chicken thighs, boneless, skinless and sliced
- 3/4 cup chicken broth
- Salt and pepper to taste
- ¼-lb spaghetti, cooked according to package instructions

Directions:
1. Press the sauté button on the Ninja Foodi and melt the butter. Whisk in the flour until it dissolves. Stir in the heavy cream, parmesan cheese, and cheddar cheese. Stir until melted. Set aside and clean the Ninja Foodi.
2. Still with the sauté button on, stir in the chicken thighs and allow to sear until lightly golden. Season with salt and pepper to taste. Stir in chicken broth and spaghetti. Pour over the cheese sauce.
3. Install pressure lid. Close Ninja Foodi, press the pressure button, choose high settings, and set time to 10 minutes.
4. Once done cooking, do a quick release. Serve and enjoy.
- **Nutrition Info:** Calories: 726; carbohydrates: 32.7g; protein: 50.5g; fat: 43.6g

111. Teriyaki Chicken & Broccoli

Servings: 3
Cooking Time: 14 Minutes
Ingredients:
- 2 (8-oz.) boneless, skinless chicken breasts
- 1 head broccoli, cut in 2-inch florets
- 1 tbsp. olive oil
- Salt and freshly ground black pepper, to taste
- ¼ C. teriyaki sauce

Directions:
1. In the pot of Ninja Foodi, place 1 C. of water.
2. In the pot, arrange the reversible rack in higher position.
3. Arrange the chicken breasts over the rack.
4. Cover the Ninja Foodi with the pressure lid and place the pressure valve to "Seal" position.
5. Select "Pressure" and set to "High" for about 2 minutes.
6. Press "Start/Stop" to begin.
7. Meanwhile, in a bowl, add the broccoli, oil salt and black pepper and toss to coat well.
8. Switch the valve to "Vent" and do a "Natural" release for about 10 minutes. Then do a "Quick" release.

9. Once all the pressure is released, open the lid
10. Coat the chicken breasts with teriyaki sauce generously.
11. Arrange the broccoli florets around the chicken breasts.
12. Now, close the Ninja Foodi with the crisping lid and select "Broil".
13. Set time to 12 minutes and select "Start/Stop" to begin.
14. Open the lid and serve the chicken breasts with alongside the broccoli.
- **Nutrition Info:** Calories: 387; Carbohydrates: 11.3g; Protein: 48.3g; Fat: 16.2g; Sugar: 5.3g; Sodium: 1000mg; Fiber: 3g

112. Spicy Beef Jerky

Servings: 6
Cooking Time: 10 Minutes
Ingredients:
- ½ pound Beef, sliced into 1/8" Thick strips
- ½ cup soy sauce
- 2 Tbsp Worcestershire sauce
- 2 tsp ground black pepper
- 1 tsp liquid smoke
- 1 tsp onion powder
- 1 tsp cayenne pepper
- ½ tsp garlic powder
- 1 tsp kosher salt

Directions:
1. Place all the ingredients in a large Ziploc bag and seal shut. Shake to mix. Leave in the fridge overnight.
2. Lay the strips on the dehydrator trays, being careful not to overlap them.
3. Place the cook and crisp lid on and set the temperature for 135 degrees for 7 hours. Once done, store in an airtight containers.
- **Nutrition Info:** Calories: 351g, Carbohydrates: 5g, Protein: 21g, Fat: 8g, Sugar: 2g, Sodium: 1530 mg

113. Chicken Meatballs Buffalo Flavored

Servings: 2
Cooking Time: 15 Minutes
Ingredients:
- ¾-pound ground chicken
- 1/4 cup almond meal
- 1/2 teaspoon salt
- 2 cloves of garlic, minced
- 2 green onions, sliced thinly
- 1 tablespoon ghee
- 2 tablespoons coconut oil, melted
- ½ cup water
- 2 tablespoons hot sauce
- Salt and pepper to taste
- 1/2 tablespoon cornstarch + 1 tablespoon water

Directions:
1. Place all ingredients in the mixing bowl except for the hot sauce, coconut oil, and cornstarch mix.
2. Mix until well combined and form small balls using your hands. Allow to set in the fridge for at least 3 hours.
3. Press the sauté button on the Ninja Foodi and heat the oil. Slowly add the meatballs and allow to sear on all sides. Add water, hot sauce, salt and pepper.
4. Install pressure lid. Close Ninja Foodi, press the pressure button, choose high settings, and set time to 10 minutes.
5. Once done cooking, do a quick release.
6. Open the lid and press the sauté button. Stir in the cornstarch slurry and allow to simmer until the sauce thickens.
7. Serve and enjoy.
- **Nutrition Info:** Calories: 356; carbohydrates: 3g; protein: 23g; fat: 28g

114. Lemon Pork Chops

Servings: 2
Cooking Time: 5 Minutes
Ingredients:
- ½ cup water
- ½ cup hot sauce
- 2 Tbsp butter
- 1/3 cup lemon juice
- 1 pound pork cutlets
- ½ tsp paprika

Directions:
1. Add all the ingredients into the cook and crisp basket and place the basket inside the Ninja Foodi.
2. Place the pressure cooker lid on top of the pot and close the pressure valve to the seal position. Set the pressure cooker function to high heat and set the timer for 5 minutes.
3. Once the coking cycle is complete, release the pressure quickly by carefully opening the steamer valve. Enjoy while hot
- **Nutrition Info:** Calories: 414g, Carbohydrates: 3g, Protein: 50g, Fat: 21g, Sugar: 1g, Sodium: 470 mg

115. Beef Jerky

Servings: 6
Cooking Time: 10 Minutes
Ingredients:
- ½ pound beef, sliced into 1/8" Thick strips
- ½ cup soy sauce
- 2 Tbsp Worcestershire sauce
- 2 tsp ground black pepper
- 1 tsp onion powder
- ½ tsp garlic powder
- 1 tsp kosher salt

Directions:

1. Place all the ingredients in a large Ziploc bag and seal shut. Shake to mix. Leave in the fridge overnight.
2. Lay the strips on the dehydrator trays, being careful not to overlap them.
3. Place the cook and crisp lid on and set the temperature for 135 degrees for 7 hours. Once done, store in an airtight container.
- **Nutrition Info:** Calories: 62g, Carbohydrates: 2g, Protein: 9g, Fat: 1g, Sugar: 1g, Sodium: 1482 mg

116. Glazed Turkey Breast

Servings: 7
Cooking Time: 1 Hour 54 Minutes
Ingredients:
- 1 (5-lb.) boneless turkey breast
- Salt and freshly ground black pepper, to taste
- ¼ C. maple syrup
- 2 tbsp. Dijon mustard
- 1 tbsp. butter, softened

Directions:
1. Season the turkey breast with salt and black pepper generously and spray with cooking spray.
2. Arrange the "Cook & Crisp Basket" in the pot of Ninja Foodi.
3. Close the Ninja Foodi with crisping lid and select "Air Crisp".
4. Press "Start/Stop" to begin and set the temperature to 350 degrees F.
5. Set the time for 5 minutes to preheat.
6. Now, place the turkey breast into "Cook & Crisp Basket".
7. Close the Ninja Foodi with the crisping lid and Select "Air Crisp".
8. Set the temperature to 350 degrees F for 50 minutes.
9. Press "Start/Stop" to begin. Flip twice, first after 25 minutes and then after 37 minutes.
10. Meanwhile, for glaze: in a bowl, mix together the maple syrup, mustard and butter.
11. Press "Start/Stop" to stop cooking and coat the turkey with the glaze evenly.
12. Close the Ninja Foodi with the crisping lid and Select "Air Crisp".
13. Set the temperature to 350 degrees F for 5 minutes.
14. Press "Start/Stop" to begin.
15. Open the lid and transfer the turkey onto a cutting board for about 5 minutes before slicing.
16. Cut into desired sized slices and serve.
- **Nutrition Info:** Calories: 362; Carbohydrates: 7.8g; Protein: 8.5g; Fat: 3.3g; Sugar: 6.7g; Sodium: 244mg; Fiber: 0.2g

117. Creamy Shredded Venison

Servings: 12
Cooking Time: 6 Hours 10 Minutes
Ingredients:
- 1 (4-lb.) venison roast
- ½ C. Italian salad dressing
- ½ can Dr. pepper soda
- 1 small onion, chopped
- 1 packet dry Italian dressing

Directions:
1. In the pot of Ninja Foodi, place all the ingredients, except dressing packets and stir to combine.
2. Close the crisping lid and select "Slow Cooker".
3. Set on "High" for about 4 hours.
4. Press "Start/Stop" to begin.
5. Now, set on "Low" for about 2-3 hours.
6. Press "Start/Stop" to begin.
7. Open the lid and with 2 forks, shred the meat.
8. Select "Sauté/Sear" setting of Ninja Foodi and stir in the dressing packets.
9. Press "Start/Stop" to begin and cook, uncovered for about 10 minutes.
10. Press "Start/Stop" to stop the cooking and serve.
- **Nutrition Info:** Calories: 290; Carbohydrates: 3.4g; Protein: 53g; Fat: 6.2g; Sugar: 2.9g; Sodium: 6mg; Fiber: 0.1g

118. Pork Ribs

Servings: 4
Cooking Time: 40 Minutes
Ingredients:
- 2 pounds boneless pork ribs
- 1 ½ cup chicken broth
- ½ tsp ground black pepper
- 1 ½ tsp paprika
- 1 tsp onion powder
- 1 tsp garlic powder
- 1 cup tomato sauce
- 1 ½ tbsp. butter, melted
- 2 Tbsp apple cider vinegar
- 1 tbsp Worcestershire sauce
- 2 tbsp stevia powder
- ½ tsp salt
- ½ tsp onion powder

Directions:
1. In a small bowl, mix together the melted butter, tomato sauce, vinegar, Worcestershire sauce, stevia, ½ tsp salt and ½ tsp onion powder.
2. Place the ribs in the Ninja Foodi bowl and sprinkle with the remaining spices. Toss to coat completely.
3. Pour the homemade BBQ sauce into the bowl with the ribs and place the pressure cooker lid on the pot. Set the timer for 30

minutes at high heat. Once the cooking cycle is complete, let the pressure naturally release from the pot, about another 15 minutes.
4. Brush the ribs with the sauce from the bottom of the pot and then place the crisper lid on the pot. Set the temperature for 400 and set the timer for 10 minutes. Let the ribs brown and then serve hot.
- **Nutrition Info:** Calories: 514g, Carbohydrates: 6g, Protein: 67g, Fat: 25g, Sugar: 4g, Sodium: 1282 mg

119. Citrus Pork Carnitas

Servings: 4
Cooking Time: 43 Minutes
Ingredients:
- 2 lb. pork butt, cut into 2-inch pieces
- Salt and freshly ground black pepper, to taste
- 1 orange, cut in half
- 1 yellow onion, peeled and cut in half
- ½ C. chicken broth

Directions:
1. Season the pork butt with salt and black pepper generously.
2. In the pot of Ninja Foodi, place the pork butt.
3. Squeeze the juice of orange halves over pork butt.
4. Place the squeezed orange halves, onion and broth over the pork.
5. Cover the Ninja Foodi with the pressure lid and place the pressure valve to "Seal" position. Select "Pressure" and set to "High" for about 20 minutes.
6. Press "Start/Stop" to begin. Switch the valve to "Vent" and do a "Quick" release.
7. Once all the pressure is released, open the lid. Remove the orange halves and onion from the pot. Select "Sauté/Sear" setting of Ninja Foodi and set "Md:Hi".
8. Press "Start/Stop" to begin and cook, uncovered for about 10-15 minutes.
9. Press "Start/Stop" to stop the cooking. Now, close the Ninja Foodi with crisping lid and select "Broil". Set time to 8 minutes and select "Start/Stop" to begin.
10. Open the lid and serve hot.
- **Nutrition Info:** Calories: 475; Carbohydrates: 8.1g; Protein: 71.9g; Fat: 15.4g; Sugar: 5.6g; Sodium: 262mg; Fiber: 1.7g

120. Beef Stew

Servings: 4
Cooking Time: 10 Minutes
Ingredients:
- 1 pound Beef Roast
- 4 cups beef broth
- 3 cloves of garlic, chopped
- 1 carrot, chopped
- 2 celery stalks, chopped
- 2 tomatoes, chopped
- ½ white onion, chopped
- ¼ tsp salt
- 1/8 tsp ground black pepper

Directions:
1. Add all the ingredients to the pot and place the pressure cooker lid on the Ninja Foodi.
2. Cook on high pressure for 10 minutes. Do a quick steam release and remove the lid.
3. Shred the chicken using two forks.
4. Serve while hot or freeze to use at a later date.
- **Nutrition Info:** Calories: 211g, Carbohydrates: 2g, Protein: 10g, Fat: 7g, Sugar: 2g, Sodium: 147 mg

121. Cauliflower Corned Beef Hash

Servings: 6
Cooking Time: 30 Minutes
Ingredients:
- 6 eggs
- 4 cups riced cauliflower
- 1 pound corned beef, diced
- ¼ cup milk
- 1 onion, chopped
- 3 Tbsp butter
- 2 cups chopped, cooked ham
- ½ cup shredded cheese

Directions:
1. Press the saute button on your Ninja Foodi and add the butter and the onions. Cook, stirring occasionally until the onions are soft, about 5 minutes.
2. Add the riced cauliflower to the pot and stir. Turn on the air crisper for 15 minutes, turning the cauliflower halfway through.
3. In a small bowl, mix the eggs and milk together then pour over the browned cauliflower.
4. Sprinkle the corned beef over the top of the egg mix.
5. Press the air crisp button again and set the timer for 10 minutes.
6. Sprinkle the cheddar cheese on top and close the lid of the Ninja Foodi for one minute to just melt the cheese. Serve while hot
- **Nutrition Info:** Calories: 322g, Carbohydrates: 3g , Protein: 20g, Fat: 26 g, Sugar: 1, Sodium: 1008 mg

122. Apple Glazed Bbq Ribs

Servings: 2
Cooking Time: 35 Minutes
Ingredients:
- 2 cups apple juice
- 1/4 cup apple cider vinegar

- 1 tsp salt
- 1-pound rack of ribs
- ½ tablespoon garlic powder
- ½ tablespoon black pepper
- 1/2 cup southern apple cider barbecue sauce
- 1/4 cup water

Directions:
1. Place all ingredients in the pot.
2. Make sure that the pork is coated with the sauce.
3. Install pressure lid.
4. Close the lid and press the pressure button. Cook for 25 minutes.
5. Do a quick release.
6. Remove the ribs from the pot and set it on a baking pan. Transfer sauce to a bowl.
7. Brush ribs with sauce and return to Ninja Foodi.
8. Roast for 5 minutes per side, while brushing with sauce after turning over.
9. Serve and enjoy.
- **Nutrition Info:** Calories: 465; carbohydrates: 29.8g; protein: 52.9g; fat: 14.9g

123. Chicken Congee

Servings: 7
Cooking Time: 65 Minutes
Ingredients:
- 6 chicken drumsticks
- 7 c. water
- 1 c. Jasmine rice
- 1 tbsp. ginger, fresh
- Salt

Directions:
1. Rinse rice under cool water for a few minutes.
2. Pour rice, water, ginger, and drumsticks into Ninja Foodi. Seal the lid.
3. Select "PRESSURE" and cook at HIGH pressure for 30 minutes.
4. When time is up, press CANCEL and wait for a natural pressure release.
5. When safe, open the lid and press "SAUTÉ".
6. Keep stirring while the congee thickens.
7. Season with salt.
8. Pull off the chicken with tongs, and throw away the bones.
9. Serve right away!
- **Nutrition Info:** 181 calories, 6g fat, 21g carbs, 12g protein

124. Shining Dinner Meal

Servings: 4
Cooking Time: 14 Minutes
Ingredients:
- 2 (12-oz.) (1½-inch thick) New York strip steaks
- 1 tsp. garlic powder
- Salt and freshly ground black pepper, to taste
- ¾ lb. asparagus, trimmed
- 1 tbsp. olive oil

Directions:
1. Season the steaks with garlic powder, salt and black pepper evenly.
2. In the pot of Ninja Foodi, place ½ C. of water.
3. In the pot, arrange the reversible rack in higher position.
4. Place the steaks over the rack. Cover the Ninja Foodi with the pressure lid and place the pressure valve to "Seal" position. Select "Pressure" and set to "High" for about 2 minutes. Press "Start/Stop" to begin.
5. Meanwhile, in a bowl, add the asparagus, oil, salt and black pepper and toss to coat well. Switch the valve to "Vent" and do a "Quick" release.
6. Once all the pressure is released, open the lid. Arrange the asparagus around the steaks. Now, close the Ninja Foodi with the crisping lid and select "Broil".
7. Set time to 12 minutes and select "Start/Stop" to begin.
8. Open the lid and transfer the steaks onto a cutting board for about 5 minutes before slicing. Cut the steaks into desired sized slices and serve alongside the asparagus.
- **Nutrition Info:** Calories: 259; Carbohydrates: 3.8g; Protein: 40.1g; Fat: 9.6g; Sugar: 1.8g; Sodium: 166mg; Fiber: 1.9g

125. Easiest Turkey Breast

Servings: 6
Cooking Time: 45 Minutes
Ingredients:
- 1 (8-lb.) bone-in turkey breast
- Salt and freshly ground black pepper, to taste
- 2 tbsp. olive oil

Directions:
1. Season the turkey breast with salt and black pepper generously and drizzle with oil.
2. Arrange the "Cook & Crisp Basket" in the pot of Ninja Foodi.
3. Close the Ninja Foodi with crisping lid and select "Air Crisp".
4. Press "Start/Stop" to begin and set the temperature to 360 degrees F.
5. Set the time for 5 minutes to preheat.
6. Now, place the turkey breast into the "Cook & Crisp Basket".
7. Close the Ninja Foodi with the crisping lid and Select "Air Crisp".
8. Set the temperature to 360 degrees F for 40-45 minutes.

9. Press "Start/Stop" to begin. After 20 minutes, flip the wings.
10. Open the lid and transfer the turkey onto a cutting board for about 5 minutes before slicing. Cut into desired sized slices and serve.
- **Nutrition Info:** Calories: 682; Carbohydrates: 0g; Protein: 150g; Fat: 7.1g; Sugar: 0g; Sodium: 562mg; Fiber: 0g

126. Subtly Sweet Chicken Breasts

Servings: 2
Cooking Time: 32 Minutes
Ingredients:
- 2 (8-oz.) frozen chicken breasts
- Salt and freshly ground black pepper, to taste
- ¼ C. honey mustard sauce
- 1 tbsp. fresh parsley, chopped

Directions:
1. In the pot of Ninja Foodi, place 1 C. of water.
2. In the pot, arrange the reversible rack in higher position.
3. Arrange the chicken breasts over the rack.
4. Cover the Ninja Foodi with the pressure lid and place the pressure valve to "Seal" position. Select "Pressure" and set to "High" for about 22 minutes.
5. Press "Start/Stop" to begin. Switch the valve to "Vent" and do a "Natural" release for about 10 minutes. Then do a "Quick" release.
6. Once all the pressure is released, open the lid
7. Coat the chicken breasts with mustard honey sauce evenly.
8. Now, close the Ninja Foodi with the crisping lid and select "Broil".
9. Set time to 10 minutes and select "Start/Stop" to begin.
10. Open the lid and serve hot with the garnishing of parsley.
- **Nutrition Info:** Calories: 499; Carbohydrates: 18.1g; Protein: 48.1g; Fat: 26.7g; Sugar: 12g; Sodium: 554mg; Fiber: 0.1g

127. Braised Chuck Roast

Servings: 10
Cooking Time: 52 Minutes
Ingredients:
- 3 lb. beef chuck roast, cut into 2-inch cubes
- Salt and freshly ground black pepper, to taste
- 2 large onions, cut into large chunks
- ¼ C. ketchup
- 2 C. beef broth

Directions:
1. Grease the pot of Ninja Foodi generously.
2. Select "Sauté/Sear" setting of Ninja Foodi and place the chuck roast into the pot.
3. Press "Start/Stop" to begin and cook, uncovered for about 5-6 minutes per side.
4. Press "Start/Stop" to stop the cooking and stir in the onion, ketchup and broth.
5. Cover the Ninja Foodi with the pressure lid and place the pressure valve to "Seal" position.
6. Select "Pressure" and set to "High" for about 40 minutes.
7. Press "Start/Stop" to begin.
8. Switch the valve to "Vent" and do a "Quick" release.
9. Once all the pressure is released, open the lid.
10. Transfer the roast onto a cutting board.
11. Cut into desired sized slices and serve.
- **Nutrition Info:** Calories: 519; Carbohydrates: 4.5g; Protein: 37g; Fat: 38.2g; Sugar: 2.8g; Sodium: 32mg; Fiber: 0.7g

128. Garlic Creamy Beef Steak

Servings: 6
Cooking Time: 1 Hour 30 Mins
Ingredients:
- ½ c. butter
- 4 minced garlic cloves
- 2 lbs. beef top sirloin steaks
- Salt and black pepper
- 1½ c. cream

Directions:
1. Rub the beef sirloin steaks with garlic, salt and black pepper.
2. Marinate the beef with butter and cream and set aside.
3. Place grill in the Ninja Foodi and transfer the steaks on it.
4. Press "Broil" and set the timer for about 30 minutes at 365 degrees F, flipping once in the middle way.
5. Dish out and serve hot.
- **Nutrition Info:** 353 calories, 24.1g fat, 3.9g carbs, 31.8g protein

129. Pork Nachos

Servings: 4
Cooking Time: 25 Minutes
Ingredients:
- 4 pork chops
- 1 cup keto salsa
- 1 tsp salt
- 1 Tbsp taco seasoning
- 4 cups grain free tortilla chips
- 1 cup shredded Mexican cheese blend
- 1 jalapeno, sliced

Directions:

1. Place the pork chops and salsa in the Ninja Foodi and place the lid on as well. Set the pressure cooker steam valve to seal and cook on high pressure for 15 minutes. Do a quick pressure release and remove the lid. Use two forks to shred the pork chops, mixing it into the sauce.
2. Add the taco seasoning and salt to the mix and stir to combine.
3. Place the tortilla chips on top of the chicken mix inside the pot. Sprinkle the shredded cheese and jalapenos over the top of the chips then close the crisper lid and set the temperature for 360 degrees for 5 minutes.
4. Remove the perfectly browned nachos and serve while warm!
- **Nutrition Info:** Calories: 221g, Carbohydrates: 4g, Protein: 21g, Fat: 13g, Sugar: 3g, Sodium: 893 mg

130. Roasted Crisp Whole Chicken

Servings: 2
Cooking Time: 25 Minutes
Ingredients:
- 1 whole Cornish Hen
- 1/2 tsp seasoned salt
- Juice of 1/2 lemon
- 1 tbsp honey
- ¼ cup hot water
- 1/4 teaspoon salt
- 1/2 teaspoon whole peppercorns (optional)
- 1 sprigs of fresh thyme
- 2 cloves of garlic
- 1 tsp canola oil

Directions:
1. Combine lemon juice, honey, water, salt, peppercorns, thyme, and garlic in pot.
2. Season the chicken inside, outside and underneath the skin with seasoned salt.
3. Place the chicken in the air crisp basket then place into the pot.
4. Install pressure lid. Close pot, choose high, and cook for 15 minutes.
5. Once done cooking, do a quick release. Remove pressure lid.
6. Brush the chicken with canola oil
7. Close the crisping lid and select roast.
8. Set the time for 15 minutes and halfway through cooking time turn chicken over.
9. The juices in the bottom of the cooking pot make a delicious sauce.
- **Nutrition Info:** Calories: 196; carbohydrates: 10.5g; protein: 24.2g; fat: 6.3g

131. Tender Chicken Thighs

Servings: 6
Cooking Time: 28 Minutes
Ingredients:
- 2 tbsp. butter
- 1 onion, chopped
- 2 lb. chicken thighs
- ¾ C. chicken broth
- Salt and freshly ground black pepper, to taste

Directions:
1. Select "Sauté/Sear" setting of Ninja Foodi and place the butter into the pot.
2. Press "Start/Stop" to begin and heat for about 2-3 minutes.
3. Add the onion and cook for about 5 minutes.
4. Press "Start/Stop" to stop cooking and stir in remaining ingredients.
5. Cover the Ninja Foodi with the pressure lid and place the pressure valve to "Seal" position.
6. Select "Pressure" and set to "High" for about 20 minutes.
7. Press "Start/Stop" to begin.
8. Switch the valve to "Vent" and do a "Quick" release.
9. Once all the pressure is released, open the lid
10. Serve hot.
- **Nutrition Info:** Calories: 333; Carbohydrates: 1.8g; Protein: 44.6g; Fat: 15.2g; Sugar: 0.9g; Sodium: 281mg; Fiber: 0.4g

132. Festive Fajita Beef

Servings: 8
Cooking Time: 7 Hours 11 Minutes
Ingredients:
- 2 tbsp. butter
- 3 bell peppers, seeded and sliced
- 2 onions, sliced
- 2 lb. beef, sliced
- 2 tbsp. fajita seasoning

Directions:
1. Select "Sauté/Sear" setting of Ninja Foodi and place the oil into the pot.
2. Press "Start/Stop" to begin and heat for about 2-3 minutes.
3. Add bell pepper and onion and cook for about 2-3 minutes.
4. Add beef and fajita seasoning and cook for about 4-5 minutes.
5. Press "Start/Stop" to stop the cooking.
6. Close the crisping lid and select "Slow Cooker".
7. Set on "Low" for about 7 hours.
8. Press "Start/Stop" to begin.
9. Open the lid and serve.
- **Nutrition Info:** Calories: 269; Carbohydrates: 7.5g; Protein: 35.2g; Fat: 10.1g; Sugar: 3.4g; Sodium: 229mg; Fiber: 1.2g

133. Creamy Tomato Chicken

Servings: 6
Cooking Time: 6 Hours
Ingredients:
- ¾ C. chicken broth
- 1 C. sour cream
- 1½ C. fresh tomatoes, chopped finely
- Salt and freshly ground black pepper, to taste
- 6 (6-oz.) boneless, skinless chicken breasts

Directions:
1. In the pot of Ninja Foodi, add all the ingredients and stir to combine.
2. Close the crisping lid and select "Slow Cooker".
3. Set on "Low" for about 6 hours.
4. Press "Start/Stop" to begin.
5. Open the lid and serve hot.
- **Nutrition Info:** Calories: 418; Carbohydrates: 3.5g; Protein: 51.4g; Fat: 20.9g; Sugar: 1.3g; Sodium: 291mg; Fiber: 0.5g

134. Asian Beef & Broccoli

Servings: 5
Cooking Time: 21 Minutes
Ingredients:
- 1½ lb. flank steak, trimmed and cut into ½-inch thick slices against the grain
- 1½ C. beef broth
- ¼ C. soy sauce
- Salt and freshly ground black pepper, to taste
- 4 C. broccoli florets

Directions:
1. In a bowl, add the steak, broth, soy sauce, salt and black pepper and mix well.
2. Refrigerate to marinate for about 15 minutes.
3. Meanwhile, in the pot of Ninja Foodi, place ½ C. of water.
4. Place the broccoli florets into "Cook & Crisp Basket".
5. Arrange the "Cook & Crisp Basket" in the pot.
6. Cover the Ninja Foodi with the pressure lid and place the pressure valve to "Seal" position.
7. Select "Steam" for 4 minutes and press "Start/Stop" to begin.
8. Switch the valve to "Vent" and do a "Quick" release.
9. Once all the pressure is released, open the lid.
10. Remove the broccoli with basket and then, discard the water from pot.
11. In the pot of Ninja Foodi, add the steak with marinade.
12. Cover the Ninja Foodi with the pressure lid and place the pressure valve to "Seal" position.
13. Select "Pressure" and set to "High" for about 12 minutes.
14. Press "Start/Stop" to begin.
15. Switch the valve to "Vent" and do a "Quick" release.
16. Once all the pressure is released, open the lid.
17. Select "Sauté/Sear" setting of Ninja Foodi and stir in the broccoli.
18. Press "Start/Stop" to begin and cook for about 5 minutes.
19. Press "Start/Stop" to stop the cooking and serve hot.
- **Nutrition Info:** Calories: 307; Carbohydrates: 6.1g; Protein: 42.2g; Fat: 12g; Sugar: 1.7g; Sodium: 1000mg; Fiber: 2g

135. Mexican Style Chicken Breast

Servings: 4 Servings
Cooking Time: 8 Minutes
Ingredients:
- 4 boneless skinless chicken breasts
- ½ cup water
- 1 cup chopped tomatoes
- ½ cup chopped onion
- 1 jalapeno, seeds removed, minced
- 1 tbsp lime juice
- ½ tsp salt
- ¼ tsp ground black pepper

Directions:
1. Place the chicken breast in the Ninja Foodi pot and add all the ingredients to the bowl.
2. Close the pressure seal lid and set the steamer valve to seal.
3. Cook on high pressure for 8 minutes then do a quick pressure release. Serve the chicken while hot.
- **Nutrition Info:** Calories: 242g, Carbohydrates: 10g, Protein: 42g, Fat: 5g, Sugar: 6g, Sodium: 655mg

136. 3-ingredients Duck Legs

Servings: 4
Cooking Time: 6 Hours
Ingredients:
- ¼ C. olive oil
- 4 duck legs
- Salt and freshly ground black pepper, to taste

Directions:
1. Season the duck legs with salt and black pepper generously.
2. In a baking dish, arrange the duck legs in a single layer and refrigerate, covered overnight.
3. In the pot of Ninja Foodi, place the oil.

4. Arrange the duck legs over oil in a single layer.
5. Close the crisping lid and select "Slow Cooker".
6. Set on "Low" for about 6 hours.
7. Press "Start/Stop" to begin.
8. Open the lid and serve.
- **Nutrition Info:** Calories: 242; Carbohydrates: 0g; Protein: 21.8g; Fat: 17.1g; Sugar: 0g; Sodium: 120mg; Fiber: 0g

137. Pork Meatballs

Servings: 4
Cooking Time: 10 Minutes
Ingredients:
- 1 tsp olive oil
- 3 cups low carb tomato sauce
- 1 ½ pounds ground pork
- 1 tbsp dried parsley
- ½ cup grated parmesan cheese
- ½ cup almond flour
- 2 eggs
- 1 tsp salt
- ½ tsp ground black pepper
- 1 tsp dried oregano
- ¼ cup water

Directions:
1. Mix the ground pork, parsley, parmesan cheese, almond flour, eggs, salt and pepper together in a bowl. Use your hands to shape into mini meatballs, about 1 inch in diameter.
2. Pour the olive oil in the bottom of the Ninja Foodi and press saute. Add the meatballs to the pot and sear for two minutes on each side to brown.
3. Add the tomato sauce to the pot and close the lid.
4. Use the pressure cooker function and cook on low pressure for 10 minutes. Once the timer goes off, let the pressure naturally release for 10 minutes then open the pot and serve hot with a toothpick.
- **Nutrition Info:** Calories: 293g, Carbohydrates: 3g, Protein: 24g, Fat: 20g, Sugar: 2g, Sodium: 1486 mg

138. Garlic Chicken In Creamy Tuscan Style

Servings: 2
Cooking Time: 15 Minutes
Ingredients:
- 1 tablespoon olive oil
- 1-pound skinless chicken breasts, halved and pounded
- 2 cloves of garlic, minced
- ½ tablespoon Italian seasoning
- 1/2 teaspoon salt
- 1/3 cup chicken stock
- 1/3 cup heavy cream
- 1/3 cup parmesan cheese
- 1/4 cup sun-dried tomato

Directions:
1. Press the sauté button on the Ninja Foodi and sear the chicken breasts on all sides.
2. Stir in the garlic, Italian seasoning, and salt.
3. Pour in the chicken stock and the rest of the ingredients.
4. Install pressure lid. Close Ninja Foodi, press the pressure button, choose high settings, and set time to 10 minutes.
5. Once done cooking, do a quick release.
6. Serve and enjoy.
- **Nutrition Info:** Calories: 521; carbohydrates: 10.8g; protein: 59.9g; fat: 26.5g

139. Ketogenic Beef Sirloin Steak

Servings: 3
Cooking Time: 22 Minutes
Ingredients:
- 3 tbsps. butter
- ½ tsp. garlic powder
- 1 lb. beef top sirloin steaks
- Salt and black pepper
- 1 minced garlic clove

Directions:
1. Press "Sauté" on Ninja Foodi and add butter and beef sirloin steaks.
2. Sauté for about 2 minutes on each side and add garlic powder, garlic clove, salt and black pepper.
3. Press "Pressure" and set the timer to 15 minutes.
4. Transfer the steaks in a serving platter and serve hot.
- **Nutrition Info:** 246 calories, 13.1g fat, 2g carbs, 31.3g protein

140. Perfect Fall Dinner Pork

Servings: 6
Cooking Time: 4 Hours
Ingredients:
- 1 medium onion, sliced
- 1½ lb. pork tenderloin
- 2 medium apples, cored and sliced
- Salt and freshly ground black pepper, to taste
- 2 C. chicken broth

Directions:
1. Grease the pot of Ninja Foodi generously.
2. In the bottom of pot, arrange the onion slices and top with the pork tenderloin, followed by apple slices.
3. Sprinkle with salt and black pepper and pour broth on top.
4. Close the crisping lid and select "Slow Cooker".

5. Set on "High" for about 4 hours.
6. Press "Start/Stop" to begin.
7. Open the lid and serve hot.
- **Nutrition Info:** Calories: 221; Carbohydrates: 12.3g; Protein: 31.7g; Fat: 4.6g; Sugar: 8.7g; Sodium: 348mg; Fiber: 2.2g

141. Richly Cheesy Sausage

Servings: 6
Cooking Time: 14 Minutes
Ingredients:
- 2 lb. pork sausages, casing removed and crumbled
- 16-oz. marinara sauce
- 10-oz. Parmesan cheese, shredded
- 16-oz. mozzarella cheese, shredded

Directions:
1. Select "Bake/Roast" of Ninja Foodi and set the temperature to 360 degrees F.
2. Press "Start/Stop" to begin and preheat the Ninja Foodi for about 10 minutes.
3. Grease the pot of Ninja Foodi generously.
4. In the prepared pot, arrange half of the sausages and top with half of the marinara sauce, followed by half of the mozzarella and Parmesan cheese.
5. Repeat the layer once.
6. Close the Ninja Foodi with crisping lid and set the time for 20 minutes.
7. Press "Start/Stop" to begin.
8. Open the lid and serve.
- **Nutrition Info:** Calories: 944; Carbohydrates: 14.8g; Protein: 67.3g; Fat: 68.4g; Sugar: 6.7g; Sodium: 2000mg; Fiber: 2g

142. Chili Chicken Wings

Servings: 4 Servings
Cooking Time: 28 Minutes
Ingredients:
- ½ cup water
- ½ cup hot sauce
- 2 Tbsp butter
- 1 ½ tbsp. apple cider vinegar
- 32 ounces frozen chicken wings
- ½ tsp paprika

Directions:
1. Add all the ingredients into the cook and crisp basket and place the basket inside the Ninja Foodi.
2. Place the pressure cooker lid on top of the pot and close the pressure valve to the seal position. Set the pressure cooker function to high heat and set the timer for 5 minutes.
3. Once the coking cycle is complete, release the pressure quickly by carefully opening the steamer valve. Enjoy while hot
- **Nutrition Info:** Calories: 311g, Carbohydrates: 0g, Protein: 24g, Fat: 23g, Sugar: 0g, Sodium: 2657 mg

143. Zingy Chicken Wings

Servings: 4
Cooking Time: 20 Minutes
Ingredients:
- 1 tbsp. fish sauce
- 1 tbsp. fresh lemon juice
- 1 tsp. sugar
- Salt and freshly ground black pepper, to taste
- 12 chicken middle wings, cut into half

Directions:
1. In In a bowl, mix together fish sauce, lime juice, sugar, salt and black pepper.
2. Add wings ad coat with mixture generously. Refrigerate to marinate for about 1 hour.
3. In the pot of Ninja Foodi, place 1 C. of water.
4. Place the chicken wings into "Cook & Crisp Basket". Arrange the "Cook & Crisp Basket" in the pot. Cover the Ninja Foodi with the pressure lid and place the pressure valve to "Seal" position.
5. Select "Pressure" and set to "High" for about 5 minutes. Press "Start/Stop" to begin. Switch the valve to "Vent" and do a "Quick" release.
6. Once all the pressure is released, open the lid
7. Now, close the Ninja Foodi with the crisping lid and select "Air Crisp".
8. Set the temperature to 390 degrees F for 13-15 minutes. Press "Start/Stop" to begin. After 7 minutes, flip the wings.
9. Meanwhile, in a large bowl, add Buffalo sauce and salt and mix well.
10. Open the lid and transfer the wings into the bowl of Buffalo sauce.
11. Then, toss the wings well to coat with the Buffalo sauce.
12. Serve immediately.
- **Nutrition Info:** Calories: 483; Carbohydrates: 17.3g; Protein: 29.5g; Fat: 32.1g; Sugar: 1.2g; Sodium: 857mg; Fiber: 0.5g

144. Tasty Sesame-honeyed Chicken

Servings: 2
Cooking Time: 16 Minutes
Ingredients:
- 1 tablespoon olive oil
- 1/2 onion, diced
- 2 cloves of garlic, minced
- 1-pound chicken breasts
- 1/4 cup soy sauce
- 2 tbsp ketchup
- 1 tsp sesame oil

- 1/4 cup honey
- ½ teaspoon red pepper flakes
- 1 tablespoon cornstarch + 1 1/2 tablespoons water
- Green onions for garnish
- 1 tablespoon sesame seeds for garnish

Directions:
1. Press the sauté button on the Ninja Foodi and heat the oil. Stir in the onion and garlic until fragrant.
2. Add the chicken breasts. Allow to sear on all sides for three minutes.
3. Stir in the soy sauce, ketchup, sesame oil, honey, and red pepper flakes.
4. Install pressure lid. Close Ninja Foodi, press the pressure button, choose high settings, and set time to 10 minutes.
5. Once done cooking, do a quick release.
6. Open the lid and press the sauté button. Stir in the cornstarch slurry and allow to simmer until the sauce thickens.
7. Garnish with green onions and sesame seeds last.
8. Serve and enjoy.
- **Nutrition Info:** Calories: 568; carbohydrates: 49.1g; protein: 50.9g; fat: 34.6g

145. Bbq Turkey Legs

Servings: 6
Cooking Time: 8 Hours
Ingredients:
- 6 turkey legs
- Salt and freshly ground black pepper, to taste
- 1 C. BBQ sauce
- 2 tbsp. prepared mustard
- 1/3 C. water

Directions:
1. Season each turkey leg with salt and black pepper generously.
2. In a bowl, add remaining ingredients and mix until well combined.
3. Grease the pot of Ninja Foodi generously.
4. In the prepared pot, place the turkey legs and top with sauce evenly.
5. Close the crisping lid and select "Slow Cooker".
6. Set on "Low" for about 7-8 hours.
7. Press "Start/Stop" to begin. Open the lid and serve.
- **Nutrition Info:** Calories: 421; Carbohydrates: 15.4g; Protein: 67.2g; Fat: 8.1g; Sugar: 10.9g; Sodium: 759mg; Fiber: 0.4g

146. Jamaican Style Curried Chicken

Servings: 2
Cooking Time: 25 Minutes
Ingredients:
- 2 tablespoons oil
- 1 tablespoon minced garlic
- 1 cup chopped onion
- 1 ½ tablespoon jamaican curry powder
- 1 scotch bonnet pepper, sliced
- ½ teaspoon ground allspice
- 3 sprigs of thyme
- 1-pound boneless chicken thighs, chunked
- Salt and pepper to taste
- 1 large potato, cut into chunks
- 1 cup water

Directions:
1. Press the sauté button on the Ninja Foodi and sauté the garlic, onion, curry powder, scotch bonnet pepper, allspice, and thyme until fragrant.
2. Stir in the chicken thighs and cook until lightly golden. Season with salt and pepper to taste. Add the potatoes and water.
3. Install pressure lid and place valve to vent position.
4. Close Ninja Foodi, press the pressure button, choose high settings, and set time to 20 minutes.
5. Once done cooking, do a quick release. Serve and enjoy.
- **Nutrition Info:** Calories: 1099; carbohydrates: 78.5g; protein: 48.6g; fat: 65.6g

147. Crispy Fried Chicken

Servings: 4
Cooking Time: 40 Minutes
Ingredients:
- 3 C. seasoned flour
- 1 C. milk
- 2 eggs
- 1 (2-2½-lb.) chicken, cut into 8 pieces
- ½ C. canola oil

Directions:
1. In a shallow bowl, place the flour.
2. In another shallow bowl, add the milk and eggs and beat well.
3. Coat the chicken with the flour, then dip into milk mixture and finally, coat with flour again.
4. Select "Sauté/Sear" setting of Ninja Foodi and place the oil into the pot.
5. Press "Start/Stop" to begin and heat for about 5 minutes.
6. Add the chicken into the pot and cook, uncovered for about 4-5 minutes per side.
7. Now, set on "High" setting and cook, uncovered for about 20 minutes, flipping occasionally.
8. With a slotted spoon, transfer the chicken pieces onto a paper towel-lined plate to drain.

9. Serve warm.
- **Nutrition Info:** Calories: 920; Carbohydrates: 93.2g; Protein: 3.2g; Fat: 3g; Sugar: 11.9g; Sodium: 1000mg; Fiber: 6.7g

148. Classic Sausage & Bell Peppers

Servings: 6
Cooking Time: 6 Hours
Ingredients:
- 1 lb. sausage, sliced
- 2 medium bell peppers, seeded and sliced
- 2 C. tomatoes, chopped finely
- 1 medium yellow onion, sliced
- Salt and freshly ground black pepper, to taste

Directions:
1. In the pot of Ninja Foodi, place all the ingredients and stir to combine.
2. Close the crisping lid and select "Slow Cooker".
3. Set on "Low" for about 6 hours.
4. Press "Start/Stop" to begin.
5. Open the lid and serve hot.
- **Nutrition Info:** Calories: 287; Carbohydrates: 7g; Protein: 15.8g; Fat: 21.7g; Sugar: 4.4g; Sodium: 598mg; Fiber: 1.6g

149. Garlicky Leg Of Lamb

Servings: 10
Cooking Time: 8 Hours
Ingredients:
- 3 lb. boneless leg of lamb, rolled
- 6 garlic cloves, minced
- Salt and freshly ground black pepper, to taste
- ½ C. beef broth
- 2-3 tbsp. fresh lemon juice

Directions:
1. In the pot of Ninja Foodi, place all the ingredients and mix well.
2. Close the crisping lid and select "Slow Cooker".
3. Set on "Low" for about 8 hours.
4. Press "Start/Stop" to begin.
5. Open the lid and transfer the leg of lamb onto a cutting board.
6. Cut the leg of lamb into desired sized pieces and serve.
- **Nutrition Info:** Calories: 258; Carbohydrates: 0.7g; Protein: 38.6g; Fat: 10.1g; Sugar: 0.1g; Sodium: 158mg; Fiber: 0.1g

150. Nutritious Beef Curry

Servings: 6
Cooking Time: 6 Hours 15 Minutes
Ingredients:
- 1¾ lb. boneless beef, cubed
- 1 C. heavy cream
- 1 large onion, quartered
- Salt and freshly ground black pepper, to taste
- 2 C. fresh spinach, chopped

Directions:
1. In the pot of Ninja Foodi, place all the ingredients except spinach and stir to combine.
2. Close the crisping lid and select "Slow Cooker".
3. Set on "High" for about 5-6 hours.
4. Press "Start/Stop" to begin.
5. Open the lid and immediately, stir in spinach.
6. Close the crisping lid and select "Slow Cooker".
7. Set on "High" for about 10-15 minutes.
8. Press "Start/Stop" to begin.
9. Open the lid and serve.
- **Nutrition Info:** Calories: 327; Carbohydrates: 3.3g; Protein: 41.1g; Fat: 15.7g; Sugar: 1.1g; Sodium: 131mg; Fiber: 0.8g

151. Chicken Soup

Servings: 4 Servings
Cooking Time: 8 Minutes
Ingredients:
- 1 pound chicken breast
- 4 cups chicken broth
- 2 cloves of garlic, chopped
- 1 carrot, chopped
- 2 celery stalks, chopped
- ½ white onion, chopped
- ¼ tsp salt
- 1/8 tsp ground black pepper
- ¼ cup shredded cheddar cheese

Directions:
1. Add all the ingredients to the pot and place the pressure cooker lid on the Ninja Foodi.
2. Cook on high pressure for 10 minutes. Do a quick steam release and remove the lid.
3. Shred the chicken using two forks.
4. Serve while hot or freeze to use at a later date.
- **Nutrition Info:** Calories: 217g, Carbohydrates: 2g, Protein: 33g, Fat: 4g, Sugar: 2g, Sodium: 755 mg

152. Garlicky-ginger Drumsticks

Servings: 2
Cooking Time: 20 Minutes
Ingredients:
- 4 chicken drumsticks
- ¼ cup water
- ½ cup soy sauce
- 2 tablespoons honey
- 2 tablespoons sear button sugar

- 2 tablespoons rice wine vinegar
- 2 cloves of garlic, minced
- 1 teaspoon minced ginger
- 1 onion, chopped

Directions:
1. Place all ingredients in the Ninja Foodi.
2. Install pressure lid. Close Ninja Foodi, press the manual button, choose high settings, and set time to 20 minutes.
3. Once done cooking, do a quick release.
4. Serve and enjoy.
- **Nutrition Info:** Calories: 277; carbohydrates: 12.3g; protein: 24.8g; fat: 14.6g

153. Flavor-packed Beef Curry

Servings: 8
Cooking Time: 6 Hours
Ingredients:
- 2 lb. boneless beef, cubed
- 1½ C. fresh tomatoes, chopped finely
- 2 C. beef broth
- 1 C. unsweetened coconut milk
- Salt and freshly ground black pepper, to taste

Directions:
1. In the pot of Ninja Foodi, place all the ingredients except spinach and stir to combine.
2. Close the crisping lid and select "Slow Cooker".
3. Set on "High" for about 5-6 hours.
4. Press "Start/Stop" to begin.
5. Open the lid and serve hot.
- **Nutrition Info:** Calories: 295; Carbohydrates: 3.2g; Protein: 36.6g; Fat: 14.6g; Sugar: 2.1g; Sodium: 291mg; Fiber: 1.1g

154. Zesty Lamb Chops

Servings: 4
Cooking Time: 40 Minutes
Ingredients:
- 4 (6-oz.) bone-in lamb chops
- 2 tbsp. all-purpose flour
- 4 tbsp. butter
- 1 C. picante sauce
- 3 tbsp. fresh lemon juice

Directions:
1. Coat the lamb chops with almond flour evenly and set aside.
2. Select "Sauté/Sear" setting of Ninja Foodi and place the butter into the pot.
3. Press "Start/Stop" to begin and heat for about 2-3 minutes.
4. Add the chops and cook, uncovered for about 4-5 minutes or until browned from both sides.
5. Press "Start/Stop" to stop the cooking and stir in the picante sauce and lemon juice.
6. Cover the Ninja Foodi with the pressure lid and place the pressure valve to "Seal" position.
7. Select "Pressure" and set to "High" for about 40 minutes.
8. Press "Start/Stop" to begin.
9. Switch the valve to "Vent" and do a "Quick" release.
10. Once all the pressure is released, open the lid.
11. Serve hot.
- **Nutrition Info:** Calories per serving: 452; Carbohydrates: 6.2g; Protein: 49.1g; Fat: 24.3g; Sugar: 2.1g; Sodium: 513mg; Fiber: 0.5g

155. Bacon 'n Broccoli Frittata

Servings: 2
Cooking Time: 20 Minutes
Ingredients:
- 1 tbsp grass-fed butter or ghee
- 1 small yellow onion, diced
- 2 fresh garlic cloves, grated or finely minced
- 1/2 cup chopped broccoli florets, cut into smaller bite-size pieces
- 2 pastured eggs
- 2 tbsp cup milk of choice (coconut milk)
- 1/2 tsp sea salt
- Zest of 1/2 lemon
- 1/2 tbsp chopped fresh Italian parsley
- 1 tsp chopped fresh thyme
- 3/4 cup shredded cheddar cheese
- 4 slices of pre-cooked crispy organic or pastured turkey bacon, crumbled
- 1 cup water

Directions:
1. Press sauté and heat oil. Once hot, sauté garlic and onions until caramelized, around 7 minutes. Add broccoli and sauté for 4 minutes. Press stop button.
2. Lightly grease the Ninja Foodi pot.
3. Whisk milk and eggs in a large mixing bowl.
4. Whisk in thyme, parsley, lemon zest, and salt.
5. Stir in broccoli mixture, bacon, and cheddar cheese. Pour into Ninja Foodi pot.
6. Close Ninja Foodi, press bake button, bake at 350 ºF for 20 minutes.
7. Serve and enjoy with a sprinkle of crumbled turkey bacon.
- **Nutrition Info:** Calories: 374; carbohydrates: 6.1g; protein: 21.2g; fat: 29.4g

156. Spicy Chicken Jerky

Servings: 6 Servings
Cooking Time: 10 Minutes

Ingredients:
- ½ pound Chicken breast, sliced into 1/8" Thick strips
- ½ cup soy sauce
- 2 Tbsp Worcestershire sauce
- 2 tsp ground black pepper
- 1 tsp liquid smoke
- 1 tsp onion powder
- 1 tsp cayenne pepper
- ½ tsp garlic powder
- 1 tsp kosher salt

Directions:
1. Place all the ingredients in a large Ziploc bag and seal shut. Shake to mix. Leave in the fridge overnight.
2. Lay the strips on the dehydrator trays, being careful not to overlap them.
3. Place the cook and crisp lid on and set the temperature for 135 degrees for 7 hours. Once done, store in an airtight containers.
- **Nutrition Info:** Calories: 42g, Carbohydrates: 2g, Protein: 4g, Fat: 1g, Sugar: 1g, Sodium: 1493 mg

157. Hawaiian Lamb Chops

Servings: 3
Cooking Time: 40 Minutes
Ingredients:
- 3 (8-oz.) lamb shoulder chops
- Salt and freshly ground black pepper, to taste
- ¼ C. brown sugar
- 4-5 pineapple slices
- ¼-½ C. pineapple juice

Directions:
1. Select "Bake/Roast" of Ninja Foodi and set the temperature to 375 degrees F.
2. Press "Start/Stop" to begin and preheat the Ninja Foodi for about 10 minutes.
3. Season the pork chops with salt and black pepper generously.
4. In the pot of Ninja Foodi, place the chops and top with the brown sugar, pineapple slices and pineapple juice.
5. Close the Ninja Foodi with crisping lid and set the time for 40 minutes.
6. Press "Start/Stop" to begin.
7. After 20 minutes of cooking, baste the chops with juices.
8. Open the lid and serve.
- **Nutrition Info:** Calories: 408; Carbohydrates: 17g; Protein: 44.3g; Fat: 18.1g; Sugar: 15.7g; Sodium: 215mg; Fiber: 0.3g

158. Mexican Cheesy Chicken Ole

Servings: 6
Cooking Time: 30 Minutes
Ingredients:
- 2 tbsps. sesame oil
- 1½ lbs. chicken breasts
- Salt and ground black pepper
- 10 oz. salsa
- 1 c. shredded Queso Añejo cheese

Directions:
1. Press the SEAR/SAUTÉ button and set to High; add olive oil. Once hot, cook the chicken breasts for a few minutes per side. Add salt, pepper, and salsa.
2. Secure the pressure lid; press the PRESSURE button and cook for 20 minutes at High Pressure. Once cooking is complete, use a quick release; remove the lid carefully.
3. Scatter shredded cheese over the chicken breasts.
4. Secure the crisping lid and choose the BROIL function. Set temperature to 390 degrees F with a time of 10 minutes; press the START/STOP button. Bon appétit!
- **Nutrition Info:** Calories 322; Fat 16.3g; Carbs 3g; Protein 38.9g

159. Italian Chicken Dinner

Servings: 6
Cooking Time: 8 Hours 15 Minutes
Ingredients:
- 1 tbsp. olive oil
- 6 skinless, boneless chicken breasts
- 4 C. fresh button mushrooms, sliced
- 1 C. chicken broth
- Salt and freshly ground black pepper, to taste

Directions:
1. Select "Sauté/Sear" setting of Ninja Foodi and place the oil into the pot.
2. Press "Start/Stop" to begin and heat for about 2-3 minutes.
3. Add the chicken and cook, uncovered for about 5 minutes per side.
4. Press "Start/Stop" to stop cooking and stir in the remaining ingredients.
5. Close the crisping lid and select "Slow Cooker".
6. Set on "Low" for about 7-8 hours.
7. Press "Start/Stop" to begin.
8. Open the lid and serve hot.
- **Nutrition Info:** Calories: 249; Carbohydrates: 1.7g; Protein: 40.3g; Fat: 8.8g; Sugar: 0.9g; Sodium: 218mg; Fiber: 0.5g

160. Sweet And Sour Chicken Wings

Servings: 4 Servings
Cooking Time: 28 Minutes
Ingredients:
- ½ cup water
- 2 Tbsp baking stevia
- 2 Tbsp butter

- 2 Tbsp lemon juice
- 32 ounces frozen chicken wings
- ½ tsp salt
- ½ tsp ground black pepper

Directions:
1. Add all the ingredients into the cook and crisp basket and place the basket inside the Ninja Foodi.
2. Place the pressure cooker lid on top of the pot and close the pressure valve to the seal position. Set the pressure cooker function to high heat and set the timer for 5 minutes.
3. Once the coking cycle is complete, release the pressure quickly by carefully opening the steamer valve. Enjoy while hot
- **Nutrition Info:** Calories: 312g, Carbohydrates: 2g, Protein: 24g, Fat: 23g, Sugar: 2g, Sodium: 985 mg

161. Creamy Turkey Breast

Servings: 6
Cooking Time: 2 Hours 10 Mins
Ingredients:
- 1½ c. Italian dressing
- 2 minced garlic cloves
- 2 lbs. bone-in turkey breast
- 2 tbsps. butter
- Salt and black pepper

Directions:
1. Mix together garlic cloves, salt and black pepper and rub the turkey breast with this mixture.
2. Grease the pot of Ninja Foodi with butter and arrange turkey breasts.
3. Top evenly with Italian dressing and press "Bake/Roast".
4. Bake for about 2 hours at 330 degrees F and dish out to serve immediately.
- **Nutrition Info:** 369 calories, 23.2g fat, 6.5g carbs, 35.4g protein

162. Family Dinner Pork Shoulder

Servings: 10
Cooking Time: 10 Minutes
Ingredients:
- 3 lb. boneless pork shoulder, trimmed and cut in 2-inch cubes
- 4 tbsp. barbecue seasoning
- 1 C. apple cider vinegar
- 1 can (6 oz.) tomato paste
- 1 (16.3-oz.) tube refrigerated biscuit dough

Directions:
1. In the pot of Ninja Foodi, place pork, barbecue seasoning and vinegar.
2. Cover the Ninja Foodi with the pressure lid and place the pressure valve to "Seal" position. Select "Pressure" and set to "High" for about 35 minutes.
3. Press "Start/Stop" to begin. Switch the valve to "Vent" and do a "Quick" release.
4. Once all the pressure is released, open the lid. Now, select "Sauté/Sear" setting of Ninja Foodi and stir in the tomato paste. Select "Md:Hi" and press "Start/Stop" to begin. Cook for about 10 minutes, stirring occasionally to shred the meat.
5. Meanwhile, tear each uncooked biscuit in 2 halves. Press "Start/Stop" to stop the cooking. Arrange the biscuit halves across the surface of the pork evenly.
6. Now, close the Ninja Foodi with crisping lid and select "Bake/Roast".
7. Set the temperature to 350 degrees F for 10 minutes.
8. Press "Start/Stop" to begin, Open the lid and serve immediately.
- **Nutrition Info:** Calories: 363; Carbohydrates: 21.9g; Protein: 39.9g; Fat: 12g; Sugar: 4.3g; Sodium: 567mg; Fiber: 1.4g

163. Quick Shredded Buffalo Chicken

Servings: 2
Cooking Time: 20 Minutes
Ingredients:
- 2 chicken breasts
- 2 tablespoons butter
- 1/4 bottle buffalo wing sauce
- 1 tablespoon honey
- 1 teaspoon cider vinegar
- 1 tablespoons tabasco sauce

Directions:
1. Place all ingredients in the Ninja Foodi.
2. Install pressure lid. Close Ninja Foodi, press the pressure button, choose high settings, and set time to 20 minutes.
3. Once done cooking, do a quick release.
4. Once cooked, take the chicken out and shred using forks.
5. Serve and enjoy.
- **Nutrition Info:** Calories: 685; carbohydrates: 23.2g; protein: 61g; fat: 38.6g

164. Ranch Flavored Tender Wings

Servings: 2
Cooking Time: 20 Minutes
Ingredients:
- 1/2 cup water
- 1/4 cup hot pepper sauce
- 2 tablespoons unsalted butter, melted
- 1/2 tablespoons apple cider vinegar
- 1-pound chicken wings
- 1/4 (1-ounce) envelope ranch salad dressing mix
- 1/2 teaspoon paprika
- Nonstick cooking spray

Directions:
1. Pour the water, hot pepper sauce, butter, and vinegar into the pot. Place the wings in the cook & crisp basket and place the basket in the pot.
2. Install pressure lid. Close pot, press pressure button, select high settings, and cook for 5 minutes.
3. Once done, do a quick release. Remove pressure lid.
4. Sprinkle the chicken wings with the dressing mix and paprika. Coat with cooking spray.
5. Close Ninja Foodi, press air crisp, set the temperature to 375 ºF, and crisp for 15 minutes. Halfway through cooking time, turnover wings.
6. Serve and enjoy.
- **Nutrition Info:** Calories: 351; carbohydrates: 1.3g; protein: 50.5g; fat: 16.0g

165. The Shiny Chicken Stock

Servings: 4
Cooking Time: 2 Hours 10 Mins
Ingredients:
- 2 lbs. meaty chicken bones
- ¼ tsp. salt
- 3½ c. water

Directions:
1. Place chicken parts in Foodi and season with salt
2. Add water, place the pressure cooker lid and seal the valve, cook on HIGH pressure for 90 minutes
3. Release the pressure naturally over 10 minutes
4. Line a cheesecloth on a colander and place it over a large bowl, pour chicken parts and stock into the colander and strain out the chicken and bones
5. Let the stock cool and let it peel off any layer of fat that might accumulate on the surface
6. Use as needed!
- **Nutrition Info:** 51 calories, 3g fat, 2g carbs. 6g protein

166. Beef Taco Casserole

Servings: 6
Cooking Time: 25 Minutes
Ingredients:
- 2 lb. ground beef
- 2 tbsp. taco seasoning
- 1 C. cheddar cheese, shredded
- 1 C. cottage cheese
- 1 C. salsa

Directions:
1. Select "Bake/Roast" of Ninja Foodi and set the temperature to 370 degrees F.
2. Press "Start/Stop" to begin and preheat the Ninja Foodi for about 10 minutes.
3. In a bowl, add the beef and taco seasoning and mix well.
4. Add cheeses and salsa and stir to combine.
5. Grease the pot of Ninja Foodi generously.
6. In the prepared pot, place the beef mixture and slightly, press to smooth the top surface.
7. Close the Ninja Foodi with crisping lid and set the time for 25 minutes.
8. Press "Start/Stop" to begin.
9. Open the lid and serve.
- **Nutrition Info:** Calories: 407; Carbohydrates: 5.3g; Protein: 56.4g; Fat: 16.5g; Sugar: 1.8g; Sodium: 734mg; Fiber: 0.7g

167. Bacon Spaghetti Squash

Servings: 4
Cooking Time: 25 Minutes
Ingredients:
- ½ pound bacon
- 1 whole spaghetti squash
- ¼ tsp salt
- ¼ tsp ground black pepper

Directions:
1. Place the bacon in the bottom of the Ninja Foodi and put the air crisper lid on top. Set the temperature to 400 and cook for 10 minutes or until crisped to your liking.
2. Remove the bacon, crumble and set aside.
3. Cut the butternut squash in half and place in the Ninja Foodi with the cut side facing upward. Close the pressure cooker lid and set the timer to 7 minutes on high pressure. When the timer is done, do a natural pressure release and then remove the lid.
4. Shred the spaghetti squash with two forks and then toss the spaghetti with the crisped bacon. Serve with the salt and pepper.
- **Nutrition Info:** Calories: 255g, Carbohydrates: 1g, Protein: 19g, Fat: 19g, Sugar: 5g, Sodium: 312 mg

168. Crispy Pork Carnitas

Servings: 6
Cooking Time: 36 Minutes
Ingredients:
- 2 tbsps. butter
- 2 oranges, juiced
- 2 lbs. pork shoulder
- Salt and black pepper
- 1 tsp. garlic powder

Directions:
1. Apply pepper and salt to the pork for seasoning.
2. Press "Sauté" on Ninja Foodi and add butter and garlic powder.

3. Sauté for about 1 minute and add seasoned pork.
4. Sauté for 3 minutes and pour orange juice.
5. Press "Pressure" and cook for about 15 minutes on High.
6. Release the pressure naturally and press "Broil".
7. Broil for about 8 minutes at 375 degrees F and dish out to serve.
- **Nutrition Info:** 506 calories, 36.3g fat, 7.6g carbs, 35.9g protein

169. Mild Flavored Rabbit

Servings: 6
Cooking Time: 6 Hours
Ingredients:
- 1 (4-lb.) rabbit, cut into pieces
- 12-14 whole red baby potatoes
- 8-10 C. chicken broth
- 3 tbsp. mixed fresh herbs (thyme, basil and parsley), chopped
- Salt and freshly ground black pepper, to taste

Directions:
1. Grease the pot of Ninja Foodi generously.
2. In the prepared pot, place all the ingredients and stir to combine.
3. Close the crisping lid and select "Slow Cooker".
4. Set on "High" for about 5-6 hours.
5. Press "Start/Stop" to begin.
6. Open the lid and serve.
- **Nutrition Info:** Calories: 851; Carbohydrates: 54.1g; Protein: 100g; Fat: 26.3g; Sugar: 7g; Sodium: 800mg; Fiber: 6.5g

170. Pulled Pork Slathered In Bbq Sauce

Servings: 2
Cooking Time: 30 Minutes
Ingredients:
- 1 teaspoon hot paprika
- 1 tablespoon light sear button sugar
- 1 teaspoon mustard powder
- ½ teaspoon ground cumin
- Salt and pepper to taste
- 1-pound pork shoulder
- 1 teaspoon vegetable oil
- 2 tbsp apple cider vinegar
- 1 tablespoon tomato paste
- 1/2 cup water

Directions:
1. Place all ingredients in the Ninja Foodi and mix all ingredients.
2. Close Ninja Foodi, press the pressure button, choose high settings, and set time to 20 minutes.
3. Once done cooking, do a complete natural release.
4. Open lid, remove pork and shred with two forks.
5. Press sauté button to render sauce until thick.
6. Return meat to pot and slather well in sauce.
7. Serve and enjoy.
- **Nutrition Info:** Calories: 622; carbohydrates: 5g; protein: 57.3g; fat: 41.4g

171. Hk Mushroom Gravy Over Chops

Servings: 2
Cooking Time: 25 Minutes
Ingredients:
- 2 bone-in pork loin chops
- 1/2 onion, chopped
- 2 cloves of garlic, minced
- 10 large cremini mushrooms, sliced
- A dash of sherry wine
- 3/4 cup chicken stock
- 1 tablespoon Worcestershire sauce
- 1 tablespoon soy sauce
- 1 tablespoon peanut oil
- 2 tbsp heavy cream
- Salt and pepper to taste
- 1 tablespoon cornstarch + 1 tablespoon water

Directions:
1. Press the sauté button on the Ninja Foodi. Place the pork chops and sear on all sides for 5 minutes each. Stir in the onion and garlic until fragrant.
2. Add the mushrooms, sherry wine, chicken stock, Worcestershire sauce, soy sauce, peanut oil and cream. Season with salt and pepper to taste.
3. Install pressure lid. Close Ninja Foodi, press the pressure button, choose high settings, and set time to 20 minutes.
4. Once done cooking, do a quick release.
5. Once the lid is open, press the sauté button and stir in cornstarch slurry. Allow to simmer until the sauce thickens.
6. Serve and enjoy.
- **Nutrition Info:** Calories: 481; carbohydrates: 10.4g; protein: 44.6g; fat: 28.9g

172. Zesty Lamb Chops(2)

Servings: 4
Cooking Time: 40 Minutes
Ingredients:
- 4 (6-oz.) bone-in lamb chops
- 2 tbsp. all-purpose flour
- 4 tbsp. butter
- 1 C. picante sauce
- 3 tbsp. fresh lemon juice

Directions:
1. Coat the lamb chops with almond flour evenly and set aside.

2. Select "Sauté/Sear" setting of Ninja Foodi and place the butter into the pot.
3. Press "Start/Stop" to begin and heat for about 2-3 minutes.
4. Add the chops and cook, uncovered for about 4-5 minutes or until browned from both sides. Press "Start/Stop" to stop the cooking and stir in the picante sauce and lemon juice.
5. Cover the Ninja Foodi with the pressure lid and place the pressure valve to "Seal" position. Select "Pressure" and set to "High" for about 40 minutes.
6. Press "Start/Stop" to begin. Switch the valve to "Vent" and do a "Quick" release.
7. Once all the pressure is released, open the lid. Serve hot.
- **Nutrition Info:** Calories: 452; Carbohydrates: 6.2g; Protein: 49.1g; Fat: 24.3g; Sugar: 2.1g; Sodium: 513mg; Fiber: 0.5g

173. Crispy Garlic-parmesan Wings

Servings: 2
Cooking Time: 20 Minutes
Ingredients:
- 1-lb chicken wings/drumettes
- Seasoned salt, to season the wings
- 1/2 cup of chicken broth
- Sauce Ingredients:
- 1 stick of salted butter, melted
- 1/2 tsp of garlic better than bouillon (or 1 tbsp of crushed garlic)
- 1/2 cup of grated parmesan cheese
- 1 tsp of garlic powder
- 1/2 tsp of black pepper
- 1/2 tsp of dried parsley flakes

Directions:
1. Lightly rub the seasoned salt on both sides of the chicken wings
2. Add the wings to the Ninja Foodi followed by the broth.
3. Install pressure lid. Close Ninja Foodi, press pressure button, select high settings, and cook for 8 minutes.
4. While the wings are pressure cooking, make the garlic parmesan sauce by combining the butter, garlic, parmesan, pepper, garlic powder and parsley flakes in a large bowl. Mix together well.
5. Once the wings are done cooking, do a quick release.
6. Transfer to bowl of sauce and discard liquid. Remove pressure lid.
7. Add the trivet to pot, spray with non-stick spray and place wings.
8. Lower the tendercrisp lid and hit "broil" and go for 8-10 minutes (the longer you go, the crispier the wings so be sure to check on them). It is a good idea to flip the wings midway through the crisping process.
9. Enjoy!

- **Nutrition Info:** Calories: 957; carbohydrates: 5.5g; protein: 63.0g; fat: 75.9g

174. Almonds Coated Lamb

Servings: 6
Cooking Time: 35 Minutes
Ingredients:
- 1¾ lb. rack of lamb
- Salt and freshly ground black pepper, to taste
- 1 egg
- 1 tbsp. breadcrumbs
- 3-oz. almonds, chopped finely

Directions:
1. Season the rack of lamb with salt and black pepper evenly and then, drizzle with cooking spray. In a shallow dish, beat the egg.
2. In another shallow dish mix together breadcrumbs and almonds.
3. Dip the rack of lamb in egg and then coat with the almond mixture.
4. Arrange the "Cook & Crisp Basket" in the pot of Ninja Foodi. Close the Ninja Foodi with crisping lid and select "Air Crisp". Press "Start/Stop" to begin and set the temperature to 220 degrees F. Set the time for 5 minutes to preheat.
5. Now, place the rack of lamb into "Cook & Crisp Basket". Close the Ninja Foodi with crisping lid and select "Air Crisp". Set the temperature to 220 degrees F for 30 minutes.
6. Press "Start/Stop" to begin. Now, set the temperature to 390 degrees F for 5 minutes. Open the lid and serve.
- **Nutrition Info:** Calories: 319; Carbohydrates: 3.9g; Protein: 31g; Fat: 19.6g; Sugar: 0.7g; Sodium: 139mg; Fiber: 1.8g

175. Holiday Luncheon Meal

Servings: 2
Cooking Time: 3 Hours
Ingredients:
- 8-oz. turkey breast, chopped
- 3½-oz. pumpkin, chopped
- 3 scallions, chopped
- ½ C. chicken broth
- Salt and freshly ground black pepper, to taste

Directions:
1. Grease the pot of Ninja Foodi generously.
2. In the prepared pot, place all ingredients and stir to combine.
3. Close the crisping lid and select "Slow Cooker".
4. Set on "High" for about 3 hours.
5. Press "Start/Stop" to begin.
6. Open the lid and serve hot.

- **Nutrition Info:** Calories: 148; Carbohydrates: 9.9; Protein: 21.5g; Fat: 2.3g; Sugar: 5.3g; Sodium: 900mg; Fiber: 3 g

176. Breaded Chicken Tenders

Servings: 4
Cooking Time: 12 Minutes
Ingredients:
- 1 C. all-purpose flour
- 3 eggs, beaten
- 2 C. Italian bread crumbs
- 1 lb. uncooked chicken tenderloins
- Kosher salt, to taste

Directions:
1. Select "Bake/Roast" of Ninja Foodi and set the temperature to 360 degrees F.
2. Press "Start/Stop" to begin and preheat the Ninja Foodi for about 10 minutes.
3. In 3 different shallow bowls, place the flour, eggs and bread crumbs respectively.
4. Coat the chicken tenders with the flour, then dip into eggs and finally, coat with bread crumbs evenly coat. Set aside.
5. In the pot of Ninja Foodi, arrange the reversible rack.
6. Arrange the chicken tenders over the rack, without overlapping.
7. Close the Ninja Foodi with the crisping lid and set time for 12 minutes.
8. Press "Start/Stop" to begin.
9. Open the lid and serve hot with the sprinkling of salt.
- **Nutrition Info:** Calories: 477; Carbohydrates: 64.1g; Protein: 38.3g; Fat: 7.2g; Sugar: 4.4g; Sodium: 1200mg; Fiber: 2.8g

177. Herb Infused Leg Of Lamb

Servings: 6
Cooking Time: 1¼ Hours
Ingredients:
- 2¼ lb. boneless leg of lamb
- 2 tbsp. olive oil
- Salt and freshly ground black pepper, to taste
- 2 fresh rosemary sprigs
- 2 fresh thyme sprigs

Directions:
1. Coat the leg of lamb with oil and sprinkle with salt and black pepper.
2. Wrap the leg of lamb with herb sprigs.
3. Arrange the "Cook & Crisp Basket" in the pot of Ninja Foodi.
4. Close the Ninja Foodi with crisping lid and select "Air Crisp".
5. Press "Start/Stop" to begin and set the temperature to 300 degrees F.
6. Set the time for 5 minutes to preheat.
7. Now, place the leg of lamb into "Cook & Crisp Basket".
8. Close the Ninja Foodi with crisping lid and select "Air Crisp".
9. Set the temperature to 300 degrees F for 75 minutes.
10. Press "Start/Stop" to begin.
11. Open the lid and transfer the leg of lamb onto a cutting board.
12. Cut into desired sized pieces and serve.
- **Nutrition Info:** Calories: 360; Carbohydrates: 0.7g; Protein: 47.8g; Fat: 17.3g; Sugar: 0g; Sodium: 157mg; Fiber: 0.5g

178. Succulent Roasted Chicken

Servings: 6
Cooking Time: 35 Minutes
Ingredients:
- 1 (5-lb.) whole chicken, necks and giblets removed
- Salt and freshly ground black pepper, to taste
- ¼ C. honey
- ¼ C. fresh lemon juice
- ¼ C. hot water

Directions:
1. Season the chicken inside, outside and underneath the skin with the salt and black pepper generously.
2. In the pot of Ninja Foodi, place the honey, lemon juice, water, salt and black pepper and mix until well combined.
3. Place the chicken into the "Cook & Crisp Basket". Arrange the "Cook & Crisp Basket" in the pot.
4. Cover the Ninja Foodi with the pressure lid and place the pressure valve to "Seal" position. Select "Pressure" and set to "High" for about 15 minutes.
5. Press "Start/Stop" to begin. Switch the valve to "Vent" and do a "Quick" release.
6. Once all the pressure is released, open the lid, Spray the chicken with the cooking spray evenly.
7. Now, close the Ninja Foodi with the crisping lid and select "Air Crisp".
8. Set the temperature to 400 degrees F for 15-20 minutes.
9. Press "Start/Stop" to begin. Open the lid and transfer the chicken onto a cutting board for about 10 minutes before carving.
10. Cut into desired sized pieces and serve.
- **Nutrition Info:** Calories: 616; Carbohydrates: 11.9g; Protein: 109.7g; Fat: 11.5g; Sugar: 11.8g; Sodium: 26mg; Fiber: 0.1g

179. Dinner Party Turkey Breast

Servings: 4
Cooking Time: 4 Hours
Ingredients:
- 1 lb. boneless turkey breast, trimmed
- 8 oz. thin-cut bacon slices
- 3 tomatoes, peeled and chopped
- ½ tsp. garlic powder

- Salt and freshly ground black pepper, to taste

Directions:
1. Wrap turkey breast with bacon slices.
2. Grease the pot of Ninja Foodi generously.
3. In the prepared pot, place the tomatoes, garlic powder, salt and black pepper and mix well.
4. Place the bacon wrapped turkey breast over tomato mixture.
5. Close the crisping lid and select "Slow Cooker".
6. Set on "High" for about 4 hours.
7. Press "Start/Stop" to begin.
8. Open the lid and transfer the turkey breast onto a cutting board.
9. Cut the turkey breast into desired sized slices and serve alongside the pan sauce.
- **Nutrition Info:** Calories: 442; Carbohydrates: 4.7g; Protein: 50.5g; Fat: 24.9g; Sugar: 2.5g; Sodium: 1300mg; Fiber: 1.1g

180. Keto Chicken Chili

Servings: 4 Servings
Cooking Time: 8 Minutes
Ingredients:
- 1 pound chicken breast
- 1 ½ cup chicken broth
- 2 cloves of garlic, chopped
- 1 jalapeno, seeds removed, diced
- 1 bell pepper, chopped
- ½ white onion, chopped
- ¼ cup heavy cream
- 4 oz cream cheese
- 1 tsp dried oregano
- ¼ tsp cayenne pepper
- ¼ tsp salt
- 1/8 tsp ground black pepper
- ¼ cup shredded cheddar cheese

Directions:
1. Place the chicken breast in the Ninja Foodi pot and sprinkle with the oregano, salt, cayenne and ground black pepper.
2. Add the broth, garlic, jalapeno, bell pepper and onion to the pot and close the pressure cooker lid.
3. Cook on high pressure for 10 minutes. Do a quick steam release and remove the lid.
4. Add the cream cheese and heavy cream and stir to blend.
5. Sprinkle the cheese on top of the chili and put the air crisper top on. Use the broil function to brown the cheese for 2 minutes.
- **Nutrition Info:** Calories: 448g, Carbohydrates: 9g, Protein: 38g, Fat: 31g, Sugar: 6g, Sodium: 1171 mg

181. Beefy Stew Recipe From Persia

Servings: 2
Cooking Time: 20 Minutes
Ingredients:
- 1 tablespoons vegetable oil
- 1 onion, chopped
- 2 cloves of garlic, minced
- ¾-pound beef stew meat, cut into chunks
- 1/2 tablespoon ground cumin
- 1/4 teaspoon saffron threads
- ½ teaspoon turmeric
- ¼ teaspoon ground cinnamon
- ¼ teaspoon ground allspice
- Salt and pepper to taste
- 2 tbsp tomato paste
- 1/2 can split peas, rinsed and drained
- 2 cups bone broth
- 1 can crushed tomatoes
- 2 tablespoon lemon juice, freshly squeezed

Directions:
1. Press the sauté button on the Ninja Foodi. Heat the oil and sauté the onion and garlic until fragrant. Add cumin, saffron, turmeric, cinnamon, and allspice. Stir in the beef and sear button for 3 minutes. Season with salt and pepper to taste.
2. Pour in the rest of the ingredients.
3. Install pressure lid. Close Ninja Foodi, press the pressure button, choose high settings, and set time to 20 minutes.
4. Once done cooking, do a quick release.
5. Serve and enjoy.
- **Nutrition Info:** Calories: 466; carbohydrates: 36g; protein: 49g; fat: 14g

182. Sweet & Sour Pork Chops

Servings: 4
Cooking Time: 16 Minutes
Ingredients:
- 6 pork loin chops
- Salt and freshly ground black pepper, to taste
- 2 tbsp. honey
- 2 tbsp. soy sauce
- 1 tbsp. balsamic vinegar

Directions:
1. With a meat tenderizer, tenderize the chops completely.
2. Sprinkle the chops with a little salt and black pepper.
3. In a large bowl, mix together remaining ingredients. Add the chops and coat with marinade generously. Refrigerate, covered for about 6-8 hours.
4. Arrange the "Cook & Crisp Basket" in the pot of Ninja Foodi. Close the Ninja Foodi with crisping lid and select "Air Crisp".
5. Press "Start/Stop" to begin and set the temperature to 355 degrees F.
6. Set the time for 5 minutes to preheat.
7. Now, place the pork chops into "Cook & Crisp Basket". Close the Ninja Foodi with crisping lid and select "Air Crisp". Set the temperature to 355 degrees F for 16 minutes, flipping once half way through.
8. Press "Start/Stop" to begin. Open the lid and serve hot.

- **Nutrition Info:** Calories: 281; Carbohydrates: 6.2g; Protein: 18.3g; Fat: 19.9g; Sugar: 5.9g; Sodium: 384mg; Fiber: 0.1g

183. Beef ' N Mushrooms In Thick Sauce

Servings: 2
Cooking Time: 35 Minutes
Ingredients:
- 1/2 tablespoon butter
- 1/2-pound beef chunks
- Salt and pepper to taste
- 1/2 cup onions, chopped
- 1/2 tablespoon garlic, minced
- 1 carrot, sliced diagonally
- 1/4 cup chopped celery
- 1/3 cup mushrooms, halved
- 1 medium potato, peeled and quartered
- 1 tablespoon Worcestershire sauce
- 1 tablespoon tomato paste
- 1/2 cup chicken broth
- 1 tablespoon all-purpose flour + 1 tablespoon water

Directions:
1. Turn on the sauté button on the Ninja Foodi and melt the butter. Sear button the beef chunks and season with salt and pepper to taste. Add the onions and garlic until fragrant.
2. Stir in the carrots, celery, mushrooms and potatoes.
3. Add the Worcestershire sauce, tomato paste, and chicken broth. Season with more salt and pepper to taste.
4. Install pressure lid. Close Ninja Foodi, press the pressure button, choose high settings, and set time to 30 minutes.
5. Once done cooking, do a quick release.
6. Open the lid and press the sauté button. Stir in the all-purpose flour and allow to simmer until the sauce thickens.
7. Serve and enjoy.
- **Nutrition Info:** Calories: 539; carbohydrates: 61.3g; protein:43.9g; fat: 13.1g

184. Zesty Lamb Chops(1)

Servings: 4
Cooking Time: 52 Minutes
Ingredients:
- 4 tbsps. butter
- 3 tbsps. lemon juice
- 4 lamb chops
- 2 tbsps. almond flour
- 1 c. picante sauce

Directions:
1. Coat the chops with almond flour and keep aside.
2. Press "Sauté" on Ninja Foodi and add butter and chops.
3. Sauté for about 2 minutes and add picante sauce and lemon juice.
4. Press "Pressure" and set the timer for 40 minutes at "Hi".
5. Release the pressure naturally and dish out to serve hot.
- **Nutrition Info:** 284 calories, 19.5g fat, 1g carbs, 24.8g protein

185. Awesome Beef Enchilada

Servings: 2
Cooking Time: 10 Minutes
Ingredients:
- 1 (12-inch) flour tortilla
- 1 C. cooked beef, shredded and divided
- 5-oz. Mexican cheese blend, shredded and divided
- 1 large Roma tomato, chopped and divided
- 2 corn tostadas, divided

Directions:
1. Arrange the tortillas onto a clean, smooth surface.
2. Place about ½ C. of shredded beef onto center of tortilla, followed by 2-oz. of the cheese, half of tomatoes and 1 tostada. Repeat the layers once and finally top with the remaining 1-oz. of cheese.
3. Gently fold tortilla over the filling in 4 layers.
4. With a broken piece of tostada, cover the center opening of the enchilada to secure the filling.
5. Arrange the "Cook & Crisp Basket" in the pot of Ninja Foodi.
6. Close the Ninja Foodi with crisping lid and select "Air Crisp".
7. Press "Start/Stop" to begin and set the temperature to 360 degrees F.
8. Set the time for 5 minutes to preheat. Coat the enchilada with cooking spray.
9. Place the enchilada, seam-side down into "Cook & Crisp Basket".
10. Close the Ninja Foodi with crisping lid and select "Air Crisp". Set the temperature to 360 degrees F for 8 minutes.
11. Press "Start/Stop" to begin. Open the lid and cut the enchilada in 2 equal sized portions. Serve warm.
- **Nutrition Info:** Calories: 441; Carbohydrates: 36.4g; Protein: 53g; Fat: 37.1g; Sugar: 2.6g; Sodium: 852mg; Fiber: 3.8g

186. Ny Strip Steak

Servings: 2
Cooking Time: 8 Minutes
Ingredients:
- 24 ounces NY Strip Steak
- 1 tsp salt
- ½ tsp ground black pepper

Directions:
1. Place the steaks on the metal trivet in the Ninja Foodi and sprinkle the salt and pepper over the top.
2. Add 1 cup of water to the pot, below the steaks.

3. Put the pressure lid on the pot and set to cook at high pressure for 1 minute. Once the timer is done, release the pressure quickly by opening the steamer valve carefully.
4. Place the air crisp lid on the pot and select the broil function and set the timer for 8 minutes for a medium cooked steak.
5. Remove from pot and serve hot
- **Nutrition Info:** Calories: 503 g, Carbohydrates: 1g, Protein: 46g, Fat: 34g, Sugar: 3g, Sodium: 1283 mg

187. Mother's Day Special Steak

Servings: 2
Cooking Time: 14 Minutes
Ingredients:
- 1 C. white flour
- 2 eggs
- 1 C. panko breadcrumbs
- Salt and freshly ground black pepper, to taste
- 2 (6-oz.) sirloin steaks, pounded

Directions:
1. In a shallow bowl, place the flour.
2. In a second shallow bowl, beat the eggs.
3. In a third shallow bowl, mix together panko, salt and black pepper.
4. Coat the steak with flour, then dip into eggs, and finally coat with the panko mixture.
5. Arrange the "Cook & Crisp Basket" in the pot of Ninja Foodi.
6. Close the Ninja Foodi with crisping lid and select "Air Crisp".
7. Press "Start/Stop" to begin and set the temperature to 360 degrees F.
8. Set the time for 5 minutes to preheat.
9. Now, place the steaks into "Cook & Crisp Basket".
10. Close the Ninja Foodi with crisping lid and select "Air Crisp".
11. Set the temperature to 360 degrees F for 10 minutes.
12. Press "Start/Stop" to begin.
13. Open the lid and serve hot.
- **Nutrition Info:** Calories: 746; Carbohydrates: 78g; Protein: 67.6g; Fat: 3g; Sugar: 1.5g; Sodium: 526mg; Fiber: 5.7g

188. Texas Steak

Servings: 6
Cooking Time: 16 Minutes
Ingredients:
- 1 (2-lb.) rib eye steak
- 2 tbsp. steak rub
- 1 tbsp. olive oil
- 2 C. beef broth

Directions:
1. Season the steak with steak rub evenly and set aside for about 10 minutes.
2. Select "Sauté/Sear" setting of Ninja Foodi and place the oil into the pot.
3. Press "Start/Stop" to begin and heat for about 2-3 minutes.
4. Add the steak and cook, uncovered for about 3 minutes per side.
5. Press "Start/Stop" to stop the cooking and stir in the broth.
6. Cover the Ninja Foodi with the pressure lid and place the pressure valve to "Seal" position.
7. Select "Pressure" and set to "High" for about 10 minutes.
8. Press "Start/Stop" to begin. Switch the valve to "Vent" and do a "Quick" release.
9. Once all the pressure is released, open the lid.
10. Serve hot.
- **Nutrition Info:** Calories: 455; Carbohydrates: 1.3g; Protein: 28.4g; Fat: 36.2g; Sugar: 0.2g; Sodium: 561mg; Fiber: 0g

189. Refreshingly Tasty Steak

Servings: 2
Cooking Time: 16 Minutes
Ingredients:
- 1 tbsp. butter
- 4 (6-oz.) flank steaks
- 1 tbsp. fresh thyme, chopped finely
- 2 tbsp. fresh lemon juice
- Salt and freshly ground black pepper, to taste

Directions:
1. Select "Sauté/Sear" setting of Ninja Foodi and place the butter into the pot.
2. Press "Start/Stop" to begin and heat for about 2-3 minutes.
3. Add the steak and cook, uncovered for about 3 minutes per side.
4. Press "Start/Stop" to stop the cooking and stir in the remaining ingredients.
5. Cover the Ninja Foodi with the pressure lid and place the pressure valve to "Seal" position.
6. Select "Pressure" and set to "High" for about 10 minutes.
7. Press "Start/Stop" to begin. Switch the valve to "Vent" and do a "Quick" release.
8. Once all the pressure is released, open the lid. Serve hot.
- **Nutrition Info:** Calories: 359; Carbohydrates: 0.6g; Protein: 47.5g; Fat: 17.1g; Sugar: 0.2g; Sodium: 156mg; Fiber: 0.3g

190. Herbed Lamb Chops

Servings: 4
Cooking Time: 10 Hours
Ingredients:
- 1 lb. lamb chops
- 1½ C. tomatoes, chopped finely
- 1 C. chicken broth
- Salt and freshly ground black pepper, to taste
- 3 tbsp. mixed fresh herbs (oregano, thyme, sage), chopped

Directions:
1. In the pot of Ninja Foodi, place all the ingredients and mix well.
2. Close the crisping lid and select "Slow Cooker".
3. Set on "Low" for about 8 hours.
4. Press "Start/Stop" to begin.
5. Open the lid and serve hot.
- **Nutrition Info:** Calories: 237; Carbohydrates: 3.8g; Protein: 33.8g; Fat: 9g; Sugar: 2g; Sodium: 319mg; Fiber: 1.4g

191. Jamaican Jerk Pork

Servings: 3
Cooking Time: 30 Minutes
Ingredients:
- 1 lb. pork shoulder
- 2 tbsp. Jamaican jerk spice blend
- 1 tbsp. butter
- ¼ C. beef broth

Directions:
1. Select "Sauté/Sear" setting of Ninja Foodi and place the butter into the pot.
2. Press "Start/Stop" to begin and heat for about 2-3 minutes.
3. Add the pork shoulder and cook, uncovered for about 10 minutes or until browned completely. Press "Start/Stop" to stop the cooking and stir in the broth.
4. Cover the Ninja Foodi with the pressure lid and place the pressure valve to "Seal" position. Select "Pressure" and set to "Low" for about 20 minutes.
5. Press "Start/Stop" to begin. Switch the valve to "Vent" and do a "Quick" release.
6. Once all the pressure is released, open the lid. Serve hot.
- **Nutrition Info:** Calories: 479; Carbohydrates: 0.1g; Protein: 35.6g; Fat: 36.3g; Sugar: 0.1g; Sodium: 194mg; Fiber: 0g

192. Filet Mignon Ala Carribé

Servings: 2
Cooking Time: 35 Minutes
Ingredients:
- 1 filet mignon
- ½ cup pineapple, chopped
- 1-piece bacon
- ¼ teaspoon jalapeno pepper
- 2 tablespoon red onions, chopped
- 2 cloves of garlic, minced
- 2 tablespoon coconut aminos or soy sauce
- 3 tablespoon honey
- ½ of a lime, juiced
- 1 tablespoon apple cider vinegar
- ¼ teaspoon ground ginger
- 1 teaspoon thyme
- ¼ teaspoon cinnamon
- 1/8 teaspoon ground cloves
- 1/8 teaspoon ground nutmeg
- Salt and pepper to taste

Directions:
1. Place all ingredients in the Ninja Foodi and mix well.
2. Install pressure lid. Close the lid and press the pressure button. Cook on high for 35 minutes.
3. Do natural pressure release to open the lid. Serve and enjoy.
- **Nutrition Info:** Calories: 345; carbohydrates: 42.7g; protein: 22.7g; fat: 9.2g

193. Pork Chili

Servings: 4
Cooking Time: 8 Minutes
Ingredients:
- 1 pound pork
- 2 cups chicken broth
- 2 cloves of garlic, chopped
- 1 bell pepper, chopped
- 1 white onion, chopped
- 4 tomatoes, chopped
- 1 tsp dried basil
- 1 tsp dried oregano
- ½ tsp tsp salt
- 1/8 tsp ground black pepper
- ¼ cup shredded cheddar cheese

Directions:
1. Place the pork in the Ninja Foodi pot and sprinkle with the oregano, salt, basil and ground black pepper.
2. Add the broth, garlic, tomato, bell pepper and onion to the pot and close the pressure cooker lid.
3. Cook on high pressure for 10 minutes. Do a quick steam release and remove the lid.
4. Add the cream cheese and heavy cream and stir to blend.
5. Sprinkle the cheese on top of the chili and put the air crisper top on. Use the broil function to brown the cheese for 2 minutes.
- **Nutrition Info:** Calories: 206g, Carbohydrates: 5g, Protein: 28g, Fat: 7g, Sugar: 3g, Sodium: 864mg

194. Beef Chili

Servings: 4
Cooking Time: 8 Minutes
Ingredients:
- 1 pound beef roast
- 2 cups beef broth
- 2 cloves of garlic, chopped
- 1 bell pepper, chopped
- 1 white onion, chopped
- 4 tomatoes, chopped
- 1 tsp dried basil
- 1 tsp dried oregano
- ½ tsp tsp salt
- 1/8 tsp ground black pepper
- ¼ cup shredded cheddar cheese

Directions:

1. Place the beef roast in the Ninja Foodi pot and sprinkle with the oregano, salt, basil and ground black pepper.
2. Add the broth, garlic, tomato, bell pepper and onion to the pot and close the pressure cooker lid.
3. Cook on high pressure for 10 minutes. Do a quick steam release and remove the lid.
4. Add the cream cheese and heavy cream and stir to blend.
5. Sprinkle the cheese on top of the chili and put the air crisper top on. Use the broil function to brown the cheese for 2 minutes.
- **Nutrition Info:** Calories: 282g, Carbohydrates: 4g, Protein: 14g, Fat: 13g, Sugar: 2g, Sodium: 1163 mg

195. Chicken Taco Filling

Servings: 8
Cooking Time: 4 Hours
Ingredients:
- ¼ C. low-sodium soy sauce
- ¼ C. blackberry jam
- ¼ C. honey
- ½ tsp. red pepper flakes, crushed
- 5 (8-oz.) boneless, skinless chicken breasts

Directions:
1. Grease the pot of Ninja Foodi generously.
2. In a bowl, add all the ingredients except the chicken breasts and mix well.
3. In the prepared pot, place the chicken breasts and top with the honey mixture.
4. Close the crisping lid and select "Slow Cooker".
5. Set on "High" for about 4 hours.
6. Press "Start/Stop" to begin.
7. Open the lid and with 2 forks, shred the meat and stir with sauce well.
8. Serve hot.
- **Nutrition Info:** Calories: 329; Carbohydrates: 15.8g; Protein: 41.6g; Fat: 10.5g; Sugar: 15.2g; Sodium: 562mg; Fiber: 0.1g

196. Jamaican Jerk Pork Roast

Servings: 3
Cooking Time: 33 Minutes
Ingredients:
- 1 tbsp. butter
- 1/8 c. beef broth
- 1 lb. pork shoulder
- 1/8 c. Jamaican jerk spice blend

Directions:
1. Season the pork with Jamaican jerk spice blend.
2. Press "Sauté" on Ninja Foodi and add butter and seasoned pork.
3. Sauté for about 3 minutes and add beef broth.
4. Press "Pressure" and cook for about 20 minutes on Low.
5. Release the pressure naturally and dish out in a platter.
- **Nutrition Info:** 477 calories, 36.2g fat, 2g carbs, 35.4g protein

197. Deliciously Spicy Turkey Legs

Servings: 2
Cooking Time: 25 Minutes
Ingredients:
- 2 turkey legs
- 5 C. chicken broth
- 3 tbsp. olive oil
- 1-2 tbsp. Mrs. Dash seasoning
- 1 tsp. paprika

Directions:
1. In the pot of Ninja Foodi, place turkey legs and top with the broth.
2. Cover the Ninja Foodi with the pressure lid and place the pressure valve to "Seal" position.
3. Select "Pressure" and set to "High" for about 15 minutes. Press "Start/Stop" to begin. Switch the valve to "Vent" and do a "Quick" release.
4. Once all the pressure is released, open the lid
5. Transfer the turkey legs onto a plate and with paper towels, pat dry them.
6. Remove broth from the pot and arrange the reversible rack in the pot.
7. Drizzle the turkey legs with oil and rub with the Mrs. Dash seasoning and paprika.
8. Place the turkey legs over the rack. Close the Ninja Foodi with the crisping lid and Select "Air Crisp". Set the temperature to 400 degrees F for 10 minutes.
9. Press "Start/Stop" to begin. After 7 minutes, flip the turkey legs.
10. Open the lid and serve.
- **Nutrition Info:** Calories: 634; Carbohydrates: 2.9g; Protein: 79.2g; Fat: 32.4g; Sugar: 1.9g; Sodium: 800mg; Fiber: 0.4g

198. Chicken Alfredo Pasta

Servings: 3
Cooking Time: 5 Minutes
Ingredients:
- 8 oz. fettuccine
- 15 oz. Alfredo sauce
- 2 c. water
- 1 c. cooked chicken, diced
- 2 tsps. chicken seasoning

Directions:
1. Break your pasta in half so it fits in the cooker.
2. Add pasta, water, and chicken seasoning to Ninja Foodi.
3. Seal the lid. Select STEAM and cook at HIGH pressure for 3 minutes.
4. When the timer beeps, press CANCEL and use a quick release.
5. Drain the pasta and add to serving bowl.
6. Mix in Alfredo sauce and chicken. Serve!

- **Nutrition Info:** 225 calories, 6.3g fat, 21.8g carbs, 20.1g protein

199. Smoky Roasted Chicken

Servings: 5
Cooking Time: 40 Minutes
Ingredients:
- 1 (4-lb.) whole chicken, necks and giblets removed
- Salt and freshly ground black pepper, to taste
- 1 tsp. liquid smoke
- 2 tbsp. chicken rub

Directions:
1. Season the chicken inside, outside and underneath the skin with the salt and black pepper generously.
2. In the pot of Ninja Foodi, place 1 C. of water and liquid smoke.
3. Place the chicken into the "Cook & Crisp Basket".
4. Arrange the "Cook & Crisp Basket" in the pot.
5. Cover the Ninja Foodi with the pressure lid and place the pressure valve to "Seal" position.
6. Select "Pressure" and set to "High" for about 15 minutes.
7. Press "Start/Stop" to begin.
8. Switch the valve to "Vent" and do a "Quick" release.
9. Once all the pressure is released, open the lid
10. Spray the chicken with the cooking spray and then, coat with half of the chicken rub.
11. Now, close the Ninja Foodi with the crisping lid and select "Air Crisp".
12. Set the temperature to 400 degrees F for 10 minutes.
13. Press "Start/Stop" to begin.
14. Again, spray the chicken with the cooking spray and then, coat with half of the chicken rub.
15. Close the Ninja Foodi with the crisping lid and cook for 10 minutes more.
16. Open the lid and transfer the chicken onto a cutting board for about 10 minutes before carving.
17. Cut into desired sized pieces and serve.
- **Nutrition Info:** Calories: 557; Carbohydrates: 1.2g; Protein: 3.2105.2g; Fat: 11g; Sugar: 0g; Sodium: 446mg; Fiber: 0g

200. French Style Duck Breast

Servings: 2
Cooking Time: 20 Minutes
Ingredients:
- 1 (10½-oz.) duck breast
- 1 tbsp. wholegrain mustard
- 1 tsp. honey
- 1 tsp. balsamic vinegar
- Salt and freshly ground black pepper, to taste

Directions:
1. Arrange the "Cook & Crisp Basket" in the pot of Ninja Foodi. Close the Ninja Foodi with crisping lid and select "Air Crisp". Press "Start/Stop" to begin and set the temperature to 365 degrees F. Set the time for 5 minutes to preheat.
2. Now, place the duck breast, skin side up into "Cook & Crisp Basket".
3. Close the Ninja Foodi with crisping lid and select "Air Crisp". Set the temperature to 365 degrees F for 15 minutes. Press "Start/Stop" to begin.
4. Meanwhile in a bowl, mix together remaining ingredients. Open the lid and coat the duck breast with the honey mixture generously.
5. Close the Ninja Foodi with crisping lid and set the temperature to 355 degrees F for 5 minutes. Press "Start/Stop" to begin.
6. Open the lid and serve hot.
- **Nutrition Info:** Calories: 229; Carbohydrates: 4.9g; Protein: 34.2g; Fat: 7.6g; Sugar: 3.3g; Sodium: 78mg; Fiber: 1.8g

FISH AND SEAFOOD RECIPES

201. Fancy "rich" Guy Smoked Lobster

Servings: 4
Cooking Time: 35 Minutes
Ingredients:
- 6 Lobster Tails
- 4 garlic cloves
- ¼ c. butter

Directions:
1. Preheat the Ninja Foodi to 400 degrees F at first
2. Open the lobster tails gently by using kitchen scissors
3. Remove the lobster meat gently from the shells but keep it inside the shells
4. Take a plate and place it
5. Add some butter in a pan and allow it melt
6. Put some garlic cloves in it and heat it over medium-low heat
7. Pour the garlic butter mixture all over the lobster tail meat
8. Let the fryer to broil the lobster at 130 degrees F
9. Remove the lobster meat from Ninja Foodi and set aside
10. Use a fork to pull out the lobster meat from the shells entirely
11. Pour some garlic butter over it if needed
- **Nutrition Info:** 160 calories, 1g fat, 3g carbs, 20g protein

202. Spicy Shrimp Soup

Servings: 4 Servings
Cooking Time: 10 Minutes
Ingredients:
- 1 pound shrimp, deveined
- 6 cups chicken broth
- 2 cloves of garlic, chopped
- 1 carrot, chopped
- 2 Bell peppers, chopped
- 2 celery stalks, chopped
- ½ white onion, chopped
- ¼ tsp salt
- ½ tsp cayenne pepper
- 1/8 tsp ground black pepper

Directions:
1. Add all the ingredients to the pot and place the pressure cooker lid on the Ninja Foodi.
2. Cook on high pressure for 10 minutes. Do a quick steam release and remove the lid.
3. Remove the chicken from the pot and shred the chicken using two forks.
4. Serve while hot or freeze to use at a later date.
- **Nutrition Info:** Calories: 150g, Carbohydrates: 2g, Protein: 36g, Fat: 0g, Sugar: 2g, Sodium: 438mg

203. Cajun Spiced Salmon

Servings: 2
Cooking Time: 8 Minutes
Ingredients:
- 2 (6-oz.) salmon steaks
- 2 tbsp. Cajun seasoning

Directions:
1. Rub the salmon steaks with the Cajun seasoning evenly and set aside for about 10 minutes.
2. Arrange the "Cook & Crisp Basket" in the pot of Ninja Foodi.
3. Close the Ninja Foodi with crisping lid and select "Air Crisp".
4. Press "Start/Stop" to begin and set the temperature to 390 degrees F.
5. Set the time for 5 minutes to preheat.
6. Now, place the salmon steaks into "Cook & Crisp Basket".
7. Close the Ninja Foodi with crisping lid and select "Air Crisp".
8. Set the temperature to 390 degrees F for 4 minutes per side.
9. Press "Start/Stop" to begin.
10. Open the lid and serve.
- **Nutrition Info:** Calories: 225; Carbohydrates: 0g; Protein: 33.1g; Fat: 10.5g; Sugar: 0g; Sodium: 225mg; Fiber: 0g

204. Coconut Curry Sea Bass

Servings: 2
Cooking Time: 3 Minutes
Ingredients:
- 1 (14.5 ounce) can coconut milk
- Juice of 1 lime
- 1 tablespoon red curry paste
- 1 teaspoon fish sauce
- 1 teaspoon coconut aminos
- 1 teaspoon honey
- 2 teaspoons sriracha
- 2 cloves garlic, minced
- 1 teaspoon ground turmeric
- 1 teaspoon ground ginger
- 1/2 teaspoon sea salt
- 1/2 teaspoon white pepper
- 1-pound sea bass, cut into 1" cubes
- 1/4 cup chopped fresh cilantro
- 2 lime wedges

Directions:
1. Whisk well pepper, salt, ginger, turmeric, garlic, sriracha, honey, coconut aminos, fish sauce, red curry paste, lime juice, and coconut milk in a large bowl.
2. Place fish in pot and pour coconut milk mixture over it.

3. Install pressure lid. Close Ninja Foodi, press pressure button, choose high settings, and set time to 3 minutes.
4. Once done cooking, do a quick release.
5. Serve and enjoy with equal amounts of lime wedge and cilantro.
- **Nutrition Info:** Calories: 749; carbohydrates: 16.6g; protein: 58.0g; fat: 50.0g

205. Lemon Pepper Salmon

Servings: 2 Servings
Cooking Time: 5 Minutes
Ingredients:
- ½ cup water
- 2 Tbsp butter
- 1/3 cup lemon juice
- 1 pound Salmon, de boned
- ½ ground black pepper

Directions:
1. Add all the ingredients into the cook and crisp basket and place the basket inside the Ninja Foodi.
2. Place the pressure cooker lid on top of the pot and close the pressure valve to the seal position. Set the pressure cooker function to high heat and set the timer for 3 minutes.
3. Once the coking cycle is complete, release the pressure quickly by carefully opening the steamer valve. Enjoy while hot
- **Nutrition Info:** Calories: 314g, Carbohydrates: 8g, Protein: 42g, Fat: 14g, Sugar: 1g, Sodium: 565g

206. Rosemary Scallops

Servings: 6
Cooking Time: 6 Minutes
Ingredients:
- ½ C. butter
- 4 garlic cloves, minced
- 2 tbsp. fresh rosemary, chopped
- 2 lb. sea scallops
- Salt and freshly ground black pepper, to taste

Directions:
1. Select "Sauté/Sear" setting of Ninja Foodi and place the butter into the pot.
2. Press "Start/Stop" to begin and heat for about 2-3 minutes.
3. Add the garlic and rosemary and cook, uncovered for about 1 minute.
4. Stir in the scallops, salt and black pepper and cook for about 2 minutes.
5. Press "Start/Stop" to stop the cooking.
6. Now, close the Ninja Foodi with crisping lid and select "Air Crisp".
7. Set the temperature to 350 degrees F for 3 minutes.

8. Press "Start/Stop" to begin. Open the lid and serve.
- **Nutrition Info:** Calories: 275; Carbohydrates: 4.9g; Protein: 25.7g; Fat: 16.7g; Sugar: 0g; Sodium: 380mg; Fiber: 0.5g

207. Salmon Stew

Servings: 3
Cooking Time: 16 Minutes
Ingredients:
- 1 c. homemade fish broth
- Salt and black pepper
- 1 chopped onion
- 1 lb. salmon fillet, cubed
- 1 tbsp. butter

Directions:
1. Season the salmon fillets with salt and black pepper.
2. Press "Sauté" on Ninja Foodi and add butter and onions.
3. Sauté for about 3 minutes and add salmon and fish broth.
4. Lock the lid and set the Ninja Foodi to "Pressure" for about 8 minutes.
5. Release the pressure naturally and dish out to serve hot.
- **Nutrition Info:** 272 calories, 14.2g fat, 4.4g carbs, 32.1g protein

208. Sweet And Sour Fish

Servings: 3
Cooking Time: 16 Minutes
Ingredients:
- 2 drops liquid stevia
- ¼ c. butter
- 1 lb. fish chunks
- 1 tbsp. vinegar
- Salt and black pepper

Directions:
1. Press "Sauté" on Ninja Foodi and add butter and fish chunks.
2. Sauté for about 3 minutes and add stevia, salt and black pepper.
3. Press "Air Crisp" and cook for about 3 minutes at 360 degrees F.
4. Dish out in a serving bowl and serve immediately.
- **Nutrition Info:** 274 calories, 15.4 fat, 2.8g carbs, 33.2g protein

209. Family Feast Shrimp

Servings: 4
Cooking Time: 20 Minutes
Ingredients:
- 1 lb. shrimp, peeled and deveined
- Salt and freshly ground black pepper, to taste
- 8-oz. coconut milk

- ½ C. panko breadcrumbs
- ½ tsp. cayenne pepper

Directions:
1. In a shallow dish, mix together the coconut milk, salt and black pepper.
2. In another shallow dish, mix together breadcrumbs, cayenne pepper, salt and black pepper.
3. Dip the shrimp in coconut milk mixture and then coat with the breadcrumbs mixture. Arrange the "Cook & Crisp Basket" in the pot of Ninja Foodi.
4. Close the Ninja Foodi with crisping lid and select "Air Crisp".
5. Press "Start/Stop" to begin and set the temperature to 350 degrees F.
6. Set the time for 5 minutes to preheat.
7. Now, place the shrimp into "Cook & Crisp Basket". Close the Ninja Foodi with crisping lid and select "Air Crisp".
8. Set the temperature to 350 degrees F for 20 minutes.
9. Press "Start/Stop" to begin. Open the lid and serve.

- **Nutrition Info:** Calories: 301; Carbohydrates: 12.5g; Protein: 28.2g; Fat: 15.7g; Sugar: 2.2g; Sodium: 393mg; Fiber: 2.3g

210. Buttered Halibut

Servings: 4
Cooking Time: 30 Minutes
Ingredients:
- 1 lb. halibut fillets
- 2 tbsp. ginger-garlic paste
- Salt and freshly ground black pepper, to taste
- 3 green chilies, chopped
- ¾ C. butter, chopped

Directions:
1. Select "Bake/Roast" of Ninja Foodi and set the temperature to 360 degrees F.
2. Press "Start/Stop" to begin and preheat the Ninja Foodi for about 10 minutes.
3. Coat the halibut fillets with ginger-garlic paste and then, season with salt and black pepper.
4. In the pot of Ninja Foodi, place the halibut fillets and top with green chilies, followed by the butter.
5. Close the Ninja Foodi with crisping lid and set the time for 30 minutes.
6. Press "Start/Stop" to begin. Open the lid and serve.

- **Nutrition Info:** Calories: 517; Carbohydrates: 2.4g; Protein: 31.5g; Fat: 41.6g; Sugar: 0.2g; Sodium: 364mg; Fiber: 0.1g

211. Bbq Shrimp

Servings: 4 Servings
Cooking Time: 12 Minutes
Ingredients:
- 1 ½ pounds Shrimp, deveined and peeled
- 1 Tbsp olive oil
- 1 tsp ground paprika
- ¼ tsp salt
- ¼ tsp ground black pepper
- 1 onion, chopped
- ¼ cup hot sauce
- 1 tsp stevia
- ¼ cup water
- 2 Tbsp vinegar

Directions:
1. Turn the Ninja Foodi on to saute and add the olive oil. Once hot, add the shrimp and sear on each side for 2 minutes.
2. Sprinkle the salt and pepper on the shrimp and then add all the remaining ingredients to the pot.
3. Cover the Foodi and use the pressure cooker function to cook the shrimp for 8 minutes under high heat pressure.
4. Release the pressure using a natural steam and serve warm or chilled

- **Nutrition Info:** Calories: 207g, Carbohydrates: 1g, Protein: 36g, Fat: 6g, Sugar: 2g, Sodium: 3633mg

212. Jambalaya

Servings: 4 Servings
Cooking Time: 10 Minutes
Ingredients:
- 1 pound shrimp, deveined, shells removed
- 2 cups chicken broth
- 2 cloves of garlic, chopped
- 2 bell peppers, chopped
- 1 white onion, chopped
- 4 tomatoes, chopped
- 1 tsp dried basil
- 1 tsp dried oregano
- ½ tsp tsp salt
- 1/8 tsp ground black pepper
- ¼ cup shredded cheddar cheese

Directions:
1. Place the shrimp in the Ninja Foodi pot and sprinkle with the oregano, salt, basil and ground black pepper.
2. Add the broth, garlic, tomato, bell pepper and onion to the pot and close the pressure cooker lid.
3. Cook on high pressure for 10 minutes. Do a quick steam release and remove the lid.
4. Add the cream cheese and heavy cream and stir to blend.
5. Sprinkle the cheese on top of the chili and put the air crisper top on. Use the broil function to brown the cheese for 2 minutes.

- **Nutrition Info:** Calories: 150g, Carbohydrates: 2g, Protein: 36g, Fat: 0g, Sugar: 2g, Sodium: 438mg

213. Butter Shrimp

Servings: 4 Servings
Cooking Time: 12 Minutes
Ingredients:
- 2 pounds shrimp, deveined and peeled
- 2 Tbsp Butter
- 1 tsp chili powder
- 1 tsp garlic powder
- ½ tsp ground black pepper
- ¼ cup parmesan cheese

Directions:
1. Place the shrimp and butter in the pot and press saute. Sear both sides of the shrimp for 2 minutes.
2. Sprinkle the chili powder, garlic powder and ground black pepper on the shrimp and mix. Sprinkle the cheese over the shrimp and place the air crisp lid on top.
3. Use the roast function set to 375 to cook the shrimp for 10 more minutes. Serve hot.
- **Nutrition Info:** Calories: 293, Carbohydrates: 2g, Protein: 66g, Fat: 13g, Sugar: 0g, Sodium: 1386 mg

214. Tomato-basil Dressed Tilapia

Servings: 2
Cooking Time: 4 Minutes
Ingredients:
- 2 (4 oz) tilapia fillets
- Salt and pepper
- 2 roma tomatoes, diced
- 2 minced garlic cloves
- 1/4 cup chopped basil (fresh)
- 1 tbsp olive oil
- 1/4 tsp salt
- 1/8 tsp pepper
- 1 tbsp Balsamic vinegar (optional)

Directions:
1. Add a cup of water in Ninja Foodi, place steamer basket, and add tilapia in basket. Season with pepper and salt.
2. Install pressure lid and place valve to vent position.
3. Close Ninja Foodi, press steam button, and set time to 2 minutes.
4. Meanwhile, in a medium bowl toss well to mix pepper, salt, olive oil, basil, garlic, and tomatoes. If desired, you can add a tablespoon of balsamic vinegar. Mix well.
5. Once done cooking, do a quick release.
6. Serve and enjoy with the basil-tomato dressing.
- **Nutrition Info:** Calories: 196; carbohydrates: 2.0g; protein: 20.0g; fat: 12.0g

215. Ketogenic Butter Fish

Servings: 3
Cooking Time: 40 Minutes
Ingredients:
- 1 lb. salmon fillets
- 2 tbsps. ginger-garlic paste
- 3 chopped green chilies
- Salt and black pepper
- ¾ c. butter

Directions:
1. Season the salmon fillets with ginger-garlic paste, salt and black pepper.
2. Place the salmon fillets in the pot of Ninja Foodi and top with green chilies and butter.
3. Press "Bake/Roast" and set the timer to 30 minutes at 360 degrees F.
4. Bake for about 30 minutes and dish out the fillets in a serving platter.
- **Nutrition Info:** 507 calories, 45.9g fat, 2.4g carbs, 22.8g protein

216. Bok Choy On Ginger-sesame Salmon

Servings: 2
Cooking Time: 6 Minutes
Ingredients:
- 1 tablespoon toasted sesame oil
- 1 tablespoons rice vinegar
- 2 tablespoons sear button sugar
- 1/2 cup shoyu (soy sauce)
- 1 garlic clove, pressed
- 1 tablespoon freshly grated ginger
- 1 tablespoon toasted sesame seed
- 2 green onions, sliced reserve some for garnish
- 2 7-oz salmon filet
- 2 baby bok choy washed well
- 1 teaspoon miso paste mixed with a 1/2 cup of water

Directions:
1. On a loaf pan that fits inside your Ninja Foodi, place salmon with skin side down.
2. In a small bowl whisk well sesame oil, rice vinegar, sear button sugar, shoyu, garlic, ginger, and sesame seed. Pour over salmon.
3. Place half of sliced green onions over salmon. Securely cover pan with foil.
4. On a separate loaf pan, place bok choy. In a small bowl, whisk well water and miso paste. Pour over bok choy and seal pan securely with foil.
5. Add water to Ninja Foodi and place trivet. Place pan of salmon side by side the bok choy pan on trivet.
6. Install pressure lid. Close Ninja Foodi, press manual button, choose high settings, and set time to 6 minutes.
7. Once done cooking, do a quick release. Serve and enjoy.

- **Nutrition Info:** Calories: 609; carbohydrates: 30.4g; protein: 56.0g; fat: 29.2g

217. Well-seasoned Catfish

Servings: 4
Cooking Time: 23 Minutes
Ingredients:
- 4 (4-oz.) catfish fillets
- ¼ C. Louisiana fish fry seasoning
- 1 tbsp. olive oil
- 1 tbsp. fresh parsley, chopped

Directions:
1. Rub the fish filets with seasoning generously and then, coat with oil.
2. Arrange the "Cook & Crisp Basket" in the pot of Ninja Foodi.
3. Close the Ninja Foodi with crisping lid and select "Air Crisp".
4. Press "Start/Stop" to begin and set the temperature to 400 degrees F.
5. Set the time for 5 minutes to preheat.
6. Now, place the fish fillets into "Cook & Crisp Basket".
7. Close the Ninja Foodi with crisping lid and select "Air Crisp".
8. Set the temperature to 400 degrees F for 23 minutes.
9. Press "Start/Stop" to begin.
10. After 10 minutes, flip the fish fillets and again after 20 minutes.
11. Open the lid and serve with the garnishing of parsley.
- **Nutrition Info:** Calories: 206; Carbohydrates: 4.7g; Protein: 17.7g; Fat: 12.1g; Sugar: 0g; Sodium: 201mg; Fiber: 0.7g

218. Easy Veggie-salmon Bake

Servings: 2
Cooking Time: 20 Minutes
Ingredients:
- 1 cup chicken broth
- 1 cup milk
- 1 salmon filet
- 2 tbsp olive oil
- Ground pepper to taste
- 1 tsp minced garlic
- 1 cup frozen vegetables
- 1/2 can of cream of celery soup
- ¼ tsp dill
- ¼ tsp cilantro
- 1 tsp Italian spice
- 1 tsp poultry seasoning
- 1 tbsp ground parmesan

Directions:
1. Press sauté button and heat oil.
2. Add the salmon and cook until white on both sides and defrosted enough to split apart, around 2 minutes per side.
3. Add the garlic and just stir into the oil then deglaze the pot with the broth for 3 minutes.
4. Add the spices, milk, vegetables, noodles and stir.
5. Add the cream of celery soup on top and just gently stir so it is mixed in enough on top to not be clumpy.
6. Install pressure lid. Close Ninja Foodi, press pressure cook button, choose high settings, and set time to 8 minutes.
7. Once done cooking, do a quick release.
8. Serve and enjoy with a sprinkle of parmesan.
- **Nutrition Info:** Calories: 616; carbohydrates: 28.7g; protein: 51.8g; fat: 32.6g

219. Green Chili Mahi-mahi Fillets

Servings: 2
Cooking Time: 10 Minutes
Ingredients:
- ¼ c. homemade green chili enchilada sauce
- 2 thawed Mahi-Mahi fillets
- 2 tbsps. butter
- Salt and pepper
- 1 c. water

Directions:
1. Pour 1 cup of water into the Ninja Foodi and set a steamer rack.
2. Grease the bottom of each mahi-mahi fillet with 1 tablespoon of butter, spreading the butter from end to end – this will prevent the fish from sticking to the rack.
3. Put the fillets on the rack. Spread 1/4 cup of enchilada sauce between each fillet using a pastry brush – cover them well.
4. Top with more enchilada sauce, if desired. Season fillets with salt and pepper. Lock the lid and close the steam valve. Press "PRESSURE", set the pressure to HIGH, and set the timer for 5 minutes.
5. When the timer beeps, quickly release the pressure and transfer the fillets into serving plates. Serve.
- **Nutrition Info:** 120 calories, 2g fat, 5g carbs, 10g protein

220. Shrimp Magic

Servings: 3
Cooking Time: 25 Minutes
Ingredients:
- 2 tbsps. butter
- ½ tsp. paprika, smoked
- 1 lb. deveined shrimps, peeled
- Lemongrass stalks
- 1 chopped red chili pepper, seeded

Directions:
1. In a bowl, combine all the ingredients except lemongrass and marinate for about 1 hour.
2. Press "Bake/Roast" and set the timer to 15 minutes at 345 degrees F.
3. Bake for about 15 minutes and dish out the fillets.
- **Nutrition Info:** 251 calories, 10.3g fat, 3g carbs, 34.6g protein

221. Sweet 'n Spicy Mahi-mahi

Servings: 2
Cooking Time: 10 Minutes
Ingredients:
- 2 6-oz mahi-mahi fillets
- Salt, to taste
- Black pepper, to taste
- 1-2 cloves garlic, minced or crushed
- 1" piece ginger, finely grated
- ½ lime, juiced
- 2 tablespoons honey
- 1 tablespoon nanami togarashi
- 2 tablespoons sriracha
- 1 tablespoon orange juice

Directions:
1. In a heatproof dish that fits inside the Ninja Foodi, mix well orange juice, sriracha, nanami togarashi, honey lime juice, ginger, and garlic.
2. Season mahi-mahi with pepper and salt. Place in bowl of sauce and cover well in sauce. Seal dish securely with foil.
3. Install pressure lid and place valve to vent position.
4. Add a cup of water in Ninja Foodi, place trivet, and add dish of mahi-mahi on trivet.
5. Close Ninja Foodi, press steam button and set time to 10 minutes.
6. Once done cooking, do a quick release.
7. Serve and enjoy.
- **Nutrition Info:** Calories: 200; carbohydrates: 20.1g; protein: 28.1g; fat: 0.8g

222. Mesmerizing Salmon Loaf

Servings: 6
Cooking Time: 6 Hours 10 Mins
Ingredients:
- 2 slightly beaten eggs
- 1 c. chicken broth
- ¼ c. shredded cheddar cheese
- 2 c. stuffing croutons, seasoned
- 7 oz. drained salmon, skinless and boneless

Directions:
1. Mix all the ingredients except salmon in a bowl then add salmon and combine it well
2. Spray the inside of the Ninja Foodi with cooking spray

3. Make it into a loaf shape
4. Cook for 4-6 hours on low heat
5. Serve and enjoy!
- **Nutrition Info:** 220 calories, 5g fat, 13g carbs, 20g protein

223. Everyday Flounder

Servings: 4 Servings
Cooking Time: 12 Minutes
Ingredients:
- 2 pounds flounder filets
- 2 Tbsp Butter
- 1 tsp garlic powder
- ½ tsp ground black pepper
- ½ tsp salt
- ¼ cup parmesan cheese

Directions:
1. Place the flounder and butter in the pot and press saute. Sear both sides of the shrimp for 2 minutes.
2. Sprinkle the salt, garlic powder and ground black pepper on the shrimp and mix. Sprinkle the cheese over the flounder and place the air crisp lid on top.
3. Use the roast function set to 375 to cook the shrimp for 10 more minutes. Serve hot.
- **Nutrition Info:** Calories: 418g, Carbohydrates: 2g, Protein: 60g, Fat: 17g, Sugar: 1g, Sodium: 1267mg

224. Cod Topped With Mediterranean-spiced Tomatoes

Servings: 6
Cooking Time: 10 Minutes
Ingredients:
- 2 frozen or fresh cod fillet
- 1 tablespoon butter
- 1/2 lemon, juiced
- ½ small onion, sliced thinly
- 1/4 teaspoon salt
- 1/4 teaspoon black pepper
- 1/2 teaspoon oregano
- ¼ tsp cumin
- ¼ tsp rosemary
- 4 roma tomatoes, diced
- ¼ cup water

Directions:
1. Press sauté and melt butter. Stir in lemon juice, onion, salt, black pepper, oregano cumin, rosemary, and diced tomatoes. Cook for 8 minutes.
2. Add fish and spoon sauce over it. Add water and press stop.
3. Install pressure lid and place valve to vent position.
4. Close Ninja Foodi, press steam button, and set time to 2 minutes.
5. Once done cooking, do a quick release. Serve and enjoy.

- **Nutrition Info:** Calories: 184; carbohydrates: 10.0g; protein: 20.7g; fat: 6.8g

225. Coconut Curry Fish

Servings: 2
Cooking Time: 15 Minutes
Ingredients:
- 1-lb fish steaks or fillets, rinsed and cut into bite-size pieces
- 1 tomato, chopped
- 1 green chiles, sliced into strips
- 1 small onions, sliced into strips
- 2 garlic cloves, squeezed
- 1/2 tbsp freshly grated ginger
- 2 bay laurel leaves
- 1 tsp ground coriander
- 1 tsp ground cumin
- ½ tsp ground turmeric
- ½ tsp chili powder
- ½ tsp ground fenugreek
- 1 cup unsweetened coconut milk
- Salt to taste

Directions:
1. Press sauté button and heat oil. Add garlic, sauté for a minute. Stir in ginger and onions. Sauté for 5 minutes. Stir in bay leaves, fenugreek, chili powder, turmeric, cumin, and coriander. Cook for a minute.
2. Add coconut milk and deglaze pot.
3. Stir in tomatoes and green chilies. Mix well.
4. Add fish and mix well. Install pressure lid and place valve to vent position.
5. Close Ninja Foodi, press pressure cook button, choose low settings, and set time to 5 minutes.
6. Once done cooking, do a quick release. Adjust seasoning to taste.
7. Serve and enjoy.
- **Nutrition Info:** Calories: 434; carbohydrates: 11.7g; protein: 29.7g; fat: 29.8g

226. Paprika Shrimp

Servings: 3
Cooking Time: 20 Minutes
Ingredients:
- 1 tsp. paprika, smoked
- 3 tbsps. butter
- 1 lb. tiger shrimps
- Salt

Directions:
1. In a bowl, mix all the above ingredients and marinate the shrimps in it.
2. Grease the pot of Ninja Foodi with butter and transfer the seasoned shrimps in it.
3. Press "Bake/Roast" and set the timer to 15 minutes at 355 degrees F.
4. Dish out shrimps from the Ninja Foodi and serve.
- **Nutrition Info:** 173 calories, 8.3g fat, 0.1g carbs, 23.8g protein

227. Black Pepper Scallops

Servings: 4 Servings
Cooking Time: 17 Minutes
Ingredients:
- 2 pounds Sea Scallops
- 2 Tbsp Butter
- 1 tsp garlic powder
- 1 tsp ground black pepper
- ¼ cup lemon juice

Directions:
1. Place the scallops and butter in the pot and press saute. Sear both sides of the shrimp for 2 minutes.
2. Sprinkle the chili powder, garlic powder and ground black pepper on the shrimp and mix. Sprinkle the cheese over the shrimp and place the air crisp lid on top.
3. Use the roast function set to 400 to cook the shrimp for 15 more minutes. Serve hot.
- **Nutrition Info:** Calories: 236 g, Carbohydrates: 11g, Protein: 34g, Fat: 7g, Sugar: 0g, Sodium: 1181 mg

228. Salmon With Orange-ginger Sauce

Servings: 2
Cooking Time: 15 Minutes
Ingredients:
- 1-pound salmon
- 1 tablespoon dark soy sauce
- 2 teaspoons minced ginger
- 1 teaspoon minced garlic
- 1 teaspoon salt
- 1 1/2 tsp ground pepper
- 2 tablespoons low sugar marmalade

Directions:
1. In a heatproof pan that fits inside your Ninja Foodi, add salmon.
2. Mix all the sauce ingredients and pour over the salmon. Allow to marinate for 15-30 minutes. Cover pan with foil securely.
3. Put 2 cups of water in Ninja Foodi and add trivet.
4. Place the pan of salmon on trivet.
5. Install pressure lid. Close Ninja Foodi, press pressure button, choose low settings, and set time to 5 minutes.
6. Once done cooking, do a quick release.
7. Serve and enjoy.
- **Nutrition Info:** Calories: 177; carbohydrates: 8.8g; protein: 24.0g; fat: 5.0g

229. Stewed Mixed Seafood

Servings: 2
Cooking Time: 35 Minutes

Ingredients:
- 1 tbsp vegetable oil
- ½ 14.5-oz can fire-roasted tomatoes
- 1/2 cup diced onion
- 1/2 cup chopped carrots, or 1 cup chopped bell pepper
- 1/2 cup water
- 1/2 cup white wine or broth
- 1 bay leaf
- 1/2 tablespoon tomato paste
- 1 tablespoon minced garlic
- 1 teaspoon fennel seeds toasted and ground
- 1/2 teaspoon dried oregano
- 1 teaspoon salt
- 1 teaspoon red pepper flakes
- 2 cups mixed seafood such as fish chunks, shrimp, bay scallops, mussels and calamari rings, defrosted
- 1 tablespoon fresh lemon juice

Directions:
1. Press sauté button on Ninja Foodi and heat oil. Once hot, stir in onion and garlic. Sauté for 5 minutes. Stir in tomatoes, bay leaves, tomato paste, oregano, salt, and pepper flakes. Cook for 5 minutes. Press stop.
2. Stir in bell pepper, water, wine, and fennel seeds. Mix well.
3. Install pressure lid. Close Ninja Foodi, press pressure button, choose high settings, and set time to 15 minutes.
4. Once done cooking, do a quick release.
5. Stir in defrosted mixed seafood. Cover and let it cook for 10 minutes in residual heat.
6. Serve and enjoy with a dash of lemon juice.
- **Nutrition Info:** Calories: 202; carbohydrates: 10.0g; protein: 18.0g; fat: 10.0g

230. Pepper Crusted Tuna

Servings: 2 Servings
Cooking Time: 5 Minutes
Ingredients:
- ½ cup water
- 2 Tbsp butter
- 1/3 cup lemon juice
- 1 pound Tuna Filets
- T tsp black peppercorns, crushed

Directions:
1. Rub the tuna with the black pepper and then place in the air crisper basket.
2. Place the basket into the Ninja Foodi.
3. Sprinkle the chili powder over the top of the salmon and then add the butter and lemon juice around the filets.
4. Place the pressure cooker lid on top of the pot and close the pressure valve to the seal position. Set the pressure cooker function to high heat and set the timer for 3 minutes.
5. Once the cooking cycle is complete, release the pressure quickly by carefully opening the steamer valve. Enjoy while hot
- **Nutrition Info:** Calories: 564g, Carbohydrates: 3g, Protein: 52g, Fat: 39g, Sugar: 1g, Sodium: 85mg

231. Salmon-pesto Over Pasta

Servings: 2
Cooking Time: 10 Minutes
Ingredients:
- 4 ounces dry pasta
- 1 cup water
- 3-ounces smoked salmon, broken up in bite sized pieces
- 1/4 lemon
- Salt and pepper
- 1/2 teaspoon grated lemon zest
- 1/2 teaspoon lemon juice
- 2 tbsp heavy cream
- Pesto-spinach sauce ingredients:
- 1 tbsp walnuts
- 1 clove garlic
- 1 cup packed baby spinach
- 1 ½ tbsp olive oil
- 1/4 cup freshly grated parmesan + more for serving/garnish
- Kosher salt and black pepper to taste
- 1 tsp grated lemon zest
- 1/4 cup heavy cream

Directions:
1. Make the sauce in blender by pulsing garlic and walnuts until chopped. Add ¼ tsp pepper, ¼ tsp salt, ½ cup parmesan, oil, and 2/3s of spinach. Puree until smooth.
2. Add butter, water, and pasta in Ninja Foodi.
3. Install pressure lid. Close Ninja Foodi, press pressure button, choose high settings, and set time to 4 minutes.
4. Once done cooking, do a quick release. Press stop and then press sauté.
5. Stir in remaining parmesan, remaining spinach, sauce, lemon juice, lemon zest, heavy cream, and smoked salmon. Mix well and sauté for 5 minutes.
6. Serve and enjoy.
- **Nutrition Info:** Calories: 465; carbohydrates: 31.0g; protein: 20.1g; fat: 29.0g

232. Wine Braised Salmon

Servings: 6
Cooking Time: 1 Hour
Ingredients:
- 1½ C. chicken broth
- ½ C. white wine
- 1 shallot, sliced thinly
- 4 (4-oz.) salmon fillets

- Salt and freshly ground black pepper, to taste

Directions:
1. In the pot of Ninja Foodi, mix together broth, shallot and lemon.
2. Arrange salmon fillets on top, skin side down and sprinkle with salt and black pepper.
3. Close the crisping lid and select "Slow Cooker".
4. Set on "Low" for about 45-60 minutes.
5. Press "Start/Stop" to begin.
6. Open the lid and serve hot.
- **Nutrition Info:** Calories: 192; Carbohydrates: 1.9g; Protein: 24g; Fat: 7.5g; Sugar: 0.5g; Sodium: 377mg; Fiber: 0g

233. Mexican Swordfish

Servings: 4 Servings
Cooking Time: 8 Minutes
Ingredients:
- 4 Swordfish Steaks
- ½ cup water
- 1 cup chopped tomatoes
- ½ cup chopped onion
- 1 tbsp lime juice
- 1 jalapeno, seeds removed, chopped
- ½ tsp salt
- ¼ tsp ground black pepper

Directions:
1. Place the swordfish in the Ninja Foodi pot and add all the ingredients to the bowl.
2. Close the pressure seal lid and set the steamer valve to seal.
3. Cook on high pressure for 8 minutes then do a quick pressure release. Serve the swordfish while hot.
- **Nutrition Info:** Calories: 177g, Carbohydrates: 8g, Protein: 23g, Fat: 6g, Sugar: 5g, Sodium: 684

234. Lemon Cod

Servings: 2 Servings
Cooking Time: 5 Minutes
Ingredients:
- ½ cup water
- 2 Tbsp butter
- 1/3 cup lemon juice
- 1 pound cod filets
- ½ tsp paprika

Directions:
1. Add all the ingredients into the cook and crisp basket and place the basket inside the Ninja Foodi.
2. Place the pressure cooker lid on top of the pot and close the pressure valve to the seal position. Set the pressure cooker function to high heat and set the timer for 3 minutes.
3. Once the coking cycle is complete, release the pressure quickly by carefully opening the steamer valve. Enjoy while hot
- **Nutrition Info:** Calories: 492g, Carbohydrates: 3g, Protein: 82g, Fat: 15g, Sugar: 1g, Sodium: 335mg

235. Seafood Gumbo New Orleans Style

Servings: 2
Cooking Time: 20 Minutes
Ingredients:
- 1 sea bass filet patted dry and cut into 2" chunks
- 1 tablespoon ghee or avocado oil
- 1 tablespoon Cajun seasoning
- 1 small yellow onion diced
- 1 small bell pepper diced
- 1 celery rib diced
- 2 roma tomatoes diced
- 1 tbsp tomato paste
- 1 bay leaf
- 1/2 cup bone broth
- ¾-pound medium to large raw shrimp deveined
- Sea salt to taste
- Black pepper to taste

Directions:
1. Press sauté button and heat oil.
2. Season fish chunks with pepper, salt, and half of Cajun seasoning. Once oil is hot, sear fish chunks for 3 minutes per side and gently transfer to a plate.
3. Stir in remaining Cajun seasoning, celery, and onions. Sauté for 2 minutes. Press stop.
4. Stir in bone broth, bay leaves, tomato paste, and diced tomatoes. Mix well. Add back fish. Install pressure lid and place valve to vent position.
5. Close Ninja Foodi, press pressure cook button, choose high settings, and set time to 5 minutes.
6. Once done cooking, do a quick release. Stir in shrimps. Cover and let it sit for 5 minutes. Open and mix well.
7. Serve and enjoy.
- **Nutrition Info:** Calories: 357; carbohydrates: 14.8g; protein: 45.9g; fat: 12.6g

236. Salsa Tuna Steaks

Servings: 4 Servings
Cooking Time: 10 Minutes
Ingredients:
- 4 Tuna Steaks, about 2 pounds
- ½ cup water
- 1 cup chopped tomatoes
- ½ cup chopped onion
- 1 tbsp lemon juice
- ½ tsp salt

- ¼ tsp ground black pepper

Directions:
1. Place the tuna in the Ninja Foodi pot and add all the ingredients to the bowl.
2. Close the pressure seal lid and set the steamer valve to seal.
3. Cook on high pressure for 8 minutes then do a quick pressure release. Serve the tuna while hot.
- **Nutrition Info:** Calories: 165g, Carbohydrates: 4g, Protein: 24g, Fat: 3g, Sugar: 3g, Sodium: 583 mg

237. Tilapia Filet Topped With Mango-salsa

Servings: 2
Cooking Time: 5 Minutes
Ingredients:
- 1 cup coconut milk
- 1/2 to 1 tablespoon Thai green curry paste
- 1 tablespoon fish sauce
- Zest of 1 lime and juice of 1/2 lime
- 2 teaspoons sear button sugar
- 1 teaspoon garlic, minced
- 1 tablespoon fresh ginger, minced
- 2 6-oz Tilapia filet
- 1 lime, cut in thin slices
- A sprinkle of cilantro leaves and chopped scallion
- Mango salsa ingredients:
- 1 mango, peeled, seeded, and diced (about 3/4 cup small dice)
- 1 fresno or jalapeno chiles, minced
- 1 scallion, finely chopped
- A handful of cilantro leaves, chopped
- Juice of 1 lime

Directions:
1. In a bowl, mix well coconut milk, Thai green curry paste, fish sauce, lime juice, lime zest, sear button sugar, garlic, and ginger. Add fish and marinate for at least an hour.
2. Meanwhile, make the mango salsa by combining all ingredients in a separate bowl. Keep in the fridge.
3. Cut two 11x11-inch foil. Place one fish fillet in each foil. Top each equally with lime, scallion and cilantro. Seal foil packets.
4. Add a cup of water in Ninja Foodi, place trivet, and add foil packets on trivet.
5. Install pressure lid. Close Ninja Foodi, press pressure button, choose high settings, and set time to 5 minutes.
6. Once done cooking, do a quick release. Serve and enjoy with mango salsa on top.
- **Nutrition Info:** Calories: 372; carbohydrates: 28.5g; protein: 29.3g; fat: 15.6g

238. Buttered Scallops

Servings: 6
Cooking Time: 25 Minutes
Ingredients:
- 4 minced garlic cloves
- 4 tbsps. freshly chopped rosemary,
- 2 lbs. sea scallops
- ½ c. butter
- Salt and black pepper

Directions:
1. Press "Sauté" on Ninja Foodi and add butter, rosemary and garlic.
2. Sauté for about 1 minute and add sea scallops, salt and black pepper.
3. Sauté for about 2 minutes and press "Air Crisp" at 350 degrees F.
4. Set the timer for about 3 minutes and dish out to serve.
- **Nutrition Info:** 279 calories, 16.8g fat, 5.7g carbs, 25.8g protein

239. Creamy Herb 'n Parm Salmon

Servings: 2
Cooking Time: 10 Minutes
Ingredients:
- 2 frozen salmon filets
- 1/2 cup water
- 1 1/2 tsp minced garlic
- 1/4 cup heavy cream
- 1 cup parmesan cheese grated
- 1 tbsp chopped fresh chives
- 1 tbsp chopped fresh parsley
- 1 tbsp fresh dill
- 1 tsp fresh lemon juice
- Salt and pepper to taste

Directions:
1. Add water and trivet in pot. Place fillets on top of trivet.
2. Install pressure lid. Close Ninja Foodi, press pressure button, choose high settings, and set time to 4 minutes.
3. Once done cooking, do a quick release.
4. Transfer salmon to a serving plate. And remove trivet.
5. Press stop and then press sauté button on Ninja Foodi. Stir in heavy cream once water begins to boil. Boil for 3 minutes. Press stop and then stir in lemon juice, parmesan cheese, dill, parsley, and chives. Season with pepper and salt to taste. Pour over salmon.
6. Serve and enjoy.
- **Nutrition Info:** Calories: 423; carbohydrates: 6.4g; protein: 43.1g; fat: 25.0g

240. Flavorsome Salmon

Servings: 2
Cooking Time: 13 Minutes
Ingredients:

- ¼ C. soy sauce
- ¼ C. honey
- 2 tsp. rice wine vinegar
- 1 tsp. water
- 2 (4-oz.) salmon fillets

Directions:
1. In a small bowl, mix together all ingredients except salmon.
2. In a small bowl, reserve about half of the mixture. Add the salmon in remaining mixture and coat well. Refrigerate, covered to marinate for about 2 hours.
3. Arrange the "Cook & Crisp Basket" in the pot of Ninja Foodi.
4. Close the Ninja Foodi with crisping lid and select "Air Crisp".
5. Press "Start/Stop" to begin and set the temperature to 355 degrees F.
6. Set the time for 5 minutes to preheat.
7. Now, place the salmon fillets into "Cook & Crisp Basket".
8. Close the Ninja Foodi with crisping lid and select "Air Crisp".
9. Set the temperature to 355 degrees F for 13 minutes.
10. Press "Start/Stop" to begin. After 8 minutes, flip the salmon fillets and coat with reserved marinade.
11. Open the lid and serve.
- **Nutrition Info:** Calories: 299; Carbohydrates: 37.4g; Protein: 24.1g; Fat: 7g; Sugar: 35.3g; Sodium: 1600mg; Fiber: 0.3g

241. Miso Glazed Salmon

Servings: 4
Cooking Time: 9 Minutes
Ingredients:
- 4 (4-oz.) (1-inch thick) frozen skinless salmon fillets
- Salt, to taste
- 2 tbsp. butter, softened
- 2 tbsp. red miso paste
- 2 heads baby bok choy, stems on, cut in half

Directions:
1. In the pot of Ninja Foodi, place ½ C. of water. In the pot, arrange the reversible rack in higher position. Season the salmon fillets with salt evenly.
2. Place the salmon fillets over the rack. Cover the Ninja Foodi with the pressure lid and place the pressure valve to "Seal" position.
3. Select "Pressure" and set to "High" for about 2 minutes.
4. Press "Start/Stop" to begin. Switch the valve to "Vent" and do a "Quick" release.
5. Meanwhile, spray the bok choy with cooking spray evenly.
6. In a bowl, add the butter and miso paste and mix well. Once all the pressure is released, open the lid. With paper towels, pat dry the salmon fillets and then, coat them with butter mixture evenly.
7. Arrange the bok choy around the salmon fillets,
8. Now, close the Ninja Foodi with crisping lid and select "Broil".
9. Set time to 7 minutes and select "Start/Stop" to begin.
10. Open the lid and serve the salmon fillets alongside the bok choy.
- **Nutrition Info:** Calories: 210; Carbohydrates: 9g; Protein: 24.2g; Fat: 9g; Sugar: 5.5g; Sodium: 897mg; Fiber: 3.4g

242. Chili Lime Salmon

Servings: 2 Servings
Cooking Time: 5 Minutes
Ingredients:
- ½ cup water
- 2 Tbsp butter
- 1/3 cup lime juice
- 1 pound Salmon, de boned
- ½ ground chili powder

Directions:
1. Add the salmon into the cook and crisp basket and place the basket inside the Ninja Foodi.
2. Sprinkle the chili powder over the top of the salmon and then add the water, butter and lime juice around the filets.
3. Place the pressure cooker lid on top of the pot and close the pressure valve to the seal position. Set the pressure cooker function to high heat and set the timer for 3 minutes.
4. Once the cooking cycle is complete, release the pressure quickly by carefully opening the steamer valve. Enjoy while hot
- **Nutrition Info:** Calories: 349g, Carbohydrates: 8g, Protein: 44g, Fat: 17g, Sugar: 1g, Sodium: 566g

243. Buffalo Fish

Servings: 6
Cooking Time: 21 Minutes
Ingredients:
- 6 tbsps. butter
- ¾ c. Franks red hot sauce
- 6 fish fillets
- Salt and black pepper
- 2 tsps. garlic powder

Directions:
1. Press "Sauté" on Ninja Foodi and add butter and fish fillets.
2. Sauté for about 3 minutes and add salt, black pepper and garlic powder.
3. Press "Bake/Roast" and bake for about 8 minutes at 340 degrees F.
4. Dish out in a serving platter and serve hot.

- **Nutrition Info:** 317 calories, 22.7g fat, 16.4g carbs, 13.6g protein

244. Pasta 'n Tuna Bake

Servings: 2
Cooking Time: 10 Minutes
Ingredients:
- 1 can cream-of-mushroom soup
- 1 1/2 cups water
- 1 1/4 cups macaroni pasta
- 1 can tuna
- 1/2 cup frozen peas
- 1/2 tsp salt
- 1 tsp pepper
- 1/2 cup shredded cheddar cheese

Directions:
1. Mix soup and water in Ninja Foodi.
2. Add remaining ingredients except for cheese. Stir.
3. Install pressure lid.
4. Close Ninja Foodi, press pressure button, choose high settings, and set time to 4 minutes.
5. Once done cooking, do a quick release.
6. Remove pressure lid.
7. Stir in cheese and roast for 5 minutes.
8. Serve and enjoy.
- **Nutrition Info:** Calories: 378; carbohydrates: 34.0g; protein: 28.0g; fat: 14.1g

245. Eggs 'n Smoked Ramekin

Servings: 2
Cooking Time: 4 Minutes
Ingredients:
- 2 eggs
- 2 slices of smoked salmon
- 2 slices of cheese
- 2 fresh basil leaves for garnish
- Olive oil

Directions:
1. Add a cup of water in Ninja Foodi and place trivet on bottom.
2. Lightly grease each ramekin with a drop of olive oil each. Spread well.
3. Crack an egg in each ramekin. Place a slice of cheese, a slice of smoked salmon, and basil leaf in each ramekin.
4. Cover each ramekin with foil and place on trivet.
5. Install pressure lid. Close Ninja Foodi, press manual button, choose low settings, and set time to 4 minutes.
6. Once done cooking, do a quick release.
7. Serve and enjoy.
- **Nutrition Info:** Calories: 239; carbohydrates: 0.9g; protein: 17.5g; fat: 18.3g

246. Veggie Fish Soup

Servings: 4 Servings
Cooking Time: 10 Minutes
Ingredients:
- 1 pound cod
- 6 cups chicken broth
- 2 cloves of garlic, chopped
- 1 carrot, chopped
- 1 Bell pepper, chopped
- 1 sweet potato, peeled, diced
- 2 celery stalks, chopped
- ½ white onion, chopped
- ¼ tsp salt
- 1/8 tsp ground black pepper
- ¼ cup shredded cheddar cheese

Directions:
1. Add all the ingredients to the pot and place the pressure cooker lid on the Ninja Foodi.
2. Cook on high pressure for 10 minutes. Do a quick steam release and remove the lid.
3. Remove the chicken from the pot and shred the chicken using two forks.
4. Serve while hot or freeze to use at a later date.
- **Nutrition Info:** Calories: 250g, Carbohydrates: 4g, Protein: 36g, Fat: 0g, Sugar: 2g, Sodium: 438mg

247. Spicy Flounder

Servings: 2 Servings
Cooking Time: 15 Minutes
Ingredients:
- 2 tsp salt
- 1 Tbsp paprika
- 1 tbsp chili powder
- 1 tsp ground black pepper
- 1 tsp onion powder
- 1 tsp garlic powder
- 1 tsp ground cumin
- 2 filets Flounder, about 1 pound
- 1 tbsp olive oil

Directions:
1. Mix all of the spices together in a bowl and then set aside.
2. Rub the flounder with the olive oil and then coat in the spice seasoning.
3. Place the spiced flounder in the cook and crisp basket and turn the Ninja Foodi to 375 degrees. Place the basket in the Foodi and set the timer for 15 minutes. Serve while hot straight out of the pot.
- **Nutrition Info:** Calories: 351g, Carbohydrates: 6g, Protein: 51g, Fat: 12g, Sugar: 6g, Sodium: 2658 mg

248. French Salmon Meal

Servings: 6
Cooking Time: 5 Hours 55 Minutes

Ingredients:
- ¾ C. green lentils
- 1 C. carrot, peeled and chopped
- 2 C. chicken broth
- Salt and freshly ground black pepper, to taste
- 6 (4-oz.) skinless, boneless salmon fillets

Directions:
1. In the pot of Ninja Foodi, place all ingredients except the salmon and stir to combine.
2. Close the crisping lid and select "Slow Cooker".
3. Set on "High" for about 5-5½ hours
4. Press "Start/Stop" to begin.
5. Open the lid and arrange a large parchment paper over lentil mixture.
6. Season the salmon fillets with salt and black pepper evenly.
7. Arrange the salmon fillets over parchment paper in a single layer.
8. Close the crisping lid and select "Slow Cooker".
9. Set on "High" for about 25 minutes.
10. Press "Start/Stop" to begin.
11. Open the lid and serve the salmon fillets with lentil mixture.
- **Nutrition Info:** Calories: 247; Carbohydrates: 16.5g; Protein: 33.3g; Fat: 4.8g; Sugar: 1.6g; Sodium: 336mg; Fiber: 7.8g

249. Salmon And Asparagus

Servings: 2 Servings
Cooking Time: 5 Minutes
Ingredients:
- ½ cup water
- 2 Tbsp butter
- 1 lemon, sliced
- 1 pound Salmon, de boned
- ½ ground black pepper
- 1 bunch asparagus, about ½ pound

Directions:
1. Add all the ingredients into the cook and crisp basket, with the asparagus on the bottom, the lemon slices layered on the salmon, and place the basket inside the Ninja Foodi.
2. Place the pressure cooker lid on top of the pot and close the pressure valve to the seal position. Set the pressure cooker function to high heat and set the timer for 3 minutes.
3. Once the cooking cycle is complete, release the pressure quickly by carefully opening the steamer valve. Enjoy while hot
- **Nutrition Info:** Calories: 342g, Carbohydrates: 13g, Protein: 46g, Fat: 14g, Sugar: 4g, Sodium: 568mg

250. Tomato Lime Tilapia

Servings: 2 Servings
Cooking Time: 5 Minutes
Ingredients:
- 2 Tbsp butter
- 1/3 cup lime juice
- 1 tomato, diced
- 1 pound Salmon, de boned
- ½ tsp salt
- ¼ tsp ground black pepper

Directions:
1. Add the tilapia into the cook and crisp basket and place the basket inside the Ninja Foodi.
2. Sprinkle the seasoning over the top of the fish and then add the tomatoes, butter and lime juice around the filets.
3. Place the pressure cooker lid on top of the pot and close the pressure valve to the seal position. Set the pressure cooker function to high heat and set the timer for 3 minutes.
4. Once the cooking cycle is complete, release the pressure quickly by carefully opening the steamer valve. Enjoy while hot
- **Nutrition Info:** Calories: 317g, Carbohydrates: 9g, Protein: 42g, Fat: 14g, Sugar: 4g, Sodium: 1726mg

SOUPS & STEWS

251. Creamy Chicken & Mushroom Soup

Servings: 6 Servings
Cooking Time: 15 Minutes
Ingredients:
- 6 chicken thighs, boneless, skinless and cut into 1-inch pieces
- 4 cups chicken broth
- 1 cup cremini mushrooms, sliced thin
- 3 carrots, peeled and chopped fine
- 2 stalks celery, chopped fine
- 1 onion, chopped fine
- ½ cup half-and-half
- ¼ cup flour
- 3 cloves garlic, chopped fine
- 2 tablespoons butter
- 2 tablespoons fresh parsley, chopped
- 1 tablespoon olive oil
- ½ teaspoon thyme
- 1 sprig rosemary
- 1 bay leaf
- Salt & pepper

Directions:
1. Add the olive oil to the pot and set to sauté on medium heat. Sprinkle the chicken with salt and pepper and add to the pot. Cook till brown, about 2-3 minutes, set aside.
2. Add the butter and let it melt. Once melted, add the vegetables and cook till tender, about 3-4 minutes. Stir in thyme and cook 1 minute more.
3. Stir in flour till lightly browned, about 1 minute. Add the broth, bay leaf, rosemary and chicken and cook, stirring constantly, till soup thickens, about 4-5 minutes.
4. Stir in the half-and-half and continue cooking till heated through, 1-2 minutes. Discard bay leaf and rosemary sprig. Serve immediately.

252. Tuscan-style Veggie Soup

Servings: 4 Servings
Cooking Time: 20 Minutes
Ingredients:
- 3 cups vegetable broth
- 2 cups kale, chopped
- 2 cups croutons
- ½ large can tomatoes, diced
- 1 can navy beans, rinsed and drained
- 1 cup water
- 1 onion, chopped
- ½ cup fresh basil, chopped
- ½ cup Parmesan cheese
- 1 tablespoon olive oil
- 1 clove garlic, chopped fine

Directions:
1. Add oil to the pot and set cooker to sauté on medium heat. Add the onion and garlic and cook, stirring often, 3 minutes. Add the broth, water, beans and tomatoes. Bring to a boil, then reduce heat to med-low.
2. Cover and cook 10 minutes. Stir in the kale and cook 5 minutes more or till kale is tender.
3. Ladle into bowls and top with croutons and Parmesan cheese.

253. Irish Lamb Stew

Servings: 6 Servings
Cooking Time: 8 Hours 15 Mins
Ingredients:
- 1 ½ pounds lamb stew meat
- 4 cups chicken broth
- 3 ½ cups cabbage, chopped
- 2 cups water
- 2 large potatoes, peeled and chopped
- 1 onion, chopped
- 1 carrot, chopped
- 1 leek, chopped
- 1 cup baby spinach
- 2 tablespoons olive oil
- 1 tablespoon fresh mint, chopped fine
- 2 sprigs rosemary
- 1 bay leaf

Directions:
1. Add 1 tablespoon of the oil to the cooking pot and set to sauté on medium heat. Sprinkle the lamb with salt and pepper and add to the pot. Cook till brown on both sides, about 8 – 10 minutes. Transfer the lamb to a plate.
2. Add the remaining oil to the pot along with the onion. Cook, stirring often, 2 minutes. Add the carrots and the leek. Cook till the vegetables start to soften, about 5 minutes.
3. Add the potatoes and the lamb to the pot. Pour in the broth and water, then add the rosemary and bay leaf. Secure the lid and select slow cooking on low. Cook 8 hours.
4. Stir in the spinach before serving. Ladle into bowls and sprinkle with mint.

254. Jamaican Chicken Stew

Servings: 6 Servings
Cooking Time: 30 Mins
Ingredients:
- Marinade
- 2 ½ – 3 pounds chicken thighs, skinless
- 1-2 green onions, chopped
- 1 teaspoon garlic, chopped fine
- ½ teaspoon ginger, grated
- ½ teaspoon white pepper
- ½ teaspoon thyme
- ½ teaspoon salt

- ½ teaspoon chicken bouillon powder
- For the stew
- 2 cups chicken broth
- 1-2 small red bell peppers, seeded and chopped
- 1 onion, chopped fine
- ¼ cup vegetable oil
- 1 tablespoon ketchup
- 2 teaspoon brown sugar
- 1 teaspoon browning sauce
- 1 teaspoon hot sauce
- 1 teaspoon smoked paprika
- ½ teaspoon thyme
- salt to taste

Directions:
1. Place chicken in a large bowl, then add all of the marinade ingredients. Mix to make sure the chicken is coated. Cover and refrigerate at least 30 minutes or overnight.
2. When ready to cook shake off any excess spice or onions from the chicken.
3. Add the oil to the cooking pot and set to sauté on medium. When the oil is hot, add the chicken and cook till chicken is browned, about 4-5 minutes. Remove the chicken to a plate and drain off excess oil.
4. Add onions, hot sauce, paprika and bell peppers to the pot. Cook, stirring often, till onion is translucent, about 2-3 minutes. Add the chicken with remaining stew ingredients and bring to a boil. Let it simmer, stirring often, till sauce thickens, about 15-20 minutes.

255. Venison Stew

Servings: 4 Servings
Cooking Time: 2 Hours
Ingredients:
- 1 pound venison stew meat
- 3 cups beef broth
- 4 slices bacon, cut into ½-inch pieces
- 1 cup dry red wine
- 2 carrots, sliced
- 1 large potato, cubed
- 1 onion, chopped
- 1 stalk celery, sliced thin
- ½ cup cold water
- 3 tablespoons flour
- ½ teaspoon salt
- ¼ teaspoon thyme
- ¼ teaspoon marjoram
- ¼ teaspoon pepper

Directions:
1. Add the bacon to the pot and set cooker to sauté on med-high heat. Cook till crispy, remove to paper towel lined plate.
2. Add the venison to the pot and cook till brown on all sides. Add the broth, wine, celery, carrots and seasonings and stir to combine. Add the lid and set the cooker to slow cooking on high. Cook one hour.
3. After one hour, add the potatoes and cook till meat and vegetables are tender.
4. Stir the flour into the cold water in a small bowl, or measuring glass. Stir into the stew and continue to cook thill thickened, about 5-10 minutes. Stir in bacon just before serving.

256. Spiced Potato-cauliflower Chowder

Servings: 2
Cooking Time: 7 Minutes
Ingredients:
- 1 head cauliflower, cut into florets
- 2 small red potatoes, peeled and sliced
- 4 cups vegetable stock
- 6 cloves of garlic, minced
- 1 onion, diced
- 1 cup heavy cream
- 2 bay leaves
- Salt and pepper to taste
- 2 stalks of green onions

Directions:
1. Place the cauliflower, potatoes, vegetable stock, garlic, onion, heavy cream, and bay leaves in the Ninja Foodi. Season with salt and pepper to taste.
2. Install pressure lid. Close Ninja Foodi, press the pressure button, choose high settings, and set time to 6 minutes.
3. Once done cooking, do a quick release.
4. Open the lid and stir in the green onions.
5. Serve and enjoy.
- **Nutrition Info:** Calories: 448; carbohydrates: 47.7g; protein: 10.1g; fat: 24.1g

257. Filling Cauli-squash Chowder

Servings: 2
Cooking Time: 12 Minutes
Ingredients:
- 1 tablespoon oil
- 1/2 onion, diced
- 1 clove garlic, minced
- 1/2-pound frozen cauliflower
- 1/2-pound frozen butternut squash
- 1 cup vegetable broth
- 1/2 teaspoon paprika
- 1/2 teaspoon dried thyme
- Salt and pepper to taste
- 1/4 cup half-and-half

Directions:
1. Press the sauté button on the Ninja Foodi and heat oil.
2. Stir in the onions and garlic. Sauté until fragrant.
3. Add the rest of the ingredients.

4. Install pressure lid. Close Ninja Foodi, press the button, choose high settings, and set time to 10 minutes.
5. Once done cooking, do a quick release.
6. Open the lid and transfer the contents into a blender. Pulse until smooth. Serve with cheese on top if desired.
7. Serve and enjoy.
- **Nutrition Info:** Calories: 103; carbohydrates:15.2 g; protein:1.9 g; fat: 3.8g

258. Chili-quinoa 'n Black Bean Soup

Servings: 2
Cooking Time: 20 Minutes
Ingredients:
- 1/2 bell pepper, diced
- 1 medium-sized sweet potatoes, peeled and diced
- 1/2 onion, diced
- 1 clove garlic, minced
- 1 stalk celery, chopped
- 1 1/3 cups vegetable broth
- 1 tablespoon tomato paste
- 1/3 cup diced tomatoes
- 1/3 can black beans, rinsed and drained
- 1 teaspoon each of paprika and cumin
- Salt to taste
- 2 tbsp quinoa
- 2 cups vegetable broth

Directions:
1. Place all ingredients in the Ninja Foodi. Give a good stir.
2. Install pressure lid.
3. Close Ninja Foodi, press the pressure button, choose high settings, and set time to 20 minutes.
4. Once done cooking, do a quick release.
5. Serve and enjoy.
- **Nutrition Info:** Calories: 377; carbohydrates: 73.7g; protein: 18.1g; fat: 1.0g

259. Tipsy Potato Chowder

Servings: 5 Servings
Cooking Time: 8 Hours
Ingredients:
- 6 cups potatoes, peeled and cubed
- 2 cups cheddar cheese, grated
- 1 ¾ cups chicken broth
- 1 can beer
- ½ cup onion, chopped
- ½ cup celery, chopped
- ½ cup carrot, chopped
- ½ cup heavy cream
- 1 clove garlic, chopped fine
- ¼ teaspoon pepper

Directions:
1. Combine all ingredients, except the cheese and cream to the cooking pot. Add lid and set to slow cooking on low. Cook 6-8 hours, stirring every so often
2. About 10 minutes before serving, coarsely mash the vegetables, leaving the soup a little chunky. Add cheese and cream and stir to combine. Cover and cook 5 minutes more or till cheese is melted. Serve.

260. Seafood Stew

Servings: 4 Servings
Cooking Time: 25 Mins
Ingredients:
- 1 pound mixed lobster, shrimp and cod
- 3 ½ cups water
- 3 ½ cups tomatoes, crushed
- 2 cups potatoes, cubed
- 1 ½ cups celery, sliced
- 1 ½ cups onions, chopped
- 1 ½ cups carrots, sliced
- ¼ cups shallots, chopped
- 4 - 6 cloves of garlic, chopped fine
- 1 teaspoon salt
- 1 teaspoon pepper
- 1 teaspoon basil
- 1 teaspoon Greek seasoning
- 1 teaspoon Sriracha sauce

Directions:
1. Place all the vegetables, except the potatoes into the cooking pot. Add tomatoes, water and seasonings. Secure lid and set to pressure cooking on high. Set timer for 10 minutes.
2. When timer goes off, use quick release to remove the lid. Add the potatoes and pressure cook another 8 minutes. Use quick release again.
3. Set to sauté on medium heat. Stir in the seafood and cook till shrimp and lobster is pink and the stew is heated through, about 5 minutes. Serve.

261. Shrimp & Mango Curry

Servings: 4 Servings
Cooking Time: 15 Minutes
Ingredients:
- 1 ¼ pounds shrimp, peeled and deveined
- 2 cups clam juice
- 1 can coconut milk
- 3 mangoes, chopped
- 1 onion, chopped
- 2 stalks celery, sliced
- 1 bunch scallions, sliced
- 4 cloves garlic, chopped fine
- 1 serrano chili, seeded and chopped fine
- 2 tablespoons curry powder
- 1 tablespoon olive oil
- 1 teaspoon thyme
- ¼ teaspoon salt

Directions:

1. Add oil to cooker and set to sauté on medium heat. Add onion and celery and cook, stirring often, till the onion begins to brown, about 3-5 minutes.
2. Add garlic, chili, curry powder and thyme, stir constantly and cook 30 seconds. Add the clam juice, coconut milk and mangoes and increase the heat to med-high. Bring to a simmer and cook, stirring often, for 5 minutes.
3. Add 3 cups of the soup to a blender and process till smooth. Return it to the pot and bring back to simmer. Add shrimp and cook till they turn pink, about 3 minutes. Stir in scallions and salt and serve.

262. Sunchoke & Asparagus Soup

Servings: 4 Servings
Cooking Time: 15 Minutes
Ingredients:
- 1 pound asparagus, cut off 1 ½ inches of the tips, discard woody ends and chop remaining into 1-inch pieces
- 3 cups vegetable broth
- ½ pound sunchokes, peeled and chopped
- 1 ½ cups potato, peeled and chopped
- 2 large shallots, peeled and sliced
- 2 tablespoons olive oil
- ½ teaspoons salt
- 1/8 teaspoon white pepper

Directions:
1. Add oil to the pot and set to sauté on medium heat. Add shallot and cook till soft. Add the vegetables along with the broth. Secure the lid and set to pressure cooking on high. Set the timer for 10 minutes. When the timer goes off, use quick release to remove the lid.
2. While the vegetables are cooking, bring a small pot of water to a boil and prepare an ice bath in a bowl. Add the asparagus tips to the boiling water and cook 2 minutes. Transfer the tips to the ice bath with a slotted spoon.
3. Once the vegetables in the cooking pot are tender, use an immersion blender to puree till smooth. Season with salt and pepper to taste.
4. To serve, ladle soup into bowls, divide the asparagus tips among them and drizzle a little olive oil over the top.

263. Sweet Potato 'n Garbanzo Soup

Servings: 2
Cooking Time: 10 Minutes
Ingredients:
- 1/2 yellow onion, chopped
- 1/2 tablespoon garlic, minced
- 1 can garbanzo beans, drained
- 1/2-pound sweet potatoes, peeled and chopped
- Salt and pepper to taste
- 1/2 teaspoon ground ginger
- 1/2 teaspoon ground cumin
- 1/2 teaspoon ground coriander
- 1/2 teaspoon ground cinnamon
- 2 cups vegetable broth
- 2 cups spinach, torn

Directions:
1. Place all ingredients in the Ninja Foodi except for the spinach.
2. Install pressure lid. Close Ninja Foodi, press the manual button, choose high settings, and set time to 10 minutes.
3. Once done cooking, do a quick release.
4. Open the lid and stir in the spinach. Press the sauté button and allow to simmer until the spinach wilts.
5. Serve and enjoy.
- **Nutrition Info:** Calories: 165; carbohydrates: 32.3g; protein: 6.3g; fat: 1.1g

264. Autumn Stew

Servings: 4 -6 Servings
Cooking Time: 8 Hours
Ingredients:
- 1 pound smoked sausage, sliced, not too thin
- 4 potatoes, peeled and quartered
- 3 carrots, peeled and chopped
- 3 stalks celery, sliced
- 2-3 turnips, peeled and cubed
- 1 small cabbage, cut into chunks
- 1 large can of tomatoes, diced
- 1 teaspoon sage
- 1 teaspoon oregano
- 1 teaspoon basil
- ½ teaspoon thyme
- ½ teaspoon rosemary
- Salt & pepper

Directions:
1. Layer the ingredients in the cooking pot; carrots, turnips, celery, potatoes and cabbage, sprinkling each layer with a little of the herbs, salt and pepper.
2. Spread tomatoes, with liquid, over cabbage and top with sausage. Sprinkle more seasonings on top.
3. Secure the lid and select slow cooking function. The stew will take 7-8 hours on low or 4-5 on high heat. The stew is done with vegetables are tender. Stir well before serving.

265. Greens & Beans Soup

Servings: 8 – 10 Servings
Cooking Time: 6 Hours
Ingredients:

- 1 pound bean soup mix, rinsed and debris removed
- 6 cups chicken broth
- 6 cups mustard or collard greens, chopped
- 2 smoked turkey wings.
- 2 cups baby Portabella mushrooms
- 1 onion, chopped
- 1 can tomatoes, diced
- 1 cup carrots, cut into chunks
- 7 cloves garlic, chopped fine
- ¾ cup red wine
- 2 tablespoons Italian seasoning
- 1 teaspoon sage
- 2 bay leaves
- Salt & pepper

Directions:
1. Add all of the ingredients, but use only half the greens, to the cooking pot. Secure lid and select slow cooking on high. Cook 5 ½ hours.
2. Remove turkey wings. When cool enough to handle, remove any meat from the bones and add it back to the soup. Add remaining greens and cook another 15 minutes. Serve topped with Parmesan cheese if desired.

266. Coconut, Apple 'n Squash Chowder

Servings: 2
Cooking Time: 15 Minutes
Ingredients:
- 3/4 cup vegetable stock
- 1 cloves of garlic, minced
- 1 small carrot, diced
- 1 granny smith apple, cored and diced
- 1/2 small squash, seeded and diced
- 1/2 onion, diced
- Salt and pepper to taste
- A pinch of ground cinnamon
- 1/4 cup canned coconut milk
- A pinch of paprika powder

Directions:
1. In the Ninja Foodi, put in the vegetable stock, garlic, carrots, apples, and squash. Season with salt and pepper to taste and sprinkle with cinnamon.
2. Install pressure lid.
3. Close Ninja Foodi, press the manual button, choose high settings, and set time to 15 minutes.
4. Once done cooking, do a quick release.
5. Open the lid and press the sauté button. Stir in the coconut milk.
6. Using an immersion blender, pulse until the mixture becomes smooth.
7. Sprinkle with paprika on top.
8. Serve and enjoy.
- **Nutrition Info:**

267. Sweet Potato & Black Bean Stew

Servings: 6 Servings
Cooking Time: 25 Minutes
Ingredients:
- 4 cups vegetable broth
- 4 cups kale, chopped
- 3 cups sweet potatoes, peeled and cubed
- 1 can black beans, rinsed and drained
- 1 large onion, chopped
- 4 cloves garlic, chopped fine
- 3 green onions, sliced thin
- 2 radishes, sliced thin
- 2 tablespoons olive oil
- 1 tablespoon lime juice
- 2 teaspoons oregano
- 1 ½ teaspoons cumin
- 1 teaspoon garlic powder
- ½. teaspoon black pepper
- ½ teaspoon salt
- ¼ teaspoon cayenne

Directions:
1. Add the oil to the pot and set to sauté on med-high heat. Add the onions and cook till translucent, about 3 minutes. Reduce heat to medium, add the garlic and seasonings and cook for 30 seconds.
2. Add the potatoes, broth, beans and salt and bring to a low boil. Cook 15 minutes, or till potatoes are tender.
3. Turn off the heat and stir in kale, green onions and lime juice. Serve.

268. Lamb Provencal

Servings: 4 Servings
Cooking Time: 40 Minutes
Ingredients:
- 1 pound lamb stew meat
- 4 cups beef broth
- 2 cups mushrooms, quartered
- 2 cups sweet potatoes, peeled and cubed
- 2 cups turnips, peeled and cubed
- 1 cup dry red wine
- 1 shallot, chopped fine
- ¾ cup flour
- 2 tablespoons olive oil
- 1 tablespoon Herbes de Provence
- 2 bay leaves
- 1 sprig rosemary
- 1 teaspoon garlic, chopped fine
- ½ teaspoon salt
- a few grinds of pepper

Directions:
1. In a large bowl, mix together flour with some salt and pepper. Add the lamb and toss to coat well.
2. Add the oil to the cooking pot and set to sauté on med-high heat. When hot, add the

lamb, shallot and garlic and cook till lamb begins to brown.
3. Add the broth, wine and seasonings and stir to combine. Secure the lid and set to pressure cooking on high. Set the timer for 30 minutes.
4. When the timer goes off, use quick release to remove the lid. Add the vegetables and secure the lid again. Cook on high pressure for 10 minutes.
5. Use quick release to remove the lid. Stir well and serve.

269. Verde Pork Stew

Servings: 6 Servings
Cooking Time: 4 – 8 Hours
Ingredients:
- 1 – 1 ½ pound pork tenderloin
- 2 cups chicken broth
- 1 16-ounce jar salsa verde
- 1 15-ounce can black beans, rinsed and drained
- 1 teaspoon cumin

Directions:
1. Place all ingredients in the cooking pot. Set to slow cooker functions. Cook 3-4 hours on high heat, or 6-8 hours on low.
2. When pork is tender, transfer it to a bowl and shred with two forks. Return it to the pot and stir to combine. Serve garnished as desired.

270. Chickpea And Potato Soup

Servings: 2
Cooking Time: 15 Minutes
Ingredients:
- 1 tablespoon olive oil
- ½ onion, chopped
- 3 cloves of garlic, minced
- ½ cup chopped tomato
- 1/8 teaspoon fennel space
- ½ teaspoon onion powder
- ¼ teaspoon garlic powder
- ½ teaspoon oregano
- ¼ teaspoon cinnamon
- ½ teaspoon thyme
- 1 large potato, peeled and cubed
- ¾ cup carrots, chopped
- 1 ½ cups cooked chickpeas
- 1 cup water
- 1 cup almond milk
- 1 cup kale, chopped
- Salt and pepper to taste

Directions:
1. Press the sauté button on the Ninja Foodi and sauté the onion and garlic until fragrant.
2. Stir in the tomatoes, fennel, onion powder, garlic powder, oregano, cinnamon, and thyme. Stir until well-combined.
3. Add the rest of the ingredients. Install pressure lid. Close Ninja Foodi, press the pressure button, choose high settings, and set time to 10 minutes.
4. Once done cooking, do a quick release. Serve and enjoy.
- **Nutrition Info:** Calories: 543; carbohydrates: 91.0g; protein: 17.7g; fat: 12g

271. Duck Ale Chili

Servings: 6 Servings
Cooking Time: 45 Minutes
Ingredients:
- 1 ½ pound duck breast
- 1 large can fire roasted tomatoes, diced
- 1 can kidney beans, rinsed and drained
- 1 can great northern beans, rinsed and drained
- 1 bottle brown ale
- 1 small can tomato paste
- 1 cup white onion, chopped fine
- 5 cloves garlic, chopped fine
- 2 tablespoons chili powder
- 1 tablespoon Worcestershire
- 1 tablespoon oregano
- 2 teaspoons cumin
- 1 teaspoon salt
- 1 teaspoon ground black pepper
- 1 teaspoon smoked paprika
- 1 teaspoon onion powder
- 1 teaspoon red pepper flakes
- ½ teaspoon cayenne pepper
- Garnishes:
- 1 cup mozzarella cheese, grated
- ½ cup chopped cilantro

Directions:
1. Score the fat on the duck and sprinkle with salt. Place, fat side down, in the cooking pot.
2. Select sauté on medium heat and sear the duck till golden brown and most of the fat has been rendered. Transfer duck to a plate.
3. Add the onions and cook till they soften, about 5 minutes. Add the duck back to the pot along with remaining ingredients.
4. Secure the lid and set to pressure cooking on high. Set the timer for 30 minutes. When the timer goes off, use manual release to remove the lid.
5. Remove the duck and shred with two forks. Return it to the pot and stir well.
6. Ladle into bowl and top with garnishes before serving.

272. White Chicken Chili

Servings: 6-8 Servings
Cooking Time: 40-50 Minutes
Ingredients:
- 4 cups chicken, cooked and chopped

- 3 ½ cups chicken broth
- 2 cans white beans, drained and rinsed
- 2 cans green chilies, diced
- 1 onion, chopped
- 2 teaspoons olive oil
- 2 teaspoons cumin
- 2 teaspoons oregano
- 1 clove garlic, chopped fine
- 1 teaspoon cayenne pepper

Directions:
1. Set cooker to sauté on med-high heat and add oil. Once oil is hot, add onion and cook 3-4 minutes or they are translucent. Add garlic and cook another minute. Add green chilies and spices and cook 2 more minutes, stirring frequently.
2. Add broth and beans. Secure lid. Set to pressure cooking function with low pressure. Set timer for 20 minutes. When timer goes off, use quick release to remove the lid.
3. Set back to sauté on low heat. Add chicken and cook 10-15 minutes, stirring occasionally. Serve garnished as desired.

273. Vegan Approver Tortilla Soup

Servings: 2
Cooking Time: 40 Minutes
Ingredients:
- 1/2 cup diced onion
- 1/2 bell pepper, diced
- 1/2 jalapeno pepper, diced
- 1 1/4 cups vegetable broth
- 1/2 can tomato sauce
- 1/4 cup salsa verde
- 1/2 tablespoon tomato paste
- 1/2 can black beans, drained and rinsed
- 1/2 can pinto beans, drained and rinsed
- 1/2 cup fresh corn kernels
- ½ teaspoon chili powder
- ½ teaspoon garlic powder
- Salt and pepper to taste
- 2 tbsp heavy cream

Directions:
1. Place all ingredients in the Ninja Foodi except for the heavy cream and give a good stir.
2. Install pressure lid. Close Ninja Foodi, press the manual button, choose high settings, and set time to 20 minutes.
3. Once done cooking, do a quick release.
4. Open the lid and press the sauté button. Stir in the heavy cream and allow to simmer for 5 minutes.
5. Serve and enjoy.
- **Nutrition Info:** Calories: 341; carbohydrates: 48.7g; protein: 8.6g; fat: 12.4g

274. Deliciously Traditional Clam Chowder

Servings: 2
Cooking Time: 17 Minutes
Ingredients:
- 2 6.5-oz cans chopped clams (reserve the clam juice)
- Water
- 2 slices bacon, chopped
- 1 1/2 tbsp butter
- 1 onion, diced
- 1 stalks celery, diced
- 1 sprig fresh thyme
- 1 cloves garlic, pressed or finely minced
- 1/2 tsp kosher salt or more
- 1/4 tsp pepper
- ½-lb potatoes, diced
- 1/2 tsp sugar
- 1/2 cup half and half
- Chopped chives, for garnish

Directions:
1. Drain the clam juice into a 2-cup measuring cup. Add enough water to make 2 cups of liquid. Set the clams and juice/water aside.
2. Press sauté button and cook bacon for 3 minutes until fat has rendered out of it, but not crispy. Add the butter, onion, celery, and thyme. Cook for 5 minutes while frequently stirring. Add the garlic, salt, and pepper. Cook for 1 minute, stirring frequently.
3. Add the potatoes, sugar (if using) and clam juice/water mixture and deglaze pot. Press stop.
4. Close Ninja Foodi, press pressure cook button, choose high settings, and set time to 4 minutes. Once done cooking, do a natural release for 3 minutes and then do a quick release. Mash the potatoes. Stir in half and half and the clams. Mix well.
5. Serve and enjoy garnished with chives.
- **Nutrition Info:** Calories: 381; carbohydrates: 32.8g; protein: 29.3g; fat: 14.7

275. Poblano Beef Stew

Servings: 4 – 6 Servings
Cooking Time: 1 Hour
Ingredients:
- 1 ½ pounds beef chuck roast, cut into 1-inch cubes
- 4 cups beef broth
- 15 ounce can fire roasted tomatoes
- 3 large poblano peppers
- 2 potatoes, cut into 1-inch cubes
- 1 onion, chopped
- 2-3 tablespoons cilantro, chopped
- 1 tablespoon olive oil
- 1 tablespoon garlic, chopped fine
- 1 ½ teaspoon ground cumin

- 1 teaspoon oregano

Directions:
1. Place the poblano chilies in the cooker. Add the Tender Crisp lid and set to broil. Cook the chilies 5-7 minutes, turning a couple of times, till skin is charred. Place them in a bowl and cover with foil. Let sit 10 minutes, then remove the skin. Remove the ribs and seeds and cut into 1-inch pieces.
2. Add the oil to the pot and set to sauté on med-high heat. Sprinkle the beef with salt and pepper and add to the pot, in batches. Cook the beef till no longer pink. Remove and set aside.
3. Add the onions and cook till they are translucent, about 3-5 minutes. Add the garlic and cook another 30 seconds. Add remaining ingredients except the potatoes and cilantro and stir to combine.
4. Secure the lid and set to pressure cooking on high. Set the timer for 40 minutes. When the timer goes off use quick release to remove the lid.
5. Add the potatoes and pressure cook on high another 8-10 minutes. Use quick release again. Stir and ladle into bowls. Top with chopped cilantro before serving.

276. Healthy Celery 'n Kale Soup

Servings: 2
Cooking Time: 35 Minutes
Ingredients:
- 1 teaspoon olive oil
- 1/2 onion, diced
- 1 clove garlic, minced
- 1 stalk celery, chopped
- 1 carrot, peeled and chopped
- 1 small potato, peeled and diced
- 1 teaspoon herbs de provence
- 1/2 can diced tomatoes
- 2 cups vegetable broth
- 2 cups green lentils, soaked overnight
- Salt and pepper to taste
- 1 cup kale, torn

Directions:
1. Press the sauté button on the Ninja Foodi and heat the oil.
2. Sauté the onion, garlic, and celery until fragrant.
3. Stir in the carrots, potatoes, herbs, tomatoes, vegetable broth and lentils. Season with salt and pepper to taste.
4. Install pressure lid. Close Ninja Foodi, press the pressure button, choose high settings, and set time to 30 minutes.
5. Once done cooking, do a quick release. Open the lid and stir in the kale while still hot. Serve and enjoy.

- **Nutrition Info:** Calories: 331; carbohydrates: 53g; protein: 23g; fat: 3g

277. Beefy White Cream Soup

Servings: 2
Cooking Time: 17 Minutes
Ingredients:
- ½ pounds stew meat
- 2 cups beef broth
- 1 1/2 tablespoons Worcestershire sauce
- ½ teaspoon Italian seasoning
- 1 teaspoon onion powder
- 1 teaspoons garlic powder
- 1/4 cup sour cream
- 3 ounces mushrooms, sliced
- Salt and pepper to taste
- 2 ounces short noodles, blanched

Directions:
1. Place the meat, broth, Worcestershire sauce, Italian seasoning, onion powder, garlic powder, sour cream, and mushrooms. Season with salt and pepper to taste.
2. Install pressure lid. Close Ninja Foodi, press the pressure button, choose high settings, and set time to 12 minutes.
3. Once done cooking, do a quick release. Open the lid and press the sauté button. Stir in the noodles and allow to simmer for 5 minutes.
4. Serve and enjoy.

- **Nutrition Info:** Calories: 599 ; carbohydrates: 65g; protein: 39.6g; fat: 20.1g

278. Sausage & Spinach Stew

Servings: 4 Servings
Cooking Time: 20 Minutes
Ingredients:
- 12 ounce Italian chicken sausage, fully cooked
- 4 cups chicken broth
- 1 bag spinach
- 1 can cannellini beans, rinsed and drained
- 1 cup ditalini pasta
- ½ cup dry white wine
- 4 cloves garlic, chopped
- 1 tablespoon olive oil
- Pepper
- Parmesan cheese

Directions:
1. Add oil to cooker and set to sauté on medium heat. Add the sausage and cook, stirring often, till brown, about 4-5 minutes. Remove to a plate.
2. Add the garlic and cook, stirring, 1 minute. Add the wine and simmer to deglaze the pan, about 1 minutes.
3. Add the broth and pasta and bring to a boil. Cook till pasta is tender, about 8-10 minutes. Stir in the beans, sausage and pepper and

cook till heated through. Turn the cooker off and stir in the spinach. Ladle into bowls and top with Parmesan cheese before serving.

279. Mushroom & Wild Rice Soup

Servings: 6 Servings
Cooking Time: 6 – 8 Hours
Ingredients:
- 1 pound mushrooms, halved
- 4 cups beef broth
- 2 carrots, cut into ½-inch pieces
- 1 cup frozen sweet peas, thawed
- 1 cup water
- 1 stalk celery, cut into ½-inch pieces
- ½ cup whole-grain wild rice
- 1 envelope onion soup mix
- 1 tablespoon sugar

Directions:
1. Layer mushrooms, rice, celery, carrots, soup mix and sugar in the cooking pot. Pour water and broth over top.
2. Add lid and set to slow cooking on low. Cook 5-8 hours.
3. Add the peas during the last 10 minutes of cooking. Serve.

280. Cheesy Onion Soup

Servings: 4 Servings
Cooking Time: 10 Minutes
Ingredients:
- 2 ¼ cups sharp cheddar cheese, grated
- 1 Vidalia onion, sliced thin
- 1 can chicken broth
- 1 cup milk
- ¼ cup celery, chopped fine
- ¼ cup dry white wine
- 2 tablespoons butter
- 2 tablespoons flour
- 1 tablespoon chives, chopped
- ½ teaspoon pepper
- ½ teaspoon dry mustard

Directions:
1. Add butter to the cooking pot and set to sauté on medium heat. Once melted, add onion and celery and cook 3 minutes, stirring often.
2. Stir in flour, pepper and mustard. Slowly stir in the milk, broth and wine. Bring to a boil and cook, stirring, one minute.
3. Stir in the cheese, reduce heat to low and while stirring constantly, cook till cheese is melted. Ladle into bowls and garnish with chopped chives.

DESSERT RECIPES

281. Easy Peasy Applesauce

Servings: 2
Cooking Time: 8 Minutes
Ingredients:
- 2 medium apples, peeled and cored
- 1 cup water
- 2 teaspoons cinnamon, ground

Directions:
1. Place the apples in the Ninja Foodi. Pour in the water.
2. Install pressure lid. Close the lid and press the manual button. Cook on high for 8 minutes.
3. Do natural pressure release and open the lid.
4. Remove the excess water. Place the apples in a blender and process until smooth.
5. Add the rest of the ingredients.
6. Serve chilled.
- **Nutrition Info:** Calories: 108; carbohydrates: 25.7g; protein: 0.5g; fat: 0.3g

282. Lemon Ricotta Cake

Servings: 6 Servings
Cooking Time: 20 Minutes
Ingredients:
- Crust: ¼ cup almond flour
- ¼ cup coconut flour
- 2 Tbsp stevia
- 2 Tbsp melted butter
- Filling: 8 oz cream cheese
- ½ cup baking stevia
- 8 ounces ricotta
- 1 egg and 2 egg yolks
- ¼ cup sour cream
- ¾ cup heavy cream
- 2 Tsp lemon zest
- 1 tsp vanilla

Directions:
1. In a small bowl, mix all the ingredients for the crust together. Press the crust into a 7" spring form pan wrapped in foil. Set aside
2. Add the cream cheese, stevia and ricotta to a food processor and blend. Add the egg and yolks and blend again. Add remaining ingredients and mix just to combine. Pour cheesecake mix on top of the prepared crust.
3. Place the pan in the Ninja Foodi bowl on top of the metal trivet. Add 2 cups of water to the bowl under the cake. Place the pressure cooker lid on and set it to high pressure for 20 minutes. Allow the pot to naturally release the pressure once he cooking time is done. Chill and then serve.
- **Nutrition Info:** Calories: 483 g, Carbohydrates: 10g, Protein: 7g, Fat: 36 g, Sugar: 4g, Sodium: 338g

283. Coconutty-blueberry Cake

Servings: 2
Cooking Time: 10 Minutes
Ingredients:
- 1/4 cup coconut flour
- 2 large eggs
- 1/2 teaspoon baking soda
- 1/4 cup coconut milk
- 1/4 teaspoon lemon zest

Directions:
1. Combine all ingredients in a mixing bowl.
2. Pour into two mugs. Cover top of mugs securely with foil.
3. Place a steam rack in the Ninja Foodi and pour a cup of water.
4. Place the mug on the steam rack.
5. Install pressure lid. Close the lid, press the steam button, and adjust the time to 10 minutes.
6. Do a natural pressure release.
- **Nutrition Info:** Calories: 259; carbohydrates: 10.3g; protein: 7.2g; fat: 20.9g

284. Carrot Pecan

Servings: 6 Servings
Cooking Time: 25 Minutes
Ingredients:
- 8 Tbsp butter
- ½ cup Baking Stevia
- 1 egg
- 1 tsp vanilla
- 1 cup almond flour
- 1 cup pecan flour
- 1 cup shredded carrots
- 2 tsp baking powder
- 1 tsp salt
- ¼ cup buttermilk

Directions:
1. Use an electric mixer to cream the butter and stevia together until they are light and fluffy.
2. Mix the vanilla and eggs in a small bowl then add to the mixer with the butter blend until just combined
3. Add the remaining dry ingredients to the mixer and fold together by hand. Add the buttermilk and mix until smooth.
4. Pour the cake batter into your Ninja Foodi and place the lid on.
5. Press the air crisp button and set the temperature to 350 degrees and program the timer to 25 minutes.
6. Once cooked, a toothpick should come out of the center of the cake cleanly. Allow to cool and serve.

- **Nutrition Info:** Calories: 334 g, Carbohydrates: 17g , Protein: 5g, Fat: 29 g, Sugar: 5g, Sodium: 722 mg

285. Strawberry Cake

Servings: 6 Servings
Cooking Time: 25 Minutes
Ingredients:
- 8 Tbsp butter
- ½ cup Baking Stevia
- 1 egg
- 1 tsp vanilla
- 2 cups almond flour
- 2 tsp baking powder
- 1 tsp salt
- 1 cup chopped strawberries
- ½ cup buttermilk

Directions:
1. Use an electric mixer to cream the butter and stevia together until they are light and fluffy.
2. Mix the vanilla and eggs in a small bowl then add to the mixer with the butter blend. Ix until just combined
3. In a separate bowl, toss the raspberries and ¼ cup almond flour to coat the berries.
4. Add the remaining dry ingredients to the mixer and fold together by hand. Add the buttermilk and mix until smooth.
5. Add the Strawberries to the batter and mix briefly.
6. Pour the cake batter into your Ninja Foodi and place the lid on.
7. Press the air crisp button and set the temperature to 350 degrees and program the timer to 25 minutes.
8. Once cooked, a toothpick should come out of the center of the cake cleanly. Allow to cool and serve.
- **Nutrition Info:** Calories: 216g, Carbohydrates: 3g , Protein: 4g, Fat: 21g, Sugar: 3g, Sodium: 538 g

286. Chocolate Peanut Butter Cups

Servings: 3
Cooking Time: 40 Minutes
Ingredients:
- 1 c. butter
- ¼ c. heavy cream
- 2 oz. chocolate, unsweetened
- ¼ c. peanut butter, separated
- 4 packets stevia

Directions:
1. Melt the peanut butter and butter in a bowl and stir in unsweetened chocolate, stevia and heavy cream.
2. Mix thoroughly and pour the mixture in a baking mold.
3. Put the baking mold in the Ninja Foodi and press "Bake/Roast".
4. Set the timer for about 30 minutes at 360 degrees F and dish out to serve.
- **Nutrition Info:** 479 calories, 51.5g fat, 7.7g carbs, 5.2g protein

287. Flourless Chocolate Brownies

Servings: 4
Cooking Time: 42 Minutes
Ingredients:
- 3 eggs
- ½ c. butter
- ½ c. chocolate chips, sugar-free
- 2 scoops stevia
- 1 tsp. vanilla extract

Directions:
1. Whisk together eggs, stevia and vanilla extract.
2. Transfer this mixture in the blender and blend until frothy.
3. Put the butter and chocolate in the pot of Ninja Foodi and press "Sauté".
4. Sauté for about 2 minutes until the chocolate is melted.
5. Add the melted chocolate mixture to the egg mixture.
6. Pour the mixture in the baking mold and transfer the baking mold in the Ninja Foodi.
7. Press "Bake/Roast" and set the timer for about 30 minutes at 360 degrees F.
8. Bake for about 30 minutes and dish out.
9. Cut into equal square pieces and serve with whipped cream.
- **Nutrition Info:** 266 calories, 26.9g fat, 2.5g carbs, 4.5g protein

288. Super Simple Chocolate Brownies

Servings: 6-8 Brownies
Cooking Time: 1-2 Hours
Ingredients:
- 1 ¼ cups semi-sweet chocolate chips
- 1 cup sugar
- 1 cup flour
- ½ cup butter
- 2 eggs + 1 egg yolk, room temperature

Directions:
1. Spray cooker with cooking spray.
2. Melt chocolate chips and butter in a large glass bowl. Add sugar and beat well. Beat in eggs, egg yolk and lastly, flour, just till combined.
3. Pour into cooker. Add lid and select slow cooking on high. Set timer for 1 hour. Brownies are done when batter is set and edges look done. Cool cut into bars.

289. Fudge Divine

Servings: 24

Cooking Time: 6 Hours 20 Minutes
Ingredients:
- ½ tsp. organic vanilla extract
- 1 c. heavy whipping cream
- 2 oz. softened butter
- 2 oz. chopped 70% dark chocolate

Directions:
1. Press "Sauté" and "Md:Hi" on Ninja Foodi and add vanilla and heavy cream.
2. Sauté for about 5 minutes and select "Lo".
3. Sauté for about 10 minutes and add butter and chocolate.
4. Sauté for about 2 minutes and transfer this mixture in a serving dish.
5. Refrigerate it for few hours and serve chilled.
- **Nutrition Info:** 292 calories, 26.2g fat, 8.2g carbs, 5.2g protein

290. Chocolate Mug Cake

Servings: 2 Servings
Cooking Time: 10 Minutes
Ingredients:
- 2/3 cup almond flour
- ¼ cup cocoa powder
- 2 eggs
- 2 Tbsp maple syrup
- 1 tsp vanilla
- ¼ tsp salt

Directions:
1. Mix all the ingredients together. Fold well to ensure no lumps.
2. Pour the batter into two 8 oz mason jars and cover the jars with foil.
3. Place the metal trivet into the Ninja Foodi and add 1 cup of water to the bowl.
4. Place the two mason jars on top of the trivet and close the pressure cooker top. Seal the steamer valve and set the timer to 10 minutes
5. Let the pressure naturally release and then open the lid and enjoy the warm cake.
- **Nutrition Info:** Calories: 208g, Carbohydrates: 22g, Protein: 10g, Fat: 11g, Sugar: 16g, Sodium: 1238mg

291. Orange-cranberry Pudding

Servings: 2
Cooking Time: 20 Minutes
Ingredients:
- 1/3 cup cranberries
- 1 tablespoon butter, softened
- 1/3 cup sugar
- 1/4 tablespoon vanilla
- 1 orange, juiced and zested
- 1 cup half and half
- 1 1/2 cups brioche, cube
- 2 egg yolks

Directions:
1. In a 6-inch square baking dish, mix well vanilla extract, half & half, orange juice, zest, juice, cranberries, and eggs. Mix thoroughly.
2. Add cubed brioche and toss well to coat in egg mixture. Let it soak for ten minutes. Cover the top with foil.
3. Prepare the Ninja Foodi by placing the inner pot inside.
4. Place wire rack inside and add 2 cups of water.
5. Place baking dish on wire rack.
6. Install pressure lid. Cover and lock lid. Press steam button. Set the timer to 15 minutes.
7. Once done cooking, press stop, and do a quick release.
8. Let it cool completely before serving.
- **Nutrition Info:** Calories: 326; carbohydrates: 48.6g; protein: 5.9g; fat: 12.0g

292. Coconut Cake

Servings: 6 Servings
Cooking Time: 25 Minutes
Ingredients:
- 8 Tbsp butter
- ½ cup Baking Stevia
- 1 egg
- 1 tsp vanilla
- 1 cup coconut flour
- ½ cup almond flour
- ½ cup shredded coconut, unsweetened
- 2 tsp baking powder
- 1 tsp salt
- 1 cup chopped strawberries
- ½ cup buttermilk

Directions:
1. Use an electric mixer to cream the butter and stevia together until they are light and fluffy.
2. Mix the vanilla and eggs in a small bowl then add to the mixer with the butter blend until just combined
3. Add the remaining dry ingredients to the mixer and fold together by hand. Add the buttermilk and mix until smooth.
4. Pour the cake batter into your Ninja Foodi and place the lid on.
5. Press the air crisp button and set the temperature to 350 degrees and program the timer to 25 minutes.
6. Once cooked, a toothpick should come out of the center of the cake cleanly. Allow to cool and serve.
- **Nutrition Info:** Calories: 197 g, Carbohydrates: 6g , Protein: 3g, Fat: 18 g, Sugar: 2g, Sodium: 559 mg

293. Meyer Lemon Hand Pies

Servings: 6 Servings

Cooking Time: 30 Minutes
Ingredients:
- 1 package refrigerated pie dough
- 1 egg, beaten
- Lemon Curd
- 4 Meyer lemons, juiced
- 8 egg yolks
- 1 ¾ cups sugar
- ½ cup butter, cold and sliced
- 2 tablespoons lemon zest
- Pinch of salt
- Icing
- 1 cup powdered sugar
- ½ lemon

Directions:
1. Place rack in the middle of the cooking pot and add 1-2 inches of water. Set the cooker to saute on med-high heat and bring to a simmer.
2. Place the yolks and sugar into a bowl that fits inside the pot but is large enough for mixing in, and whisk vigorously till smooth. Add the juice and salt and whisk till smooth again.
3. Once the water reaches a simmer, reduce the heat to med-low and place the bowl on the rack. Cook, whisking constantly, 20-22 minutes, it should be a light yellow color, do not let it boil. Remove from heat and whisk in the zest.
4. Add butter, one piece at a time, and whisk to combine after each addition. Let cool. Transfer to an airtight container and refrigerate overnight.
5. When ready to make the pies, unfold the pie crust on a lightly floured surface. Roll to a ¼-inch thickness. Use a cookie cutter to cut out 6 circles and place them on a baking sheet. Place 1 tablespoon of the lemon curd in the center of each circle and brush the edges with beaten egg. Fold dough over the filling using a fork to seal the edges. Brush the top of the pies with beaten egg and sprinkle sugar over.
6. Place pies, 2 at a time, in the basket of the air fryer. Add the Tender Crisp lid and set the temperature to 380 degrees. Bake 8-10 minutes, or till golden brown. Let pies cool.
7. Place the powdered sugar in a small bowl and whisk in lemon juice till desired consistency. Drizzle over cooled pies and let sit till the glaze sets. Serve.

294. Turtle Fudge Pudding

Servings: 6 Servings
Cooking Time: 2 ½ - 3 Hours
Ingredients:
- 1 2/3 cups hot water
- 1 ½ cups Bisquick
- 1 cup sugar
- ¾ cup caramel topping
- ½ cup unsweetened baking cocoa
- ½ cup milk
- ½ cup pecans, chopped

Directions:
1. Place rack in the bottom of the cooking pot. Lightly spray a deep baking dish that will fit inside the cooker.
2. In a large bowl, mix Bisquick, ½ cup sugar and the cocoa till combined. Stir in milk and ½ the caramel till well blended. Pour into prepared baking dish and lower on to the rack.
3. Pour the hot water over the top of the chocolate mixture and sprinkle with the remaining ½ cup sugar.
4. Add the lid and set to slow cooking on low. Cook 2 ½ - 3 hours or the top springs back when lightly touched. Turn off the cooker and let stand, uncovered 20 minutes. Serve warm drizzled with remaining caramel and sprinkle with pecans.

295. Key Lime Curd

Servings: 6 Servings
Cooking Time: 10 Minutes
Ingredients:
- 3 oz butter
- ½ cup baking stevia
- 2 eggs
- 2 egg yolks
- 2/3 cup key lime juice
- 2 tsp lime zest

Directions:
1. Blend the butter and stevia then add in the eggs slowly, creating an emulsion.
2. Add the key lime juice and zest and the separate into mason jars
3. Add 1 ½ cups of water to the bottom of the Ninja Foodi and place the mason jars on top of the metal trivet inside the pot.
4. Place the pressure cooker lid on the pot and set the pressure cooker function to high pressure for 10 minutes. Let the pressure release naturally after the cooking time is completed.
5. Let cool and then enjoy.
- **Nutrition Info:** Calories: 151g, Carbohydrates: 3g, Protein: 3g, Fat: 15g, Sugar: 1g, Sodium: 109mg

296. Choco-coffee Cake

Servings: 2
Cooking Time: 25 Minutes
Ingredients:
- 4 tbsp granulated sweetener
- 3 small eggs
- 1/8 teaspoon salt

- 2 tbsp almond flour
- 1 1/4 tablespoons unsweetened cocoa powder
- 1/2 teaspoon vanilla extract
- 1 tablespoon instant coffee crystals
- 2 tbsp heavy cream
- 1-ounce unsweetened chocolate
- 1/4 cup butter
- Coconut oil spray

Directions:
1. Grease sides and bottom of Ninja Foodi with cooking spray.
2. Press sauté button. Add butter and chocolate. Mix well. Make sure to mix constantly so as the bottom doesn't burn. Once fully incorporated, press stop to keep warm.
3. Meanwhile, in a small bowl whisk well vanilla, coffee crystals, and heavy cream.
4. In another bowl, mix well salt, almond flour, and cocoa powder.
5. In a mixing bowl, beat eggs until thick and pale, around 5 minutes while slowly stirring in sweetener.
6. While beating, slowly drizzle and mix in melted butter mixture.
7. Mix in the almond flour mixture and mix well.
8. Add the coffee mixture and beat until fully incorporated.
9. Pour batter into Ninja Foodi.
10. Cover pot, press bake button, and bake for 20 minutes at 350 ºF.
- **Nutrition Info:** Calories: 407; carbohydrates: 27.9g; protein: 3.6g; fat: 31.2g

297. Banana Bundt Cake

Servings: 4 -6 Servings
Cooking Time: 30 Minutes
Ingredients:
- 1 cup flour
- 1 ripe banana, mashed
- 1/3 cup brown sugar, packed
- ¼ cup butter, soft
- 1 egg
- 2-3 tablespoons walnuts, chopped
- 2 tablespoons honey
- ½ teaspoon cinnamon
- Pinch of salt

Directions:
1. Preheat air fryer to 320 degrees. Lightly spray a small ring cake pan with cooking spray.
2. Place the butter and sugar in a mixing bowl and beat till creamy. Add egg, banana and honey and stir till smooth.
3. Add the dry ingredients and stir to mix well. Pour into prepared pan.
4. Add the rack to the bottom of the cooking pot and place pan on it. Add the Tender Crisp lid and bake 30 minutes or it passes the toothpick test.
5. Carefully remove the pan from the cooker and let cool 10 minutes before transferring to a serving plate. Garnish if desired.

298. Blueberry & Peach Streusel Pie

Servings: 6-8 Servings
Cooking Time: 20 - 35 Minutes
Ingredients:
- 1 pie crust
- 3 peaches, peeled and sliced
- 1 ½ cups fresh blueberries, rinsed & dried
- 2-3 tablespoons tapioca, quick cooking
- 1 ½ tablespoons honey
- 1 tablespoon lemon zest
- 1 tablespoon lemon juice
- 1 egg white, lightly beaten
- 1 ½ teaspoons vanilla
- 1 teaspoon cinnamon
- Streusel Topping:
- ½ cup butter, cubed
- ½ cup quick cooking oats
- ½ cup sugar
- ¼ cup flour
- ¼ cup almonds, chopped

Directions:
1. Preheat air fryer to 340 degrees. Lightly oil a ceramic pie plate that fits inside the cooker.
2. Add the fruit, spices, zest, juice and tapioca to a large bowl and stir well.
3. Add the topping ingredients to a bowl and mix with a fork, or pastry cutter, till it comes together.
4. Roll the pie crust out, or if store bought, unfold it into the prepared pan. Brush the entire crust with the egg white. Add the fruit mixture and spread evenly.
5. Sprinkle the topping over the fruit. Add the rack to the cooking pot and place the pie on it. Bake 20-35 minutes and the crust is cooked. Cool and serve.

299. Blackberry Brioche Bread Pudding

Servings: 4-6 Servings
Cooking Time: 30 – 46 Minutes
Ingredients:
- 4 cups brioche bread cubes, loosely packed
- ½ pint blackberries, rinse and pat dry
- 1 cup milk
- 2 eggs
- ½ cup sugar
- 1 teaspoon vanilla
- pinch of salt

Directions:

1. Lightly spray the cooking pot with cooking spray.
2. Place the bread cubes and berries in the pot.
3. In a mixing bowl, whisk remaining ingredients together and pour over the bread and berries.
4. Add the Tender Crisp lid and set to 350 degrees. Bake 45 minutes, or till the pudding puffs up and is starting to brown on top. Serve warm.

300. Cherry Cobbler

Servings: 10 – 12 Servings
Cooking Time: 5 – 8 Hours
Ingredients:
- 1 box yellow cake mix
- 2 cans cherry pie filling
- ½ cup butter, melted
- ½ cup almonds, sliced and toasted
- 1 tablespoon water

Directions:
1. Lightly spray the cooking pot with cooking spray.
2. Dump the pie filling into the pot. Sprinkle the cake mix over the cherries then add the almonds.
3. Drizzle the melted butter over the top. Using knife, cut through the ingredients to marble them do not mix. Sprinkle water over the top.
4. Place 2-3 paper towels over the cooker then add the lid. Set to slow cooking. The cobbler will be done in 3-5 hours on high, or 5-8 hours on low. Cobbler is done with the cake parts are set but not sticky. Serve warm.

301. Crème Brûlée

Servings: 4
Cooking Time: 25 Minutes
Ingredients:
- 1 c. heavy cream
- ½ tbsp. vanilla extract
- 3 egg yolks
- 1 pinch salt
- ¼ c. stevia

Directions:
1. Mix together egg yolks, vanilla extract, heavy cream and salt in a bowl and beat until combined.
2. Divide the mixture into 4 greased ramekins evenly and transfer the ramekins in the basket of Ninja Foodi.
3. Press "Bake/Roast" and set the timer for about 15 minutes at 365 degrees F.
4. Remove from the Ninja Foodi and cover the ramekins with a plastic wrap.
5. Refrigerate to chill for about 3 hours and serve chilled.

- **Nutrition Info:** 149 calories, 14.5g fat, 1.6g carbs, 2.6g protein

302. Hot Fudge Cake

Servings: 6 Servings
Cooking Time: 2 – 2 ½ Hours
Ingredients:
- 1 ½ cups hot water
- 1 cup flour
- ¾ cup brown sugar, packed
- ½ cup sugar
- ½ cup milk
- ½ cup nuts, chopped
- ¼ cup baking cocoa
- 2 tablespoons baking cocoa
- 2 tablespoons vegetable oil
- 2 teaspoons baking powder
- 1 teaspoon vanilla
- ½ teaspoon salt

Directions:
1. Lightly spray the pot with cooking spray.
2. In a medium bowl mix flour, sugar, 2 tablespoons cocoa, baking powder and salt together. Stir in milk, oil and vanilla till smooth. Stir in nuts and spread the batter evenly in the cooking pot.
3. In a small bowl, whisk together brown sugar, ¼ cup cocoa and hot water till smooth. Pour over batter in the cooking pot.
4. Add the lid and select slow cooking on high. Cook the cake 2 – 2 1/2 hours or it passes the toothpick test.
5. Turn off the cooker and let the cake rest, uncovered 30-40 minutes. Serve.

303. Bananas Foster

Servings: 6 – 8 Servings
Cooking Time: 2 Hours
Ingredients:
- 7 bananas, not too ripe, sliced into ½-inch pieces
- 6 tablespoons honey
- Juice of 1 lemon
- 2 tablespoons coconut oil, melted
- 1 teaspoon rum extract
- ½ teaspoon cinnamon
- 1 tablespoon coconut oil, melted (unrefined coconut oil)
- 3 tablespoon honey
- Juice from 1/2 lemon
- 1/4 teaspoon cinnamon
- 5 bananas, medium firmness, 1/2" slices
- 1/2 teaspoon 100% Rum Extract (optional)

Directions:
1. Add the coconut oil, honey, lemon juice and cinnamon to the cooking pot. Stir to combine. Add bananas and toss gently to coat. Add the lid and set to slow cooking on low. Cook 1 ½ - 2 hours.

2. Just before serving, add the rum extract. Serve over vanilla ice cream, or topped with whip cream.

304. Chocolatey 'n Peanut Butter Cakes

Servings: 2
Cooking Time: 15 Minutes
Ingredients:
- 1/2 can black beans, drained and rinsed
- 1/4 cup cocoa powder, unsweetened
- 1/4 cup egg whites
- 2 tbsp canned pumpkin
- 2 tbsp unsweetened applesauce
- 2 tbsp sear button sugar
- 1/2 teaspoon vanilla extract
- ¾ teaspoon baking powder
- ¼ teaspoon salt
- 1 1/2 tablespoon peanut butter baking chips

Directions:
1. Place all the ingredients except the peanut butter chips inside a food processor. Process until smooth.
2. Add the peanut butter chips and fold until evenly distributed within the batter.
3. Place the batter in a ramekin sprayed with cooking oil.
4. Place a steam rack in the Ninja Foodi and add 1 cup water.
5. Place the ramekins with the batter onto the steamer rack.
6. Install pressure lid. Close the lid and press the manual button. Cook on high for 10 minutes.
7. Do natural pressure release.
8. Serve chilled.
- **Nutrition Info:** Calories: 246; carbohydrates: 34.9g; protein: 12.0g; fat: 6.5g

305. Raspberry Mug Cake

Servings: 2 Servings
Cooking Time: 10 Minutes
Ingredients:
- 2/3 cup almond flour
- 2 eggs
- 2 Tbsp maple syrup
- 1 tsp vanilla
- 1/8 tsp salt
- 1 cup fresh raspberries

Directions:
1. Mix all the ingredients together except the raspberries. Fold well to ensure no lumps.
2. Fold in raspberries
3. Pour the batter into two 8 oz mason jars and cover the jars with foil.
4. Place the metal trivet into the Ninja Foodi and add 1 cup of water to the bowl.
5. Place the two mason jars on top of the trivet and close the pressure cooker top. Seal the steamer valve and set the timer to 10 minutes
6. Let the pressure naturally release and then open the lid and enjoy the warm cake.
- **Nutrition Info:** Calories: 215g, Carbohydrates: 10g, Protein: 9g, Fat: 10g, Sugar: 16g, Sodium: 82mg

306. Sweet Sticky Coco-rice

Servings: 2
Cooking Time: 20 Minutes
Ingredients:
- 1/2 cup Thai sweet rice
- ¾ cup water
- 1/2 can full fat coconut milk
- A pinch of salt
- 2 tablespoons pure sugar
- 1/4 teaspoon cornstarch + 1 tablespoon water
- 1 small mango, sliced
- Sesame seeds for garnish

Directions:
1. Place rice and water in the Ninja Foodi.
2. Install pressure lid. Close the lid and press the pressure button. Cook on high for 5 minutes.
3. Turn off the Ninja Foodi and do natural pressure release for 10 minutes.
4. While the rice is cooking, place the coconut milk, salt, and sugar in a saucepan. Heat over medium heat for 10 minutes while stirring constantly.
5. Once the Ninja Foodi lid can be open, add the coconut milk mixture. Stir well. Place a clean kitchen towel over the opening of the lid and let it rest for 10 minutes.
6. Meanwhile, mix cornstarch with water and add to the rice. Press the sauté button and mix until the rice becomes creamy and thick.
7. Serve with mango slices and sesame seeds.
- **Nutrition Info:** Calories: 318; carbohydrates: 36.5g; protein: 3.5g; fat: 17.5g

307. Reece's Cookie Bars

Servings: 8-10 Bars
Cooking Time: 1-2 Hours
Ingredients:
- 1 1/3 cup graham cracker crumbs
- 1 cup chocolate chips
- 1 cup peanut butter chips
- 1 can sweetened condensed milk
- ½ cup butter, melted

Directions:
1. In a small bowl, mix together cracker crumbs and butter.

2. Spray cooker with cooking spray. Press cracker mixture on the bottom. Pour milk over crust then sprinkle both chips over the milk.
3. Add lid and select slow cooking on high. Set timer for 1 hour. Bars are done with edges are golden brown. Let cool then cut into bars.

308. Surprising Campfire S'mores

Servings: 4
Cooking Time: 14 Minutes
Ingredients:
- 4 Graham Crackers
- 4 marshmallows
- 2 (1½ oz. each) chocolate bars

Directions:
1. Place Cook and Crisp basket in the pot, close crisping lid
2. Pre-heat your pot by setting it to 350 degrees F on Air Crisp mode, for 5 minutes
3. Break graham crackers into half and place half of the chocolate bar on one half of Graham Cracker
4. Add marshmallow and top with remaining graham cracker half
5. Repeat with remaining ingredients to create the S'Mores
6. Use aluminum foil to wrap each S'More individually, place all 4 foil-wrapped S'Mores in your pre-heated Cook and Crisp Basket
7. Place Crisping Lid and select the Air Crisp mode, cook for 4 minutes at 350 degrees F
8. Carefully unwrap the S'mores, serve and enjoy!
- **Nutrition Info:** 152 Calories, 7g fat, 24g carbs, 1g protein

309. Strawberry Chocolate Chip Mug Cake

Servings: 2 Servings
Cooking Time: 10 Minutes
Ingredients:
- 2/3 cup almond flour
- 2 eggs
- 2 Tbsp maple syrup
- 1 tsp vanilla
- 1/8 tsp salt
- ½ cup chopped strawberries
- ¼ cup dark chocolate chips

Directions:
1. Mix all the ingredients together except the strawberries and chocolate chips. Fold well to ensure no lumps.
2. Fold in strawberries and chocolate chips.
3. Pour the batter into two 8 oz mason jars and cover the jars with foil.
4. Place the metal trivet into the Ninja Foodi and add 1 cup of water to the bowl.
5. Place the two mason jars on top of the trivet and close the pressure cooker top. Seal the steamer valve and set the timer to 10 minutes
6. Let the pressure naturally release and then open the lid and enjoy the warm cake.
- **Nutrition Info:** Calories: 326g, Carbohydrates: 35g, Protein: 8g, Fat: 18g, Sugar: 26g, Sodium: 228mg

310. Scrumptiously Molten Lava Cake

Servings: 3
Cooking Time: 6 Minutes
Ingredients:
- 1 egg
- 4 tablespoon sugar
- 2 tablespoon olive oil
- 4 tablespoon milk
- 4 tablespoon all-purpose flour
- 1 tablespoon cacao powder
- ½ teaspoon baking powder
- Pinch of salt
- Powdered sugar for dusting

Directions:
1. Grease two ramekins with butter or oil. Set aside
2. Pour 1 cup of water in the Ninja Foodi and place the steamer rack.
3. In a medium bowl, mix all the ingredients except the powdered sugar. Blend until well combined.
4. Pour in the ramekins. Place the ramekins in the Ninja Foodi.
5. Install pressure lid and close. Press the pressure button and cook on high for 6 minutes.
6. Once the Ninja Foodi beeps, remove the ramekin.
7. Sprinkle powdered sugar once cooled.
8. Serve and enjoy.
- **Nutrition Info:** Calories: 290; carbohydrates: 30.0g; protein: 5.2g; fat: 16.6g

311. Pineapple Pecan Bread Pudding

Servings: Serves 4
Cooking Time: 30 – 35 Minutes
Ingredients:
- 2 cups French bread, cubed
- 14 ounce can crushed pineapple, drained
- 1 cup sugar
- ½ cup butter, soft
- 4 eggs
- ¼ cup pecans, chopped
- ½ teaspoon cinnamon

Directions:
1. Butter a 1 ½ quart baking dish that fits inside the cooking pot. Add the rack to the bottom of the pot.

2. In a large bowl, on medium speed, beat butter sugar and cinnamon for 1 minutes, scraping sides of the bowl frequently. Add eggs and beat 2 minutes, or till light and fluffy. Fold in remaining ingredients and pour into prepared baking dish.
3. Place the dish on the rack and add the Tender Crisp lid. Set the temperature to 330 degrees and bake 30-35 minutes, or it passes the toothpick test. Serve warm dusted with powdered sugar.

312. Chocolate Cheese Cake(2)

Servings: 6
Cooking Time: 25 Minutes
Ingredients:
- 2 c. softened cream cheese
- 2 eggs
- 2 tbsps. cocoa powder
- 1 tsp. pure vanilla extract
- ½ c. swerve

Directions:
1. Place eggs, cocoa powder, vanilla extract, swerve and cream cheese in an immersion blender and blend until smooth.
2. Pulse to mix well and transfer the mixture evenly into mason jars.
3. Put the mason jars in the insert of Ninja Foodi and lock the lid.
4. Press "Bake/Roast" and bake for about 15 minutes at 360 degrees F.
5. Place in the refrigerator for 2 hours before serving and serve chilled.
- **Nutrition Info:** 244 calories, 24.8g fat, 2.1g carbs, 4g protein

313. Cream Crepes

Servings: 6
Cooking Time: 26 Minutes
Ingredients:
- 1½ tsps. Splenda
- 3 organic eggs
- 3 tbsps. coconut flour
- ½ cup heavy cream
- 3 tbsps. melted coconut oil, divided

Directions:
1. Mix together 1½ tablespoons of coconut oil, Splenda, eggs and salt in a bowl and beat until well combined.
2. Add the coconut flour slowly and continuously beat.
3. Stir in the heavy cream and beat continuously until well combined.
4. Press "Sauté" on Ninja Foodi and pour about ¼ of the mixture in the pot.
5. Sauté for about 2 minutes on each side and dish out.
6. Repeat with the remaining mixture in batches and serve.
- **Nutrition Info:** 145 calories, 13.1g fat, 4g carbs, 3.5g protein

314. Excellent Strawberry Toast Pastries

Servings: 8
Cooking Time: 30 Minutes
Ingredients:
- 1 refrigerated pie crust, at room temperature
- ¼ c. simple strawberry jam
- Vanilla icing
- Rainbow sprinkles

Directions:
1. Place Cook and Crisp basket in the pot and close the crisping lead, pre-heat at 350 degrees F on Air Crisp mode for 5 minutes
2. Roll out pie crust on a lightly floured surface, shaping it into a large rectangle, cut dough into 8 rectangles
3. Spoon a tablespoon of jam to the center of each of 4 dough rectangles, leaving ½ inch border
4. Brush edges of filled dough with water, top each with the other 4 dough rectangles and gently press edges to seal
5. Place pastries in your pre-heated basket and coat with cooking spray
6. Arrange pastries in the Cook and Crisp basket in a single layer
7. Close crisping lid and Air Crisp for 10 minutes at 350 degrees F
8. Repeat until all pastries are done, frost pastries with vanilla icing and top with sprinkles
9. Enjoy!
- **Nutrition Info:** 363 calories, 15g fat, 55g carbs, 2g protein

315. Balsamic Roasted Strawberries

Servings: 4 Servings
Cooking Time: 10 Minutes
Ingredients:
- 4 Cups whole Strawberries
- ½ cup balsamic vinegar
- 2 Tbsp stevia

Directions:
1. Place all the ingredients into the pot of the Ninja Foodi and close the crisper lid.
2. Press the air crisp button and set the temperature to 350 degrees and program the timer to 10 minutes.
3. Serve hot or chilled
- **Nutrition Info:** Calories: 172g, Carbohydrates: 21g, Protein: 0g, Fat: 0g, Sugar: 37g, Sodium: 20mg

316. Almond Cheese Cake

Servings: 6 Servings
Cooking Time: 20 Minutes

Ingredients:
- Crust: ½ cup almond flour
- 2 Tbsp stevia
- 2 Tbsp melted butter
- Filling: 16 oz cream cheese
- ½ cup baking stevia
- 1 egg
- 2 egg yolks
- ¼ cup sour cream
- ¾ cup heavy cream
- 1 tsp almond extract

Directions:
1. In a small bowl, mix all the ingredients for the crust together. Press the crust into a 7" spring form pan wrapped in foil. Set aside
2. Add the cream cheese, stevia and cocoa powder to a food processor and blend. Add the egg and yolks and blend again. Add remaining ingredients and mix just to combine. Pour cheesecake mix on top of the prepared crust.
3. Place the pan in the Ninja Foodi bowl on top of the metal trivet. Add 2 cups of water to the bowl under the cake. Place the pressure cooker lid on and set it to high pressure for 20 minutes. Allow the pot to naturally release the pressure once he cooking time is done. Chill and then serve.
- **Nutrition Info:** Calories: 474g, Carbohydrates: 10g, Protein:8g, Fat: 46g, Sugar: 4g, Sodium: 338g

317. Coconut Cream Cake

Servings: 8 – 10 Servings
Cooking Time: 35 – 45 Minutes
Ingredients:
- 1 box vanilla cake mix
- 1 box instant coconut pudding
- 1 ½ cups coconut
- 1 cup sour cream
- 1 cup coconut milk, unsweetened
- 4 eggs
- ½ cup coconut oil
- 2 teaspoons coconut extract
- Glaze
- 1 cup powdered sugar
- Enough milk for the desired consistency

Directions:
1. Lightly spray a Bundt cake pan that will fit inside the cooking pot with cooking spray.
2. In a large mixing bowl, beat together all ingredients except the coconut. Stir the coconut in by hand.
3. Pour the batter into the prepared pan and lower into the cooking pot. Add the Tender Crisp lid and set the temperature to 320 degrees. Bake 35 – 40 minutes or till it passes the toothpick test.
4. Carefully remove the cake from the pot and let cool 10 minutes. Transfer to a serving plate.
5. Make the glaze, and toast some additional coconut for garnish. Drizzle the glaze over the cake and top with toasted coconut.

318. Almond Cake

Servings: 8 Servings
Cooking Time: 25 Minutes
Ingredients:
- 8 Tbsp butter
- ½ cup Baking Stevia
- 1 egg
- 1 tsp vanilla
- 2 cups almond flour
- 2 tsp baking powder
- 1 tsp salt
- 1 cup chopped Almonds
- ½ cup buttermilk

Directions:
1. Use an electric mixer to cream the butter and stevia together until they are light and fluffy.
2. Mix the vanilla and eggs in a small bowl then add to the mixer with the butter blend until just combined
3. Add the remaining dry ingredients to the mixer and fold together by hand. Add the buttermilk and mix until smooth.
4. Add the almonds to the batter and mix briefly.
5. Pour the cake batter into your Ninja Foodi and place the lid on.
6. Press the air crisp button and set the temperature to 350 degrees and program the timer to 25 minutes.
7. Once cooked, a toothpick should come out of the center of the cake cleanly. Allow to cool and serve.
- **Nutrition Info:** Calories: 295 g, Carbohydrates: 6g, Protein: 7g, Fat: 29 g, Sugar: 1g, Sodium: 165 mg

319. Chocolate Cheese Cake(1)

Servings: 6 Servings
Cooking Time: 20 Minutes
Ingredients:
- Crust: ¼ cup almond flour
- ¼ cup coconut flour
- 2 Tbsp stevia
- 2 Tbsp melted butter
- Filling: 16 oz cream cheese
- ½ cup baking stevia
- 1/3 cup cocoa powder
- 1 egg and 2 egg yolks
- ¼ cup sour cream
- ¾ cup heavy cream
- 6 oz melted chocolate

- 1 tsp vanilla

Directions:
1. In a small bowl, mix all the ingredients for the crust together. Press the crust into a 7" spring form pan wrapped in foil. Set aside
2. Add the cream cheese, stevia and cocoa powder to a food processor and blend. Add the egg and yolks and blend again. Add remaining ingredients and mix just to combine. Pour cheesecake mix on top of the prepared crust.
3. Place the pan in the Ninja Foodi bowl on top of the metal trivet. Add 2 cups of water to the bowl under the cake. Place the pressure cooker lid on and set it to high pressure for 20 minutes. Allow the pot to naturally release the pressure once he cooking time is done. Chill and then serve.

- **Nutrition Info:** Calories: 474 g, Carbohydrates: 10g , Protein: 8g, Fat: 46 g, Sugar: 4g, Sodium: 338 g

320. Lemon Mousse

Servings: 2
Cooking Time: 22 Minutes
Ingredients:
- 1 oz. softened cream cheese
- ½ c. heavy cream
- 1/8 c. fresh lemon juice
- ½ tsp. lemon liquid stevia
- 2 pinches salt

Directions:
1. Mix together cream cheese, heavy cream, lemon juice, salt and stevia in a bowl.
2. Pour into the ramekins and transfer the ramekins in the pot of Ninja Foodi.
3. Press "Bake/Roast" and bake for about 12 minutes at 350 degrees F.
4. Pour into the serving glasses and refrigerate for at least 3 hours before serving.

- **Nutrition Info:** 305 calories, 31g fat, 2.7g carbs, 5g protein

321. Chocolate Pecan Pie

Servings: 8 – 10 Servings
Cooking Time: 35 Minutes
Ingredients:
- 1 pie crust
- 1 cup corn syrup
- 1 cup semisweet chocolate chips
- 1 cup coconut
- 1 cup pecans, chopped
- 3 eggs
- 1/3 cup sugar
- 1/3 cup brown sugar, packed
- 1/3 cup butter, melted
- 1 teaspoon vanilla
- ¼ teaspoon salt

Directions:
1. Unfold the pie crust into a pie plate that fits inside the cooking pot. Place the rack on the bottom of the pot.
2. In a mixing bowl, combine eggs, syrup, sugars, butter, vanilla and salt.
3. Layer the chocolate chips, coconut and pecans on the bottom of the pie crust. Pour the egg mixture evenly on top. Cover the pastry edge with foil and place the pie on the rack in the pot.
4. Add the Tender Crisp lid and set to 350 degrees. Bake 20 minutes then remove the foil and bake another 15 minutes or till set. Carefully remove from the pot and cool completely.

322. Nutty Cinnamon 'n Cranberry Cake

Servings: 2
Cooking Time: 25 Minutes
Ingredients:
- 2 tbsp cashew milk (or use any dairy or non-dairy milk you prefer)
- 1 medium egg
- 1/2 tsp vanilla extract
- 1/2 cup almond flour
- 2 tbsp monk fruit (or use your preferred sweetener)
- 1/4 tsp baking powder
- 1/4 tsp cinnamon
- 1/8 tsp salt
- 3 tbsp fresh cranberries
- 2 tbsp cup chopped pecans

Directions:
1. In blender, add all wet ingredients: and mix well. Add all dry ingredients: except for cranberries and pecans. Blend well until smooth.
2. Lightly grease baking pot of Ninja Foodi with cooking spray. Pour in batter. Drizzle cranberries on top and then followed by pecans.
3. For 20 minutes, cook on 330 ºF.
4. Let stand for 5 minutes.
5. Serve and enjoy.

- **Nutrition Info:** Calories: 98; carbs: 11.7g; protein: 1.7g; fat: 4.9g

323. Lemon Sponge Pie

Servings: 8 Servings
Cooking Time: 35 – 40 Minutes
Ingredients:
- 1 pie crust
- 1 ½ cups sugar
- 1 cup milk
- 2/3 cups lemon juice
- 1/3 cup flour
- 3 eggs, separated
- ¼ teaspoon salt

Directions:

1. Place the rack in the bottom of the cooking pot. Unfold the pie crust into a pie pan that fits inside the pot.
2. In a large mixing bowl, beat egg whites till stiff peaks form, set aside.
3. In a separate mixing bowl, beat yolks, lemon juice and milk till combined. Add sugar, flour and salt and beat till smooth.
4. Fold lemon mixture into egg whites, until thoroughly blended. Pour into pie crust. Carefully lower the dish onto the rack in the pot. Add the Tender Crisp lid and set temperature to 330 degrees. Bake 35-40 minutes, or till golden brown.
5. Carefully remove the pie from the pot and cool completely. Cover loosely and refrigerate till the filling sets. Serve.

324. Individual S'mores Pies

Servings: 6 – 12 Pies
Cooking Time: 10 Minutes
Ingredients:
- 2 sheets of puff pastry, thawed
- 2 chocolate bars
- 1 cup mini marshmallows
- ½ cup graham cracker crumbs
- 1 egg, lightly beaten

Directions:
1. Roll out the pastry dough on a lightly floured surface. Cut into 2-3 inch squares, or the size you desire.
2. In the center of half the squares, place a piece of chocolate, some marshmallows and graham crumbs. Moisten the edges of the pastry with water and add the remaining squares on top. Press the edges together. Brush the tops with egg wash.
3. Place 2-3 pies in the air fryer basket at a time, add the Tender Crisp lid and set the temperature to 330 degrees. Bake 5-7 minutes or till the outside is puffed and golden brown. Cool slightly before serving. You can drizzle the tops with melted chocolate or melted marshmallow cream.

325. Noodle Kugel

Servings: 10 Servings
Cooking Time: 6 Hours
Ingredients:
- 1 pound egg noodles, uncooked
- 1 bag frozen peaches, thawed and chopped
- 1 can coconut milk
- 1 cup sugar
- 3 eggs
- ¼ cup raisins
- 3 tablespoons orange liquor
- 2 teaspoons cinnamon

Directions:
1. Soak raisins in the liquor in a small bowl for 20 minutes.
2. Lightly spray the pot with cooking spray. Add milk, sugar, 1 teaspoon cinnamon and eggs to the pot and stir to combine.
3. Add the noodles, raisins with liquor and peaches to the egg mixture and stir to combine. Sprinkle the remaining teaspoon of cinnamon on the top. Add the lid and set slow cooking on low heat. Cook 6 hours.

326. Vanilla Yogurt

Servings: 2
Cooking Time: 3 Hours 20 Minutes
Ingredients:
- ½ c. full-fat milk
- ¼ c. yogurt starter
- 1 c. heavy cream
- ½ tbsp. pure vanilla extract
- 2 scoops stevia

Directions:
1. Pour milk in the pot of Ninja Foodi and stir in heavy cream, vanilla extract and stevia.
2. Allow the yogurt to sit and press "Slow Cooker" and cook on Low for about 3 hours.
3. Add the yogurt starter in 1 cup of milk and return this mixture to the pot.
4. Lock the lid and wrap the Ninja Foodi in two small towels.
5. Let sit for about 9 hours and allow the yogurt to culture.
6. Dish out in a serving bowl or refrigerate to serve.
- **Nutrition Info:** 292 calories, 26.2g fat, 8.2g carbs, 5.2g protein

327. Caramel Apple Chimichangas

Servings: 1 Dozen
Cooking Time: 6 Mins
Ingredients:
- 12 10-inch flour tortillas
- 7 Granny Smith apples, peeled, cored and sliced
- 1 lemon, juice and zest
- ¾ cup light brown sugar
- ¼ cup flour
- ¾ teaspoon ground cinnamon
- Cinnamon sugar
- Caramel sauce

Directions:
1. Preheat air fryer to 400 degrees.
2. Mix the brown sugar, flour and cinnamon together in small bowl.
3. In a large bowl, toss the apples with the lemon juice, then stir in the sugar mixture making sure to coat all of the apples.
4. Warm the tortillas so they are soft enough to fold. Place ½ - ¾ cup apples in the center

of tortilla and fold like a burrito. You can seal the edge with water or use toothpicks.
5. Lightly spray the outsides with cooking spray and sprinkle with the cinnamon sugar.
6. Cook them in batches in the fryer, 6-7 minutes, turning halfway through.
7. Drizzle with the caramel sauce, or serve them with the caramel sauce for dipping.

328. Nut Porridge

Servings: 4
Cooking Time: 20 Minutes
Ingredients:
- 4 tsps. melted coconut oil
- 1 c. halved pecans
- 2 c. water
- 2 tbsps. stevia
- 1 c. raw cashew nuts, unsalted

Directions:
1. Put the cashew nuts and pecans in the food processor and pulse until chunked.
2. Put the nuts mixture into the pot and stir in water, coconut oil and stevia.
3. Press "Sauté" on Ninja Foodi and cook for about 15 minutes.
4. Dish out and serve immediately.
- **Nutrition Info:** 260 calories, 22.9g fat, 12.7g carbs, 5.6g protein

329. Fruity And Tasty Vegan Crumble

Servings: 2
Cooking Time: 15 Minutes
Ingredients:
- 1 medium apple, finely diced
- ½ cup frozen blueberries, strawberries, or peaches
- ¼ cup plus 1 tablespoon sear button rice flour
- 2 tablespoons sugar
- ½ teaspoon ground cinnamon
- 2 tablespoons nondairy butter

Directions:
1. Lightly grease pot of Ninja Foodi with cooking spray.
2. Spread frozen blueberries and apple slices on bottom of pot.
3. In a bowl, whisk well butter, cinnamon, sugar, and flour. Sprinkle over fruit. If needed, sprinkle extra flour to cover exposed fruit.
4. For 15 minutes, bake at 350 ºF
5. Serve and enjoy.
- **Nutrition Info:** Calories: 281; carbs: 40.1g; protein: 2.0g; fat: 12.5g

330. Crunchy Cinnamon Topped Peaches

Servings: 2
Cooking Time: 30 Minutes
Ingredients:
- 2 cups sliced peaches, frozen
- 1 1/2 tablespoons sugar
- 1 tablespoon flour, white
- 1/2 teaspoon sugar, white
- 2 tbsp flour, white
- 3 tbsp oats, dry rolled
- 1 1/2 tablespoons butter, unsalted
- 1/2 teaspoons cinnamon
- 1 ½ tablespoons pecans, chopped

Directions:
1. Lightly grease the pot of Ninja Foodi with cooking spray. Mix in a tsp cinnamon, 2 tbsp flour, 3 tbsp sugar, and peaches.
2. For 20 minutes, bake on 300 ºF.
3. Mix the rest of the ingredients: in a bowl. Pour over peaches.
4. Bake for 10 minutes more at 330 ºF.
5. Serve and enjoy.
- **Nutrition Info:** Calories: 435; carbs: 74.1g; protein: 4.3g; fat: 13.4g

OTHER FAVORITE RECIPES

331. Ninja Foodi Chili

Servings: 4
Cooking Time: 30 Minutes
Ingredients:
- 2 tablespoons olive oil
- 1 onion, chopped
- 2 cloves of garlic, minced
- 2 pound ground beef
- 1 green bell pepper, chopped
- 1 jalapeno pepper, chopped
- 2 cans red kidney beans, rinsed and drained
- 2 cans diced tomatoes, undrained
- 3 tablespoons tomato paste
- 1 tablespoon sugar
- 2 teaspoons unsweetened cocoa powder
- ¼ teaspoon crushed red pepper flakes
- 2 tablespoons chili powder
- 2 teaspoons ground cumin
- ½ teaspoon salt
- 2 cups water

Directions:
1. Press the Sear/Sauté button and then the START button.
2. Heat the oil and sauté the garlic and onion until fragrant.
3. Stir in the ground beef and cook for another 2 minutes.
4. Add in the rest of the ingredients.
5. Close the pressure lid and set the vent to SEAL.
6. Press the Pressure button and adjust the cooking time to 30 minutes.
- **Nutrition Info:** Calories: 285; Carbohydrates: 35.3g; Protein: 22.3g; Fat: 14.9g; Sugar: 13.8g; Sodium: 790mg

332. Steamed Lemon Grass Crab Legs

Servings: 4
Cooking Time: 25 Minutes
Ingredients:
- 2 tablespoons vegetable oil
- 3 cloves of garlic, minced
- 1 piece fresh ginger root, crushed
- 1 stalk lemon grass, crushed
- 2 tablespoons fish sauce
- 1 tablespoon oyster sauce
- 2 pounds frozen Alaskan king crab
- Salt and pepper to taste

Directions:
1. Place the FoodiTM Cook &CrispTM reversible rack inside the ceramic pot.
2. Pour water into the pot.
3. Combine all ingredients in a big Ziploc bag and marinate for at least 30 minutes.
4. Place the crabs on the reversible rack.
5. Close the pressure lid and set the vent to SEAL.
6. Press the Steam button and adjust the cooking time to 25 minutes.
- **Nutrition Info:** Calories: 564; Carbohydrates: 5.3g; Protein: 89.1g; Fat: 20.7g; Sugar: 2.2g; Sodium: 1023mg

333. Easy Chow Mein Topped With Green Onions

Servings: 2
Cooking Time: 15 Minutes
Ingredients:
- 4 oz chow mein noodles
- 2 tablespoons peanut oil
- 4 green onions, chopped, white and green parts separated
- 3 cloves garlic, minced
- 1 teaspoon ginger, minced
- 1 small bell pepper, thinly sliced
- Sauce ingredients:
- 1/4 cup chicken broth
- 2 tablespoons shaoxing wine, or dry sherry
- 2 tablespoons oyster sauce
- 1 tablespoon soy sauce
- 1/2 teaspoon sesame oil

Directions:
1. In a small bowl, whisk well all sauce ingredients.
2. Boil noodles according to package instructions. Pour into colander and run under tap water to stop the cooking process. Drain well.
3. In Ninja Foodi, press sauté button and heat 3 tbsps oil. Heat for 4 minutes. Once hot add noodles and cook for a minute.
4. Stir in ginger and garlic. Cook for a minute until fragrant.
5. Stir in bell pepper and cook for 2 minutes.
6. Add sauce and toss noodles to coat well.
7. Serve and enjoy.
- **Nutrition Info:** Calories: 441; carbohydrates: 49.9g; protein: 6.6g; fat: 23.8g

334. Steamed Brisket In Guinness

Servings: 8
Cooking Time: 50 Minutes
Ingredients:
- 3 ½ cups Irish stout beer (Guinness)
- 2 bay leaves
- 1 tablespoon salt
- 1 tablespoon ground black pepper
- 2 teaspoons paprika
- 1 teaspoon dried basil
- 1 teaspoon dried oregano
- 1 teaspoon garlic powder

- 1 teaspoon onion powder
- 4 pounds beef brisket
- 2 large onions, sliced
- 2 tablespoons cornstarch
- 3 tablespoons water

Directions:
1. Place the FoodiTM Cook &CrispTM reversible rack inside the ceramic pot.
2. Pour the Guinness in the pot. Stir in the bay leaves.
3. In a small bowl, combine the salt, black pepper, paprika, dried basil, oregano, garlic powder, and onion powder. This will be the dry rub.
4. Season the beef brisket with the dry rub. Place the beef brisket on the reversible rack.
5. Close the pressure lid and set the vent to SEAL.
6. Press the Steam button and adjust the cooking time to 50 minutes.
7. Do quick pressure release. Once the lid is open, remove the beef. Take out the basket as well. Press the Sear/Sauté button and allow the sauce to simmer.
8. Stir in the onions and cornstarch until the sauce thickens.
9. Pour the sauce over the steamed beef.
- **Nutrition Info:** Calories: 714; Carbohydrates: 83.4g; Protein: 46.2g; Fat: 21.7g; Sugar: 0.9g; Sodium: 693mg

335. Lemon Pepper Wings

Servings: 4 Servings
Cooking Time: 20 Minutes
Ingredients:
- 2 ½ pounds chicken wing pieces
- 1 cup flour
- 1/3 cup butter
- 1 teaspoon lemon pepper
- ½ teaspoon salt
- ½ teaspoon black pepper

Directions:
1. Mix flour with salt in pepper in a large bowl. Add wing pieces, in small batches to flour and toss to coat each piece well.
2. Spray the fryer basket lightly with cooking spray. Add wings, in batches, to basket and place in the cooker. Lock the Tender Crisp lid in place and set temperature to 360 degrees.
3. Cook for 10 minutes, then turn the wings over and cook an additional 10 minutes or till they are golden brown.
4. Place the butter in a medium mixing bowl and melt in the microwave. Stir in the lemon pepper seasoning and then add cooked wings and toss to coat.
5. Serve with your favorite dipping sauce.

336. Fragrant Steamed Pork

Servings: 2
Cooking Time: 45 Minutes
Ingredients:
- 2 boneless pork chops
- 2 tablespoons fresh orange juice
- 2 cups water
- ¼ teaspoon ground cloves
- ¼ teaspoon ground coriander
- ¼ teaspoon ground cinnamon
- 1 pinch cayenne pepper

Directions:
1. Place all ingredients in a Ziploc bag and marinate in the fridge for at least 2 hours.
2. Place the FoodiTM Cook &CrispTM reversible rack inside the ceramic pot.
3. Pour water into the pot.
4. Place the marinated meat on the reversible rack.
5. Close the pressure lid and set the vent to SEAL.
6. Press the Steam button and adjust the cooking time to 45 minutes.
- **Nutrition Info:** Calories: 104; Carbohydrates: 2.2g; Protein: 12.7g; Fat: 4.6g; Sugar: 0.3g; Sodium: 33mg

337. Hot Pepper Jelly Cheese Dip With Bacon

Servings: 2 Cups
Cooking Time: 35 Minutes
Ingredients:
- 1 10.5 ounce jar hot pepper Jelly
- 1 package cream cheese, soft
- 1 cup sharp cheddar cheese, grated
- 4 slices bacon, cooked crisp and crumbled
- 1 clove garlic, chopped fine
- 1/2 teaspoon salt

Directions:
1. Beat cream cheese in a large bowl till creamy. Add cheddar, garlic, and salt and mix well. Stir in ½ the jelly till well combined.
2. Lightly grease a baking dish that will fit inside the cooker. Pour the mixture in the dish.
3. Place the rack in the bottom of the cooker and place the dip on top. Lock on the Tender Crisp lid and set the temperature to 350 degrees.
4. Bake 35 – 40 minutes or till hot and bubbly. Carefully remove the dip from the cooker
5. Slightly melt the remaining jelly in the microwave and spread over the top of the dip and top with the bacon. Serve warm with crackers or pita chips.

338. Ninja Foodie Short Ribs

Servings: 8

Cooking Time: 60 Minutes
Ingredients:
- 1 bottle (750mL) red wine
- 4 pounds beef short ribs
- 3 tablespoons unsalted butter
- 1 ½ cups onion, chopped
- 3 cloves of garlic, minced
- 1 cup minced carrots
- 2 sprigs fresh rosemary
- 2 cups chicken stock
- Salt and pepper to taste

Directions:
1. Place all ingredients in the pot except for the hard-boiled eggs.
2. Close the pressure lid and set the vent to SEAL.
3. Press the Pressure button and adjust the cooking time to 60 minutes.
4. Do natural pressure release.
- **Nutrition Info:** Calories: 436; Carbohydrates: 13.2g; Protein: 15.9g; Fat: 35.5g; Sugar: 5.8g; Sodium: 277mg On

339. Beer Braised Brisket
Servings: 8 – 10 Servings
Cooking Time: 8 Hours
Ingredients:
- 5 pound beef brisket
- 1 large can tomatoes, diced
- 1 bottle of Modelo beer
- 1 medium onion, sliced thin
- 3 cloves garlic, chopped fine
- 1 tablespoon plus 1 teaspoon oregano
- 1 tablespoon salt
- 1 tablespoon freshly ground black pepper

Directions:
1. Place the onion on the bottom of the cooking pot. Add brisket, fat side up, if you need to cut it into pieces to fit the pot then that is okay. Add the tomatoes, undrained and beer. Sprinkle the garlic and seasonings on the top.
2. Secure the lid and select the slow cooker function on low heat. Cook 8 hours, or till beef is fork tender.
3. Carefully transfer the brisket to a cutting board and slice or shred it. Return it to the pot and stir before serving.

340. Mediterranean Spinach With Cheese
Servings: 6
Cooking Time: 20 Minutes
Ingredients:
- 4 tbsps. butter
- 2 lbs. boiled and chopped spinach
- Salt and black pepper
- 2/3 c. pitted Kalamata olives, halved
- 1½ c. grated feta cheese
- 4 tsps. Freshly grated lemon zest

Directions:
1. Mix together spinach, butter, salt and black pepper in a bowl.
2. Place the basket in the Ninja Foodi and add seasoned spinach.
3. Press "Air Crisp" and set the timer to 15 minutes at 340 degrees F.
4. Dish out from the Ninja Foodi and stir in the olives, lemon zest and feta cheese to serve.
- **Nutrition Info:** 247 calories, 18.7g fat, 7.2g carbs, 9.9g protein

341. Lamb Marsala
Servings: 2 Servings
Cooking Time: 1 Hour 40 Minutes
Ingredients:
- 2 lamb shanks
- 1 cup chicken stock
- 2/3 cup Marsala wine
- 1 onion, chopped
- 8 cloves garlic, halved
- 4 bay leaves
- 2 tablespoons tomato paste
- 2 twigs rosemary
- Salt & pepper to taste
- Olive oil

Directions:
1. Trim off the excess fat from the lamb. Rub them with salt and pepper.
2. Set the cooker to sauté on med-high heat and add a splash of olive oil. When the oil is hot add the onions and garlic and cook till almost translucent, stirring often. Stir in the tomato paste and cook 2-3 minutes more.
3. Add lamb shanks, one at a time, and brown on both sides. Add both shanks to the pot, making sure they are meat side down. Add the bay leaves, wine, rosemary and chicken stock and bring to a boil.
4. Secure the lid and select pressure cooking on high. Set the timer for 45 minutes.
5. When the timer goes off, use quick release to remove the lid. Flip the lamb and secure the lid again. Cook another 25 minutes.
6. Quick release the lid and set the cooker back to sauté on medium heat. Cook another 10 – 15 minutes till the sauce is thick and sticky, being sure to glaze the lamb every few minutes. Serve.

342. Deliciously Dehydrated Apple Chips
Servings: 4
Cooking Time: 12 Hours
Ingredients:
- 2 Golden Delicious apples, cored and sliced
- 1 ½ teaspoons white sugar
- ½ teaspoon ground cinnamon

Directions:

1. Place in the ceramic pot the FoodiTM Cook &CrispTM dehydrating tray.
2. Season the apples with white sugar and cinnamon
3. Place the apples on the dehydrating tray.
4. Close the crisping lid and press the Dehydrate button before pressing the START button.
5. Adjust the cooking time to 12 hours.
- **Nutrition Info:** Calories: 28; Carbohydrates: 6.9g; Protein: 0.1g; Fat: 0g; Sugar: 3.6g; Sodium: 1mg

343. Louisiana Style Banana Foster

Servings: 4
Cooking Time: 6 Minutes
Ingredients:
- ½ C. butter
- 1 C. dark brown sugar
- 1 tsp. ground cinnamon
- 4 small bananas, peeled, halved lengthwise, then cut in half again
- ½ C. rum

Directions:
1. Select "Sauté/Sear" setting of Ninja Foodi and set "Md:Hi".
2. Press "Start/Stop" to begin and preheat for 5 minutes.
3. In the pot, place butter, brown sugar, and cinnamon in the pot and cook until butter and brown sugar dissolve, stirring continuously.
4. Add bananas and place the sauce over them.
5. Cook for about 2 minutes or until edges start to soften.
6. Stir in the rum and cook for about 2 minutes.
7. Press "Start/Stop" to stop the cooking.
8. Serve immediately.
- **Nutrition Info:** Calories per serving: 512; Carbohydrates: 63g; Protein: 1.6g; Fat: 23.4g; Sugar: 2.1g; Sodium: 175mg; Fiber: 3.4g

344. Bacon And Cabbage

Servings: 4 Servings
Cooking Time: 11 Minutes
Ingredients:
- 1 head of cabbage, core removed
- 3 sliced bacon
- 4 Tbsp butter
- 2 cups chicken broth
- 1 tsp salt
- ½ tsp black pepper

Directions:
1. Use the saute function to cook the bacon strips for about 8 minutes, flipping halfway through. Add the butter to the pot and stir to melt.
2. Chopp the cabbage and place it into the pot with the cooked bacon.
3. Add the chicken broth, salt and pepper to the bowl and stir to combine everything.
4. Place the pressure cooker lid on the Ninja Foodie and set the steamer valve to seal. Pressure cook for three minutes on high heat then quickly release the steam by opening the steamer valve carefully.
5. Serve the bacon cabbage while hot.
- **Nutrition Info:** Calories: 236g, Carbohydrates: 1g, Protein: 5g, Fat: 14g, Sugar: 2g, Sodium: 801 mg

345. Dessert Fruity Tacos

Servings: 2
Cooking Time: 5 Minutes
Ingredients:
- 2 soft shell tortillas
- 4 tbsp. strawberry jelly
- ¼ C. blueberries
- ¼ C. raspberries
- 2 tbsp. powdered sugar

Directions:
1. Spread 2 tbsp. of strawberry jelly over each tortilla
2. Top each with berries evenly and sprinkle with powdered sugar.
3. Arrange the "Cook & Crisp Basket" in the pot of Ninja Foodi.
4. Close the Ninja Foodi with crisping lid and select "Air Crisp".
5. Press "Start/Stop" to begin and set the temperature to 300 degrees F.
6. Set the time for 5 minutes to preheat.
7. Now, place the tortillas into "Cook & Crisp Basket".
8. Close the Ninja Foodi with crisping lid and select "Air Crisp".
9. Set the temperature to 300 degrees F for 5 minutes.
10. Press "Start/Stop" to begin.
11. Open the lid and serve
- **Nutrition Info:** Calories per serving: 202; Carbohydrates: 49.2g; Protein: 1.7g; Fat: 0.9g; Sugar: 34.5g; Sodium: 11mg; Fiber: 3g

346. Simple Pot Roast And Potatoes

Servings: 6
Cooking Time: 50 Minutes
Ingredients:
- 3 pounds beef rump roast
- 1/3 cup all-purpose flour
- ¼ cup olive oil
- 2 packages dry onion soup mix
- 2 ½ cups water
- 3 onions, peeled and cut into wedges
- 8 potatoes, peeled and halved
- Salt and pepper to taste

Directions:
1. Season the beef with salt and pepper. Dredge in flour.
2. Press the Sear/Sauté button and then the START button.
3. Heat the oil and sear the beef on all sides for at least 2 minutes.
4. Add the rest of the ingredients.
5. Close the pressure lid and set the vent to SEAL.
6. Press the Pressure button and adjust the cooking time to 50 minutes.
- **Nutrition Info:** Calories: 700; Carbohydrates: 71.3g; Protein: 47.6g; Fat: 24.9g; Sugar: 21.7g; Sodium: 935mg

347. French Onion Soup

Servings: 4 Servings
Cooking Time: 35 Minutes
Ingredients:
- 2 Tbsp butter
- 2 onions, sliced
- 1 tbsp tomato paste
- 1 tbsp soy sauce
- 1 tbsp Worcestershire sauce
- 3 cups beef stock
- 1 tsp salt
- ½ tsp pepper
- 2 cups mozzarella cheese

Directions:
1. Place the butter in the bottom of the Foodi pot and turn the machine on to sear. Add the onions after the butter has melted and stir together. Cook for about 10 minutes, stirring occasionally.
2. Add the Worcestershire sauce, tomato paste and soy sauce to the pot and mix. Cook for another 5 minutes then add the remaining ingredients except the mozzarella cheese.
3. Close the pressure cooker lid and set the steamer valve to seal. Cook the soup on high pressure for 10 minutes. Once cooked, do a quick pressure release and remove the lid.
4. Sprinkle the soup with the mozzarella cheese and put the crisper lid on top. Set the Ninja Foodi to broil and the timer for 6 minutes. Once the cheese has browned, serve immediately.
- **Nutrition Info:** Calories: 252g, Carbohydrates: 5g, Protein: 16g, Fat: 18g, Sugar: 4g, Sodium: 1604 mg

348. Zucchini Cream Cheese Fries

Servings: 4
Cooking Time: 20 Minutes
Ingredients:
- 1 lb. zucchini, sliced
- Salt
- 1 c. cream cheese
- 2 tbsps. olive oil

Directions:
1. Put zucchini in a colander and add salt and cream cheese.
2. Put oil and zucchini in the pot of Ninja Foodi and lock the lid.
3. Press "Air Crisp" and set the timer to 10 minutes at 365 degrees F.
4. Dish out from the Ninja Foodi and serve.
- **Nutrition Info:** 374 calories, 36.6g fat, 7.1g carbs, 7.7g protein

349. Elegant Mushroom Sautee

Servings: 8
Cooking Time: 25 Minutes
Ingredients:
- 1 lb. white button mushrooms, stems trimmed
- 2 tbsps. butter, unsalted
- ½ tsp. salt
- ¼ c. water

Directions:
1. Quarter medium mushrooms and cut any large mushrooms into eight
2. Put mushrooms, butter, and salt in your Foodi's inner pot
3. Add water and lock pressure lid, making sure to seal the valve
4. Cook on HIGH pressure for 5 minutes, quick release pressure once did
5. Once done, set your pot to Sauté mode on HIGH mode and bring the mix to a boil over 5 minutes until all the water evaporates
6. Once the butter/water has evaporated, stir for 1 minute until slightly browned
7. Enjoy!
- **Nutrition Info:** 50 calories, 4g fat, 2g carbs, 2g protein

350. Thai Sweet Pork

Servings: 6 Servings
Cooking Time: 15 Minutes
Ingredients:
- 2 pounds pork shoulder, cut into ¼" x 2" strips
- 3 large shallots, sliced not too thin
- ¼ cup brown sugar
- ¼ cup palm sugar
- 3 cloves garlic, chopped fine
- 3 tablespoons soy sauce
- 2 tablespoons vegetable oil
- 2 tablespoons sweet soy sauce
- 2 tablespoons fish sauce
- 1 teaspoon ground chili paste
- ¼ teaspoon white pepper
- Rice
- 1 ½ cups Jasmine rice, rinsed
- 1 can coconut milk
- ¼ cup water

- 1 teaspoon salt

Directions:
1. Set cooker to sauté on med-high heat. Add oil and shallots and cook two minutes. Add garlic and cook another 30 seconds.
2. Add soy sauce, fish sauce, chili paste, pepper and half the sugars and simmer 3 minutes.
3. Add the pork and stir to coat.
4. Place the rack in the pot and place a pan on top. Add the rice ingredients and cover with foil, poke holes in the foil to vent.
5. Secure the lid and set to pressure cooking on high. Set timer for 6 minutes. When timer goes off, use manual release to remove the lid.
6. Remove the pan of rice and set aside. Stir in the remaining sugars and set the cooker back to sauté on medium heat. Cook the sauce, stirring often, till it has thickened. Serve the pork over the rice garnished with chopped scallions and crispy, caramelized onions.

351. Ninja Foodi Cola Roast

Servings: 8
Cooking Time: 2 Hours
Ingredients:
- 4 pounds beef sirloin roast
- 1 can cola
- 3 cups water
- 1 clove of garlic, minced
- 1 bay leaf
- Salt and pepper to taste

Directions:
1. Place in the ceramic pot the FoodiTM Cook &CrispTM basket insert.
2. Place all ingredients in a bowl and allow the beef to soak in the cola for at least overnight.
3. Place the marinated beef in the basket insert.
4. Close the crisping lid and press the Bake/Roast button before pressing the START button.
5. Adjust the cooking time to 2 hours.
- **Nutrition Info:** Calories: 416; Carbohydrates: 12.7g; Protein: 38.8g; Fat: 23.3g; Sugar: 6.9g; Sodium: 736mg

352. Cheesy Spinach Bake

Servings: 6
Cooking Time: 15 Minutes
Ingredients:
- 2 lb. fresh spinach, chopped
- 4 tbsp. butter, melted
- Salt and freshly ground black pepper, to taste
- 1 C. feta cheese, crumbled
- 1 tsp. fresh lemon zest, grated

Directions:
1. In a bowl, add the spinach, butter, salt and black pepper and mix well.
2. Arrange the "Cook & Crisp Basket" in the pot of Ninja Foodi.
3. Close the Ninja Foodi with crisping lid and select "Air Crisp".
4. Press "Start/Stop" to begin and set the temperature to 340 degrees F.
5. Set the time for 5 minutes to preheat.
6. Now, place the spinach mixture into "Cook & Crisp Basket".
7. Close the Ninja Foodi with crisping lid and select "Air Crisp".
8. Set the temperature to 340 degrees F for 15 minutes.
9. Press "Start/Stop" to begin.
10. Open the lid and immediately, stir in the cheese and lemon zest.
11. Serve hot.
- **Nutrition Info:** Calories: 169; Carbohydrates: 6.6g; Protein: 8g; Fat: 13.6g; Sugar: 1.7g; Sodium: 480mg; Fiber: 3.4g

353. Cauliflower Gratin

Servings: 4 Servings
Cooking Time: 15 Minutes
Ingredients:
- 1 cup water
- 1 large cauliflower head, cup into florets
- 2 tsp salt
- ¼ tsp ground nutmeg
- ½ cup grated parmesan cheese
- ½ cup heavy cream
- 1 Tbsp coconut flour

Directions:
1. Add the water, cauliflower, salt and nutmeg to the bowl and place the lid on the machine, setting the steamer valve to seal. Use the pressure cooker function to cook the cauliflower on high pressure for 2 minutes. Do a quick pressure release and remove the lid once the timer is done.
2. In a separate bowl, mix together the cream and coconut flour. Add this mix to the pot and stir Press the saute button and bring the mix to a boil.
3. Sprinkle the cheese over the top and lower the air crisper lid. Set the temperature to 400 degrees and set the timer for 10 minutes. Cook until browned and then serve hot.
- **Nutrition Info:** Calories: 357g, Carbohydrates: 11g, Protein: 23g, Fat: 26g, Sugar: 7g, Sodium: 2071 mg

354. Pork Loin With Onion Beer Sauce

Servings: 4 – 6 Servings
Cooking Time: 40 Minutes
Ingredients:

- 1 ½ pound pork loin
- 1 ½ cups dark beer
- 1 large onion, sliced
- 2 cloves garlic, chopped fine
- 3 tablespoons water
- 2 tablespoons cornstarch
- 1 tablespoon olive oil
- 1 tablespoon Dijon mustard
- 2 bay leaves

Directions:
1. Set cooker to sauté on medium heat and add oil. Once oil is hot, add onions and cook till tender. Add the pork loin and brown on all sides, transfer to a plate.
2. Add the beer and stir to deglaze the pan. Stir in the mustard, garlic and bay leaves and add the pork loin back to the pot.
3. Secure the lid and switch to pressure cooking on high. Set the timer for 35 minutes. When the timer goes off, use manual release to remove the lid.
4. Dissolve the cornstarch in the water. Remove the pork and set the cooker back to sauté on med-high heat. Add the cornstarch mixture to the pot and cook till sauce thickens.
5. Slice the pork and serve with the onion beer sauce.

355. Hard Steamed Eggs

Servings: 12
Cooking Time: 15 Minutes
Ingredients:
- 12 eggs

Directions:
1. Place the FoodiTM Cook &CrispTM reversible rack inside the ceramic pot.
2. Pour water into the pot.
3. Place the eggs gently on the baking insert.
4. Close the pressure lid and set the vent to SEAL.
5. Press the Steam button and adjust the cooking time to 10 minutes.
6. Do quick pressure release.
7. Place the eggs in iced water for about 20 minutes to easily peel off the shell.
- **Nutrition Info:** Calories: 72; Carbohydrates: 0.4g; Protein: 6.3g; Fat: 5g; Sugar: 0g; Sodium: 70mg

356. Broiled Cranberry Pork

Servings: 6
Cooking Time: 1 Hour And 30 Minutes
Ingredients:
- 3 pounds boneless pork loin roast
- 1 can cranberry sauce
- 1/3 cup French salad dressing
- 1 onion, sliced

Directions:
1. Place in the ceramic pot the pork loin roast and pour the cranberry sauce and French salad dress. Top with onions.
2. Close the crisping lid and press the Bake/Roast button before pressing the START button.
3. Adjust the cooking time to 1hour and 30 minutes.
- **Nutrition Info:** Calories: 375; Carbohydrates: 32.9g; Protein: 26.8g; Fat: 15.1g; Sugar: 19.8g; Sodium: 184mg

357. Jalapeno & Cheese Wontons

Servings: 16 – 20 Pieces
Cooking Time: 15 Minutes
Ingredients:
- 1 package wonton wrappers
- 1 package cream cheese, soft
- 3 jalapenos, remove ribs and seeds and chop fine
- ½ cup cheddar cheese, grated
- Coarse salt

Directions:
1. In a bowl, combine cream cheese, jalapenos, and cheddar cheese.
2. Lay out wrappers on a work surface. Moisten with a dab of water and spoon about 1 ½ teaspoons filling on each.
3. Pull two opposite corners up over filling and pinch together. Repeat with other corners. Spray the wontons lightly with cooking spray.
4. Spray the cooking pot with and add the wontons, you will have to cook them in batches.
5. Lock the Tender Crisp lid in place and set temperature to 350 degrees. Cook 8 minutes or till they are golden brown and crisp.
6. Sprinkle with salt and serve warm

358. Spiced Roasted Broccoli

Servings: 2
Cooking Time: 20 Minutes
Ingredients:
- 2 cups broccoli florets
- 1 yellow bell pepper, sliced
- 1 teaspoon garlic powder
- 1 tablespoon steak seasoning
- 2 teaspoons chili powder
- 1 tablespoon extra-virgin olive oil
- Salt and pepper to taste

Directions:
1. Place in the ceramic pot the FoodiTM Cook &CrispTM basket insert.
2. Toss all ingredients in a mixing bowl.
3. Place the vegetables in the basket.

4. Close the crisping lid and press the Bake/Roast button before pressing the START button.
5. Adjust the cooking time to 20 minutes.
6. Give the basket a shake to roast the vegetables evenly
- **Nutrition Info:** Calories: 76; Carbohydrates: 8g; Protein: 2.1g; Fat: 3.9g; Sugar: 0.6g; Sodium: 718mg

359. Quinoa 'n Lime-cilantro Salad

Servings: 2
Cooking Time: 15 Minutes
Ingredients:
- 1 cup quinoa, rinsed and drained
- 1 ¼ cups vegetable broth
- 2 tablespoons lime juice
- Zest from one lime, grated
- ½ cup chopped cilantro
- Salt to taste

Directions:
1. In the Ninja Foodi, place the quinoa and vegetable broth.
2. Install pressure lid. Close Ninja Foodi, press the pressure button, choose high settings, and set time to 15 minutes.
3. Once done cooking, do a quick release.
4. Open the lid and fluff the quinoa using fork. Transfer to a bowl and let it cool.
5. Assemble the salad by adding into the quinoa the remaining ingredients.
6. Serve and enjoy.
- **Nutrition Info:** Calories: 101; carbohydrates: 19g; protein: 4g; fat: 1g

360. Stunning Broccoli Florets

Servings: 6
Cooking Time: 16 Minutes
Ingredients:
- 4 tbsps. butter
- Salt and black pepper
- 2 lbs. broccoli florets
- 1 c. whipping cream

Directions:
1. Arrange the basket in the bottom of Ninja Foodi and add water.
2. Place the broccoli florets on top of the basket and lock the lid.
3. Press "Pressure" and cook for about 5 minutes.
4. Release the pressure quickly and replace the pot with the basket.
5. Transfer the broccoli florets in the pot and top with salt, black pepper and butter.
6. Press "Air Crisp" and cook for about 3 minutes at 360 degrees F.
7. Dish out to serve immediately.
- **Nutrition Info:** 178 calories, 14.4g fat, 9.6g carbs, 4.7g protein

361. Chili Tomatoes 'n Black Beans

Servings: 2
Cooking Time: 13 Minutes
Ingredients:
- 1 teaspoon olive oil
- 1/2 onion, diced
- 1/2 bell pepper, diced
- 1/2 teaspoon dried oregano
- 1 clove garlic, minced
- 1 tablespoon chili powder
- 1 teaspoon ground cumin
- 1 can cooked black beans, drained
- 1/2 can tomatoes
- 1/2 jalapeno pepper, minced
- Salt and pepper to taste
- 1/2 cup water

Directions:
1. Press the sauté button on the Ninja Foodi and heat the olive oil.
2. Once hot, stir in the onion, bell pepper, oregano, and garlic until fragrant.
3. Stir in the rest of the ingredients.
4. Install pressure lid. Close Ninja Foodi, press the manual button, choose high settings, and set time to 10 minutes.
5. Once done cooking, do a quick release.
6. Serve and enjoy.
- **Nutrition Info:** Calories: 309; carbohydrates: 50.4g; protein: 17.2g; fat: 4.3g

362. Eggplant Parmesan

Servings: 4 Servings
Cooking Time: 11 Minutes
Ingredients:
- 1 medium eggplant, sliced about ¼ inch thick
- 2 cups Keto Tomato Sauce
- 1½ cup water
- 1/2 cup shredded mozzarella cheese
- ¼ tsp red pepper flakes

Directions:
1. Place one cup of water in the bottom of the Ninja Foodi and then layer the eggplant slices inside the pot. Spread some of the tomato sauce across the eggplant when you are halfway through and continue layering
2. Pour the remaining sauce over the eggplant once it is all in the pot and sprinkle with the cheese and red pepper flakes. 'Place the lid on the Foodi and use the pressure cooking function, set on high pressure for eleven minutes.
3. Once the timer is done, use the quick pressure release, open the lid and serve.
- **Nutrition Info:** Calories: 132g, Carbohydrates: 13g, Protein: 6g, Fat: 4g, Sugar: 8g, Sodium: 134mg

363. Chicken-parm Fettucine Alfredo

Servings: 2
Cooking Time: 10 Minutes
Ingredients:
- 1 1/2 tbsp butter, cut in a few small pieces
- 2 cloves garlic, pressed/minced
- 1 cup chicken broth
- 4 oz fettuccine noodles, broken in half
- 1/2-lb small chicken breasts, uncooked cut larger breasts in half
- 1/2 cup heavy cream
- 1/2 tsp salt (or more to taste)
- 1/2 tsp pepper
- 1/4 cup parmesan cheese, grated

Directions:
1. Place the butter and garlic in the pot. Pour chicken broth.
2. Sprinkle in the fettuccine noodles, in a random pattern, and gently press them down.
3. If adding chicken: add the chicken breasts, and space evenly over the noodles. Pour the cream over them, then sprinkle with the salt and pepper.
4. Install pressure lid. Close Ninja Foodi, press pressure button, choose high settings, and set time to 5 minutes.
5. Once done cooking, do a quick release.
6. Stir in parmesan and mix well. Let it rest for 5 minutes.
7. Serve and enjoy.
- **Nutrition Info:** Calories: 726; carbohydrates: 50.8g; protein: 42.7g; fat: 39.1g

364. Spicy Green Beans

Servings: 4 Servings
Cooking Time: 10 Minutes
Ingredients:
- 1 pound green beans, ends trimmed
- 1 Tbsp coconut oil
- 1 tsp coconut aminos
- 1 tsp rice wine vinegar
- 1 garlic clove, chopped
- ¾ tsp red pepper flakes

Directions:
1. Toss all the ingredients together in a bowl and let sit for 10 minutes to marinate.
2. Add the green beans into the crisp and cook basket and set the air crisper to 400 degrees F for 10 minutes.
3. Remove the green beans and serve hot
- **Nutrition Info:** Calories: 69g, Carbohydrates: 9g, Protein: 2g, Fat: 4g, Sugar: 4g, Sodium: 30 mg

365. Scalloped Pineapple

Servings: 8 – 10 Servings
Cooking Time: 35 Minutes
Ingredients:
- 20 ounce can pineapple tidbits, reserve ¼ cup juice,
- 20 ounce can crushed pineapple, drained
- 40 Ritz crackers, crushed
- 2 cups sharp cheddar cheese, grated
- ½ cup sugar
- ½ cup butter, melted
- 6 tablespoons flour

Directions:
1. In a mixing bowl, combine all ingredients except the cracker crumbs and the butter.
2. Lightly spray the cooking pot with cooking spray. Add the pineapple mixture.
3. In a small bowl, combine the crackers crumbs and butter. Sprinkle over the top of the pineapple mixture.
4. Add the Tender Crisp lid and set the temperature to 350 degrees. Bake 35 minutes or till top is golden brown. Serve warm.

366. Coffee-flavored Chuck Roast

Servings: 8
Cooking Time: 2 Hours
Ingredients:
- 2 tablespoons butter
- 4 pounds chuck roast
- 1 tablespoon butter
- 1 onion, chopped finely
- 6 cups brewed coffee
- Salt and pepper to taste

Directions:
1. Place all ingredients in a bowl and allow the chuck roast to marinate for at least overnight in the fridge.
2. Place in the ceramic pot the Foodi™ Cook & Crisp™ basket insert.
3. Place the marinated roast on the basket insert.
4. Close the crisping lid and press the Bake/Roast button before pressing the START button.
5. Adjust the cooking time to 2 hours.
- **Nutrition Info:** Calories: 690; Carbohydrates: 8g; Protein: 59.7g; Fat: 46.5g; Sugar: 2.4g; Sodium: 501mg

367. Simple Beer-marinated Pork Roast

Servings: 8
Cooking Time: 2 Hours
Ingredients:
- 4 pounds pork shoulder roast, scored
- 2 cans beer
- 2 bay leaves
- 3 sprigs fresh rosemary
- Salt and pepper to taste

Directions:

1. Place in the ceramic pot the FoodiTM Cook &CrispTM basket insert.
2. In a large bowl, mix all ingredients and allow the pork to marinate in the fridge for at least overnight.
3. Place the marinated pork in the basket.
4. Close the crisping lid and press the Bake/Roast button before pressing the START button.
5. Adjust the cooking time to 2 hours.
- **Nutrition Info:** Calories: 476; Carbohydrates: 38.5g; Protein: 30.8g; Fat: 22g; Sugar: 15.8g; Sodium: 931mg

368. Apple Butter Pork Loin

Servings: 4
Cooking Time: 1 Hour And 30 Minutes
Ingredients:
- 2 pounds boneless pork loin roast
- 2 cups apple juice
- ½ cup apple butter
- ¼ cup brown sugar
- 2 tablespoons water
- ¼ teaspoon ground cinnamon
- ¼ teaspoon ground cloves
- Salt and pepper to taste

Directions:
1. Place in the ceramic pot the FoodiTM Cook &CrispTM basket insert.
2. Season the pork loin with salt and pepper.
3. Place the pork in a roasting pan that will fit inside the basket insert.
4. Pour over the apple juice and cover with aluminum foil.
5. Close the crisping lid and press the Bake/Roast button before pressing the START button.
6. Adjust the cooking time to 1hour and 30 minutes.
7. Meanwhile, place the apple butter, sugar, water, cinnamon, and cloves in a saucepan until it thickens.
8. Halfway through the cooking time, brush the pork loin with the sauce.
- **Nutrition Info:** Calories: 591; Carbohydrates: 25.7g; Protein: 64.9g; Fat: 25.4g; Sugar: 16.4g; Sodium: 151mg

369. Herb Roasted Pork Loin With Potatoes

Servings: 8
Cooking Time: 2 Hours
Ingredients:
- 4 pounds pork loin, fat trimmed
- 2 tablespoons olive oil
- ½ teaspoon dried thyme
- ½ teaspoon garlic powder
- Salt and pepper to taste
- 6 medium potatoes, peeled and quartered
- 1 ½ teaspoons chopped fresh chives

Directions:
1. Place in the ceramic pot the FoodiTM Cook & CrispTM basket insert.
2. Season the pork loin with olive oil, thyme, garlic powder, salt and pepper.
3. Place in the basket insert and place the potatoes on the side. Season with salt and pepper and garnish with fresh chives.
4. Close the crisping lid and press the Bake/Roast button before pressing the START button.
5. Adjust the cooking time to 2 hours.
- **Nutrition Info:** Calories: 345; Carbohydrates: 29.5g; Protein: 28.9g; Fat: 12.3g; Sugar: 6.6g; Sodium: 53mg

370. Cinnamon Apple Chips

Servings: 2 Servings
Cooking Time: 10 Minutes
Ingredients:
- 1 medium apple, sliced thin
- ¼ teaspoon cinnamon
- ¼ teaspoon nutmeg

Directions:
1. Place all ingredients into a mixing bowl and toss to coat the apple slice.
2. Place the apples in the fryer basket, in one layer and add to the cooker.
3. Lock the Tender Crisp lid in place and set the temperature to 375 degrees.
4. Cook for 8 minutes, turning over halfway through
5. Serve immediately or store in an airtight container.

371. Roasted Whole Chicken

Servings: 4
Cooking Time: 60 Minutes
Ingredients:
- ½ cup salt
- 10 cups water
- 2 pounds whole rotisserie chicken
- 1 sprig rosemary
- 1 tablespoon sage

Directions:
1. Dissolve the salt in water to make a brine in a deep bowl or stock pot.
2. Soak the chicken and put in the rosemary and sage.
3. Allow the chicken to marinate in the brine for overnight.
4. Place in the ceramic pot the FoodiTM Cook & CrispTM reversible rack.
5. Place the chicken on the rack.
6. Close the crisping lid and press the Bake/Roast button before pressing the START button.
7. Adjust the cooking time to 1hour.

- **Nutrition Info:** Calories: 406; Carbohydrates: 0.9g; Protein: 34.2g; Fat: 29.5g; Sugar: 0g; Sodium: 899mg

372. Dad's Beef Jerky

Servings: 4
Cooking Time: 12 Hours
Ingredients:
- ½ cup soy sauce
- ¼ cup Worcestershire sauce
- ½ teaspoon liquid seasoning
- 1 teaspoon hot pepper sauce
- 1 teaspoon garlic powder
- 1 teaspoon onion powder
- ½ teaspoon black pepper
- ½ cup brown sugar
- 2 pounds beef sirloin, cut into strips

Directions:
1. Place in the ceramic pot the FoodiTM Cook &CrispTM dehydrating tray.
2. Mix all ingredients in a mixing bowl and allow to marinate in the fridge for at least 2 hours.
3. Place the marinated beef slices on the dehydrating tray.
4. Close the crisping lid and press the Dehydrate button before pressing the START button.
5. Adjust the cooking time to 12 hours.
- **Nutrition Info:** Calories: 216; Carbohydrates: 6.9g; Protein: 34.2g; Fat: 5.7g; Sugar: 2.4g; Sodium: 993mg

373. Lemony Steamed Fish

Servings: 6
Cooking Time: 15 Minutes
Ingredients:
- 6 halibut fillets
- 1 tablespoon dried dill weed
- 1 tablespoon onion powder
- 2 teaspoons dried parsley
- ¼ teaspoon paprika
- A pinch of salt
- 1 pinch lemon pepper
- 1 pinch garlic powder
- 2 tablespoons lemon juice

Directions:
1. Place the FoodiTM Cook &CrispTM reversible rack inside the ceramic pot.
2. Pour water into the pot.
3. Season the halibut fillets with dill weed, onion powder, dried parsley, paprika, salt, pepper, garlic powder, and lemon juice.
4. Place the seasoned fish fillets on the reversible rack.
5. Close the pressure lid and set the vent to SEAL.
6. Press the Steam button and adjust the cooking time to 15 minutes.

- **Nutrition Info:** Calories: 137; Carbohydrates: 1.9g; Protein: 29.7g; Fat: 1.1g; Sugar: 0.2g; Sodium: 184mg

374. Easy Baked Beef & Pasta

Servings: 6 Servings
Cooking Time: 20 Mins
Ingredients:
- 1 ½ pounds ground beef
- 28 ounce can tomatoes, crushed
- 2 cups Mozzarella cheese, grated
- 2 cups Fusilli pasta, cooked
- ½ cup onion, chopped
- ¼ cup Parmesan cheese, grated
- 4 teaspoons garlic, chopped fine
- 2 teaspoons oregano
- ¼ teaspoon red pepper flakes
- fresh parsley for garnish

Directions:
1. Set the cooker to sauté on medium heat. Add ground beef and cook till no longer pink. Stir in onion, garlic, oregano and red pepper flakes. Add salt and pepper to taste.
2. Stir in pasta, tomatoes and half the Mozzarella cheese. Sprinkle the remaining Mozzarella and the Parmesan over the top.
3. Add the Tender Crisp lid and set the temperature to 350 degrees. Bake for 20 minutes, or till heated through and cheese is golden brown. Serve with chopped fresh parsley sprinkled on the top.

375. Amazing Beef Sauerbraten

Servings: 4
Cooking Time: 40 Minutes
Ingredients:
- 2 tablespoons shortening or olive oil
- 2 pounds beef stew meat
- 5 cups water
- 1 cup white vinegar
- 3 bay eaves
- 3 tablespoons cornstarch
- 4 tablespoons all-purpose flour
- Salt and pepper to taste

Directions:
1. Press the Sear/Sauté button and then the START button.
2. Heat the oil and brown the beef stew meat on all sides for at least 3 minutes.
3. Close the pressure lid and set the vent to SEAL.
4. Press the Pressure button and adjust the cooking time to 40 minutes.
5. Do natural pressure release to open the lid.
6. Once the lid is open, press the Sear/Sauté button and stir in the cornstarch slurry.
7. Allow to simmer until the sauce thickens.

- **Nutrition Info:** Calories: 746; Carbohydrates: 3.1g; Protein: 59.2g; Fat: 55.2g; Sugar: 0.5g; Sodium: 150mg

376. Pressure Cooker Red Beans And Sausages

Servings: 4
Cooking Time: 40 Minutes
Ingredients:
- ½ pound smoked sausages, sliced
- 2 cloves of garlic, minced
- 1 stalk celery, chopped
- ½ green bell pepper, chopped
- 1 pound dried red beans, rinsed
- 1 bay leaf
- 2 tablespoons Cajun seasoning
- 1 teaspoon dried parsley
- ¼ teaspoon ground cumin
- 5 cups water
- Salt and pepper to taste

Directions:
1. Season the beef with salt and pepper. Dredge in flour.
2. Press the Sear/Sauté button and then the START button.
3. Place the sausage in the pot and allow fat to render.
4. Sauté the onion and celery until fragrant.
5. Stir in the rest of the ingredients.
6. Close the pressure lid and set the vent to SEAL.
7. Press the Pressure button and adjust the cooking time to 40 minutes.
- **Nutrition Info:** Calories: 298; Carbohydrates: 16g; Protein: 17g; Fat: 18.4g; Sugar: 6.3g; Sodium: 1511mg

377. Tasty Mushroom Ala Bourguignon

Servings: 2
Cooking Time: 10 Minutes
Ingredients:
- 1 teaspoon oil
- 1 onion, chopped
- 3 cloves of garlic, minced
- 2 carrots, cut into thick strips
- 5 cups mushrooms, halved
- 1 cup red wine
- 4 tablespoons tomato paste
- 1 teaspoon dried marjoram
- 1 cup vegetable broth
- 3 teaspoons italian herbs
- Salt and pepper to taste
- 1 tablespoon cornstarch + 2 tablespoons water

Directions:
1. Press the sauté button on the Ninja Foodi and heat the oil. Stir in the onion and garlic until fragrant.
2. Add the carrots and mushrooms and allow to sweat. Stir in the rest of the ingredients except for the cornstarch slurry.
3. Install pressure lid. Close Ninja Foodi, press the manual button, choose high settings, and set time to 5 minutes.
4. Once done cooking, do a quick release.
5. Open the lid and press the sauté button. Stir in the cornstarch slurry and allow to simmer until the sauce thickens.
6. Serve and enjoy.
- **Nutrition Info:** Calories: 171; carbohydrates: 25.1g; protein: 10.2g; fat: 3.3g

378. Baked Beans

Servings: 10 Servings
Cooking Time: 40 Minutes
Ingredients:
- 1 pound dried navy beans, rinsed
- ½ pound bacon, cut into 3-inch pieces
- 2 ½ cups water
- 1 cup onion, chopped
- ½ cup ketchup
- ¼ cup brown sugar
- 2 tablespoons molasses
- 1 teaspoon dry mustard
- ½ teaspoon salt
- ¼ teaspoon pepper

Directions:
1. Add beans to the cooking pot with enough water to cover them completely. Secure the lid and select pressure cooking on high. Cook for 1 minute, then let rest for one hour. Drain and rinse the beans and discard any that are floating.
2. Set the cooker to sauté on med-high heat. Add the bacon and cook till crisp. Transfer the bacon to a paper towel lined plate and set aside.
3. Add the onion and cook till tender, scraping up the brown bits on the bottom of the pot.
4. Add all of the ingredients, except the bacon to the onions and stir to combine. Set the cooker back to pressure cooking on high and cook 35 minutes.
5. When the timer goes off wait 10 minutes, then use quick release to remove the lid. Check to see if the beans are tender, if not cook a few minutes longer.
6. Set the cooker back to sauté on medium heat and stir in the bacon. Cook, stirring often, till sauce thickens to desired consistency. Serve or store in the refrigerator.

379. Vegetarian-approved Meatballs In Bbq Sauce

Servings: 2

Cooking Time: 10 Minutes
Ingredients:
- ¼ cup water
- 1-pound frozen vegan meatballs
- 3/4 cup barbecue sauce
- 1/2 can cranberry sauce
- Salt and pepper to taste

Directions:
1. Place all ingredients in the Ninja Foodi and give a good stir.
2. Install pressure lid. Close Ninja Foodi, press the manual button, choose high settings, and set time to 10 minutes.
3. Once done cooking, do a quick release.
4. Serve and enjoy.
- **Nutrition Info:** Calories: 357; carbohydrates: 68.1g; protein: 17.1g; fat: 1.8g

380. Easy Garlic Broiled Chicken

Servings: 6
Cooking Time: 30 Minutes
Ingredients:
- ½ cup butter
- 3 tablespoons minced garlic
- ¼ teaspoon black pepper
- 1 tablespoon dried parsley
- 6 boneless chicken thighs
- Dried parsley

Directions:
1. Place in the ceramic pot the FoodiTM Cook &CrispTM reversible tray.
2. Place all ingredients in a Ziploc bag and allow to marinate in the fridge for at least 3 hours.
3. Close the crisping lid and press the Broil button before pressing the START button.
4. Adjust the cooking time to 30 minutes.
- **Nutrition Info:** Calories: 284; Carbohydrates: 2.3g; Protein: 16.8g; Fat: 23g; Sugar: 0.7g; Sodium: 615mg

381. Makhanidaal (butterfly Lentils)

Servings: 5
Cooking Time: 43 Minutes
Ingredients:
- 2 teaspoons vegetable oil
- 1 onion, finely chopped
- 2 cloves of garlic, minced
- 1 teaspoon cumin seeds
- 2 teaspoons ground coriander
- 1 teaspoon garam masala
- ½ teaspoon chili powder
- ½ teaspoon ground turmeric
- 2 tomatoes, chopped
- 1 cup dry black lentils, soaked overnight
- ¼ cup split chickpeas, soaked overnight
- ¼ cup red kidney beans, soaked overnight
- 3 cups water
- Salt and pepper to taste
- 2 teaspoons butter
- 2 teaspoons yogurt

Directions:
1. Press the Sear/Sauté button and then the START button.
2. Heat the oil and sauté the onion and garlic until fragrant.
3. Stir in the cumin, coriander, garam masala, chili powder, and turmeric. Stir for 2 minutes until lightly toasted.
4. Stir in the tomatoes. Add the beans and water. Season with salt and pepper to taste.
5. Close the pressure lid and set the vent to SEAL.
6. Press the Pressure button and adjust the cooking time to 40 minutes.
7. Do quick pressure release. Once open, stir in butter and yogurt before serving.
- **Nutrition Info:** Calories: 341; Carbohydrates: 51.7g; Protein: 19g; Fat: 6.4g; Sugar: 10.8g; Sodium: 71mg

382. Luncheon Green Beans

Servings: 4
Cooking Time: 15 Minutes
Ingredients:
- 1 lb. fresh green beans
- 2 tbsps. butter
- 1 minced garlic clove
- Salt and freshly ground black pepper
- 1½ c. water

Directions:
1. Put all the ingredients in the pot of Ninja Foodi and lock the lid.
2. Press "Pressure" and cook for about 5 minutes.
3. Release the pressure quickly and dish out to serve hot.
- **Nutrition Info:** 87 calories, 5.9g fat, 8.4g carbs, 2.2g protein

383. Bacon Cheeseburger Dip

Servings: 8 Servings
Cooking Time: 30 Mins
Ingredients:
- 1 pound ground beef
- 1 package cream cheese, soft
- 2 cups cheddar cheese, grated
- 10 ounce can of Rotel tomatoes with green chilies
- 1 cup sour cream
- 2/3 cup bacon, cooked crisp and crumbled

Directions:
1. Set the cooker to the sauté function on med-high. Add ground beef and cook through, breaking it up while cooking. Drain the fat.

2. Combine remaining ingredients in a large bowl and mix till well combined. Stir in ground beef.
3. Pour into a baking dish that will fit inside the cooking pot. Add the Tender Crisp lid and lock into place.
4. Set the temperature to 350 degrees. Bake for 20 – 25 minutes or hot and bubbly.
5. Serve with your favorite chips or crackers for dipping.

384. Breakfast Oats With Apricots 'n Nuts

Servings: 2
Cooking Time: 6 Minutes
Ingredients:
- 1 ½ cups water
- 1 cup chopped strawberries, for topping
- 1 cup freshly squeezed orange juice
- 1 cup steel cut oats
- 1 tbsp chopped dried apricots
- 1 tbsp dried cranberries
- 1 tbsp raisins
- 1/4 tsp ground cinnamon
- 1/8 tsp salt
- 2 tbsp butter
- 2 tbsp pure maple syrup
- 3 tbsp chopped pecans, for topping

Directions:
1. Lightly grease Ninja Foodi insert with cooking spray and then add all ingredients except for pecans. Mix well.
2. Install pressure lid.
3. Close Ninja Foodi, press pressure button, choose high settings, and set time to 6 minutes.
4. Once done cooking, do a quick release.
5. Transfer to two bowl and evenly divide toppings on bowl.
6. Serve and enjoy.
- **Nutrition Info:** Calories: 507; carbohydrates: 72.4g; protein: 11.1g; fat: 19.2g

385. Cauliflower Mash

Servings: 6
Cooking Time: 15 Minutes
Ingredients:
- 1 tbsp. softened butter
- ½ c. feta cheese
- Salt and black pepper
- 1 large head cauliflower, chopped
- 1 minced garlic clove
- 2 tsps. freshly minced chives

Directions:
1. Arrange the basket in the bottom of Ninja Foodi and add water.
2. Place the cauliflower pieces on top of the basket and lock the lid.
3. Press "Pressure" and cook for about 5 minutes.
4. Release the pressure quickly and dish out in a bowl.
5. Transfer the cauliflower in an immersion hand blender along with rest of the ingredients.
6. Blend until desired texture is achieved and dish out to serve.
- **Nutrition Info:** 124 calories, 9.3g fat, 6.1g carbs, 5.4g protein

386. Air Fried Zucchini Chips

Servings: 3
Cooking Time: 15 Minutes
Ingredients:
- 1 cup panko bread crumbs
- ¾ cup grated Parmesan cheese
- 1 medium zucchini, sliced thinly
- 1 large egg, beaten

Directions:
1. Place in the ceramic pot the FoodiTM Cook &CrispTM basket.
2. Mix the panko bread crumbs and parmesan cheese. Set aside.
3. Dip the zucchini in egg before dredging in the panko mixture.
4. Place the dredged zucchini in the basket.
5. Close the crisping lid and press the Air Crisp button before pressing the START button.
6. Adjust the cooking time to 15 minutes.
- **Nutrition Info:** Calories: 187; Carbohydrates: 21.1g; Protein: 10.8g; Fat: 6.6g; Sugar: 4.9g; Sodium: 384mg

387. Homemade Sweet Yogurt

Servings: 8
Cooking Time: 30 Minutes
Ingredients:
- 16 C. whole milk
- 2 tbsp. plain yogurt with active live cultures
- ½ C. honey
- 1 tbsp. vanilla extract

Directions:
1. In the pot of Ninja Foodi, place the milk.
2. Cover the Ninja Foodi with the pressure lid and place the pressure valve to "Seal" position.
3. Select "Sauté/Sear" setting of Ninja Foodi and set to "Medium".
4. Press "Start/Stop" to begin and cook for about 30 minutes, stirring frequently.
5. Press "Start/Stop" to stop the cooking.
6. Let the milk to cool to 110 degrees F, astirring frequently.
7. With a slotted spoon, gently skim off the fat from the top surface.
8. Add the yogurt and beat until well combined.

9. Cover the Ninja Foodi with the pressure lid and place the pressure valve to "Seal" position for 8 hours.
10. Open the lid and transfer the yogurt into a glass container.
11. Refrigerate to chill for about 4 hours.
12. Add the honey and vanilla extract and stir until well combined.
13. Refrigerate, covered before serving.
- **Nutrition Info:** Calories per serving: 365; Carbohydrates: 40g; Protein: 16g; Fat: 15.9g; Sugar: 43.6g; Sodium: 199mg; Fiber: 0g

388. Chinese Style Steamed Fish

Servings: 3
Cooking Time: 25 Minutes
Ingredients:
- 1 ½ pounds halibut, cut into 4 pieces
- 3 green onions, chopped
- 2 fresh mushrooms, sliced
- 6 leaves napa cabbage, slice
- 2 slices fresh ginger root, chopped
- 2 clove of garlic, chopped
- ¼ cup soy sauce
- 1/8 cup water
- ¼ cup crushed red pepper flakes
- ½ cup fresh cilantro sprigs for garnish

Directions:
1. Place the FoodiTM Cook &CrispTM reversible rack inside the ceramic pot.
2. Pour water into the pot.
3. In a big aluminum foil, place the halibut and arrange the rest of the ingredients on top of the halibuts.
4. Fold the aluminum foil and crimp the edges.
5. Place on the reversible rack.
6. Close the pressure lid and set the vent to SEAL.
7. Press the Steam button and adjust the cooking time to 25 minutes.
- **Nutrition Info:** Calories: 210; Carbohydrates: 5.2g; Protein: 37.7g; Fat: 4.2g; Sugar: 2.1g; Sodium: 636mg

389. Vanilla-espresso Flavored Oats

Servings: 2
Cooking Time: 20 Minutes
Ingredients:
- 1/2 cup milk
- 1/2 cup steel cut oats
- 1 teaspoon espresso powder
- 1/4 teaspoon salt
- 1 1/4 cups water
- 1 tablespoon sugar
- 1 teaspoon vanilla extract
- Finely grated chocolate

Directions:
1. Mix well salt, espresso powder, sugar, oats, milk, and water in Ninja Foodi.
2. Install pressure lid and place valve to vent position.
3. Close Ninja Foodi, press steam button, and set time to 2 minutes.
4. Once done cooking, do a natural release for 10-minutes and then do a quick release.
5. Uncover pot and stir in vanilla extract. Spoon into bowls.
6. Garnish with grated chocolate.
7. Serve and enjoy.
- **Nutrition Info:** Calories: 198; carbohydrates: 27.6g; protein: 6.5g; fat: 6.8g

390. Cheesy Artichoke & Crab Dip

Servings: 4 Cups
Cooking Time: 30 Minutes
Ingredients:
- 1 pound lump crab meat
- 14 ounce can artichoke hearts, drained
- ¾ cups cheddar cheese, grated
- 1/3 cup Parmesan cheese
- 6 tablespoons sour cream
- 6 tablespoons mayonnaise
- 2 tablespoons chives, chopped
- 1-2 teaspoons hot sauce
- 1 teaspoon lemon juice

Directions:
1. Chop the artichokes and crab and place them in a mixing bowl. Add the remaining ingredients and mix till combined. Transfer to a baking dish that will fit inside the cooking pot.
2. Add the Tender Crisp lid and lock into place. Set the temperature for 400 degrees and bake 30 minutes or till cheese is melted and top is golden brown.
3. Serve with your favorite chips, crackers or toasted bread

391. Dehydrated Beet Chips

Servings: 5
Cooking Time: 8 Hours
Ingredients:
- 3 large beets, peeled and sliced
- ¼ cup water
- ¼ cup apple cider vinegar
- 1 tablespoon olive oil
- A dash of salt flakes

Directions:
1. Place in the ceramic pot the FoodiTM Cook & CrispTM dehydrating tray.
2. Soak the beets in water and apple cider vinegar.
3. Let it sit for a few hours in the fridge.
4. Drain the beets and pat dry using a paper towel.
5. Season the beets with oil and salt flakes.

6. Close the crisping lid and press the Dehydrate button before pressing the START button.
7. Adjust the cooking time to 8 hours.
- **Nutrition Info:** Calories: 117; Carbohydrates: 17.9g; Protein: 3g; Fat: 3.7g; Sugar: 2.4g; Sodium: 14466mg

392. Crispy Fried Green Tomatoes

Servings: 2
Cooking Time: 7 Minutes
Ingredients:
- 1 cup panko bread crumbs
- 6 tablespoons cornstarch
- 1 teaspoon dried basil, ground
- 1 teaspoon dried oregano, ground
- 1 teaspoon granulated onion
- Salt and pepper to taste
- 2 medium-sized green tomato, sliced
- 1 teaspoon cooking oil

Directions:
1. In a mixing bowl, combine the panko bread crumbs, cornstarch, basil, oregano, onion, salt and pepper.
2. Dredge the tomato slices in the bread crumb mixture.
3. Brush with oil and arrange on the Cook & Crisp basket.
4. Place the Cook & Crisp basket in the Ninja Foodi.
5. Close the lid and cook for 7 minutes at 330 ºF.
- **Nutrition Info:** Calories: 269; carbs: 54.1g; protein: 5.4g; fat: 3.4g

393. Simple Roasted Veggie Stock

Servings: 1 Quart
Cooking Time: 110 Minutes
Ingredients:
- 1 quartered onion
- 2 large carrots, peeled and chopped
- 1 tbsp. vegetable oil
- 12 oz. sliced mushroom
- ¼ tsp. salt
- 3½ c. water

Directions:
1. Take cook and crisp basket out of the inner pot, close crisping lid and let it pre-heat for 3 minutes at 400 degrees F on Bake/Roast settings
2. While the pot heats up, add onion, carrot chunks in the Cook and Crisp basket and drizzle vegetable oil, toss well
3. Place basket back into the inner pot, close crisping lid and cook for 15 minutes at 400 degrees F on Bake/Roast mode
4. Make sure to shake the basket halfway through
5. Remove basket from pot and add onions, carrots, mushrooms, water and season with salt
6. Lock pressure lid and seal the valves, cook on HIGH pressure for 60 minutes
7. Release the pressure naturally over 10 minutes
8. Line a cheesecloth on a colander and place it over a large bowl, pour vegetables and stock into the colander
9. Strain the stock and discard veggies
10. Enjoy and use as needed!
- **Nutrition Info:** 45 calories, 4g fat, 3g carbs, 0g protein

394. Seafood Casserole

Servings: 6 Servings
Cooking Time: 15 Mins
Ingredients:
- 1 pound large shrimp, peeled and deveined
- 1 ½ cups ziti, cooked
- 1 cup lump crab meat
- 1 can chicken broth
- 1 cup sour cream
- ¾ cup Colby jack cheese, grated
- 1/3 cup sweet onion, chopped
- ¼ cup jalapenos, seeded and chopped
- ¼ cup flour
- 2 tablespoons butter
- 2 tablespoons sherry
- 2 cloves garlic, chopped fine
- ½ teaspoon Old Bay seasoning
- ¼ teaspoon white pepper
- Chopped cilantro for garnish

Directions:
1. Sprinkle the shrimp with the Old Bay seasoning and toss to coat.
2. Add butter to the cooking pot and set to sauté on med-low heat. When the butter melts, add onion, garlic and jalapenos and cook till tender, stirring often.
3. Add the seafood, sherry and broth and cook till shrimp are pink.
4. In a mixing bowl, whisk together the sour cream, pepper and flour. Add to seafood mixture and stir well. Reduce heat to low and cook till thickened.
5. Stir in the pasta then top with the cheese. Add the Tender Crisp lid and set the temperature to 350 degrees. Bake 10 – 15 minutes till heated through and cheese it bubbly and starts to brown. Serve garnished with chopped cilantro.

395. Tasty Asparagus Fries

Servings: 6
Cooking Time: 10 Minutes
Ingredients:
- 1 large egg

- 1 teaspoon honey
- 1 cup panko bread crumbs
- ½ cup grated parmesan cheese
- 12 asparagus spears, cleaned and trimmed
- ¼ cup stone-ground mustard
- ¼ cup Greek yogurt
- A pinch of cayenne pepper

Directions:
1. Place in the ceramic pot the FoodiTM Cook &CrispTM basket.
2. Mix in a bowl the egg and honey. Whisk until well combined. Set aside.
3. In another bowl, combine the bread crumbs and parmesan cheese. Set aside.
4. Dip the asparagus spears in the egg mixture before dredging in the breadcrumbs.
5. Place in the basket.
6. Close the crisping lid and press the Air Crisp button before pressing the START button.
7. Adjust the cooking time to 10 minutes.
8. While the spears are cooking, combine the mustard, yogurt and cayenne pepper. This will be the dipping sauce.
9. Serve the asparagus with the dipping sauce.
- **Nutrition Info:** Calories: 140; Carbohydrates: 18g; Protein: 7.5g; Fat: 4.2g; Sugar: 2.4g; Sodium: 356mg

396. Low-carb Zucchini Chips

Servings: 4
Cooking Time: 12 Hours
Ingredients:
- 2 large zucchinis, thinly sliced
- 1 tablespoon olive oil
- Salt to taste

Directions:
1. Place in the ceramic pot the FoodiTM Cook & CrispTM dehydrating tray.
2. Season the zucchini with olive oil, salt and taste.
3. Place the zucchini on the dehydrating tray.
4. Close the crisping lid and press the Dehydrate button before pressing the START button.
5. Adjust the cooking time to 12 hours.
- **Nutrition Info:** Calories: 130; Carbohydrates: 10.8g; Protein: 3.9g; Fat: 7.9g; Sugar: 0.2g; Sodium: 192mg On

397. Mexican Beef And Vegetable Stew

Servings: 6
Cooking Time: 30 Minutes
Ingredients:
- 3 tablespoons vegetable oil
- ½ onion, chopped
- 2 cloves of garlic, minced
- 2 pounds beef chuck roast, cut into chunks
- ½ teaspoon paprika
- ½ teaspoon salt
- ¼ teaspoon pepper
- ¼ teaspoon cumin
- ¼ teaspoon dried Mexican oregano
- 2 cans Hunts Diced Tomatoes
- 1 quart beef broth
- 2 bay leaves
- ½ teaspoon crushed red pepper flakes
- 3 large potatoes, peeled and quartered
- 2 carrots, peeled and sliced
- 2 cups frozen corn

Directions:
1. Place the ceramic pot in the Ninja Foodi base and press the Sear/Sauté button. Press the START button.
2. Heat the oil and sauté the onions and garlic until fragrant. Stir in the beef chuck roast and continue stirring for 3 minutes. Season with paprika, salt, pepper, cumin, and oregano. Add in the tomatoes and the rest of the ingredients.
3. Place the pressure lid and make sure that the vent is set to the SEAL position. Press the Pressure button. Cook for 30 minutes.
- **Nutrition Info:** Calories: 419; Carbohydrates: 25.3g; Protein: 28.6g; Fat: 22.5g; Sugar: 6.4g; Sodium: 1238mg

398. The Easy Watermelon Jerky

Servings: 1 Cup
Cooking Time: 12 Hours 10 Minutes
Ingredients:
- 1 c. seedless watermelon, cubed

Directions:
1. Arrange watermelon cubes in single layer in the Cook and Crisp basket
2. Place the basket in the pot and close the crisping lid
3. Press the Dehydrate button and let it dehydrate for 12 hours at 135 degrees F
4. Once the dehydrating is done, remove the basket from pot and transfer jerky to your Air Tight container, serve and enjoy!
- **Nutrition Info:** 46 calories, 0g fat, 12g carbs, 1g protein

399. Cheesy Mozzarella Sticks

Servings: 1
Cooking Time: 15 Minutes
Ingredients:
- ½ cup water
- ¼ cup all-purpose flour
- 5 tablespoons cornstarch
- 1 tablespoon cornmeal
- 1 teaspoon garlic salt
- ½ teaspoon salt
- 1 cup panko bread crumbs
- 1 tablespoon Italian seasoning blend
- 5 ounce mozzarella cheese, cut into strips
- 1 tablespoon all-purpose flour

- Cooking spray

Directions:
1. Place in the ceramic pot the FoodiTM Cook &CrispTM basket.
2. In a mixing bowl, combine the water, ¼ cup all-purpose flour, cornstarch, cornmeal, garlic salt, and salt. Mix until well-blended. Set aside.
3. In another bowl, mix the bread crumbs and Italian seasoning mix. Set aside.
4. Dust the mozzarella cheese with 1 tablespoon all-purpose flour.
5. Dip the dusted mozzarella cheese in the egg mixture before dredging in the flour mixture.
6. Place gently inside the basket.
7. Close the crisping lid and press the Air Crisp button before pressing the START button.
8. Adjust the cooking time to 15 minutes.
9. Halfway through the cooking time, open the lid and give the basket a shake.

- **Nutrition Info:** Calories: 270; Carbohydrates: 39.2g; Protein: 12.9g; Fat: 6.8g; Sugar: 13.7g; Sodium: 936mg

400. Southwest Chicken Egg Rolls

Servings: 6 Pieces
Cooking Time: 20 Minutes
Ingredients:
- 6 egg roll wrappers
- 1 cup Mexican blend cheese, grated
- ½ cup chicken, cooked and shredded
- ½ cup red onion, chopped fine
- ½ cup bell pepper, chopped fine
- ½ cup fire roasted tomatoes, drained
- ½ avocado, chopped fine
- 1 teaspoon chili powder
- 1 teaspoon olive oil
- Water

Directions:
1. Set cooker to saute setting on med-high heat. Add olive oil and red onion. Cook, stirring frequently till onion becomes translucent.
2. Add bell peppers and cook 2-3 minutes. Add tomatoes and cook an additional 2-3 minutes, stirring frequently.
3. Transfer vegetables to a bowl and mix in the remaining ingredients till blended.
4. Place wrappers on a work surface. Place about 2 tablespoons of filling near one corner. Fold the corner closest to the filling over it. Fold both side corners toward the center and roll it up. Seal with water. Lightly spray the rolls with cooking spray on both sides.
5. Wipe out the cooker. Lightly spray the rack with cooking spray and place it into the pot. Place egg rolls on the rack and lock the Tender Crisp lid in place.
6. Set the temperature for 375 degrees and cook egg rolls for 8 minutes. Flip them over and cook another 8 minutes or till golden brown.

401. Chicken Poblano

Servings: 4 Servings
Cooking Time: 3 Hours
Ingredients:
- 1 package chicken thighs, boneless and skinless
- 3 Poblano chilies, seeded and sliced thin
- 1 cup onions, sliced thin
- ½ cup heavy whipping cream
- 3 cloves garlic, chopped fine
- 3 tablespoons taco seasoning
- 2 tablespoons olive oil
- ½ teaspoon salt
- ¼ teaspoon ground black pepper

Directions:
1. Set the cooker to sauté on med-high heat. Add 1 tablespoon of the oil and heat. Add chilies, onions and garlic and cook, stirring often, 6 -7 minutes, till tender crisp. Remove and set aside.
2. Heat the remaining oil and add chicken. Cook 4 -5 minutes, till browned on the outside.
3. Select slow cooker function on low heat. Add the onion mix to the chicken along with the seasoning, salt and pepper. Stir to combine.
4. Secure the lid and cook 2-3 hours, or chicken is cooked through. Stir in the cream and cook another 15 minutes. Stir before serving.

402. Creamy Braised Oxtails

Servings: 6 Servings
Cooking Time: 1 Hour 5 Mins
Ingredients:
- 2 pounds oxtails
- 1 onion, chopped
- 1 cup beef broth
- ½ cup heavy cream
- ¼ cup sake
- 4 cloves garlic, chopped
- 2 tablespoons chili bean sauce
- 1 teaspoon Chinese five spice
- 1 teaspoon bacon fat, or butter
- Salt and pepper

Directions:
1. Set the cooker to sauté on medium heat and add bacon fat.
2. Sprinkle the oxtails with salt and pepper and brown on all sides, about 3-5 minutes each sides.

3. Add onion and garlic and continue cooking another 3-5 minutes. Add the sake to deglaze the pot and cook 1-2 minute to reduce the liquid.
4. Add the broth, chili bean sauce and five spice. Secure the lid and select the pressure cooking setting on high. Set the timer for 60 minutes. When the timer goes off, use the quick release to remove the lid.
5. Put it back on the sauté setting on low heat and bring the oxtails to a simmer. Add the cream and simmer about 5 minutes or till the sauce has thickened. Serve.

403. Light Luncheon Meal

Servings: 4
Cooking Time: 12 Minutes
Ingredients:
- 1 lb. green beans, washed and trimmed
- 1 tsp. butter, melted
- 1 tbsp. fresh lemon juice
- ¼ tsp. garlic powder
- Salt and freshly ground black pepper, to taste

Directions:
1. In a large bowl, add all ingredients and toss to coat well.
2. Arrange the "Cook & Crisp Basket" in the pot of Ninja Foodi.
3. Close the Ninja Foodi with crisping lid and select "Air Crisp".
4. Press "Start/Stop" to begin and set the temperature to 400 degrees F.
5. Set the time for 5 minutes to preheat.
6. Now, place the green beans mixture into "Cook & Crisp Basket".
7. Close the Ninja Foodi with crisping lid and select "Air Crisp".
8. Set the temperature to 400 degrees F for 12 minutes.
9. Press "Start/Stop" to begin.
10. Open the lid and serve warm.
- **Nutrition Info:** Calories: 45; Carbohydrates: 8.3g; Protein: 2.1g; Fat: 1.1g; Sugar: 1.7g; Sodium: 53mg; Fiber: 3.9g

404. Pressure Cooker Lamb Stew

Servings: 6
Cooking Time: 75 Minutes
Ingredients:
- 2 tablespoons olive oil
- 2 cloves of garlic, minced
- 2 ½ pounds lamb, cut into cubes
- 1 tablespoon dried marjoram
- 1 tablespoon dried parsley
- 1 teaspoon dried chives
- 1 tablespoon all spice powder
- 2 cups water
- 1 bay leaf
- 16 baby carrots
- 8 potatoes, cut into chunks
- Salt and pepper to taste

Directions:
1. Press the Sear/Sauté button and then the START button.
2. Heat the oil and sauté the garlic until fragrant.
3. Add in the lamb and stir in the marjoram, parsley, chives, and all spice. Season with salt and pepper to taste.
4. Stir in the rest of the ingredients.
5. Close the pressure lid and set the vent to SEAL.
6. Press the Pressure button and adjust the cooking time to 75 minutes.
- **Nutrition Info:** Calories: 480; Carbohydrates: 29.8g; Protein: 32.7g; Fat: 25.5g; Sugar: 5.8g; Sodium: 644mg

405. Flavorsome Baked Bananas

Servings: 4
Cooking Time: 10 Minutes
Ingredients:
- 4 firm bananas, peeled and halved
- ¼ cup maple syrup
- 1 tablespoons ground cinnamon
- 1 piece fresh ginger, grated
- 1 ½ teaspoon nutmeg

Directions:
1. Place in the ceramic pot the FoodiTM Cook &CrispTM reversible rack.
2. In a bowl, season the bananas with maple syrup, ground cinnamon, ginger, and nutmeg.
3. Place the bananas on the rack.
4. Close the crisping lid and press the Bake/Roast button before pressing the START button. Adjust the cooking time to 10 minutes.
- **Nutrition Info:** Calories: 183; Carbohydrates: 42.2g; Protein:1.4 g; Fat: 0.9g; Sugar: 24.7g; Sodium: 3mg

406. Salsa Verde Slow Cooker Dip

Servings: 8 – 10 Servings
Cooking Time: 2 Hours
Ingredients:
- ½ cup salsa verde
- ½ cup green chilies, diced
- ½ package cream cheese, soft
- ½ cup white American cheese, cubed
- ½ cup white cheddar cheese, cubed
- ½ cup pepper Jack cheese, cubed
- ¼ cup milk

Directions:
1. Combine all ingredients in mixing bowl and mix till combined.

2. Pour into a small baking dish that will fit inside the cooker.
3. Lock the lid in place and select slow cooker function on high. Set the timer for 2 hours, but stir the dip every 30 minutes. Cook till all the cheese is completely melted.

407. Crispy Fried Crumbed Fish

Servings: 4
Cooking Time: 20 Minutes
Ingredients:
- 4 flounder fillets
- 1 egg, beaten
- 1 cup dry bread crumbs
- ¼ cup vegetable oil
- 1 lemon, sliced
- Salt and pepper

Directions:
1. Place in the ceramic pot the FoodiTM Cook &CrispTM basket.
2. Season the flounder fillet with salt and pepper.
3. Dip in egg and dredge in flour.
4. Carefully place in the basket and brush generously with oil.
5. Close the crisping lid and press the Air Crisp button before pressing the START button.
6. Adjust the cooking time to 20 minutes.
7. Serve with sliced lemons.
- **Nutrition Info:** Calories: 357; Carbohydrates: 22.5g; Protein: 26.9g; Fat: 17.7g; Sugar: 4.2g; Sodium: 309mg

408. Spanish Rice Pudding

Servings: 10
Cooking Time: 7 Minutes
Ingredients:
- 6½ C. cold whole milk, divided
- 2 C. long grain white rice
- ½ C. granulated sugar
- 3 cinnamon sticks
- 10½-oz. sweetened condensed milk

Directions:
1. In the pot of Ninja Foodi, place 6 C. of milk, rice sugar and cinnamon sticks and stir to combine.
2. Cover the Ninja Foodi with the pressure lid and place the pressure valve to "Seal" position.
3. Select "Pressure" and set to "High" for about 2 minutes.
4. Press "Start/Stop" to begin.
5. Switch the valve to "Vent" and do a "Natural" release for about 10 minutes. Then do a "Quick" release.
6. Once all the pressure is released, open the lid.
7. Select "Sauté/Sear" setting of Ninja Foodi and stir in the condensed milk.
8. Press "Start/Stop" to begin and cook for about 5 minutes, stirring frequently.
9. Press "Start/Stop" to stop the cooking and stir in the remaining milk.
10. Set the pot aside to cool for about 15 minutes.
11. Serve warm.
- **Nutrition Info:** Calories per serving: 363; Carbohydrates: 62.9g; Protein: 10.1g; Fat: 8g; Sugar: 34.6g; Sodium: 103mg; Fiber: 0.5g

409. Braised Artichokes

Servings: 6 Servings
Cooking Time: 29 Minutes
Ingredients:
- 6 large artichokes, stems peeled, outer leaves removed and halved
- 2 lemons, quartered
- 4-6 cloves garlic, crushed
- 4 thyme sprigs
- ½ cup extra-virgin olive oil
- Salt and freshly ground pepper, to taste

Directions:
1. Fill a large bowl with cold water and squeeze the juice from the quarters of one lemon into it. As you are prepping the artichokes, drop them in the bowl to prevent discoloration. Make sure to remove the furry choke and cut 1 inch off the top. Just before cooking, drain the artichokes and pat dry with paper towels.
2. Set cooker to sauté on med-high heat. Add the oil. Sprinkle the cut sides of the artichokes with salt and pepper. Working in batches, lay them cut side down in the pot and cook till browned, about 6 – 10 minutes.
3. Place all of the artichokes back in the pot along with remaining ingrediets. Secure the lid and select pressure cooking on high. Set the timer for 9 minutes. When the timer goes off, use quick release to remove the lid.
4. Transfer the artichokes to a serving bowl and squeeze the juice of the cooked lemons over them. Serve.

410. Savory Roasted Vegetables

Servings: 16
Cooking Time: 20 Minutes
Ingredients:
- 8 zucchinis, peeled and chopped
- 1 eggplant, diced
- 8 carrots, peeled and diced
- 16 cherry tomatoes, halved
- 2 red onions, sliced
- 1 red bell pepper, sliced
- 1 yellow bell pepper, sliced
- ½ cup olive oil
- 1 teaspoon dried rosemary

- 1 teaspoon dried thyme
- 2 bay leaves, crushed
- 1 teaspoon dried oregano
- 2 cloves of garlic, minced
- 2 tablespoons fresh lemon juice
- 1 teaspoon grated lemon zest
- Salt and pepper to taste

Directions:
1. Place in the ceramic pot the FoodiTM Cook &CrispTM basket insert.
2. Toss all ingredients in a mixing bowl.
3. Place in the basket insert.
4. Close the crisping lid and press the Bake/Roast button before pressing the START button.
5. Adjust the cooking time to 20 minutes.
6. Give the basket a shake to evenly roast the vegetables.
- **Nutrition Info:** Calories: 78; Carbohydrates: 7.3g; Protein: 1.5g; Fat:4.7 g; Sugar: 0.6g; Sodium: 11mg

411. Buffalo Air Fried Chicken

Servings:2
Cooking Time: 30 Minutes
Ingredients:
- ½ cup plain fat-free Greek yogurt
- 1 egg, beaten
- 1 tablespoon hot sauce
- 1 cup panko bread crumbs
- 1 tablespoon paprika
- 1 tablespoon garlic pepper seasoning
- 1 tablespoon cayenne pepper
- 1 pound skinless chicken breasts, cut into strips

Directions:
1. Place the FoodiTM Cook &CrispTM basket in the ceramic pot.
2. In a bowl, combine together the yogurt, eggs, and hot sauce. Set aside.
3. Mix the bread crumbs, paprika, garlic pepper seasoning, and cayenne pepper. Set aside.
4. Dip the chicken in the egg mixture before dredging in the breadcrumb mixture.
5. Place the chicken pieces in the basket.
6. Close the crisping lid and press the Air Crisp button before pressing the START button.
7. Adjust the cooking time to 30 minutes.
8. Open the lid halfway through the cooking time to flip the chicken for even cooking.
- **Nutrition Info:** Calories: 255; Carbohydrates: 22.1g; Protein: 31.2g; Fat: 4.6g; Sugar: 6.9g; Sodium: 696mg

412. Vegetable Masala Indian Style

Servings: 2
Cooking Time: 25 Minutes
Ingredients:
- 1 tablespoon olive oil
- 3 black whole peppercorns
- 2 green cardamoms
- 2 whole cloves
- 1 bay leave
- 1/4 cup tomato puree
- 1 teaspoon coriander powder
- 1/2 teaspoon garam masala
- ¼ teaspoon red chili powder
- 1/4 teaspoon turmeric powder
- 1/4 cup water
- 1/2 cup coconut milk
- ½ teaspoon sugar
- 1 small potato, peeled and chopped
- Salt and pepper to taste
- ¼ lemon, juiced
- 1 tablespoon chopped cilantro

Directions:
1. Press the sauté button on the Ninja Foodi and heat the oil.
2. Stir in the whole peppercorns, cardamoms, cloves, and bay leaf until fragrant.
3. Add in the tomato puree, coriander powder, garam masala, chili powder, and turmeric powder.
4. Stir in water, coconut milk, sugar and potatoes. Season with salt and pepper to taste.
5. Install pressure lid. Close Ninja Foodi, press the button, choose high settings, and set time to 20 minutes. Once done cooking, do a quick release.
6. Open the lid and stir in the lemon juice and cilantro. Serve and enjoy.
- **Nutrition Info:** Calories: 261; carbohydrates: 14g; protein: 4g; fat: 21g

413. Delicate Stuffed Tomatoes

Servings: 2
Cooking Time: 15 Minutes
Ingredients:
- 2 large tomatoes
- ½ C. broccoli, chopped finely
- ½ C. cheddar cheese, shredded
- 1 tbsp. unsalted butter, melted
- ½ tsp. dried thyme, crushed

Directions:
1. Carefully, cut the top of each tomato and scoop out pulp and seeds.
2. In a bowl, mix together chopped broccoli and cheese.
3. Stuff each tomato with broccoli mixture evenly.
4. Arrange the "Cook & Crisp Basket" in the pot of Ninja Foodi.
5. Close the Ninja Foodi with crisping lid and select "Air Crisp".
6. Press "Start/Stop" to begin and set the temperature to 355 degrees F.

7. Set the time for 5 minutes to preheat.
8. Now, place the stuffed tomatoes into "Cook & Crisp Basket" and drizzle with the butter.
9. Close the Ninja Foodi with crisping lid and select "Air Crisp".
10. Set the temperature to 355 degrees F for 15 minutes.
11. Press "Start/Stop" to begin.
12. Open the lid and serve with the garnishing of thyme.
- **Nutrition Info:** Calories: 206; Carbohydrates: 9.1g; Protein: 9.4g; Fat: 15.6g; Sugar: 5.3g; Sodium: 233mg; Fiber: 2.9g

414. Chipotle Chicken Bowls

Servings: 4 Servings
Cooking Time: 6 Minutes
Ingredients:
- 1 pound chicken, boneless, skinless and cut into bite sized pieces
- 4 cups tomatoes, diced in juice
- 1 can black beans, drain and rinse
- 1 small onion, chopped
- 1 cup jasmine rice, uncooked
- ½ cup water
- ½ lime, juiced
- 2 tablespoons butter
- 1 tablespoon chipotle peppers in adobo, pureed
- 2 teaspoons salt
- ½ teaspoon black pepper

Directions:
1. Place all ingredients, except the beans, into the cooking pot. Stir to combine.
2. Secure the lid and select pressure cooking on high. Set timer for 6 minutes. When the timer goes off, use quick release to remove the lid.
3. Stir in the beans and serve.

415. Easy Foiled Baked Salmon

Servings: 2
Cooking Time: 20 Minutes
Ingredients:
- 2 salmon fillets
- 2 cloves of garlic, minced
- 6 tablespoons olive oil
- 1 teaspoon dried basil
- 1 teaspoon salt
- 1 teaspoon ground black pepper
- 1 tablespoon lemon juice
- 1 tablespoon fresh parsley, chopped

Directions:
1. Place in the ceramic pot the FoodiTM Cook &CrispTM reversible rack.
2. On a large foil, place the salmon fillets and season with the rest of the ingredients.
3. Do not fold the aluminum foil.
4. Place the foil - fish and all - on the reversible tray.
5. Close the crisping lid and press the Bake/Roast button before pressing the START button.
6. Adjust the cooking time to 20 minutes or until the fish is flaky.
- **Nutrition Info:** Calories: 619; Carbohydrates: 2.9g; Protein: 36.3g; Fat: 51.3g; Sugar: 0.3g; Sodium: 1235mg

416. Capers 'n Olives On Red Sauce Pasta

Servings: 2
Cooking Time: 7 Minutes
Ingredients:
- 2 cloves garlic minced
- 2 cups pasta sauce
- 1 ½ cups water
- 1 1/2 cups pasta such as penne or fusilli
- 1/4 teaspoon crushed red pepper flakes
- 1 tablespoon capers
- 1/4 cup kalamata olives sliced
- Salt to taste
- Pepper to taste

Directions:
1. Press sauté and add a splash of water. Add garlic and sauté for 30 seconds. Press stop.
2. Stir in olives, capers, crushed red pepper flakes, pasta, water, and pasta sauce. Mix well.
3. Install pressure lid. Close Ninja Foodi, press pressure button, choose high settings, and set time to 5 minutes.
4. Once done cooking, do a quick release.
5. Mix well and adjust seasoning to taste
6. Serve and enjoy.
- **Nutrition Info:** Calories: 450; carbohydrates: 85.9g; protein: 10.0g; fat: 7.3g

417. Juicy Corned Beef

Servings: 4
Cooking Time: 15 Minutes
Ingredients:
- 1 can corned beef
- ¼ green bell pepper, chopped
- ¼ onion, chopped
- 1 teaspoon vegetable oil
- 2 teaspoons tomato paste
- ¼ teaspoon dried thyme
- Salt and pepper to taste

Directions:
1. Place the FoodiTM Cook &CrispTM reversible rack inside the ceramic pot.
2. Pour water into the pot.
3. Place in a heat-proof dish the rest of the ingredients. Stir to combine.
4. Place the dish on the reversible rack.

5. Close the pressure lid and set the vent to SEAL.
6. Press the Steam button and adjust the cooking time to 15 minutes.
- **Nutrition Info:** Calories: 223; Carbohydrates: 1.7g; Protein: 23.1g; Fat: 13.7g; Sugar: 0.4g; Sodium: 869mg

418. Steamed Broccoli And Carrots With Lemon

Servings: 3
Cooking Time: 8 Minutes
Ingredients:
- 1 cup broccoli florets
- ½ cup carrots, julienned
- 2 tablespoons lemon juice
- Salt and pepper to taste

Directions:
1. Place the FoodiTM Cook &CrispTM reversible rack inside the ceramic pot.
2. Pour water into the pot.
3. Toss everything in a mixing bowl and combine.
4. Place the vegetables on the reversible rack.
5. Close the pressure lid and set the vent to SEAL.
6. Press the Steam button and adjust the cooking time to 10 minutes.
7. Do quick pressure release.
- **Nutrition Info:** Calories: 35; Carbohydrates: 8.1g; Protein: 1.7g; Fat: 0.3g; Sugar: 0.7g; Sodium: 497mg

419. Heart-felt Caramelized Onions

Servings: 4
Cooking Time: 65 Minutes
Ingredients:
- 2 tbsps. butter, unsalted
- 3 sliced onions
- 2 tbsps. water
- 1 tsp. salt

Directions:
1. Set your pot to Sauté mode and adjust the heat to Medium, pre-heat the inner pot for 5 minutes
2. Add butter and melt, add water, salt, onions, and stir well
3. Lock pressure lid into place, making sure that the pressure valve is locked
4. Cook on HIGH pressure for 30 minutes
5. Quick release the pressure once done
6. Remove the lid and set the pot to Sauté mode, let it sear in the Medium-HIGH mode for about 15 minutes until the liquid is almost gone
7. Enjoy!
- **Nutrition Info:** 110 calories, 6g fat, 14g carbs, 2g protein

420. Filipino-style Bistek Tagalog

Servings: 4
Cooking Time: 33 Minutes
Ingredients:
- 2 tablespoons vegetable oil
- 3 cloves of garlic, minced
- 1 onion, chopped finely
- 2 pounds flank steak, cut into thin strips
- 1 cup chicken broth
- Juice from 1 lemon
- ¼ cup soy sauce
- 1 laurel leaf
- 3 tablespoons sugar
- Black pepper to taste
- 1 red onion, cut into rings
- 2 tablespoons cornstarch
- 3 tablespoons water

Directions:
1. Press the Sear/Sauté button and then the START button.
2. Heat the oil and sauté the garlic and onion until fragrant.
3. Stir in the beef until lightly golden and stir in the chicken stock, lemon juice, soy sauce, bay leaf, sugar, and black pepper.
4. Close the pressure lid and set the vent to SEAL.
5. Press the Pressure button and adjust the cooking time to 30 minutes.
6. Once done, do quick pressure release to open the lid.
7. Once the lid is open, press the Sear/Sauté button and add in the onion rings and cornstarch slurry.
8. Allow to simmer until the sauce thickens.
- **Nutrition Info:** Calories: 486; Carbohydrates: 24.3g; Protein: 33.2g; Fat: 28.4g; Sugar: 10.8g; Sodium: 891mg

421. Lemon Orzo With Asparagus

Servings: 6 Servings
Cooking Time: 5 Mins
Ingredients:
- 1 pound asparagus, tips only
- 3 cups water
- 1 cup orzo pasta, uncooked
- ¾ cup Parmesan cheese
- ¼ cup butter
- 2-3 tablespoons fresh lemon juice
- 2 tablespoons garlic, chopped fine
- salt and pepper to taste

Directions:
1. Cook pasta according to package directions, adding asparagus during the last 3 minutes of cooking. Drain.
2. Set cooker to sauté on medium heat. Add butter and let melt. Add the garlic and cook, stirring often, 2 minutes. Turn off the heat

and stir in lemon juice and cheese. Add pasta and toss to coat. Serve immediately.

422. Chinese Steamed Buns

Servings: 8
Cooking Time: 30 Minutes
Ingredients:
- 1 tablespoon active dry yeast
- 1 teaspoon white sugar
- ¼ cup all-purpose flour
- ¼ cup warm water
- ½ cup water
- 1 ½ cups all-purpose flour
- ¼ teaspoon salt
- 2 tablespoons white sugar
- 1 tablespoon vegetable oil
- ½ teaspoon baking powder

Directions:
1. Place the FoodiTM Cook &CrispTM reversible rack inside the ceramic pot. Pour water into the pot.
2. In a mixing bowl, mix together the dry yeast, white sugar, ¼ cup all-purpose flour, and ¼ cup water. Allow the yeast to activate for 10 minutes. This is evident with bubbles forming on top.
3. In another bowl, combine ½ cup water, 1 ½ cups all-purpose flour, salt, white sugar, vegetable oil, and baking powder. Add in the activated yeast mixture.
4. Fold the mixture until you form a dough.
5. On a floured surface, pour the dough and knead for at least 10 minutes using your hands until it becomes springy. Cover the bowl with warm towel and allow to rest for 2 hours.
6. Once risen, knead the dough and cut into 8 equal parts. Cover with warm towel and allow to rest for another 2 hours.
7. Place on the reversible rack. Close the pressure lid and set the vent to SEAL.
8. Press the Steam button and adjust the cooking time to 30 minutes.
- **Nutrition Info:** Calories: 44; Carbohydrates: 8.4g; Protein: 1.1g; Fat:0.6 g; Sugar:1.4 g; Sodium: 35mg

423. Ninja Foodi Chinese Ribs

Servings:13
Cooking Time: 35 Minutes
Ingredients:
- 3 tablespoons paprika
- 1 tablespoon garlic powder
- ½ teaspoon ground black pepper
- ½ teaspoon salt
- 6 ½ pounds pork ribs
- 2 tablespoons vegetable oil
- 3 cups water
- ¾ cup ketchup
- ¼ cup brown sugar
- ¼ cup Chinese vinegar

Directions:
1. In a bowl, combine the paprika, garlic powder, black pepper, and salt.
2. Sprinkle on to the pork ribs and rub to coat everything with the spices.
3. Press the Sear/Sauté button and then the START button.
4. Heat the oil and stir in the pork ribs. Allow to brown for 5 minutes.
5. Stir in the rest of the ingredients.
6. Close the pressure lid and set the vent to SEAL.
7. Press the Pressure button and adjust the cooking time to 30 minutes.
- **Nutrition Info:** Calories: 768; Carbohydrates: 31.9g; Protein: 56.9g; Fat: 45.8g; Sugar: 14.6g; Sodium: 889mg

424. Sole Steamed With Tomatoes And Leeks

Servings: 2
Cooking Time: 25 Minutes
Ingredients:
- 2 fillets of sole
- 1 tablespoon olive oil
- 1cup chopped leeks
- ½ teaspoon minced garlic
- ½ cup dry white wine
- 3 tomatoes, chopped
- ½ teaspoon dried thyme
- 1 teaspoon dill weed

Directions:
1. Place the FoodiTM Cook &CrispTM reversible rack inside the ceramic pot.
2. Pour water into the pot.
3. Get a big aluminum foil and place the sole fillets in the middle.
4. Add in the rest of the ingredients and season with salt and pepper to taste.
5. Fold the aluminum foil and crimp the edges.
6. Place on the reversible rack.
7. Close the pressure lid and set the vent to SEAL.
8. Press the Steam button and adjust the cooking time to 25 minutes.
- **Nutrition Info:** Calories: 285; Carbohydrates: 15.9g; Protein: 34.2g; Fat: 9.3g; Sugar: 2.4g; Sodium: 161mg

425. Ninja Foodie Pressure Cooked Adobo

Servings: 4
Cooking Time: 30 Minutes
Ingredients:
- 2 pounds chicken breasts and thighs, bones removed
- ½ cup soy sauce
- ¼ cup rice vinegar

- 2 tablespoons brown sugar
- 1 bay leaf
- 8 hard-boiled egg, peeled
- Salt and pepper to taste

Directions:
1. Place all ingredients in the pot except for the hard-boiled eggs.
2. Close the pressure lid and set the vent to SEAL.
3. Press the Pressure button and adjust the cooking time to 30 minutes.
4. Do natural release.
5. Before serving, place the hard-boiled eggs.
- **Nutrition Info:** Calories: 489; Carbohydrates: 21.3g; Protein: 54.5g; Fat: 20.6g; Sugar: 14g; Sodium: 979mg

426. Scrumptious Sausage Dinner

Servings: 10
Cooking Time: 15 Minutes
Ingredients:
- 2 ½ pounds smoked sausage, sliced
- 2 pounds hammocks, sliced
- 4 large potatoes, peeled and cut into large chunks
- 6 turnips, peeled and cut into chunks
- 6 carrots, peeled and cut into chunks
- 2 onions, cut into large chunks
- 1 large cabbage, quartered
- 1 teaspoon salt

Directions:
1. Place the FoodiTM Cook &CrispTM reversible rack inside the ceramic pot.
2. Pour water into the pot.
3. Arrange all ingredients on the reversible rack and season with salt to taste.
4. Close the pressure lid and set the vent to SEAL.
5. Press the Steam button and adjust the cooking time to 15 minutes.
- **Nutrition Info:** Calories: 625; Carbohydrates: 42.5g; Protein: 31.4g; Fat: 36.6g; Sugar:8.3 g; Sodium: 1536mg

427. Easy 'n Crispy Egg Rolls

Servings:12
Cooking Time: 10 Minutes
Ingredients:
- 2 cups frozen corn, thawed
- 1 can black beans, rinsed and drained
- 1 can spinach, drained
- 1 ½ cups shredded jalapeno Jack cheese
- 1 cup sharp cheddar cheese, shredded
- 1 can diced green chilies, drained
- 4 green onions, sliced
- 1 teaspoon salt
- 1 teaspoon ground cumin
- 1 teaspoon chili powder
- 1 package egg roll wrapper
- Cooking spray

Directions:
1. Place in the ceramic pot the FoodiTM Cook &CrispTM basket.
2. In a mixing bowl, combine all the ingredients except for the egg roll wrapper and cooking spray. Mix to combine.
3. Place an egg roll wrapper on a flat surface. Place ¼ cup of the filling in the center of the wrapper. Moisten the edges of the wrapper with water and fold then roll to create the spring roll. Do the same thing with the other egg wrappers.
4. Place the spring rolls in the basket and brush with oil.
5. Close the crisping lid and press the Air Crisp button before pressing the START button.
6. Adjust the cooking time to 10 minutes.
7. Open the crisping lid and flip the spring rolls to cook evenly.
- **Nutrition Info:** Calories: 220; Carbohydrates: 27g; Protein: 10.6g; Fat: 7.7g; Sugar: 7.4g; Sodium: 632mg

428. Creamy Cheesy Polenta

Servings: 4 Servings
Cooking Time: 4 Hrs
Ingredients:
- 3 cups vegetable broth
- 1 cup coarse cornmeal
- 1 cup half and half
- ¼ cup cheese, grated

Directions:
1. Combine the broth and cornmeal in the cooking pot. Secure the lid and select slow cooking on low heat. Cook 3 -4 hours, being sure to stir it every 30 minutes.
2. Add the half-and-half, stir well and turn the heat up to high and cook another 30 minutes. Stir in the cheese till melted. Serve.

429. Baked Teriyaki Chicken

Servings:12
Cooking Time: 40 Minutes
Ingredients:
- 1 tablespoon cornstarch
- 1 tablespoon cold water
- ½ cup white sugar
- ½ cup soy sauce
- ¼ cup apple cider vinegar
- 1 clove of garlic, minced
- ½ teaspoon ground ginger
- ¼ teaspoon ground black pepper
- 12 skinless chicken thighs

Directions:
1. Mix together the cornstarch, cold water, white sugar, soy sauce, apple cider vinegar, garlic, ground ginger, and black pepper.

2. Place the mixture in a saucepan and simmer on low heat until the sauce thickens.
3. Season the chicken with salt and pepper.
4. Place in the ceramic pot the FoodiTM Cook & CrispTM reversible rack.
5. Place the chicken on the reversible tray and brush the chicken with the sauce.
6. Close the crisping lid and press the Bake/Roast button before pressing the START button.
7. Adjust the cooking time to 40 minutes.
- **Nutrition Info:** Calories: 267; Carbohydrates: 19.9g; Protein: 24.7g; Fat: 9.8g; Sugar: 15.2g; Sodium: 1282mg

430. Kids Favorite Pasta

Servings: 6
Cooking Time: 2 Hours
Ingredients:
- 2 egg whites
- 1½ C. milk
- 2 tsp. tapioca starch
- 2 C. whole wheat penne pasta
- 4-oz. cheddar cheese, shredded

Directions:
1. In a bowl, add egg whites, milk and tapioca starch and beat until well combined.
2. Add remaining ingredients and stir to combine.
3. In the pot of Ninja Foodi, place the pasta mixture
4. Close the crisping lid and select "Slow Cooker".
5. Set on "Low" for about 1½-2 hours.
6. Press "Start/Stop" to begin.
7. Open the lid and serve warm.
- **Nutrition Info:** Calories: 395; Carbohydrates: 60g; Protein: 17.2g; Fat: 9.6g; Sugar: 5.6g; Sodium: 170mg; Fiber: 6.7g

431. Appetizing Baked Pompano

Servings: 3
Cooking Time: 40 Minutes
Ingredients:
- 1 cup soy sauce
- ½ cup rice cooking wine
- 5 tablespoons olive oil, divided
- 2 teaspoons hoisin sauce
- 2 teaspoons fish sauce
- 2 teaspoons oyster sauce
- 1 lime, halved
- 1 shallot, died
- 1 piece ginger, grated
- 1 ½ pounds whole pompano fish, gutted and cleaned
- 1 teaspoon dill
- 2 cups Napa cabbage leaves
- Salt and pepper to taste

Directions:
1. Place in the ceramic pot the FoodiTM Cook &CrispTM reversible rack.
2. In a big dish, place soy sauce, wine, half of the olive oil, hoisin sauce, fish sauce, oyster sauce, lime, shallot, and ginger.
3. Place the pompano fish in the dish and brush with the marinade. Allow to marinate in the fridge for at least 2 hours.
4. Take the fish out and place on the rack. Brush with the remaining half of the oil and season with dill, salt, and pepper.
5. Close the crisping lid and press the Bake/Roast button before pressing the START button. Adjust the cooking time to 40 minutes.
6. Once cooked, place the fish on a bed of napa cabbage.
- **Nutrition Info:** Calories: 501; Carbohydrates: 13.4g; Protein: 36.8g; Fat: 33.3g; Sugar:4.6 g; Sodium: 998mg

432. Greek Style Stew

Servings: 5
Cooking Time: 53 Minutes
Ingredients:
- 1 tablespoon olive oil
- 2 pound beef stew meat, cubed
- 1 onion, chopped
- 2 cloves of garlic, chopped
- Salt and pepper to taste
- ¼ cup red wine
- ½ cup beef broth
- 1 tablespoon tomato paste
- ½ teaspoon dried rosemary
- ½ teaspoon dried oregano
- 2 bay leaves
- 1/8 teaspoon ground cinnamon
- 1 pinch ground cloves
- 1 ½ teaspoons brown sugar
- 1 can plum tomatoes
- ½ cup water
- 2 potatoes, peeled and chopped

Directions:
1. Press the Sear/Sauté button and then the START button.
2. Heat the oil in the inner pot and stir in the meat, onion, and garlic. Season with salt and pepper to taste. Keep stirring for at least 3 minutes.
3. Add in the rest of the ingredients and give a good stir.
4. Close the pressure lid and set the vent to SEAL.
5. Press the Pressure button and adjust the cooking time to 50 minutes.
- **Nutrition Info:** Calories: 288; Carbohydrates: 26.8g; Protein: 15.9g; Fat: 13g; Sugar: 10.2g; Sodium: 367mg

433. Mexican Pork In Annatto Sauce

Servings: 10
Cooking Time: 75 Minutes
Ingredients:
- 3 ounces achiote paste or annatto powder
- 1 white onion, chopped
- 2 cloves of garlic, minced
- 2 cups orange juice
- ½ cup lemon juice
- ¼ cup white vinegar
- 2 tablespoons salt
- 1 tablespoon ground black pepper
- 1 tablespoon Mexican oregano
- 5 pounds pork shoulder roast

Directions:
1. Place all ingredients in the Ninja Foodi Pot.
2. Close the pressure lid and set the vent to SEAL.
3. Press the Pressure button and adjust the cooking time to 75 minutes.
4. Do natural pressure release.
- **Nutrition Info:** Calories: 414; Carbohydrates: 8.3g; Protein: 37.6g; Fat: 25.6g; Sugar: 4.9g; Sodium: 122mg

434. Asian Spiced Chicken Wings

Servings: 2 Servings
Cooking Time: 30 Mins
Ingredients:
- 8 chicken wings
- 2 tablespoons soy sauce
- 2 tablespoons Chinese spice
- Salt & pepper

Directions:
1. Add the soy sauce, spice, salt and pepper to a large mixing bowl and stir to combine.
2. Add the wings and toss to coat well.
3. Place the rack in the bottom of the cooker. Place the chicken on it and pour any remaining sauce over it.
4. Add the Tender Crisp lid and set the temperature to 350 degrees.
5. Cook for 15 minutes, then turn the chicken over and cook another 15 minutes. Serve with your favorite dipping sauce.

435. Carrot Pudding

Servings: 4 Servings
Cooking Time: 2 – 4 Hours
Ingredients:
- 4 cups carrots, grated
- 1 small onion, grated
- 1 cup heavy cream
- 1 egg, beaten
- 1 tablespoon sugar
- 1 teaspoons salt
- 1 teaspoon nutmeg

Directions:
1. Place the carrots and onion in the cooking pot.
2. Whisk the remaining ingredients together in a mixing bowl, then pour over vegetables. Secure the lid and select slow cooking function. If using low heat, set the timer for 4 hours, or two hours on high.
3. When the timer goes off check to see if the carrots are tender. If not, cook a while longer. When the carrots are done, use an immersion blender, and pulse till the mixture resembles pudding. Serve warm.

436. Bbq Oysters With Bacon

Servings: 12 Oysters
Cooking Time: 10 Mins
Ingredients:
- 1 dozen fresh oysters, shucked and left on the half shell
- Rock salt
- 1 pound thick cut bacon, sliced into thin strips
- 1/3 cup ketchup
- ¼ cup Worcestershire sauce
- Juice of ½ lemon
- 1 teaspoon horseradish
- Dash of your favorite hot sauce
- Lime wedges for garnish

Directions:
1. Line a shallow baking dish that will fit inside the cooker with rock salt. Place the oysters snugly into the salt, you will have to cook them in batches.
2. In a large bowl, combine remaining ingredients and mix well.
3. Add a dash of Worcestershire to each oyster then top with bacon mixture.
4. Use the Tender Crisp lid and lock into place. Set the temperature to broil and cook 10 minutes, or till bacon is crisp.
5. Serve with lime wedges.

437. Cheese Casserole

Servings: 6
Cooking Time: 37 Minutes
Ingredients:
- 16 oz. marinara sauce
- 10 oz. shredded parmesan
- 2 tbsps. olive oil
- 16 oz. shredded mozzarella cheese
- 2 lbs. scrambled sausages

Directions:
1. Grease the pot of Ninja Foodi with olive oil and arrange half of the scrambled sausages.
2. Layer with half of the marinara, followed by half of the mozzarella and Parmesan cheese.
3. Top with the remaining half of the scrambled sausages, marinara, mozzarella and Parmesan cheese.

4. Press "Bake/Roast" and set the timer to 20 minutes at 360 degrees F.
5. Remove from the Ninja Foodi after 20 minutes and dish out to serve.
- **Nutrition Info:** 521 calories, 38.8g fat, 6g carbs, 35.4g protein

438. Cheesy Cauliflower

Servings: 5
Cooking Time: 35 Minutes
Ingredients:
- 1 tbsp. prepared mustard
- 1 head cauliflower
- 1 tsp. avocado mayonnaise
- ½ c. grated Parmesan cheese
- ¼ c. butter, chopped

Directions:
1. Press "Sauté" on Ninja Foodi and add butter and cauliflower.
2. Sauté for about 3 minutes and add rest of the ingredients.
3. Lock the lid and set the Ninja Foodi to "Pressure" for about 30 minutes.
4. Release the pressure naturally and dish out to serve hot.
- **Nutrition Info:** 155 calories, 13.3g fat, 3.8g carbs, 6.7g protein

439. Buffalo Cauliflower Bites

Servings: 4 Servings
Cooking Time: 35 Minutes
Ingredients:
- 6 cups Cauliflower florets
- 1 ½ cups water
- 1/3 cup hot sauce
- 1 ½ cups cornstarch
- ½ cup almond flour
- 2 tsp baking powder
- 1 tsp garlic powder
- 1 tsp salt
- ½ tsp black pepper
- 2 eggs

Directions:
1. Add the cauliflower and ½ cup of the water to the bowl of the Ninja Foodi. Place the lid on the machine and use the pressure cooker on low pressure to cook the cauliflower for 2 minutes. Once the cooking is complete, do a quick pressure release, and remove the lid. Cool the cauliflower in the fridge.
2. In a small bowl, mix together the corn starch, almond flour, baking powder, garlic powder, salt, eggs and pepper. Add the remaining cup of water and mix until smooth.
3. Toss the chilled cauliflower in the batter then place the coated cauliflower on a separate tray and cool in the freezer for about 30 minutes.
4. Place the chilled cauliflower in the cook and crisp basket in one layer, try not to overlap.
5. Preheat the Ninja Foodi using the air crisp setting to 350 degrees.
6. Place the cauliflower basket into the Ninja Foodi and close the crisper lid. Set the timer to twenty minutes. Remove the cauliflower once cooked and toss with the hot sauce. Serve immediately.
- **Nutrition Info:** Calories: 72g, Carbohydrates: 5g, Protein: 5g, Fat: 4g, Sugar: 2g, Sodium: 1405mg

440. Spicy Pressure Cooker Short Ribs

Servings: 4
Cooking Time: 45 Minutes
Ingredients:
- 1 habanero pepper, minced
- 1 ½ teaspoons black pepper
- 1 teaspoon paprika
- ½ teaspoon ground cumin
- 2 pounds beef short ribs
- 1 can cola
- 2 tablespoons apple cider vinegar
- 1 tablespoon raspberry jam
- 1 tablespoon Worcestershire sauce
- 1 tablespoon brown sugar
- 2 teaspoons canola oil
- ½ onion, diced
- 4 cloves of garlic, minced
- 2 tablespoons water
- 2 tablespoons cornstarch

Directions:
1. In a Ziploc bag, place the habanero, black pepper, paprika, cumin, beef short ribs, cola, apple cider vinegar, raspberry jam, Worcestershire sauce, and sugar. Marinate for at least 2 hours in the fridge.
2. Press the Sear/Sauté button and press the START button.
3. Heat the olive oil and sauté the onion and garlic until fragrant. Stir in the marinated beef (liquid included) and adjust the moisture.
4. Place the pressure lid and set the vent to the SEAL position. Press the Pressure button.
5. Adjust the cooking time to 45 minutes.
6. Once cooking is done, do natural pressure release to open the lid.
7. Open the lid and press the Sear/Sauté button and stir in the cornstarch slurry.
8. Allow to simmer until the sauce thickens.
- **Nutrition Info:** Calories: 582; Carbohydrates: 24.1g; Protein: 22g; Fat: 44.1g; Sugar: 10.4g; Sodium: 224mg

441. Ninja Foodi Pressure Cooked Barbecue Chicken

Servings: 4

Cooking Time: 20 Minutes
Ingredients:
- 2 pounds boneless chicken thighs
- 1 teaspoon ground paprika
- 1 onion, minced
- ½ cup chili sauce
- ½ cup water
- 2 tablespoons vinegar
- Salt and pepper to taste

Directions:
1. Place all ingredients in the pot except for the hard-boiled eggs.
2. Close the pressure lid and set the vent to SEAL.
3. Press the Pressure button and adjust the cooking time to 20 minutes.
4. Do natural release.
- **Nutrition Info:** Calories: 215; Carbohydrates: 7g; Protein: 19.8g; Fat: 11.9g; Sugar: 1.2g; Sodium: 313mg

442. Asparagus Bites

Servings: 3
Cooking Time: 25 Minutes
Ingredients:
- 1 c. asparagus
- ½ c. coconut, desiccated
- ½ c. feta cheese

Directions:
1. Place the coconut in a shallow dish and coat asparagus with coconut evenly.
2. Place coated asparagus in the pot of Ninja Foodi and top with feta cheese.
3. Press "Air Crisp" and set the timer to 10 minutes at 360 degrees F.
4. Remove from the Ninja Foodi and dish out to serve.
- **Nutrition Info:** 135 calories, 10.3g fat, 5g carbs, 7g protein

443. Buffalo Chicken Soup

Servings: 4 Servings
Cooking Time: 20 Minutes
Ingredients:
- 1 tsp olive oil
- ½ cup chopped onion
- ½ cup chopped celery
- 3 garlic cloves, minced
- 1 ½ cup chicken broth
- 1 cup shredded cooked chicken
- 1 Tbsp Buffalo Sauce
- 4 oz cream cheese
- 1/3 cup cream

Directions:
1. Press the saute button on your Ninja Foodi and then add the oil, onion and celery to the pot. Stir and cook until the veggies are soft, about 8 minutes.
2. Add the garlic and cook for one more minute.
3. Add the chicken, broth and buffalo sauce and stir everything together.
4. Place the lid on the Ninja Foodi and seal the pot. Use the pressure cooker function and cook on high pressure for 5 minutes. Once the timer goes off, let the pressure naturally release. Open the lid.
5. Add the cream cheese and cream to the pot and stir until it is melted into the soup. Enjoy while hot.
- **Nutrition Info:** Calories: 244g, Carbohydrates: 5g, Protein: 13g, Fat: 22g, Sugar: 3g, Sodium: 480mg

444. Easy Ninja Foodi Pot Roast

Servings: 6
Cooking Time: 60 Minutes
Ingredients:
- 2 tablespoons vegetable oil
- 3 pounds boneless beef chuck roast, trimmed
- 1 tablespoon onion powder
- 1 can beef broth
- 1 ½ tablespoons Worcestershire sauce
- 1 onion, cut into wedges
- 4 carrots, peeled and sliced
- 4 large potatoes, peeled and cut into bite-sized pieces
- Salt and pepper to taste

Directions:
1. Press the Sear/Sauté button on the Ninja Foodi. Press the START button.
2. Heat the oil and sear the beef chuck roast for 2 minutes on each side. Season with salt, pepper, and onion powder.
3. Once golden, stir in the rest of the ingredients.
4. Close the pressure lid and set the vent to SEAL position. Press the Pressure button and adjust the cooking time to 60 minutes.
5. Press the START button and cook until done.
- **Nutrition Info:** Calories: 450; Carbohydrates: 38.3g; Protein: 25.1g; Fat: 21.8g; Sugar: 10.2g; Sodium: 311mg

445. Fried Meatballs With Tomato Sauce

Servings: 2
Cooking Time: 20 Minutes
Ingredients:
- 1 small onion
- 1 pound minced beef
- 1 tablespoon chopped parsley
- 1 tablespoon chopped thyme leaves
- 1 egg, beaten
- 3 tablespoons bread crumbs
- ¾ cup of your favorite tomato sauce
- Salt and pepper to taste

Directions:
1. Place in the ceramic pot the FoodiTM Cook &CrispTM basket.
2. In a mixing bowl, combine all ingredients except for the tomato sauce.
3. Form small balls using your hands.
4. Place the balls in the basket.
5. Close the crisping lid and press the Air Crisp button before pressing the START button.
6. Adjust the cooking time to 20 minutes.
7. Give the basket a shape halfway through the cooking time to evenly cook the food.
8. Once cooked, pour over your favorite tomato sauce on top.
- **Nutrition Info:** Calories: 231; Carbohydrates: 12.1g; Protein: 15.1g; Fat: 13.5g; Sugar: 5.3g; Sodium:267 mg

446. Mini Meatballs

Servings: 4 Servings
Cooking Time: 10 Minutes
Ingredients:
- 1 tsp olive oil
- 3 cups low carb tomato sauce
- 1 ½ pounds ground beef
- 1 tbsp dried parsley
- ½ cup grated parmesan cheese
- ½ cup almond flour
- 2 eggs
- 1 tsp salt
- ½ tsp ground black pepper
- 1 tsp dried oregano
- ¼ cup water

Directions:
1. Mix the ground beef, parsley, parmesan cheese, almond flour, eggs, salt and pepper together in a bowl. Use your hands to shape into mini meatballs, about 1 inch in diameter.
2. Pour the olive oil in the bottom of the Ninja Foodi and press saute. Add the meatballs to the pot and sear for two minutes on each side to brown.
3. Add the tomato sauce to the pot and close the lid.
4. Use the pressure cooker function and cook on low pressure for 10 minutes. Once the timer goes off, let the pressure naturally release for 10 minutes then open the pot and serve hot with a toothpick.
- **Nutrition Info:** Calories: 639g, Carbohydrates: 6g, Protein: 60g, Fat: 38g, Sugar: 8g, Sodium: 198g

447. Crunchy Tortilla Chips

Servings: 6
Cooking Time: 3 Minutes
Ingredients:
- 8 corn tortillas, cut into triangle
- 1 tbsp. olive oil
- Salt, to taste

Directions:
1. Coat the tortilla chips pieces with oil evenly.
2. Arrange the "Cook & Crisp Basket" in the pot of Ninja Foodi.
3. Close the Ninja Foodi with crisping lid and select "Air Crisp".
4. Press "Start/Stop" to begin and set the temperature to 390 degrees F.
5. Set the time for 5 minutes to preheat.
6. Now, place the tortilla chips pieces into "Cook & Crisp Basket".
7. Close the Ninja Foodi with crisping lid and select "Air Crisp".
8. Set the temperature to 390 degrees F for 3 minutes.
9. Press "Start/Stop" to begin.
10. Open the lid and serve warm.
- **Nutrition Info:** Calories per serving: 90; Carbohydrates: 14.3g; Protein: 1.8g; Fat: 3.2g; Sugar: 0.3g; Sodium: 42mg; Fiber: 2g

448. Cheesy Green Chili Rice

Servings: 6 – 8 Servings
Cooking Time: 1 -2 Hours
Ingredients:
- 4-5 cups long-grain white rice, cooked
- 2 cans green chilies, diced
- 2 cups scallions, sliced thin
- 1 ½ cups plus 3 tablespoons Mozzarella cheese, grated
- 1 cup sour cream
- 2 tablespoons Parmesan cheese
- 1-2 tablespoons green hot sauce

Directions:
1. Place the rice and scallions in a large bowl and stir together.
2. In a separate bowl, combine sour cream, chilies with their juice, hot sauce and 1 ½ cups of the Mozzarella cheese.
3. Mix the cheese mixture into the rice.
4. Lightly spray the cooking pot with cooking spray. Add the rice mixture and press down to make sure it is in an even layer. Top with remaining Mozzarella and the Parmesan cheese.
5. Secure the lid and select slow cooking on high heat. Cook 1-2 hours or till bubbling hot and cheese is melted. Serve.

449. Roasted Corn

Servings: 4 – 6 Servings
Cooking Time: 10 Minutes
Ingredients:
- 4 ears of corn, shucked and cut into thirds
- 2 - 3 teaspoons vegetable oil
- salt and pepper to taste

Directions:

1. Place corn in a large bowl and drizzle with oil. Toss being sure to coat each piece. Sprinkle with salt and pepper.
2. Place the corn in the basket for the air fryer, you may have to cook these in batches. Add the Tender Crisp lid and set the temperature to 400 degrees. Cook 10 minutes. Serve.

450. Crab Frittata

Servings: 4 Servings
Cooking Time: 50 Mins
Ingredients:
- 2 cups lump crabmeat
- 4 eggs
- 1 cup half and half
- 1 cup Parmesan cheese, grated
- 1 cup green onions, chopped
- 1 teaspoon salt
- 1 teaspoon pepper
- 1 teaspoon sweet smoked paprika
- 1 teaspoon Italian seasoning

Directions:
1. Whisk egg and half-and-half together in a large bowl. Add seasonings and Parmesan and stir to mix.
2. Stir in the onions and crab meat.
3. Wrap some foil around the base of a springform pan that will fit inside the cooking pot. Pour the egg mixture into the pan.
4. Place the rack in the pot and add 2 cups of water. Place the pan on the rack and secure the lid. Select pressure cooking on high and set the timer for 40 minutes.
5. When the timer goes off, let sit for 10 minutes. Then use quick release to remove the lid. Carefully remove the pan and remove the outer ring. Serve warm or at room temperature.

451. Ginger-soy On Tuna Fish

Servings: 4
Cooking Time: 20 Minutes
Ingredients:
- 2 pounds fresh tuna steaks
- ½ cup soy sauce
- ½ cup sherry
- ½ cup vegetable oil
- 1 bunch green onions, chopped
- ½ cup minced ginger root
- 3 cloves garlic, minced
- Salt and pepper to taste

Directions:
1. Marinate the tuna steaks in soy sauce, sherry and vegetable oil. Allow to marinate in the fridge for at least 2 hours.
2. Place the FoodiTM Cook & CrispTM reversible rack inside the ceramic pot.
3. Pour the marinade into the pot.
4. In a large foil, place the tuna in the middle and top with green onions, ginger, and garlic. Season with more salt and pepper if desired.
5. Close the foil and place the tuna steak packets on the reversible rack.
6. Close the pressure lid and set the vent to SEAL.
7. Press the Steam button and adjust the cooking time to 20 minutes.
8. Do quick pressure release.
9. Once the lid is open, remove the tuna packets and the reversible rack.
10. Press the Sear/Sauté button and allow the sauce the simmer until reduced.
11. Brush the tuna steaks with the reduced sauce.
- **Nutrition Info:** Calories: 275; Carbohydrates: 7.1g; Protein: 28.3g; Fat: 14.8g; Sugar: 1.4g; Sodium: 1330mg

452. Creamy Tomato-basil Soup

Servings: 2
Cooking Time: 9 Minutes
Ingredients:
- 1 tablespoon olive oil
- 1 onion, chopped
- 2 medium carrots, peeled and chopped
- 1 can fire roasted tomatoes
- ¾ cup vegetable broth
- 2 teaspoons dried basil
- 1 teaspoon salt
- 2 teaspoons sugar
- 1/2 cup cashew nuts, soaked

Directions:
1. Press the sauté button on the Ninja Foodi and heat the oil.
2. Stir in the onions and carrots for 3 minutes.
3. Add the rest of the ingredients.
4. Install pressure lid. Close Ninja Foodi, press the pressure button, choose high settings, and set time to 6 minutes.
5. Once done cooking, do a quick release.
6. Open the lid and transfer the contents into a blender. Pulse until smooth.
7. Serve and enjoy.
- **Nutrition Info:** Calories: 415; carbohydrates: 27.7g; protein: 8.8g; fat: 29.9g

453. Spicy Honey Mustard Pork Roast

Servings: 6
Cooking Time: 1 Hour And 30 Minutes
Ingredients:
- 3 pounds pork roast
- ¼ cup honey
- 2 tablespoons Dijon mustard
- 2 tablespoons black pepper

- ½ teaspoon salt
- ½ teaspoon dried thyme

Directions:
1. Place in the ceramic pot the FoodiTM Cook & CrispTM reversible rack.
2. Score the pork roast with a knife and place on a circular baking dish that will fit in the Ninja Foodi.
3. In a mixing bowl, mix together the rest of the ingredients until well-blended.
4. Brush the pork with the spice rub.
5. Place the pork in a baking dish on the rack.
6. Close the crisping lid and press the Bake/Roast button before pressing the START button.
7. Adjust the cooking time to 1hour and 30 minutes.
- **Nutrition Info:** Calories: 242; Carbohydrates: 14.1g; Protein: 26.5g; Fat: 8.8g; Sugar: 7.9g; Sodium: 366mg

454. Brekky Bacon 'n Egg Risotto

Servings: 2
Cooking Time: 10 Minutes
Ingredients:
- 1 1/2 cups chicken broth
- 1/3 cup chopped onion
- 2 eggs
- 2 tablespoons grated parmesan cheese
- 3 slices center cut bacon, chopped
- 3 tablespoons dry white wine
- 3/4 cup arborio rice
- Chives, for garnish
- Salt and pepper, to taste

Directions:
1. Press sauté button and cook bacon to a crisp, around 6 minutes.
2. Stir in onion and sauté for 3 minutes. Add rice and sauté for a minute.
3. Pour in wine and deglaze pot. Continue sautéing until wine is completely absorbed by rice, around 5 minutes.
4. Stir in chicken broth.
5. Install pressure lid. Close Ninja Foodi, press pressure button, choose high settings, and set time to 5 minutes.
6. Meanwhile, cook eggs sunny side up to desired doneness.
7. Once done cooking, do a quick release. Stir in pepper, salt, and parmesan.
8. Divide risotto evenly on to two plates, add egg, and sprinkle with chives.
9. Serve and enjoy.
- **Nutrition Info:** Calories: 211; carbohydrates: 16.0g; protein: 12.0g; fat: 11.0g

455. Tomato ' N Eggplant Pasta

Servings: 3
Cooking Time: 25 Minutes
Ingredients:
- 1 tablespoon olive oil
- 1 red onion, chopped
- 2 cloves of garlic, chopped
- 1 eggplant, chopped
- 1 can chopped tomatoes
- 1-pound pasta
- Enough vegetable broth to cover the pasta
- ¼ cup black olives, pitted and sliced
- Salt and pepper to taste

Directions:
1. Press the sauté button on the Ninja Foodi and heat the oil. Sauté the onions and garlic until fragrant before adding the eggplants. Allow the eggplants to wilt before adding the rest of the ingredients.
2. Install pressure lid. Close Ninja Foodi, press the pressure button, choose high settings, and set time to 20 minutes.
3. Once done cooking, do a quick release.
4. Serve and enjoy.
- **Nutrition Info:** Calories: 394; carbohydrates: 73g; protein: 12g; fat: 6g

456. Broiled & Buttered Scallops

Servings: 3
Cooking Time: 20 Minutes
Ingredients:
- 1 ½ pounds bay scallops, removed from shells
- 1 tablespoon garlic salt
- 2 tablespoons melted butter
- 2 tablespoon lemon juice

Directions:
1. Place in the ceramic pot the FoodiTM Cook &CrispTM basket insert.
2. In a mixing bowl, combine all ingredients until the scallops are coated with the seasoning.
3. Place in the basket insert.
4. Close the crisping lid and press the Broil button before pressing the START button.
5. Adjust the cooking time to 20 minutes.
- **Nutrition Info:** Calories: 265; Carbohydrates: 6.8g; Protein: 38.3g; Fat: 9.4g; Sugar: 2.3g; Sodium: 2232mg

457. Chinese Steamed Fish

Servings: 2
Cooking Time: 10 Minutes
Ingredients:
- 1 pound red snapper fillets
- 1 tablespoon grated ginger
- 1 tablespoon soy sauce
- 2 tablespoons sesame oil
- 2 shiitake mushrooms, sliced thinly
- 1 tomato, quartered
- ½ fresh red chili pepper, chopped

- 2 sprigs of cilantro, chopped
- Salt and pepper to taste

Directions:
1. Place the FoodiTM Cook &CrispTM reversible rack inside the ceramic pot.
2. Pour a cup of water in the pot.
3. One a heat-proof ceramic bowl, place the fish and season with salt, pepper, ginger, and soy sauce.
4. Pour over sesame oil and add mushrooms, tomatoes, and red chili on top.
5. Place the ceramic dish with the fish on the reversible rack.
6. Close the pressure lid and set the vent to SEAL.
7. Press the Steam button and adjust the cooking time to 10 minutes.
8. Do quick pressure release.
9. Serve with chopped cilantro
- **Nutrition Info:** Calories: 290; Carbohydrates: 5.9g; Protein: 48.3g; Fat: 8.1g; Sugar: 0.8g; Sodium: 1187mg

458. Southwest Short Ribs

Servings: 4-6 Servings
Cooking Time: 45 Minutes
Ingredients:
- 3 pounds beef short ribs, trim off fat
- 1 pound yams, peeled and cubed
- 14.5 ounce can tomatoes, diced
- 1 cup red onion, chopped
- 1 cup green beans, thawed
- 1 cup corn, thawed
- 1 cup beef stock
- 1 cup pale ale
- 4 cloves garlic, chopped fine
- 2 teaspoons olive oil
- 2 teaspoons cumin
- 1 teaspoon salt
- 1 teaspoon Ancho chili powder
- ½ teaspoon pepper
- ½ teaspoon coriander

Directions:
1. Add the oil to the cooking pot and set to sauté on med-high heat. Sprinkle the ribs with salt and pepper and cook, in batches, till brown on each side. Transfer to a plate and set aside. Drain all but 1 tablespoon fat.
2. Add the onions and garlic and cook 2 minutes, stirring often. Add the beef stock and ale and deglaze the pan.
3. Add the yam, tomatoes, cumin, chili powder and coriander and stir well. Place the ribs back in the pot and secure the lid. Set to pressure cooking on high. Set the timer for 35 minutes.
4. When the timer goes off, use the manual release to remove the lid. Use a slotted spoon to remove the ribs and vegetables, placing them in two separate serving bowls.
5. Set the cooker back to sauté on med-high heat and cook sauce till it reduces and is thickened. To serve, place 2 ribs on the succotash and drizzle with sauce.

459. Cheesy 'n Milky Haddock

Servings: 4
Cooking Time: 20 Minutes
Ingredients:
- 4 haddock fillets
- ¾ cup milk
- 2 teaspoons salt
- ¾ cup bread crumbs
- ¼ cup grated Parmesan cheese
- ¼ teaspoon ground dried thyme
- ¼ cup butter, melted

Directions:
1. Place in the ceramic pot the FoodiTM Cook &CrispTM reversible rack.
2. Dip the haddock fillets in milk then season with salt. Set aside.
3. In a mixing bowl, combine the bread crumbs, parmesan cheese, and ground thyme.
4. Dredge the fillets in the bread crumbs mixture.
5. Place the fish on the reversible rack.
6. Brush with butter on all sides.
7. Close the crisping lid and press the Bake/Roast button before pressing the START button.
8. Adjust the cooking time to 20 minutes.
- **Nutrition Info:** Calories: 321; Carbohydrates: 17g; Protein: 27.7g; Fat: 15.7g; Sugar: 8.4g; Sodium: 1546mg

460. Pressure Cooker Pork Tenderloin

Servings: 3
Cooking Time: 40 Minutes
Ingredients:
- ¼ cup fresh cilantro leaves
- ¼ cup lime juice
- 2 cloves of garlic
- ½ teaspoon red pepper flakes
- ¼ teaspoon salt
- 1 pound pork tenderloin
- ¾ cup chicken broth
- ¼ cup lemon juice

Directions:
1. Place all ingredients in the pot except for the hard-boiled eggs.
2. Close the pressure lid and set the vent to SEAL.
3. Press the Pressure button and adjust the cooking time to 40 minutes.
4. Do natural pressure release.

- **Nutrition Info:** Calories: 231; Carbohydrates: 4.9g; Protein: 40.3g; Fat: 5.5g; Sugar: 1.3g; Sodium: 480mg

461. Nutty Brussels Sprouts

Servings: 8
Cooking Time: 16 Minutes
Ingredients:
- 2 lbs. trimmed Brussels sprouts, halved
- 1 c. chopped almonds
- 1 tbsp. melted butter, unsalted

Directions:
1. Arrange the basket in the bottom of Ninja Foodi and add water.
2. Place the Brussels sprout on top of the basket and lock the lid.
3. Press "Pressure" and cook for about 3 minutes.
4. Release the pressure quickly and replace the pot with the basket.
5. Transfer the Brussels sprout in the pot and top with almonds and butter.
6. Press "Air Crisp" and cook for about 3 minutes at 350 degrees F.
7. Dish out to serve.
- **Nutrition Info:** 130 calories, 7.8g fat, 8.9g carbs, 6.4g protein

462. Ninja Foodi Baked Fudge

Servings: 6
Cooking Time: 50 Minutes
Ingredients:
- 2 cups white sugar
- ½ cup all-purpose flour
- ½ cup cocoa powder
- 4 eggs, beaten
- 1 cup butter, melted
- 2 teaspoons vanilla extract
- 1 cup chopped pecans

Directions:
1. Place in the ceramic pot the FoodiTM Cook &CrispTM reversible rack.
2. Close the crisping lid and press the Broil button before pressing the START button to preheat the Ninja Foodi.
3. In a bowl, sift together the sugar, flour, and cocoa. Add in eggs, melted butter, vanilla, and pecans. Mix to combine everything.
4. Pour the batter into a baking pan that will fit inside the Ninja Foodi.
5. Place in the preheated Ninja Foodi and close the crisping lid.
6. Press the Bake/Roast button before pressing the START button.
7. Adjust the cooking time to 50 minutes.
- **Nutrition Info:** Calories: 397; Carbohydrates: 40.7g; Protein: 4.3g; Fat: 24.1g; Sugar: 25.3g; Sodium: 159mg

463. Flaky Broiled Salmon

Servings: 4
Cooking Time: 20 Minutes
Ingredients:
- 1 clove of garlic, chopped
- 2 tablespoons olive oil
- 4 salmon fillets
- ½ cup butter
- 2 tablespoons Worcestershire sauce
- 2 tablespoons lemon juice
- ¼ cup white wine
- 1 teaspoon ground black pepper
- 1 teaspoon garlic salt
- 1 ½ teaspoon fines herbs
- ¼ cup fresh dill

Directions:
1. Place in the ceramic pot the FoodiTM Cook &CrispTM reversible tray.
2. In a Ziploc bag, combine all ingredients and allow the salmon to marinate in the fridge for at least 2 hours.
3. Place the salmon fillets on the reversible tray.
4. Close the crisping lid and press the Broil button before pressing the START button.
5. Adjust the cooking time to 20 minutes.
- **Nutrition Info:** Calories: 519; Carbohydrates: 4g; Protein: 36.4g; Fat: 39.7g; Sugar: 1.2g; Sodium: 772mg

464. Chinese Pork Roast

Servings: 8
Cooking Time: 1 Hour And 30 Minutes
Ingredients:
- 4 pounds pork roast, trimmed
- ¾ cup soy sauce
- ½ cup dry sherry
- 1/3 cup honey
- 2 cloves of garlic, minced
- ½ teaspoon ground ginger

Directions:
1. Place in the ceramic pot the FoodiTM Cook &CrispTM reversible rack.
2. Place all ingredients in a bowl and allow the meat to marinate in the fridge for at least 12 hours.
3. Place the marinated meat on the rack.
4. Close the crisping lid and press the Bake/Roast button before pressing the START button.
5. Adjust the cooking time to 1 hour and 30 minutes.
6. Meanwhile, put the marinade in a saucepan and bring to a simmer until the sauce has reduced.
7. Halfway through the cooking time, baste the pork with sauce.

- **Nutrition Info:** Calories: 345; Carbohydrates: 15.1g; Protein: 22.3g; Fat: 21.5g; Sugar: 8.6g; Sodium: 1310mg

465. Root Veggie Mix

Servings: 6 Servings
Cooking Time: 15 Minutes
Ingredients:
- 1 tsp kosher salt
- ½ tsp ground black pepper
- 2 Tbsp olive oil
- 3 cloves garlic
- 1 Tbsp thyme, fresh, minced
- 3 large carrots, peeled and chopped
- 3 large parsnips, peeled, chopped
- 1 cup pearl onions

Directions:
1. Toss all the ingredients together in a medium sized bowl.
2. Place the veggies in the crisper bowl and lower them into the Ninja Foodi. Close the crisper lid and set the temperature to 350 degrees for 15 minutes.
3. Open the lid and serve the veggies warm.
- **Nutrition Info:** Calories: 84, Carbohydrates: 9g, Protein: 1g, Fat: 5g, Sugar: 4g, Sodium: 248g

466. Steamed Egg Chawan Mushi

Servings: 2
Cooking Time: 20 Minutes
Ingredients:
- 2 eggs
- 1 cup cool chicken stock
- 1 dash sake
- ½ teaspoon soy sauce
- ½ cup chicken meat, chopped
- 1 shiitake mushroom, sliced
- 2 sprigs parsley, chopped

Directions:
1. Place the FoodiTM Cook &CrispTM reversible rack inside the ceramic pot.
2. Pour a cup of water in the pot.
3. In a mixing bowl, whisk together the eggs, chicken stock, sake, and soy sauce until well-combined.
4. Pour into heat-proof ramekins.
5. Top each egg mixture with chicken and mushroom slices.
6. Place on the reversible rack.
7. Close the pressure lid and set the vent to SEAL.
8. Press the Steam button and adjust the cooking time to 20 minutes.
9. Once cooked, garnish with chopped parsley.
- **Nutrition Info:** Calories: 156; Carbohydrates: 3.3g; Protein: 17.3g; Fat: 8.1g; Sugar: 1.4g; Sodium: 527mg

467. Chicken Potato & Broccoli Casserole

Servings: 6 -8 Servings
Cooking Time: 40 Minutes
Ingredients:
- 3 pounds red potatoes, cut into 1-inch pieces
- 3 cups chicken, cooked and chopped
- 2-3 cups broccoli florets
- 4 slices bacon, cooked and crumbled
- 2 cups cheddar cheese, grated
- 1 cup sour cream
- 4 tablespoons butter, soft
- 1 teaspoon salt
- ½ teaspoon freshly ground black pepper
- ½ teaspoon garlic powder
- ½ teaspoon paprika

Directions:
1. Place the potatoes and 1 cup of water in the cooking pot. Secure the lid and select pressure cooking on high. Cook the potatoes 8 minutes. Use quick release and drain the potatoes. Mash them and set aside.
2. Place the broccoli and 1 cup of water in the pot and repeat above, cooking the broccoli for 3 minutes. Drain and set aside.
3. Lightly spray the cooking pot with cooking spray. Add the mashed potatoes to the hot pot and stir in the butter, sour cream and seasonings. Stir to combine.
4. Add the broccoli, bacon, chicken and half the cheese. Stir to mix well. Sprinkle the remaining cheese on top.
5. Switch to the Tender Crisp lid and set to 350 degrees. Bake 20 – 25 minutes, or till the casserole is heated through and the cheese has melted. Serve.

468. Seafood With Chorizo 'n Chicken Spanish Rice

Servings: 2
Cooking Time: 30 Minutes
Ingredients:
- 1/4-lb chicken breast, diced
- 2 oz. Spicy chorizo
- 1 tbsp olive oil
- ½ onion, diced
- 1/4 tsp marjoram
- 1/4 tsp cumin
- 1/8 tsp whole saffron
- 1/2 cup long-grain rice, uncooked
- 1 1/2 cups chicken stock
- 2 cloves garlic, minced
- 1/4-lb whole shrimp
- ¼-lb clams, in the shell, drained
- ¼ cup green peas; frozen
- Salt
- 1/2 lemon, wedged

Directions:

1. Press sauté and heat oil.
2. Sauté saffron, cumin, marjoram, and onions for a minute.
3. Stir in chorizo and chopped chicken, cook for 8 minutes.
4. Stir in rice and cook for a minute. Add water and chicken stock. Deglaze pot.
5. Install pressure lid and place valve to vent position.
6. Close Ninja Foodi, press steam button, and set time to 10 minutes.
7. Once done cooking, do a quick release.
8. Press stop, press sauté button. Stir in salt, garlic, clams, green peas and shrimp. Cook for 3 minutes.
9. Press stop and let it sit for 5 more minutes to continue cooking.
10. Serve and enjoy with lemon wedges.
- **Nutrition Info:** Calories: 563; carbohydrates: 49.9g; protein: 40.8g; fat: 22.2g

469. Tasty 'n Easy To Make Baked Potatoes

Servings: 2
Cooking Time: 35 Minutes
Ingredients:
- 2 medium russet potato
- 2 teaspoon canola oil
- 1/2 teaspoon onion powder
- Salt and pepper to taste
- 2 tablespoons cream cheese
- 2 tablespoons chopped chives

Directions:
1. Brush the potatoes until clean.
2. Place the Cook & Crisp basket in the Ninja Foodi and add potatoes.
3. Brush with oil on all surface and season with onion powder, salt, and pepper.
4. Close the Ninja Foodi and cook for 35 minutes at 350 ºF.
5. Once cooked, slice through the potato and serve with cream cheese and chives.
- **Nutrition Info:** Calories: 413; carbs: 72.3g; protein:10.2 g; fat: 9.2g

470. Summertime Mousse

Servings: 2
Cooking Time: 12 Minutes
Ingredients:
- 4-oz. cream cheese, softened
- ½ C. heavy cream
- 2 tbsp. fresh lemon juice
- 2 tbsp. honey
- 2 pinches salt

Directions:
1. Select "Bake/Roast" of Ninja Foodi and set the temperature to 350 degrees F.
2. Press "Start/Stop" to begin and preheat the Ninja Foodi for about 10 minutes.
3. In a bowl, add all the ingredients and mix until well combined.
4. Transfer the mixture into 2 ramekins.
5. In the pot of Ninja Foodi, arrange the ramekins.
6. Close the Ninja Foodi with crisping lid and set the time for 12 minutes.
7. Press "Start/Stop" to begin.
8. Open the lid and set the ramekins aside to cool.
9. Refrigerate for at least 3 hours before serving.
- **Nutrition Info:** Calories per serving: 369; Carbohydrates: 20g; Protein: 5.1g; Fat: 31g; Sugar: 17.7g; Sodium: 338mg; Fiber: 0.1g

471. Olive-brined Air Fryer Turkey Breasts

Servings: 7
Cooking Time: 45 Minutes
Ingredients:
- ½ cup salt
- 6 cups water
- ½ cup butter milk
- 3 ½ pounds boneless turkey breasts
- 1 sprig rosemary
- 2 sprigs thyme

Directions:
1. Place all ingredients in a large bowl or stock pot and allow the turkey to soak in the brine for at least 24 hours.
2. Rinse the turkey and pat dry.
3. Place in the ceramic pot the FoodiTM Cook & CrispTM basket
4. Place the turkey breasts in the basket.
5. Close the crisping lid and press the Air Crisp button before pressing the START button.
6. Adjust the cooking time to 45 minutes.
- **Nutrition Info:** Calories: 135; Carbohydrates: 1.4g; Protein: 30.2g; Fat: 0.9g; Sugar:0 g; Sodium: 62mg

472. Crispy Brussel Sprouts

Servings: 4 Servings
Cooking Time: 14 Minutes
Ingredients:
- 4 cups Brussel sprouts
- 2 Tablespoons olive oil
- 1 tsp salt
- ½ tsp pepper

Directions:
1. Cut the Brussel sprouts in half and toss together with the olive oil, salt and pepper.
2. Place the cook and crisp pot inside the Ninja Foodi. Close the crisper lid and set the pot to 400 degrees F using the air crisp function.
3. Add the Brussel Sprouts to the basket and set the timer for 6 minutes.

4. Open the lid, mix the Brussel sprouts inside the pot and then cook for another 8 minutes to get nice and crispy.
- **Nutrition Info:** Calories: 62g, Carbohydrates: 0g, Protein: 0g, Fat: 7g, Sugar: 0g, Sodium: 35g

473. Crispy Sweet Potato Fries

Servings: 2
Cooking Time: 15 Minutes
Ingredients:
- 2 large sweet orange sweet potatoes, peeled and cut into thick strips
- 2 tablespoons olive oil
- 1 teaspoon paprika
- 1 teaspoon garlic powder
- Salt and pepper to taste
- 1 ripe avocado, flesh scooped
- 2 tablespoons sour cream
- 2 tablespoons fresh cilantro, chopped
- Juice from ½ lime
- ½ teaspoon garlic, minced

Directions:
1. Place the sweet potatoes in a bowl and season with oil, paprika, garlic powder, salt, and pepper.
2. Toss to coat.
3. Add ingredients to the Cook & Crisp basket.
4. Close the Ninja Foodi and cook for 15 minutes at 330 ºF.
5. Halfway through the cooking time, give the basket a shake.
6. Meanwhile, prepare the avocado dip by combining the rest of the ingredient in a food processor.
7. Dip the sweet potatoes in the avocado dressing.
- **Nutrition Info:** Calories: 506; carbs: 52g; protein: 7.1g; fat: 30 g

474. Tiger Shrimp A La Bang Bang

Servings: 2
Cooking Time: 15 Minutes
Ingredients:
- ½ cup mayonnaise
- ¼ cup sweet chili oil
- 1 pound raw shrimps, peeled and deveined
- ¼ cup all-purpose flour
- 1 cup panko bread crumbs
- 1 head loose leaf lettuce
- 2 green onions, chopped

Directions:
1. Place in the ceramic pot the FoodiTM Cook &CrispTM basket.
2. In a bowl, combine the mayonnaise and sweet chili oil. Reserve half of it as dipping sauce.
3. Dust the shrimps with all-purpose flour and dip in half of the mayonnaise mixture.
4. Dredge the shrimps in panko bread crumbs.
5. Close the crisping lid and press the Air Crisp button before pressing the START button.
6. Adjust the cooking time to 15 minutes.
7. Serve on top of lettuce and garnish with green onions.
- **Nutrition Info:** Calories: 442; Carbohydrates: 32.7g; Protein: 23.9g; Fat: 23.9g; Sugar: 10.8g; Sodium: 894mg

475. Jicama Fries

Servings: 4 Servings
Cooking Time: 10 Minutes
Ingredients:
- 1 medium jicama
- 3 Tbsp olive oil
- ½ tsp salt
- ¼ tsp ground black pepper

Directions:
1. Peel the jicama and cup it into ¼ inch strips.
2. Toss the slices with the oil, salt and pepper.
3. Place the strips in the air crisp basket, put the basket into the Ninja Foodie and put the air crisp lid on the machine.
4. Set the temperature to 390 degrees F and the timer for 20 minutes. Toss the fries occasionally to brown evenly. Serve hot
- **Nutrition Info:** Calories: 101g, Carbohydrates: 3g, Protein: 0g, Fat: 10g, Sugar: 2g, Sodium: 583g

476. Roasted Beets

Servings: 4 Servings
Cooking Time: 15 Minutes
Ingredients:
- 1 cup water
- 4 whole beets
- ½ tsp salt
- 1/8 tsp black pepper
- 1 tbsp olive oil

Directions:
1. Add the water to the Ninja Foodi Pot and place the metal trivet inside as well.
2. Rinse the beets and then place in the pot on top of the trivet.
3. Close the lid and seal then use the pressure cooker function set at high heat for 15 minutes.
4. Once the timer has gone off, let the steam release naturally.
5. Open the lid and remove the beets and peel with your hand, the skin should come right off.
6. Slice and toss in a bowl with the olive oil, salt and black pepper
- **Nutrition Info:** Calories: 65g, Carbohydrates: 8g, Protein: 1g, Fat: 4g, Sugar: 7g, Sodium: 645mg

477. Buttery Corn

Servings: 2
Cooking Time: 20 Minutes
Ingredients:
- 2 ears corn on the cob
- Salt and freshly ground pepper, to taste
- 2 tbsp. butter, softened and divided

Directions:
1. Season the corn with salt and black pepper and then, rub with half of butter.
2. Arrange the "Cook & Crisp Basket" in the pot of Ninja Foodi.
3. Close the Ninja Foodi with crisping lid and select "Air Crisp".
4. Press "Start/Stop" to begin and set the temperature to 320 degrees F.
5. Set the time for 5 minutes to preheat.
6. With a piece of foil, wrap each cob and place into "Cook & Crisp Basket".
7. Close the Ninja Foodi with crisping lid and select "Air Crisp".
8. Set the temperature to 320 degrees F for 20 minutes.
9. Press "Start/Stop" to begin.
10. Open the lid and transfer the cobs into a bowl.
11. Coat with the remaining butter and serve.
- **Nutrition Info:** Calories per serving: 234; Carbohydrates: 29g; Protein: 5.1g; Fat: 13.3g; Sugar: 5g; Sodium: 182mg; Fiber: 4.2g

478. Steamed Egg Chawanmushi

Servings: 2
Cooking Time: 20 Minutes
Ingredients:
- 2 eggs
- 1 cup cool chicken stock
- 1 dash sake
- ½ teaspoon soy sauce
- ½ cup chicken meat, chopped
- 1 shiitake mushroom, sliced
- 2 sprigs parsley, chopped

Directions:
1. Place the FoodiTM Cook &CrispTM reversible rack inside the ceramic pot.
2. Pour a cup of water in the pot.
3. In a mixing bowl, whisk together the eggs, chicken stock, sake, and soy sauce until well-combined.
4. Pour into heat-proof ramekins.
5. Top each egg mixture with chicken and mushroom slices.
6. Place on the reversible rack.
7. Close the pressure lid and set the vent to SEAL.
8. Press the Steam button and adjust the cooking time to 20 minutes.
9. Once cooked, garnish with chopped parsley.
- **Nutrition Info:** Calories per serving: 156; Carbohydrates: 3.3g; Protein: 17.3g; Fat: 8.1g; Sugar: 1.4g; Sodium: 527mg

479. Crispy Kale Chips In Ninja Foodi

Servings: 2
Cooking Time: 7 Minutes
Ingredients:
- 3 cups kale leaves, stem removed
- 1 tablespoon olive oil
- Salt and pepper to taste

Directions:
1. In a bowl, combine all of the ingredients: and toss to coat the kale leaves with oil, salt and pepper.
2. Arrange kale leaves on the double layer rack and insert inside the Ninja Foodi.
3. Close the Ninja Foodi and cook it to 7 minutes at 370 ºF.
4. Allow to cool before serving.
- **Nutrition Info:** Calories: 85; carbs: 4.2g; protein: 1.35g; fat: 6.9g

480. Avocado Chips

Servings: 4
Cooking Time: 20 Minutes
Ingredients:
- 4 tbsps. butter
- 4 raw avocados, peeled and sliced
- Salt and black pepper

Directions:
1. Season the avocado slices with salt and black pepper.
2. Grease the pot of Ninja Foodi with butter and add avocado slices.
3. Press "Air Crisp" and set the timer to 10 minutes at 350 degrees F.
4. Remove from the Ninja Foodi and dish out to serve.
- **Nutrition Info:** 391 calories, 38.2g fat, 15g carbs, 3.5g protein

481. Crunchy Onion Rings

Servings: 2
Cooking Time: 10 Minutes
Ingredients:
- ¾ cup all-purpose flour
- ½ cup cornstarch
- 2 teaspoons baking powder
- 1 teaspoon salt
- 1 large onion, cut into rings
- 1 cup milk
- 1 egg, beaten
- 1 cup bread crumbs
- A dash of garlic powder
- A dash of paprika
- Cooking spray

Directions:

1. Place in the ceramic pot the FoodiTM Cook &CrispTM basket.
2. In a large bowl, toss together all-purpose flour, cornstarch, baking powder, salt, and onion rings. Toss until the onion rings have been coated with flour.
3. In another bowl, mix the milk and egg. Set aside.
4. In another bowl, mix the breadcrumbs, garlic powder and paprika. Set aside.
5. Dip each floured onion ring in the milk mixture before dredging in the breadcrumbs.
6. Place the onion rings in the basket.
7. Close the crisping lid and press the Air Crisp button before pressing the START button.
8. Adjust the cooking time to 10 minutes.
9. Be sure to flip the onion rings halfway through the cooking time for even cooking.
- **Nutrition Info:** Calories: 319; Carbohydrates: 59.7g; Protein: 10.2g; Fat: 4.3g; Sugar: 10.5g; Sodium: 1069mg

482. Spicy Short Ribs

Servings: 4
Cooking Time: 60 Minutes
Ingredients:
- 2 teaspoons canola oil
- 1 onion, diced
- 4 cloves of garlic, minced
- 2 pounds beef short ribs
- 1 teaspoon paprika
- 1 teaspoon cumin
- 2 tablespoons apple cider vinegar
- 1 can cola
- 1 tablespoon raspberry jam
- 1 tablespoon Worcestershire sauce
- 1 tablespoon sugar
- 2 tablespoons cornstarch
- 2 tablespoons water
- Salt and pepper to taste

Directions:
1. Press the Sear/Sauté button and then the START button. Heat the oil and sauté the onion and garlic until fragrant.
2. Stir in the beef short ribs and season with salt, pepper, paprika, and cumin.
3. Stir until all sides are lightly golden.
4. Add in the apple cider vinegar, cola, raspberry jam, Worcestershire sauce, and sugar.
5. Close the pressure lid and set the vent to SEAL.
6. Press the Pressure button and adjust the cooking time to 60 minutes.
7. Do quick pressure release. Once the lid is open, press the Sear/Sauté button and stir in the cornstarch slurry. Allow to simmer until the sauce thickens.
- **Nutrition Info:** Calories: 471; Carbohydrates: 45.1g; Protein: 22g; Fat: 22.5g; Sugar: 21.9g; Sodium: 624mg

483. Spicy 'n Steamy Shrimps

Servings: 2
Cooking Time: 10 Minutes
Ingredients:
- pound tiger prawns with shell
- 1 packet Old Bay seasoning
- 1 jar cocktail sauce

Directions:
1. Place the FoodiTM Cook &CrispTM reversible rack inside the ceramic pot.
2. Pour a cup of water in the pot.
3. Season the prawns with Old Bay seasoning.
4. Place the shrimps on the reversible rack.
5. Close the pressure lid and set the vent to SEAL.
6. Press the Steam button and adjust the cooking time to 10 minutes.
7. Do quick pressure release.
8. Serve with cocktail sauce.
- **Nutrition Info:** Calories: 360; Carbohydrates: 38.8g; Protein: 41.1g; Fat: 4.4g; Sugar: 10.9g; Sodium: 1250mg

484. Easy Crab Wontons

Servings: 16 Pieces
Cooking Time: 10 Minutes
Ingredients:
- 16 wonton wrappers
- ¾ cup lump crab meat
- 2 green onions, chopped
- 3 tablespoons cream cheese, soft
- Black pepper
- Old Bay seasoning

Directions:
1. Combine all ingredients in a mixing bowl and mix well
2. Lay out wrappers on a work surface. Moisten with a dab of water and spoon about 1 ½ teaspoons filling on each.
3. Pull two opposite corners up over filling and pinch together. Repeat with other corners. Spray the wontons lightly with cooking spray.
4. Spray the cooking pot with and add the wontons, you will have to cook them in batches.
5. Lock the Tender Crisp lid in place and set temperature to 350 degrees. Cook 8 minutes or till they are golden brown and crisp.
6. Serve with your favorite dipping sauce or enjoy them on their own.

485. Herbed Pork Rump Roast

Servings: 4

Cooking Time: 1 Hour And 30 Minutes
Ingredients:
- 2 tablespoons olive oil
- ½ teaspoon thyme
- ½ teaspoon garlic powder
- 1 ½ teaspoons chopped chives
- 2 pounds pork rump
- Salt and pepper to taste

Directions:
1. Place in the ceramic pot the FoodiTM Cook & CrispTM reversible rack.
2. In a bowl, mix together olive oil, thyme, garlic powder, chives, salt, and pepper. This will be the seasoning.
3. Rub the pork rump with the seasoning.
4. Close the crisping lid and press the Bake/Roast button before pressing the START button.
5. Adjust the cooking time to 1 hour and 30 minutes.
- **Nutrition Info:** Calories: 518; Carbohydrates: 0.9g; Protein: 47.3g; Fat: 36.1g; Sugar: 0g; Sodium: 852mg

486. Southwest's Chickpea Gumbo

Servings: 2
Cooking Time: 12 Minutes
Ingredients:
- 1/2 tablespoon olive oil
- 1 teaspoon minced garlic
- 3/4 cup chopped onion
- 1 celery rib, chopped
- 1 tsp oregano
- ½ teaspoon cayenne pepper
- 1/3 cup cooked chickpeas
- 1 1/2 cups vegetable broth
- 1/2 cup frozen okra
- 1/2 red bell pepper, chopped
- 1/2 can diced tomatoes, drained
- 1 tablespoon apple cider vinegar
- ½ cups tomato sauce
- 1/2 cup cauliflower, cut into florets
- Salt and pepper to taste

Directions:
1. Press the sauté button on the Ninja Foodi and heat the oil. Sauté the garlic, onions, and celery until fragrant.
2. Stir in the rest of the ingredients.
3. Install pressure lid. Close Ninja Foodi, press the manual button, choose high settings, and set time to 10 minutes.
4. Once done cooking, do a quick release.
5. Serve and enjoy.
- **Nutrition Info:** Calories: 227; carbohydrates: 29.2g; protein: 13.2g; fat: 6.3g

487. Easy-steam Lobster Tails

Servings: 4
Cooking Time: 10 Minutes
Ingredients:
- 4 6-ounces lobster tails
- Salt and pepper to taste
- ½ cup butter

Directions:
1. Place the FoodiTM Cook &CrispTM reversible rack inside the ceramic pot.
2. Pour a cup of water in the pot.
3. Season the lobster tails with salt and pepper to taste.
4. Place the seasoned lobster tails on the reversible rack.
5. Close the pressure lid and set the vent to SEAL.
6. Press the Steam button and adjust the cooking time to 10 minutes.
7. Do quick pressure release.
8. Once the lid is open, take the lobster tail out and serve with butter on top.
- **Nutrition Info:** Calories: 353; Carbohydrates: 0.9g; Protein: 32.2g; Fat: 24.5g; Sugar: 0.2g; Sodium: 1987mg

488. Salt-encrusted Prime Rib Roast

Servings: 8
Cooking Time: 45 Minutes
Ingredients:
- 2 cups salt
- 4 pounds prime rib roast
- 1 tablespoon black pepper

Directions:
1. Place in the ceramic pot the FoodiTM Cook &CrispTM reversible rack.
2. In a roasting pan that will fit in the Ninja Foodi, place the salt. Place the roast on top of the bed of salt. Season the pork with black pepper.
3. Place the pan with the meat on the rack.
4. Close the crisping lid and press the Bake/Roast button before pressing the START button.
5. Adjust the cooking time to 45 minutes.
- **Nutrition Info:** Calories: 382; Carbohydrates: 1.2g; Protein: 36.1g; Fat: 25.8g; Sugar: 0g; Sodium: 3092mg

489. Baked Calamari & Shrimp Pasta

Servings: 4 Servings
Cooking Time: 45 Mins
Ingredients:
- 1 squid, cut into rings
- ½ pound shrimp, deveined and peeled
- 3 cups milk
- 2 cups mushrooms, sliced
- 1 ½ cups mozzarella cheese, grated
- 1 ¼ cups pasta, cooked
- 4 cloves garlic, chopped fine
- 3 tablespoons butter

- 3 tablespoons flour
- 2 tablespoons olive oil
- 2 teaspoons white rum
- ½ teaspoon thyme
- ¼ teaspoon chicken bouillon
- ¼ teaspoon nutmeg
- sea salt and pepper to taste

Directions:
1. In a small bowl, add shrimp and 1 teaspoon rum, salt and pepper and mix well.
2. In another small bowl, repeat with the squid.
3. Set the cooker to sauté on med-high heat and add 1 tablespoon of the oil. Once the oil is warm add the garlic and cook till fragrant, about 1 minute. Add mushrooms and cook, stirring often, till they are cooked through and no liquid remains. Transfer to a plate or bowl and set aside.
4. Add ½ tablespoon of oil to the cooking pot and cook shrimp till both sides are pink but they are not cooked through. Remove to bowl and set aside.
5. Add the remaining oil and squid and cook till it turns white but is not cooked through. Remove to bowl and set aside.
6. Turn the temperature down to med-low and add butter. Once the butter is melted, whisk in flour till completely combined. Cook and stir for about 2 minutes before adding milk. Stir while turning the heat up to med and continue to cook till mixture is boiling. Turn the heat back to med-low and stir in salt, pepper, bouillon, thyme and nutmeg. Simmer about 5 minutes, or sauce thickens.
7. Turn off the sauté function. Stir the pasta into the sauce. Top with a layer of shrimp, then the calamari, the mushrooms and finally the mozzarella. Secure the Tender Crisp lid and select bake at 350 degrees.
8. Cook the casserole 15 – 20 minutes, or till heated through and cheese is melted and browned. Serve.

490. Pressure Cooker Fenugreek Chicken

Servings: 8
Cooking Time: 30 Minutes
Ingredients:
- 2 tablespoons cooking oil
- 6 pounds whole chicken, cut into 8 pieces
- Salt and pepper to taste
- ½ teaspoon garam masala
- 1 teaspoon cumin seeds
- 1 cinnamon stick
- 1 black cardamom pod
- 4 whole cloves
- 1 onion, sliced
- 4 green chili pepper, halved
- 1 cup water
- ½ cup fenugreek leaves

Directions:
1. Press the Sear/Sauté button and then the START button.
2. Heat the oil and sear the chicken on all sides.
3. Season with salt, pepper, garam masala and cumin seeds.
4. Add in the rest of the ingredients except for the fenugreek leaves.
5. Close the pressure lid and set the vent to SEAL.
6. Press the Pressure button and adjust the cooking time to 25 minutes.
7. Do quick pressure release.
8. Once the lid is open, add the fenugreek leaves last.
- **Nutrition Info:** Calories: 305; Carbohydrates: 8g; Protein: 36.7g; Fat: 14g; Sugar: 2g; Sodium: 395mg

491. Broiled Short Ribs

Servings: 8
Cooking Time: 45 Minutes
Ingredients:
- 4 pounds boneless beef short ribs
- Salt and pepper to taste
- 1/3 cup molasses
- 2/3 ketchup
- ¼ cup fresh lemon juice
- 1 tablespoon dry mustard
- ½ teaspoon chili powder
- ½ teaspoon garlic powder

Directions:
1. Place in the ceramic pot the FoodiTM Cook & CrispTM reversible tray.
2. Combine all ingredients in a mixing bowl and allow to marinate in the fridge for at least 12 hours.
3. Close the crisping lid and press the Broil button before pressing the START button.
4. Adjust the cooking time to 45 minutes.
- **Nutrition Info:** Calories: 357; Carbohydrates: 16.4g; Protein: 31.2g; Fat: 18.5g; Sugar: 8.3 g; Sodium: 287mg

492. Wonderful Side Dish

Servings: 2
Cooking Time: 12 Minutes
Ingredients:
- 1 lb. Brussels sprouts, cut in half
- 2 tbsp. olive oil
- 2 garlic cloves, minced
- Salt and freshly ground black pepper, to taste

Directions:
1. In a bowl, add all the ingredients and toss to coat well.
2. Arrange the "Cook & Crisp Basket" in the pot of Ninja Foodi.

3. Close the Ninja Foodi with crisping lid and select "Air Crisp".
4. Press "Start/Stop" to begin and set the temperature to 390 degrees F.
5. Set the time for 5 minutes to preheat.
6. Now, place the Brussels sprout into "Cook & Crisp Basket".
7. Close the Ninja Foodi with crisping lid and select "Air Crisp".
8. Set the temperature to 390 degrees F for 12 minutes, shaking once after 6 minutes.
9. Press "Start/Stop" to begin.
10. Open the lid and serve
- **Nutrition Info:** Calories: 111; Carbohydrates: 10.8g; Protein: 4g; Fat: 7.4g; Sugar: 2.5g; Sodium: 67mg; Fiber: 4.3g

493. Unique Apple Pastries

Servings: 8
Cooking Time: 10 Minutes
Ingredients:
- ½ large apple, peeled, cored and chopped
- 1 tsp. fresh orange zest, grated finely
- ½ tbsp. white sugar
- ½ tsp. ground cinnamon
- 7.05-oz. prepared frozen puff pastry

Directions:
1. In a bowl, mix together all ingredients except puff pastry.
2. Cut the pastry in 16 squares.
3. Place about a tsp. of the apple mixture in the center of each square.
4. Fold each square into a triangle and press the edges slightly with wet fingers.
5. Then with a fork, press the edges firmly.
6. Arrange the "Cook & Crisp Basket" in the pot of Ninja Foodi.
7. Close the Ninja Foodi with crisping lid and select "Air Crisp".
8. Press "Start/Stop" to begin and set the temperature to 390 degrees F.
9. Set the time for 5 minutes to preheat.
10. Now, place the pastries into "Cook & Crisp Basket".
11. Close the Ninja Foodi with crisping lid and select "Air Crisp".
12. Set the temperature to 390 degrees F for 10 minutes.
13. Press "Start/Stop" to begin.
14. Open the lid and serve warm.
- **Nutrition Info:** Calories per serving: 119; Carbohydrates: 11.3g; Protein: 1.5g; Fat: 7.6g; Sugar: 1.9g; Sodium: 50mg; Fiber: 0.7g

494. Spicy Cauliflower Bites

Servings: 4 Servings
Cooking Time: 10 Mins
Ingredients:
- 1 cup panko bread crumbs
- 1 cup ranch dressing
- ½ head of cauliflower, separated into florets
- ½ cup hot sauce
- 1 egg
- ½ teaspoon salt
- ½ teaspoon garlic powder
- Black pepper

Directions:
1. Place the egg in a medium bowl and mix in the salt, pepper and garlic. Place the panko crumbs into a small bowl.
2. Dip the florets first in the egg then into the panko crumbs.
3. Place the basket into the cooker and add breaded cauliflower. Lock the Tender Crisp lid in place and set the temperature to 400 degrees.
4. Cook the cauliflower for 8 – 10 minutes, shaking half way through, or till crisp and golden brown.
5. Mix the ranch dressing with the hot sauce and serve it for dipping.

495. Hearty Egg And Sausage Bake

Servings: 6
Cooking Time: 30 Minutes
Ingredients:
- 1 ½ pounds bulk pork sausages, sliced
- 1 ½ cups milk
- 8 eggs, beaten
- ¾ teaspoon dry mustard
- 1 can condensed cream of mushroom soup
- 8 slices of bread, torn into small squares
- 2 cups shredded mozzarella cheese

Directions:
1. Place the ceramic tray in the Ninja Foodi.
2. Place the sausages in the pot.
3. In a bowl, combine the milk, eggs, mustard and mushroom soup.
4. Pour the egg mixture into the ceramic pot and add the bread pieces.
5. Top with mozzarella cheese.
6. Close the crisping lid and press the Bake/Roast button before pressing the START button.
7. Adjust the cooking time to 30 minutes.
- **Nutrition Info:** Calories: 159; Carbohydrates: 14.7g; Protein: 20.5g; Fat: 22g; Sugar: 7.3g; Sodium: 976mg

496. Asparagus, Shrooms 'n Shrimp Risotto

Servings: 4
Cooking Time: 20 Minutes
Ingredients:
- 2 tsp olive oil
- 1 small onion, diced
- 3/4 cup arborio rice
- 1 cup sliced cremini or white button mushrooms
- 1/4 cup dry white wine

- 1 1/2 cups chicken broth
- 1 tbsp butter
- 1/2 cup chopped asparagus
- 1/4 lb shrimp, defrosted if frozen, peeled and deveined
- 1/4 cup grated parmigiano-reggiano cheese
- 1/2 tsp fresh black pepper

Directions:
1. Press sear button and heat oil. Sauté onions for 3 minutes.
2. Stir in mushrooms and rice. Cook for 5 minutes.
3. Add wine and deglaze pot for a minute.
4. Add chicken broth. Press stop.
5. Install pressure lid and place valve to vent position.
6. Close Ninja Foodi, press steam button, and set time to 6 minutes.
7. Once done cooking, do a 5-minute natural release and then a quick release.
8. Press stop, press sear button, stir in asparagus and butter. Cook for a minute.
9. Add shrimps and stirring frequently, cook for 3 minutes.
10. Stir in cheese.
11. Serve and enjoy.
- **Nutrition Info:** Calories: 430; carbohydrates: 30.3g; protein: 23.2g; fat: 24.0g

497. Bangladeshi Beef Curry

Servings: 4
Cooking Time: 45 Minutes
Ingredients:
- 3 tablespoons olive oil
- 1 onion, chopped
- 6 cloves of garlic, minced
- 5 green chili peppers, sliced
- 1 teaspoon ginger paste
- 3 whole cardamom seeds
- 2 whole cloves
- 1 ½ inch cinnamon sticks
- 1 teaspoon ground cumin
- 1 teaspoon ground coriander
- 1 teaspoon ground turmeric
- 1 teaspoon garlic powder
- 2 pounds boneless beef chuck, cut into chunks
- 1 cup water
- Salt and pepper to taste

Directions:
1. Season the beef with salt and pepper. Dredge in flour.
2. Press the Sear/Sauté button and then the START button.
3. Heat the oil and sauté the onion and garlic until fragrant. Stir in the rest of the ingredients except for the beef and water.
4. Keep stirring for 3 minutes until the toasted.
5. Stir in the beef and cook for 2 minutes. Pour in water and season with salt and pepper to taste. Close the pressure lid and set the vent to SEAL.
6. Press the Pressure button and adjust the cooking time to 45 minutes.
- **Nutrition Info:** Calories: 322; Carbohydrates: 8.8g; Protein: 19.5g; Fat: 23.1g; Sugar: 0.8g; Sodium: 50mg

498. Holiday Brussels Sprouts With Nuts & Cranberries

Servings: 8 Servings
Cooking Time: 2 Hours 30 Mins
Ingredients:
- 4 cups Brussels sprouts, halved
- 4 cups butternut squash, cut into 1-inch cubes
- 1 red onion, cut into large chunks
- 1 cup cranberries
- ½ cup pecans
- Maple Cinnamon Sauce
- ¼ cup maple syrup
- 2 tablespoons apple cider vinegar
- 1 teaspoon cinnamon
- ½ teaspoon salt
- ¼ teaspoon nutmeg

Directions:
1. Add the Brussels sprouts, squash and onion to the cooking pot and toss together. Secure the lid and select slow cooking on high. Cook 2 – 2 ½ hours, stirring every hour.
2. After 2 hours check for doneness, sprouts should be tender-crisp and squash should be tender without being mushy.
3. In a small saucepan, stir the sauce ingredients together over med-high heat. Bring to a boil, reduce heat and simmer, stirring often, 5 minutes, or till thickened.
4. Just before serving add the cranberries to the vegetables in the pot and cook another 5 minutes.
5. To serve, transfer vegetables to a serving bowl and pour the sauce over, toss to coat. Top with pecans.

499. Parmesan 'n Garlic Fries

Servings: 2
Cooking Time: 15 Minutes
Ingredients:
- 2 russet potatoes, scrubbed and julienned into thick strips
- 1 tablespoon olive oil
- 1 tablespoon salt
- ¼ cup parmesan cheese, grated
- ½ teaspoon garlic powder
- 2 tablespoons chopped parsley

Directions:

1. Place the potatoes in a bowl and add the rest of the ingredients.
2. Toss to combine all ingredients.
3. Add ingredients to the Cook & Crisp basket.
4. Close the Ninja Foodi and cook for 15 minutes.
5. Halfway through the cooking time, give a good shake.
- **Nutrition Info:** Calories: 417; carbs: 69g; protein: 11.7g; fat: 10.5g

500. Garden Fresh Veggie Combo

Servings: 5
Cooking Time: 35 Minutes
Ingredients:
- 6 tsp. olive oil, divided
- ½ lb. carrots, peeled and sliced
- 2 lb. zucchini, sliced
- 1 tbsp. fresh basil, chopped
- Salt and freshly ground black pepper, to taste

Directions:
1. In a bowl, mix together 2 tsp. of oil and carrots.
2. Arrange the "Cook & Crisp Basket" in the pot of Ninja Foodi.
3. Close the Ninja Foodi with crisping lid and select "Air Crisp".
4. Press "Start/Stop" to begin and set the temperature to 400 degrees F.
5. Set the time for 5 minutes to preheat.
6. Now, place the carrots into "Cook & Crisp Basket".
7. Close the Ninja Foodi with crisping lid and select "Air Crisp".
8. Set the temperature to 400 degrees F for 5 minutes. Press "Start/Stop" to begin.
9. Meanwhile, in a large bowl, mix together remaining oil, zucchini, basil, salt and black pepper.
10. Open the lid and place the zucchini mixture into basket with carrots.
11. Close the Ninja Foodi with crisping lid and set the time for 30 minutes.
12. Press "Start/Stop" to begin. Toss the vegetable mixture 2-3 times during the coking. Open the lid and serve.
- **Nutrition Info:** Calories: 96; Carbohydrates: 10.6g; Protein: 2.6g; Fat: 5.9g; Sugar: 5.4g; Sodium: 80mg; Fiber: 3.1g

501. Cheesy Shepherd's Pie

Servings: 6 Servings
Cooking Time: 30 Minutes
Ingredients:
- 1 pound ground beef
- 3 medium russet potatoes, peeled and cut into 1-inch cubes
- 3 carrot, chopped
- 1 cup onion, chopped fine
- 1 cup mushrooms, chopped
- 1 cup peas, frozen
- 1 cup water
- 1 cup beef broth
- 1 cup cheddar cheese, grated
- 1 egg
- 2 tablespoons butter
- 2 tablespoons Worcestershire
- 2 tablespoons flour
- 1 ½ teaspoons salt
- 1 teaspoon garlic powder
- 1 teaspoon pepper

Directions:
1. Add potatoes and water to cooking pot. Secure lid and select pressure cooking on high. Set timer for 8 minutes. When the timer goes off, drain the potatoes and place them in a large mixing bowl.
2. Add the egg, garlic powder, ½ teaspoon salt and butter and blend together with a hand mixer. Set aside.
3. Set the cooker to sauté on med-high heat and add the ground beef. Cook, stirring often, till no longer pink. Drain the grease. Add Worcestershire, vegetables, salt and pepper and stir to combine.
4. In a small measuring cup, stir the flour and broth together then add to beef mixture. Cook, stirring often, about 3 minutes or till sauce begins to thicken. Transfer to a baking dish that will fit inside the cooking pot.
5. Top the beef mixture with the mashed potatoes in an even layer. Cover the dish with foil.
6. Rinse out the cooking pot and add the rack to it. Add ½ cups water then place the baking dish on the rack. Secure the lid and select pressure cooking on high. Set the timer for 10 minutes.
7. Use quick release to remove the lid. Carefully remove the dish from the pot, unless you are going to broil the top. Remove the foil and sprinkle the cheese on top. Let rest for 10 minutes before serving.

502. Butter-lemon On Walleye Pickerel

Servings: 8
Cooking Time: 20 Minutes
Ingredients:
- 8 fillets walleye pickerel
- ¼ cup clarified butter
- ¼ cup lemon juice
- 1 large onion, sliced into rings
- Salt and pepper to taste

Directions:
1. Place the FoodiTM Cook &CrispTM reversible rack inside the ceramic pot.

2. Pour a cup of water in the pot.
3. On a large aluminum foil, place the pickerel and pour over the butter, lemon juice, salt and pepper.
4. Garnish with onion rings on top.
5. Close the aluminum foil and crimp the edges.
6. Place on the reversible rack.
7. Close the pressure lid and set the vent to SEAL.
8. Press the Steam button and adjust the cooking time to 20 minutes.
- **Nutrition Info:** Calories: 336; Carbohydrates: 4.8g; Protein: 43.9g; Fat: 15.6g; Sugar: 2.8g; Sodium: 118mg

503. Artichoke Dip

Servings: 6 Servings
Cooking Time: 6 Minutes
Ingredients:
- ¼ cup chicken broth
- 4 oz cream cheese
- 5 ounces chopped spinach
- 1 cup canned artichoke hearts
- ½ cup sour cream
- 1 clove garlic
- ½ tsp onion powder
- 6 ounces parmesan cheese, grated
- 6 ounces Swiss cheese

Directions:
1. Add all the ingredients to the Ninja Foodi Pot except the parmesan cheese and Swiss cheese.
2. Close the lid and set the steamer valve to seal. Use the pressure cooker function and cook the dip on high pressure for 4 minutes. Do a quick pressure release and open the pot.
3. Add the cheeses, reserving a small amount of each, and mix. Sprinkle the final cheese over the top of the dip and lower the crisper plate over the dip.
4. Use the broil function for 2 minutes to brown the cheese. Serve hot!
- **Nutrition Info:** Calories: 427g; Carbohydrates: 10g, Protein: 22g, Fat: 32g, Sugar: 2g, Sodium: 812mg

504. Rum Spiced Nuts

Servings: 3 Cups
Cooking Time: 10 Minutes
Ingredients:
- 3 cups mixed nuts
- 2 tablespoons butter
- 2 tablespoons dark rum
- 2 tablespoons sugar
- 1 tablespoon salt
- 2 teaspoons curry powder
- 1 teaspoon ancho chile powder
- 1 teaspoon cinnamon
- 1 teaspoon cumin

Directions:
1. Set the cooker to sauté on medium heat. Add nuts and cook to lightly toast them, about 3-5 minutes, stirring frequently.
2. Add the butter and rum to the nuts and cook, stirring frequently, till most of the liquid evaporates and the nuts are glassy.
3. In a large bowl, add remaining ingredients and stir to combine. Add the glazed nuts and toss well to coat.
4. Dump the nuts onto a large baking sheet to cool. Serve immediately or store in an airtight container.

505. Crusty Sweet Potato Hash

Servings: 4
Cooking Time: 10 Minutes
Ingredients:
- 2 large sweet potatoes, cut into small cubes
- 2 slices of bacon, cut into small pieces
- 2 tablespoons olive oil
- 1 tablespoon smoked paprika
- 1 teaspoon salt
- 1 teaspoon ground black pepper
- 1 teaspoon dill weed

Directions:
1. Place in the ceramic pot the FoodiTM Cook &CrispTM basket.
2. Combine all ingredients in a bowl and give a good stir.
3. Form small patties using your hands.
4. Place the patties in the basket.
5. Close the crisping lid and press the Air Crisp button before pressing the START button.
6. Adjust the cooking time to 10 minutes.
7. Flip the patties halfway through the cooking time for even cooking.
- **Nutrition Info:** Calories: 195; Carbohydrates: 31.4g; Protein: 3.7g; Fat: 6g; Sugar: 15.9g; Sodium: 446mg

506. Beef, Veggie 'n Barley Stew

Servings: 2
Cooking Time: 30 Minutes
Ingredients:
- ¾-lb stew beef, cut into 1-inch cubes
- 2 tsp olive oil
- 1/2 tsp salt
- 1/2 tsp ground pepper
- 1/4 cup red wine
- 1 cup beef broth
- 1 clove garlic, finely diced
- 1/4 cup onion, diced
- 1 tbsp tomato paste
- 1/2 tsp dried thyme
- 1 bay leaf
- 1/2 tsp Italian seasoning

- 1 tomato, chopped
- 1/2 cup carrots, 1/2" pieces
- 1/2 cup potatoes, diced 1/2" pieces
- 2 tbsp barley

Directions:
1. Press sear button and heat oil. Once hot, add beef and season with pepper and salt. Cook until browned, around 8 minutes.
2. Add wine and deglaze pot.
3. Stir in broth, garlic, onion, tomato paste, thyme, bay leaf, Italian seasoning, diced tomatoes, carrots, potatoes and barley. Mix well.
4. Install pressure lid. Close Ninja Foodi, press pressure button, set on high for 20 minutes.
5. Once done cooking, do a quick release.
6. Mix well and discard bay leaf.
7. Serve and enjoy.
- **Nutrition Info:** Calories: 379; carbohydrates: 26.9g; protein: 41.2g; fat: 11.8g

507. Cajun Style Blue Crabs

Servings: 6
Cooking Time: 10 Minutes
Ingredients:
- 1 cup beer
- ¼ cup vinegar
- 12 medium-sized blue crabs
- 1 tablespoon Old Bay seasoning

Directions:
1. Place the FoodiTM Cook &CrispTM reversible rack inside the ceramic pot.
2. Pour the beer and vinegar in the pot.
3. Season the crabs with Old Bay seasoning.
4. Place the crabs on the reversible rack.
5. Close the pressure lid and set the vent to SEAL.
6. Press the Steam button and adjust the cooking time to 10 minutes.
7. Do quick pressure release.
8. Discard the beer and vinegar mixture.
- **Nutrition Info:** Calories: 118; Carbohydrates: 2.3g; Protein: 21.5g; Fat: 2.5g; Sugar: 0.8g; Sodium: 954mg

508. Cool Beet Chips

Servings: 8
Cooking Time: 8 Hours 10 Mins
Ingredients:
- ½ beet, peeled and sliced

Directions:
1. Arrange beet slices in single layer in the Cook and Crisp basket
2. Place the basket in the pot and close the crisping lid
3. Press the Dehydrate button and let it dehydrate for 8 hours at 135 degrees F
4. Once the dehydrating is done, remove the basket from pot and transfer slices to your Air Tight container, serve and enjoy!
- **Nutrition Info:** 35 calories, 0g fat, 8g carbs, 1g protein

509. Chive 'n Parsnips Chowder

Servings: 2
Cooking Time: 10 Minutes
Ingredients:
- 10-oz parsnips, trimmed and peeled
- 1 clove garlic, minced
- 1 tbsp raw cashews
- 1 1/4 cup vegetable broth
- ¼ lemon, juiced, freshly squeezed
- 2 tbsp fresh chives, chopped
- Salt and pepper to taste

Directions:
1. Place all ingredients in the Ninja Foodi
2. Install pressure lid. Close Ninja Foodi, press the pressure button, choose high settings, and set time to 10 minutes.
3. Once done cooking, do a quick release.
4. Open the lid and use an immersion blender to pulse everything until smooth.
5. Serve and enjoy.
- **Nutrition Info:** Calories: 199; carbohydrates: 29.9g; protein: 3.5g; fat: 7.2g

510. Sugar-glazed Carrots

Servings: 6
Cooking Time: 8 Minutes
Ingredients:
- 8 large carrots, peeled and chopped
- 2 tbsps. butter, unsalted
- 1 tbsp. sugar
- 1 tbsp. rice vinegar, unseasoned

Directions:
1. Preparing the ingredients.
2. Put the carrots in the Ninja Foodi; add enough cool tap water that they're submerged by 2 inches.
3. High pressure for 3 minutes. Lock the lid onto the pot.
4. Pressure release. Use the quick-release method to return the pot's pressure to normal.
5. Finish the dish. Unlock and open the pot. Drain the carrots. Turn the Ninja Foodi to its "browning" function. Add the butter; when it has melted, stir in the sugar and cook until it melts and becomes bubbly, stirring all the while, less than 1 minute.
6. Add the carrots and vinegar; toss over the heat for 1 minute to glaze the carrots evenly and thoroughly.
- **Nutrition Info:** 83 calories, 3g fat, 14g carbs, 1g protein

511. Zucchini Pasta With Walnuts & Basil

Servings: 3 – 4 Servings
Cooking Time: 10 Minutes
Ingredients:
- 4 large zucchini, peeled
- ½ cup walnuts, chopped
- 1/3 cup bacon grease
- ¼ cup fresh basil, chopped
- 2 cloves garlic, chopped fine
- 2 teaspoons salt

Directions:
1. If you have a vegetable spiralizer, use it to create zucchini noodles. If you don't, cut the zucchini, lengthwise into long, thin strips that resemble spaghetti noodles. Place in a colander and sprinkle with salt, toss to coat. Place over the kitchen sink for 1 hour to extract the water.
2. Rinse the zucchini thoroughly till no salt remains. Drain on paper towels.
3. Set the cooker to saute on med-high heat and add the bacon grease. Once it is hot, add garlic and zucchini and cook, stirring often, about 4-5 minutes or it is al dente.
4. Stir in basil and walnuts and cook another 2 minutes. Serve.

512. Squash With Cherries

Servings: 6 – 8 Servings
Cooking Time: 1 Hour
Ingredients:
- 3 cups butternut squash, peeled and cut into 1-inch cubes
- 10 slivers lemon peel
- 1 cup apple juice
- 3 cinnamon sticks
- 2 vanilla beans
- ½ cup dried cherries
- ½ teaspoon sea salt

Directions:
1. Place all ingredients in the cooking pot and toss to combine.
2. Add the Tender Crisp lid and set the temperature to 350 degrees. Bake 45 minutes to 1 hour, or till squash is tender and the top is golden brown. Serve.

513. Pressure Cooker Pasta Stew

Servings: 6
Cooking Time: 20 Minutes
Ingredients:
- 1 pound lean ground beef
- 1 cloves of garlic, minced
- 1 onion, chopped
- 1 package bow tie pasta
- 1 can tomato sauce
- 1 can stewed tomatoes
- 1 teaspoon oregano
- 1 teaspoon Italian seasoning
- 1 cup mozzarella cheese
- 1 cup ricotta cheese
- Salt and pepper to taste

Directions:
1. Season the beef with salt and pepper. Dredge in flour.
2. Press the Sear/Sauté button and then the START button.
3. Sauté the beef until some of the fat has rendered. Stir in the garlic and onions until fragrant.
4. Add in the pasta, tomatoes, oregano, and Italian seasoning. Season with salt and pepper to taste. Stir in the rest of the ingredients.
5. Close the pressure lid and set the vent to SEAL.
6. Press the Pressure button and adjust the cooking time to 10 minutes.
7. Do quick pressure release.
8. Once the lid is open, press the Sear/Sauté button then the START button.
9. Stir in the cheese and allow to simmer for another 5 minutes.
- **Nutrition Info:** Calories: 469; Carbohydrates: 53g; Protein: 29.3g; Fat: 15.5g; Sugar: 24.3g; Sodium: 567mg

514. Fall-time Vegetarian Dish

Servings: 8
Cooking Time: 4 Hours
Ingredients:
- 1 (3 lb.) butternut squash, peeled, seeded and cut into cubes
- 3 apples, peeled, cored and chopped
- ½ C. dried cranberries
- ½ white onion, chopped
- 1 tbsp. ground cinnamon

Directions:
1. Grease the pot of Ninja Foodi generously.
2. In the prepared pot, add all the ingredients and stir to combine.
3. Close the crisping lid and select "Slow Cooker".
4. Set on "High" for about 4 hours.
5. Press "Start/Stop" to begin.
6. Open the lid and serve.
- **Nutrition Info:** Calories: 129; Carbohydrates: 33.4g; Protein: 2g; Fat: 0.3g; Sugar: 13g; Sodium: 8mg; Fiber: 6.3g

515. Orange Lobster Tail

Servings: 2
Cooking Time: 25 Minutes
Ingredients:
- ¼ cup wine
- 1 cup orange juice
- 2 lobster tails, shells removed
- 6 cubes of butter

- Salt to taste

Directions:
1. Place the wine, orange juice, and lobster tails in a Ziploc bag. Allow to marinate in the fridge.
2. Place the FoodiTM Cook &CrispTM reversible rack inside the ceramic pot.
3. Pour the marinade in the pot and place the lobster tails on the reversible rack.
4. Close the pressure lid and set the vent to SEAL.
5. Press the Steam button and adjust the cooking time to 20 minutes.
6. Do quick pressure release.
7. Once the lid is open, take out the lobster tails and the reversible rack.
8. Press the Sear/Sauté button and heat the marinade until it thickens. This will be the sauce.
9. Once the sauce thickens, pour over on to the lobster tails.
10. Garnish with butter cubes.
- **Nutrition Info:** Calories: 517; Carbohydrates: 15.4g; Protein: 26.5g; Fat: 38.8g; Sugar: 7.9g; Sodium: 770mg

516. Eggs Stuffed With Avocado & Watercress

Servings: 6
Cooking Time: 15 Minutes
Ingredients:
- ½ tbsp. fresh lemon juice
- 1 medium ripe avocado, peeled, pitted and chopped
- 6 organic eggs, boiled, peeled and halved
- Salt
- ½ c. freshly trimmed watercress

Directions:
1. Set a steamer basket to the bottom of the Ninja Foodi and pour water.
2. Put the watercress on the basket and lock the lid.
3. Set the Ninja Foodi to "Pressure" for about 3 minutes.
4. Release the pressure quickly and drain the watercress completely.
5. Remove the egg yolks and transfer into a bowl.
6. Add watercress, avocado, lemon juice and salt and mash with a fork completely.
7. Place the egg whites in a serving dish and fill the egg whites with watercress mixture.
- **Nutrition Info:** 132 calories, 10.9g fat, 3.3g carbs, 6.3g protein

517. Spicy Salmon Jerky

Servings: 6
Cooking Time: 12 Hours
Ingredients:
- 3 pounds salmon fillets, skin removed
- 1 cup soy sauce
- 2 tablespoons molasses
- 2 tablespoons white sugar
- 2 tablespoons Worcestershire sauce
- 2 tablespoons lemon juice
- 1 ½ tablespoons ground black pepper
- 2 teaspoons liquid smoke seasoning
- 12 dashes of hot sauce

Directions:
1. Place in the ceramic pot the FoodiTM Cook & CrispTM dehydrating tray.
2. Mix all ingredients in a mixing bowl and allow to marinate in the fridge for at least 2 hours.
3. Place the marinated salmon fillets on the dehydrating tray.
4. Close the crisping lid and press the Dehydrate button before pressing the START button.
5. Adjust the cooking time to 12 hours.
- **Nutrition Info:** Calories: 227; Carbohydrates: 7.5g; Protein: 25.6g; Fat: 10.5g; Sugar: 3.2g; Sodium: 1317mg

518. Balsamic Roasted Pork Loin

Servings: 4
Cooking Time: 1 Hour And 30 Minutes
Ingredients:
- 2 tablespoons steak seasoning rub
- ½ cup balsamic vinegar
- ½ cup olive oil
- 2 pounds boneless pork loin roast

Directions:
1. Place in the ceramic pot the FoodiTM Cook &CrispTM reversible rack.
2. Mix the steak seasoning rub, balsamic vinegar, and olive oil.
3. Rub the pork loin roast with the seasoning.
4. Close the crisping lid and press the Bake/Roast button before pressing the START button.
5. Adjust the cooking time to 1 hour and 30 minutes.
- **Nutrition Info:** Calories: 297; Carbohydrates: 3.1g; Protein: 18.3g; Fat: 23.4g; Sugar: 0.8g; Sodium: 732 mg

519. Soy-glazed Mushrooms

Servings: 4 Servings
Cooking Time: 10 Minutes
Ingredients:
- 2 cups mushrooms, sliced
- 4 tablespoons butter
- 3 cloves garlic, chopped fine
- 1-3 teaspoons soy sauce

Directions:
1. Set cooker to sauté on med-high heat. Add butter and let melt. Add mushrooms,

stirring to coat. Cook till mushrooms release their liquid then add garlic and continue to cook, stirring often, till the liquid has evaporated and the mushrooms are golden brown.
2. Drizzle on desired amount of soy sauce and stir. Serve.

520. Steamed Garlic Prawn Chinese Style

Servings: 10
Cooking Time: 20 Minutes
Ingredients:
- 20 large tiger prawns, shells not removed
- 2 tablespoons soy sauce
- 5 cloves of garlic, minced
- 1 tablespoon brandy

Directions:
1. Place all ingredients in a Ziploc bag and marinate in the fridge for at least 2 hours.
2. Place the FoodiTM Cook &CrispTM reversible rack inside the ceramic pot.
3. Pour water into the pot.
4. Place the marinated shrimps on the reversible rack.
5. Close the pressure lid and set the vent to SEAL.
6. Press the Steam button and adjust the cooking time to 20 minutes.
- **Nutrition Info:** Calories: 67; Carbohydrates: 1.8g; Protein: 12.1g; Fat: 1.8g; Sugar: 0.5g; Sodium: 574mg

521. Sausage Onions & Peppers

Servings: 4 Servings
Cooking Time: 4 Hours
Ingredients:
- 1 pound Italian sausage, casings removed
- 1-2 cans tomatoes, diced
- 1 large onion, chopped
- 1 green pepper, seeded and chopped
- 3-4 cloves garlic, chopped fine
- ½ teaspoon salt

Directions:
1. Set cooker to sauté on med-high heat. Add sausage and brown, breaking up into large chunks.
2. Add remaining ingredients and secure the lid. Set to slow cooking on high and cook for 4 hours. Serve.

522. Authentic French Potato Gratin

Servings: 4
Cooking Time: 20 Minutes
Ingredients:
- 2 large potatoes, sliced thinly
- 5½ tbsp. cream
- 2 eggs
- 1 tbsp. plain flour
- ½ C. cheddar cheese, grated

Directions:
1. Arrange the "Cook & Crisp Basket" in the pot of Ninja Foodi.
2. Close the Ninja Foodi with crisping lid and select "Air Crisp".
3. Press "Start/Stop" to begin and set the temperature to 355 degrees F.
4. Set the time for 5 minutes to preheat.
5. Now, place the potatoes into "Cook & Crisp Basket".
6. Arrange the "Cook & Crisp Basket" in the pot.
7. Close the Ninja Foodi with crisping lid and select "Air Crisp".
8. Set the temperature to 355 degrees F for 10 minutes.
9. Press "Start/Stop" to begin.
10. Meanwhile, in a bowl, add cream, eggs and flour and mix until a thick sauce forms.
11. Remove the potatoes from the basket.
12. Now, divide the potato slices in 4 ramekins evenly and top with the egg mixture evenly, followed by the cheese.
13. Arrange the ramekins into the "Cook & Crisp Basket".
14. Close the Ninja Foodi with crisping lid and select "Air Crisp".
15. Set the temperature to 390 degrees F for 10 minutes.
16. Press "Start/Stop" to begin.
17. Open the lid and serve warm.
- **Nutrition Info:** Calories: 233; Carbohydrates: 31.3g; Protein: 9.7g; Fat: 8g; Sugar: 2.7g; Sodium: 135mg; Fiber: 4.5g

523. Steamed Mussels With Fennel And Tomatoes

Servings: 8
Cooking Time: 15 Minutes
Ingredients:
- 2 shallots, chopped
- 4 cloves of garlic, chopped
- 1 bulb fennel, sliced
- 1 tomato, cubed
- ½ cup white wine
- ½ cup heavy cream
- 4 pounds mussels, cleaned
- 1/3 cup basil leaves, torn
- Salt to taste

Directions:
1. Place everything in a large Ziploc bag and allow the mussels to soak in the marinade.
2. Place the FoodiTM Cook &CrispTM reversible rack inside the ceramic pot.
3. Pour water into the pot.
4. Place the mussels and the vegetables (except the marinade) on the reversible rack.

5. Close the pressure lid and set the vent to SEAL.
6. Press the Steam button and adjust the cooking time to 15 minutes.
7. Meanwhile, pour the marinade on a saucepan and heat over medium flame until the sauce thickens.
8. Serve the sauce over the clams.
- **Nutrition Info:** Calories: 270; Carbohydrates: 15.7g; Protein: 16.3g; Fat: 15.7g; Sugar: ,4.7g; Sodium: 245mg

524. Sweet & Spicy Balsamic Beef

Servings: 6 – 8 Servings
Cooking Time: 6 – 8 Hours
Ingredients:
- 3-4 pound beef roast, boneless
- 1 can beef broth
- ½ onion, chopped fine
- ½ cup balsamic vinegar
- 5 cloves garlic, chopped fine
- 3 tablespoons honey
- 1 tablespoon soy sauce
- 1 tablespoon Worcestershire sauce
- 1 teaspoon red chili flakes

Directions:
1. Place all ingredients, except the roast, into the cooking pot. Stir well. Add roast and turn to coat.
2. Add the lid and select slow cooking on low and cook 6-8 hours. When the beef is done, remove to a plate and shred, using two forks. Add it back to the sauce and serve.

525. Red Wine Braised Short Ribs

Servings: 10
Cooking Time: 60 Minutes
Ingredients:
- 5 pounds beef short ribs, cut into chunks
- 2/3 cup all-purpose flour
- 2 tablespoons olive oil
- 2 onions, chopped
- 2 cloves of garlic, minced
- 2 stalks of celery, chopped
- 2 tablespoons tomato paste
- 3 carrots, peeled and sliced
- 4 cup beef stock
- 1 cup dry red wine
- Salt and pepper to taste

Directions:
1. Season the ribs with salt and pepper.
2. Dredge the meat on all-purpose flour.
3. Press the Sear/Sauté button and then the START button.
4. Heat the oil and sear the meat on all sides for at least 3 minutes.
5. Sauté the onion and garlic until fragrant. Stir in the celery until wilted.
6. Add the rest of the ingredients.
7. Close the pressure lid and set the vent to SEAL.
8. Press the Pressure button and adjust the cooking time to 60 minutes.
- **Nutrition Info:** Calories: 592; Carbohydrates: 23.2g; Protein: 51.1g; Fat: 32.7g; Sugar: 15.9g; Sodium: 986mg

526. Coconut Carrots

Servings: 4 Servings
Cooking Time: 16 Minutes
Ingredients:
- 4 cups sliced carrots
- 2 Tablespoons coconut oil
- 1 tsp salt
- ½ tsp pepper

Directions:
1. Cut the carrots in half and toss together with the coconut oil, salt and pepper.
2. Place the cook and crisp pot inside the Ninja Foodi. Close the crisper lid and set the pot to 400 degrees F using the air crisp function.
3. Add the carrots to the basket and set the timer for 8 minutes.
4. Open the lid, mix the carrots inside the pot and then cook for another 8 minutes to get nice and crispy.
- **Nutrition Info:** Calories: 113g, Carbohydrates: 12g, Protein: 1g, Fat: 7g, Sugar: 6g, Sodium: 122mg

527. Flaky Fish With Ginger

Servings: 2
Cooking Time: 15minutes
Ingredients:
- 1 pound halibut fillet, skin removed
- 1 teaspoon salt to taste
- 1 tablespoon fresh ginger, sliced thinly
- 3 tablespoons green onion
- 1 tablespoon dark soy sauce
- 1 tablespoon peanut oil
- 2 teaspoons sesame oil

Directions:
1. Place the FoodiTM Cook &CrispTM reversible rack inside the ceramic pot.
2. Pour a cup of water in the pot.
3. Season the halibut fillets with salt to taste.
4. Place in a heat-proof ceramic dish. Drizzle with the rest of the ingredients.
5. Place the ceramic dish with the fish inside on the reversible rack.
6. Close the pressure lid and set the vent to SEAL.
7. Press the Steam button and adjust the cooking time to 15 minutes.
8. Do quick pressure release.
- **Nutrition Info:** Calories: 352; Carbohydrates: 2g; Protein: 48.1g; Fat: 16.8g; Sugar: 0.2g; Sodium: 1908mg

528. Sumptuous Breakfast Frittata

Servings: 2
Cooking Time: 15 Minutes
Ingredients:
- ¼ pounds breakfast sausage, cooked and crumbled
- 4 eggs, beaten
- ½ cup Mexican cheese blend of your choice
- 2 tablespoons red bell pepper, diced
- 1 green onion, chopped
- A pinch of cayenne pepper

Directions:
1. Into the ceramic pot, place all ingredients until well-combined.
2. Close the crisping lid and press the Air Crisp button before pressing the START button.
3. Adjust the cooking time to 20 minutes.
- **Nutrition Info:** Calories: 383; Carbohydrates: 2.9g; Protein: 31.2g; Fat: 27.4g; Sugar: 0.2g; Sodium:443 mg

529. Tastiest Cauliflower

Servings: 4
Cooking Time: 13 Minutes
Ingredients:
- 1 medium head cauliflower
- ¼ C. olive oil
- 4 garlic cloves, minced
- 2 tbsp. capers, minced
- ½ C. Parmesan cheese, grated

Directions:
1. With a knife, cut an X into the cauliflower head, slicing about halfway down.
2. In the pot of Ninja Foodi, place ½ C. of water.
3. Place the cauliflower head into "Cook & Crisp Basket".
4. Arrange the "Cook & Crisp Basket" in the pot.
5. Cover the Ninja Foodi with the pressure lid and place the pressure valve to "Seal" position.
6. Select "Pressure" and set to "Low" for about 3 minutes.
7. Press "Start/Stop" to begin.
8. Switch the valve to "Vent" and do a "Quick" release.
9. Meanwhile, in a small bowl, add the oil, garlic and capers and mix well.
10. Once all the pressure is released, open the lid.
11. Place the oil mixture over the cauliflower evenly and sprinkle with the Parmesan cheese.
12. No, close the Ninja Foodi with crisping lid and select "Air Crisp".
13. Set the temperature to 390 degrees F for 10 minutes.
14. Press "Start/Stop" to begin.
15. Open the lid and serve warm.
- **Nutrition Info:** Calories: 172; Carbohydrates: 5.1g; Protein: 5.4g; Fat: 15.5g; Sugar: 1.6g; Sodium: 317mg; Fiber: 1.9g

530. Pressure Cooker Pork Carnitas

Servings: 4
Cooking Time: 60 Minutes
Ingredients:
- 2 pounds pork butt, chopped into large cubes
- 1 teaspoon salt
- ½ teaspoon oregano
- ½ teaspoon cumin
- 1 orange, cut in half and juiced
- 6 cloves of garlic, peeled and crushed
- 1 cup chicken broth

Directions:
1. Place the ceramic pot in the Ninja Foodi base and place all ingredients.
2. Put the pressure lid and make sure that the vent is on the SEAL position.
3. Press the Pressure button.
4. Adjust the cooking time for 60 minutes.
5. Once cooked, take the pork out and shred using forks.
6. Serve with the sauce.
- **Nutrition Info:** Calories: 321; Carbohydrates: 8g; Protein: 43g; Fat: 13g; Sugar: 4g; Sodium: 838mg

531. Speedy Paella

Servings: 6 Servings
Cooking Time: 25 Minutes
Ingredients:
- 1 pound Spanish chorizo, cut into ½-inch slices
- 1 pound shrimp, deveined but leave tails and shell on
- 1 pound Little neck clams, scrubbed
- 4 cups chicken broth
- 2 cups long grain rice
- 1 cup roasted red peppers, sliced
- 1 onion, chopped
- ½ cup green olives, pitted
- ½ cup dry white wine
- 3 cloves garlic, chopped fine
- 2 tablespoons olive oil
- 1 teaspoon smoked paprika
- ½ teaspoon saffron threads, crumbled
- Salt & pepper

Directions:
1. Set the cooker to sauté on med-high heat and add the oil. Once the oil is hot, add the chorizo and cook till browned on both sides, about 3 minutes. Transfer to a plate and set aside.
2. Add the onion and garlic and cook till translucent, about 3 – 4 minutes. Season

with salt and pepper. Add the wine and deglaze the pan. Continue cooking till wine is reduced by half, about 2 minutes.
3. Add the rice, paprika and saffron and cook till rice is well coated, about 1 minute. Add the broth and a pinch of salt. Secure the lid and set to pressure cooking on high. Set the timer for 5 minutes.
4. Once the timer goes off, use quick release to remove the lid. Add the shrimp and clams to the pot. Cover and cook on high pressure for 6 minutes, or till shrimp are pink and clams have opened. Use quick release to remove the lid again.
5. Discard any unopened clams. Add the chorizo, olives and red peppers and stir to combine. Serve.

532. Celery Root Fried Crisped

Servings: 2
Cooking Time: 10 Minutes
Ingredients:
- ½ celeriac or celery root, cut into sticks
- 3 cups of water
- 1 tablespoon lime juice
- 1/3 cup mayonnaise
- 1 tablespoon mustard
- 1 teaspoon powdered horseradish
- 1 tablespoon olive oil
- Salt and pepper to taste

Directions:
1. Place in the ceramic pot the FoodiTM Cook &CrispTM basket.
2. Place the celery root slices in water and lime juice. Allow to soak for 1 hour.
3. Drain the celery roots and pat dry with a paper towel. Season with salt and pepper to taste.
4. Place in the basket.
5. Close the crisping lid and press the Air Crisp button before pressing the START button.
6. Adjust the cooking time to 10 minutes.
7. Give the basket a shake halfway through the cooking time.
8. While the celery roots are frying, mix the rest of the ingredients in a bowl. This will be the dipping sauce.
9. Serve the celery roots with the dipping sauce.
- **Nutrition Info:** Calories: 176; Carbohydrates: 13g; Protein: 1.8g; Fat: 12.9g; Sugar: 2.1g; Sodium: 259mg

533. Vegan-approved Fajita Pasta

Servings: 2
Cooking Time: 9 Minutes
Ingredients:
- 1 teaspoon oil
- 2 cloves of garlic, minced
- 1/3 cup chopped bell peppers
- 1/3 cup black beans, cooked
- 1/2 teaspoon taco seasoning mix
- 1 1/3 cups pasta, cooked according to package instruction
- 2/3 cup commercial enchilada sauce
- Salt and pepper to taste

Directions:
1. Press the sauté button on the Ninja Foodi and heat the oil. Stir in the garlic and bell peppers and allow to wilt for 3 minutes.
2. Add the rest of the ingredients.
3. Install pressure lid. Close Ninja Foodi, press the manual button, choose high settings, and set time to 6 minutes.
4. Once done cooking, do a quick release.
5. Serve and enjoy.
- **Nutrition Info:** Calories: 282; carbohydrates: 52.1g; protein: 10.4g; fat: 3.5g

534. Crispy 'n Tasty Cauliflower Bites

Servings: 4
Cooking Time: 10 Minutes
Ingredients:
- 3 cloves of garlic, minced
- 1 tablespoon olive oil
- ½ teaspoon salt
- ½ teaspoon smoked paprika
- 4 cups cauliflower florets

Directions:
1. Place in the ceramic pot the FoodiTM Cook &CrispTM basket.
2. Place all ingredients in a bowl and toss to combine.
3. Place the seasoned cauliflower florets in the basket.
4. Close the crisping lid and press the Air Crisp button before pressing the START button.
5. Adjust the cooking time to 10 minutes.
6. Give the basket a shake for even cooking
- **Nutrition Info:** Calories: 130; Carbohydrates: 12.4g; Protein: 4.3g; Fat: 7g; Sugar: 0.7g; Sodium: 642mg

535. Healthy Asparagus Bake

Servings: 8
Cooking Time: 25 Minutes
Ingredients:
- 4 cups asparagus spears, trimmed
- 12 dinner rolls
- 1 ½ cup diced cheese
- 2 ½ cups cooked ham
- 6 eggs, beaten
- 3 cups milk
- 3 tablespoons minced onion
- Salt and pepper to taste

Directions:
1. Place the ceramic pot in the Ninja Foodi.

2. Place the asparagus spears in the ceramic pot.
3. Add in a layer of dinner rolls, cheese, and ham.
4. In a bowl, combine the eggs and milk. Whisk until well-combined.
5. Pour the egg mixture over the layer of the ingredients.
6. Stir in the onion and season with salt and pepper to taste.
7. Close the crisping lid and press the Bake/Roast button before pressing the START button.
8. Adjust the cooking time to 25 minutes.
- **Nutrition Info:** Calories: 239; Carbohydrates: 15.1g; Protein: 15.3g; Fat: 13g; Sugar: 6.7g; Sodium: 825mg

536. Zucchini Fries

Servings: 4 Servings
Cooking Time: 25 Minutes
Ingredients:
- 2 Zucchinis
- 2 tsp salt
- ½ tsp ground black pepper
- 2 cups almond flour
- 3 eggs
- 1 cup grated parmesan cheese
- 1 Tbsp garlic powder
- 2 tsp onion powder

Directions:
1. Cut the zucchini into strips about ¼ inch wide and 3 inches long. Sprinkle with the salt and let sit for about 20 minutes then pat dry to take any extra moisture off of the fries.
2. Add the almond flour and ground black pepper to a bowl and put the eggs in a separate small bowl and whisk briefly.
3. In a third small bowl, mix the parmesan, garlic powder and onion powder together.
4. Dip the fries one at a time in the flour then in the egg mix and finally in the cheese mix and set coated fries aside on a plate. Dip all the fries.
5. Place the fries in the cook and crisp basket and then put the basket inside the pot. Lose the crisper lid and set the temperature to 375 degrees F and set the timer for 12 minutes.
6. After 12 minutes has passed, open the Ninja Foodi, flip the fries and continue to crisp for another 12 minutes.
7. Serve fries while hot.
- **Nutrition Info:** Calories: 575g, Carbohydrates: 12g, Protein: 47g, Fat: 38g, Sugar: 6g, Sodium: 2916 mg

537. Kale Chips

Servings: 4 Servings
Cooking Time: 10 Minutes
Ingredients:
- 1 bunch curly leaf kale, chopped, stems removed
- ¼ tsp garlic powder
- ¼ tsp baking stevia
- 1 ½ tsp salt
- 3 Tbsp olive oil

Directions:
1. Toss the kale leaves in the olive oil and then add the dry seasonings and toss again.
2. Place the kale on a dehydrating rack inside the Ninja Foodi, being careful not to overlap the leaves too much.
3. Place the lid on the Foodi and set the dehydrator function to 135 degrees for 7 hours.
4. Remove the lid once the time has completed and allow the chips to cool. Store in an air tight container.
- **Nutrition Info:** Calories: 108g, Carbohydrates: 2g, Protein: 1g, Fat: 10g, Sugar: 1g, Sodium: 618 mg

538. Mixed Nuts

Servings: 5
Cooking Time: 20 Minutes
Ingredients:
- 1 tbsp. melted butter
- ½ c. raw cashew nuts
- 1 c. raw almonds
- 1 c. raw peanuts
- Salt

Directions:
1. Place the nuts in the pot of Ninja Foodi and lock the lid.
2. Press "Air Crisp" and set the timer to 10 minutes at 350 degrees F.
3. Remove the nuts into a bowl and add melted butter and salt.
4. Toss to coat well and return the nuts mixture into the Ninja Foodi.
5. Press "Bake/Roast" and bake for about 5 minutes.
6. Dish out to serve.
- **Nutrition Info:** 189 calories, 16.5g fat, 6.6g carbs, 6.8g protein

539. Pumpkin & Bacon Risotto

Servings: 6 Servings
Cooking Time: 1 Hour
Ingredients:
- 4 ½ cups chicken broth
- 6 strips bacon, chopped
- 1 ½ cups onion, chopped
- 1 cup Arborio rice, uncooked
- ½ cup Parmesan cheese
- ¼ cup pumpkin puree
- 2 tablespoons parsley, chopped

- 1 tablespoon olive oil
- salt and black pepper

Directions:
1. Set cooker to sauté on med-high heat and add oil. When the oil is hot, add bacon and onions and cook till onions are tender and bacon starts to crisp, about 15 minutes.
2. Add the rice, salt and pepper. Cook, stirring often, 5 minutes. Stir in broth and cook another 10 minutes.
3. Reduce the heat to low and cover. Cook 25 minutes, or till rice is done. Stir the pumpkin in during the last 5 minutes of cooking.
4. Turn the heat up to med-high and stir in the cheese. Cook, uncovered, till most of the liquid is gone. Serve immediately garnished with the chopped parsley and additional Parmesan cheese.

540. Loaded Nachos

Servings: 4 Servings
Cooking Time: 25 Minutes
Ingredients:
- 2 chicken breasts, boneless and skinless
- 1 cup keto salsa
- 1 tsp salt
- 1 Tbso taco seasoning
- 4 cups grain free tortilla chips
- 1 cup shredded Mexican cheese blend
- 1 jalapeno, sliced

Directions:
1. Place the chicken and salsa in the Ninja Foodi and place the lid on as well. Set the pressure cooker steam valve to seal and cook on high pressure for 15 minutes. Do a quick pressure release and remove the lid. Use two forks to shred the chicken, mixing it into the sauce.
2. Add the taco seasoning and salt to the mix and stir to combine.
3. Place the tortilla chips on top of the chicken mix inside the pot. Sprinkle the shredded cheese and jalapenos over the top of the chips then close the crisper lid and set the temperature for 360 degrees for 5 minutes.
4. Remove the perfectly browned nachos and serve while warm!
- **Nutrition Info:** Calories: 198g; Carbohydrates: 3g, Protein: 20g, Fat: 10g, Sugar: 4g, Sodium: 1016mg

541. Portuguese Steamed Clams

Servings: 12
Cooking Time: 15 Minutes
Ingredients:
- 1 can diced tomatoes
- 1 large onion, cut into wedges
- 1 ½ pounds chorizo, sliced into chunks
- 5 pounds clams, shells scrubbed
- 2 cups white wine
- ¼ cup olive oil
- Salt and pepper to taste

Directions:
1. Place the tomatoes at the bottom of the ceramic bowl.
2. Add the large onions and the chorizo on top.
3. Put on top the clams.
4. Pour over the white wine and season with salt and pepper to taste.
5. Close the pressure lid and set the vent to SEAL.
6. Press the Steam button and adjust the cooking time to 15 minutes.
7. Do quick pressure release.
8. Drizzle the clams with olive oil before serving.
- **Nutrition Info:** Calories: 630; Carbohydrates: 9.1g; Protein: 29.9g; Fat: 52.6g; Sugar: 3.6g; Sodium: 1567 mg

542. Spicy Red Potatoes

Servings: 6 – 8 Servings
Cooking Time: 3 -4 Hours
Ingredients:
- 3 pounds red potatoes, quartered
- 1 packet taco seasoning
- 2 tablespoons olive oil
- 2 tablespoons butter
- 1 tablespoon red pepper flakes
- salt and pepper to taste

Directions:
1. Spray the cooking pot with cooking spray. Add all of the ingredients and stir well to coat the potatoes.
2. Add the lid and select slow cooking on high. Cook 3-4 hours, stirring the potatoes every hour. At the 3 hour mark check for doneness, when they are fork tender they are done. Serve.

543. Duck Confit

Servings: 4 Servings
Cooking Time: 2 Hours
Ingredients:
- 4 duck legs, drumsticks and thighs
- 4 sprigs fresh thyme
- 4 cloves garlic, smashed
- 2 bay leaves, halved
- 1 tablespoon salt
- ¼ teaspoon peppercorns, lightly crushed
- ¼ teaspoon allspice berries, lightly crushed

Directions:
1. Line a baking sheet with paper towels. Place all the spices, salt and pepper in a large mixing bowl and stir to combine. Add the duck legs and toss to coat evenly. Lay them in a single layer on the baking sheet and

refrigerate at least 24 hours, or up to 3 days.. Do not cover.
2. Brush the garlic and thyme off the duck, set it aside for later. Set the cooker to sauté on med-high heat.
3. Add the duck legs and sear till golden brown on all sides and the fat starts to render, about 5 – 10 minutes per side. Scatter the reserved garlic and thyme over the duck.
4. Secure the lid and select pressure cooking on high. Set the timer for 40 minutes. Use manual release to remove the lid. Flip the legs over and cook another 30 minutes. Again use manual release to remove the lid.
5. Let it cool completely then cover the pot and refrigerate. When the liquid cools the fat will separate from the stock, save the stock for soups or other recipes for later.
6. When ready to serve, scrape the fat off the duck and lay it on a baking sheet. Broil it till the skin is crispy, about 3 – 5 minutes. Serve.

544. Popular Finger Food

Servings: 3
Cooking Time: 12 Minutes
Ingredients:
- 3 tbsp. white flour
- 2 eggs
- 3 tbsp. milk
- ½ C. plain breadcrumbs
- ½ lb. mozzarella cheese block, cut into 3x½-inch sticks

Directions:
1. In a shallow dish, place the flour.
2. In a second shallow dish, add eggs and milk and beat well.
3. In a third shallow dish, place the breadcrumbs.
4. Coat the Mozzarella sticks with flour, then dip in egg mixture and finally, coat with the breadcrumbs.
5. Arrange the Mozzarella sticks onto a cookie sheet and freezer for about 1-2 hours.
6. Arrange the "Cook & Crisp Basket" in the pot of Ninja Foodi.
7. Close the Ninja Foodi with crisping lid and select "Air Crisp".
8. Press "Start/Stop" to begin and set the temperature to 400 degrees F.
9. Set the time for 5 minutes to preheat.
10. Now, place the mozzarella sticks into "Cook & Crisp Basket".
11. Close the Ninja Foodi with crisping lid and select "Air Crisp".
12. Set the temperature to 400 degrees F for 12 minutes.
13. Press "Start/Stop" to begin.
14. Open the lid and serve

- **Nutrition Info:** Calories per serving: 162; Carbohydrates: 20.1g; Protein: 8.7g; Fat: 5.1g; Sugar: 2.1g; Sodium: 209mg; Fiber: 1g

545. Easy Broiled Lobster Tails

Servings: 2
Cooking Time: 20 Minutes
Ingredients:
- 2 ounces fresh lobster tails
- 1 tablespoon olive oil
- 1 teaspoon lemon pepper seasoning

Directions:
1. Place in the ceramic pot the FoodiTM Cook & CrispTM reversible tray.
2. Season the lobster tails with olive oil and lemon-pepper seasoning.
3. Place the lobster tails on the tray.
4. Close the crisping lid and press the Broil button before pressing the START button.
5. Adjust the cooking time to 20 minutes.

- **Nutrition Info:** Calories: 208; Carbohydrates: 1.1g; Protein: 32g; Fat: 8.3g; Sugar: 0.4g; Sodium: 734mg

546. Korean Chicken

Servings: 6 Servings
Cooking Time: 3 -4 Hours
Ingredients:
- 2 pounds chicken thighs, boneless and skinless
- ¼ cup soy sauce
- ¼ cup honey
- 4 cloves garlic, chopped fine
- 2 tablespoons Korean chili paste
- 2 tablespoons toasted sesame oil
- 2 tablespoons fresh ginger, grated
- 2 teaspoons cornstarch
- Pinch of red pepper flakes
- For the Mango Salsa:
- 2 ripe mangoes, peeled, pitted, and diced
- ¼ red onion, chopped fine
- Juice of 1 lime
- 1 jalapeno pepper, seeded and chopped fine
- 1 tablespoon cilantro, chopped
- Drizzle of honey
- Salt, to taste

Directions:
1. Add the soy sauce, honey, chili paste, sesame oil, ginger, garlic and pepper flakes to the cooking pot, stir to combine. Add the chicken and turn to coat in the sauce.
2. Secure the lid and select slow cooking function on low. Cook 3 – 4 hours or till chicken is cooked through.
3. While the chicken is cooking, make the salsa. Add the mango, jalapeno, onion and cilantro to a bowl. Juice the lime over the top and add honey to taste. Stir, cover and refrigerate till ready to serve.

4. When the chicken is cooked, transfer it to a plate. Set the cooker to sauté on med-low heat. Whisk the cornstarch into ¼ cup of cold water and add to the sauce. Cook, stirring constantly, about 5 minutes or till thick and glossy.
5. Shred the chicken and add it back to the sauce, stirring to coat. Serve with the salsa and garnish with sesame seeds or chopped scallions if desired.

547. Teriyaki Green Beans & Mushrooms

Servings: 4 – 6 Servings
Cooking Time: 10 Minutes
Ingredients:
- 1 pound fresh green beans, cut into 1-inch pieces
- 1 ¼ cups mushrooms, sliced
- 1 shallot, diced
- ¼ cup teriyaki sauce
- 3 tablespoons butter
- 1 teaspoon garlic, chopped fine
- ½ teaspoon sesame seeds

Directions:
1. Add butter to the cooker and set to sauté on med-high heat. Once butter melts, add beans, mushrooms and shallot. Cook till the vegetables start to soften, about 4-5 minutes.
2. Add garlic and cook another 30 seconds. Add teriyaki sauce and cook 5 minutes, or till green beans are done. Sprinkle with sesame seeds before serving.

548. Herb Roasted Pork

Servings: 10
Cooking Time: 2 Hours
Ingredients:
- 1 teaspoon sage
- ½ teaspoon salt
- ¼ teaspoon pepper
- 1 clove of garlic, crushed
- 5 pounds boneless pork loin, scored
- ½ cup sugar
- 1 tablespoon cornstarch
- ¼ cup vinegar
- ¼ cup water
- 2 tablespoons soy sauce

Directions:
1. Place in the ceramic pot the FoodiTM Cook &CrispTM reversible rack.
2. In a bowl, combine the sage, salt, pepper, and garlic.
3. Rub all over the pork and place the pork on the reversible rack.
4. Close the crisping lid and press the Bake/Roast button before pressing the START button.
5. Adjust the cooking time to 2 hours.
6. Meanwhile, place the remaining ingredients in a saucepan and heat until the sauce thickens.
7. Serve the roasted pork with the sauce.
- **Nutrition Info:** Calories: 461; Carbohydrates: 13.9g; Protein: 45.8g; Fat: 24.6g; Sugar: 4.3g; Sodium: 470mg

549. Great Snacking Nuts

Servings: 20
Cooking Time: 14 Minutes
Ingredients:
- ½ C. unsalted butter
- 1½ C. walnuts
- 1½ C. cashews
- 3 tsp. ground cinnamon
- ½ C. powdered sugar

Directions:
1. Select "Sauté/Sear" setting of Ninja Foodi and place the butter into the pot.
2. Press "Start/Stop" to begin and heat for about 2-3 minutes.
3. Add the nuts and cook, uncovered for about 15 minutes.
4. Press "Start/Stop" to stop the cooking and stir in the cinnamon and sugar.
5. Close the crisping lid and select "Slow Cooker".
6. Set on "High" for about 2-2½ hours.
7. Press "Start/Stop" to begin.
8. Open the lid and transfer the nuts into a bowl to cool before serving.
- **Nutrition Info:** Calories per serving: 170; Carbohydrates: 7.6g; Protein: 3.9g; Fat: 14.9g; Sugar: 3.6g; Sodium: 35mg; Fiber: 1.1g

550. Almond Cheddar Cornbread

Servings: 6 Servings
Cooking Time: 25 Minutes
Ingredients:
- 1 ¼ cup almond flour
- ¾ cup coconut flour
- 2 Tbsp baking stevia
- 2 tsp baking powder
- 2 tsp salt
- 1 egg
- 1 cup whole milk
- ½ cup canned corn, drained
- ¼ cup coconut oil
- 1 cup cheddar cheese

Directions:
1. Pre heat the Ninja Foodi by closing the crisper lid and pressing the broil button, setting the timer for 10 minutes.
2. In a separate bowl, mix together all the dry ingredients. Then add the remaining wet ingredients and stir until the batter is smooth. Pour the batter into a greased eight

inch baking pan and set inside the preheated Ninja Foodi on top of the reversible rack.
3. Close the crisper lid again and use the bake function, set at 350 degrees, for 25 minutes. Once the bread begins to turn golden brown, remove it from the Foodi and allow to cool before serving.
- **Nutrition Info:** Calories: 621g, Carbohydrates: 7g, Protein: 14g, Fat: 57g, Sugar: 8g, Sodium: 1022 mg

551. Veggie 'n Shrimp Fried Rice

Servings: 2
Cooking Time: 30 Minutes
Ingredients:
- 1 tablespoon oil, divided
- 1 small onion, peeled and diced
- 2 tablespoons of garlic
- 2 eggs, whisked
- 1/2 cup uncooked basmati rice
- 2 teaspoons of soy sauce
- 1 cup of chicken broth
- ½ cup of mixed frozen vegetables
- 1/2-pound frozen shrimp
- 1/2 cup of water

Directions:
1. Add rice, water, and stock in Ninja Foodi.
2. Install pressure lid and place valve to vent position.
3. Close Ninja Foodi, press steam button and set timer to 8 minutes.
4. Once done cooking, do a 5-minute natural release and then a quick release. Transfer rice to a bowl.
5. Press stop, press sauté button and add 1/2 tbsp oil.
6. Once hot, scramble eggs for 4 minutes. Transfer to a bowl and cut into small pieces.
7. Add remaining oil and once hot sauté garlic for a minute. Stir in onions and cook for another 3 minutes.
8. Add shrimps and cook until opaque, around 5 minutes.
9. Stir in frozen vegetables and cook until heated through around 3 minutes.
10. Stir in rice. Add soy sauce. Mix well and cook for 2 minutes.
11. Serve and enjoy.
- **Nutrition Info:** Calories: 463; carbohydrates: 47.2g; protein: 39.1g; fat: 13.1g

552. Vegetable And Tilapia Dinner

Servings: 6
Cooking Time: 15 Minutes
Ingredients:
- 1 teaspoon olive oil
- 6 tilapia fillets
- 1 pinch Greek seasoning
- 4 stalks celery, halved
- 1 cup fresh baby carrots
- 1 bell pepper, cut into chunks
- ½ onion, sliced
- Salt and pepper to taste

Directions:
1. Place the FoodiTM Cook &CrispTM reversible rack inside the ceramic pot.
2. Pour water into the pot.
3. Brush oil on to the tilapia fillets.
4. Season with Greek seasoning, salt and pepper.
5. Place the tilapia fillets on the basket.
6. Layer the vegetables on top.
7. Close the pressure lid and set the vent to SEAL.
8. Press the Steam button and adjust the cooking time to 15 minutes.
- **Nutrition Info:** Calories: 134; Carbohydrates: 4.4g; Protein: 23.6g; Fat: 2.4g; Sugar: 0.8g; Sodium: 126mg

553. Pressure Cooker Bone-in Pork Chops With Vegetables

Servings: 4
Cooking Time: 30 Minutes
Ingredients:
- 4 ¾-inch bone-in pork chops
- Salt and pepper to taste
- ¼ cup butter, divided
- 1 cup baby carrots
- 4 whole potatoes, peeled and halved
- 1 onion, chopped
- 1 cup vegetable broth
- 3 tablespoons Worcestershire sauce

Directions:
1. Season the beef with salt and pepper. Dredge in flour.
2. Press the Sear/Sauté button and then the START button.
3. Season the pork with salt and pepper to taste.
4. Put half of the butter in the pot and sear the pork for at least 2 minutes on both sides.
5. Stir in the carrots, potatoes, onions, vegetable broth, and Worcestershire sauce.
6. Close the pressure lid and set the vent to SEAL.
7. Press the Pressure button and adjust the cooking time to 30 minutes.
8. Do natural pressure release.
9. Once the lid is open, stir in the remaining butter.
- **Nutrition Info:** Calories: 577; Carbohydrates: 60.3g; Protein: 34.6g; Fat: 21.9g; Sugar: 20.6g; Sodium: 404mg

554. Veal Marengo

Servings: 8 Servings
Cooking Time: 20 Minutes
Ingredients:
- 4 pounds lean veal, cubed
- 1 pound mushrooms, quartered
- 1 ½ cups chicken broth
- 1 cup plus 2 tablespoons dry white wine
- 1 cup onion, chopped
- 1 cup celery, chopped
- 1 cup tomato sauce
- 2 long strips orange zest
- 2 sprigs fresh parsley
- 4 tablespoons light olive oil
- 2 tablespoons butter
- 2 tablespoons fresh lemon juice
- 2 teaspoons cornstarch
- 1 teaspoon garlic, chopped fine
- ½ teaspoon thyme
- Salt & pepper
- Chopped parsley for garnish

Directions:
1. Pat veal dry with paper towel and sprinkle with salt and pepper.
2. Add 2 tablespoons olive oil to the cooking pot and set to sauté on med-high heat. Working in batches, brown meat on all sides and transfer to a plate.
3. Add remaining oil to the pot along with onion, garlic and celery. Cook, stirring often, about 5 minutes or onion is tender. Add zest, bay leaf, thyme, broth and 1 cup wine. Bring to a boil and simmer 1 minute.
4. Add the veal back to the pot with the tomato sauce. Top with parsley sprigs, do not stir.
5. Secure the lid and select pressure cooking on high. Set the timer for 20 minutes. When the timer goes off, use quick release to remove the lid. Use a slotted spoon to remove the veal. Discard the bay leaf and orange zest.
6. Use an immersion blender to puree the sauce and season with salt if needed.
7. In a small mixing bowl, whisk the cornstarch and 2 tablespoons wine together. Stir into the sauce to thicken.
8. In a large skillet, over med-high heat, melt the butter. Add the mushrooms and lemon juice and cook till mushrooms soften, about 3-4 minutes. Add to the sauce along with the veal. Serve garnished with chopped parsley.

555. Marinated Tofu

Servings: 4
Cooking Time: 25 Minutes
Ingredients:
- 2 tbsp. low-sodium soy sauce
- 2 tbsp. fish sauce
- 1 tsp. sesame oil
- 12-oz. extra-firm tofu, drained and cubed into 1-inch size
- 1 tsp. butter, melted

Directions:
1. In a large bowl, add soy sauce, fish sauce and sesame oil and mix until well combined.
2. Add tofu cubes and toss to coat well.
3. Set aside to marinate for about 30 minutes, tossing occasionally.
4. Arrange the "Cook & Crisp Basket" in the pot of Ninja Foodi.
5. Close the Ninja Foodi with crisping lid and select "Air Crisp".
6. Press "Start/Stop" to begin and set the temperature to 355 degrees F.
7. Set the time for 5 minutes to preheat.
8. Now, place the tofu cubes into "Cook & Crisp Basket" and drizzle with the butter.
9. Close the Ninja Foodi with crisping lid and select "Air Crisp".
10. Set the temperature to 355 degrees F for 25 minutes.
11. Press "Start/Stop" to begin. Flip the tofu after every 10 minutes during the cooking. Open the lid and serve
- **Nutrition Info:** Calories: 102; Carbohydrates: 2.5g; Protein: 9.4g; Fat: 7.1g; Sugar: 1.3g; Sodium: 1100mg; Fiber: 0.3g

www.ingramcontent.com/pod-product-compliance
Lightning Source LLC
Chambersburg PA
CBHW081414080526
44589CB00016B/2531